Visual Techniques Applied in Social Research

Florentina Scârneci-Domnişoru (ed.)

Visual Techniques Applied in Social Research

PETER LANG

Bibliographic Information published by the Deutsche Nationalbibliothek
The Deutsche Nationalbibliothek lists this publication in the Deutsche Nationalbibliografie; detailed bibliographic data is available online at http://dnb.d-nb.de.

Library of Congress Cataloging-in-Publication Data
A CIP catalog record for this book has been applied for at the Library of Congress.

cover image @pixabay.com

Printed by CPI books GmbH, Leck

ISBN 978-3-631-79561-3 (Print)
E-ISBN 978-3-631-80719-4 (E-PDF)
E-ISBN 978-3-631-80720-0 (EPUB)
E-ISBN 978-3-631-80721-7 (MOBI)
DOI 10.3726/b16351

Peter Lang – Berlin · Bern · Bruxelles · New York · Oxford · Warszawa · Wien

This publication has been peer reviewed.

www.peterlang.com

Contents

Florentina Scârneci-Domnișoru
Introduction 7

Florentina Scârneci-Domnișoru
I The relevance of visual data in social research 21

Codrina Csesznek
II Studying social change through the *re-photography technique* in a rural Romanian community 59

Marinela-Cristina Șimon
III Are the volunteers different from non-volunteers? A comparative analysis based on visual data (drawings) 129

Ada Ioana Dobrescu
IV A visual perspective on adolescent identity 157

Diana-Cristina Bódi
V Using the drawing to identify post-retirement identity transformations 189

Daniela Sorea
VI God, as the children of Romania draw It 229

Mihaela Gotea
VII Exploring social workers' perceptions of their marital partners in different family life stages, using visual methodology 281

Ioana-Anisa Atudorei
VIII Studying students' moral emotions by visual techniques 321

Giuseppina Cersosimo
IX Concluding notes: Applications and developments in visual techniques 359

List of Figures 377

List of Tables 387

Florentina Scârneci-Domnişoru

Introduction

This book is the result of a project by which I intended to bring visual data within the social research in Romania and to illustrate the relevance of this type of data in the process of scientific knowledge production. In brief, this is the context which led to the materialization of this volume.

At the end of 2016, I published the first book in Romanian that referred to visual data and the ways of collecting, processing, analyzing, and interpreting them. I have expressed then my surprise and regret that, although elsewhere the visual data are increasingly present in social research, in our country they are almost completely ignored.

In 2017, 'Transilvania' University of Braşov launched the first grant competition for young researchers to encourage the formation of research teams. That was the moment when the idea of promoting visual research among my colleagues crossed my mind. I planned to make a team, train it, and prepare its members to be independent in conducting research with visual components. Thus, I hoped that, by their help, I could spread knowledge related to the use of images in research and to the idea of using visual data in different projects and studies about the Romanian society. And by this book, I would like to show the conclusions I came to with reference to the advantages and disadvantages of using visual data in social studies and in relation to the significance of visual data in the context of social research.

So I teamed up with seven of my colleagues, all having earned the title of doctor in sociology and holding the position of lecturers or associate professors at the Faculty of Sociology and Communication at the above-mentioned university. I wrote the financing application that was approved (so the book was written and published with financial support from 'Transilvania' University of Braşov by the research grant for young researchers No. 8037 from 14.07.2017). This book is the result of the work of each member of the team. I will come to what it contains and to the presentation of the team after I briefly present what we originally intended with this project and what we have achieved.

Therefore, by the project 'Applying Visual Techniques in Social Research' I intended to change the fact that the visual is almost inexistent in the studies in Romania and I tried to align the social research from here to the latest methodological developments in the field. I claimed that introducing the visual research techniques in our country would enrich the arsenal of social scientists in Romania, and by the results obtained after their application, it would contribute to the advancement of knowledge in the field. The main argument that I offered in support of these claims was that visual data (photography, drawing, or film) are, in many respects, superior to other types of data gathered in the research. For example, they can reveal surprising details and elements that take place too fast to be noticed, they present the reality in a holistic way and they are less selective than the observations, they facilitate the elimination of cultural and linguistic barriers between the researcher and those that are studied, they are more accessible than the academic speeches, they are memorable, they capture the ineffable, they facilitate empathic understanding, and they are evocative (these are only some of the characteristics used in the literature to describe the images). Moreover, visual data are quite easy to collect, and they offer the diversity of data gathered in the research ensuring an important type of triangulation; they represent a fascinating way of collecting data for the researcher and a welcoming attempt of involving the participants more easily in research. In addition, images facilitate the collection of verbal data by interviewing, and the use of visual data in the presentation of the research results makes them be spectacular, exciting, and easy to understand.

Photos have long been used by social scientists all over the world, for example, in researching social and economic inequality, social change, perceptions, studying family history, or some biographical themes, etc. Drawings are frequently used in studies which refer to the description of different experiences the subjects are experiencing (e.g., divorce, emigration, hospitalization, dismissal, incarceration, change of leadership in an organization, etc.), in studies that address sensitive topics (e.g. understanding the disease, description of pain, knowledge about HIV/AIDS), etc. Films are similarly used in ethnographic, ethno-methodological, and cultural studies, in market studies, in the study of poverty, drug use, professional interactions, etc.

The specialty literature suggests the great potential of visual data in as far as the advancement of social knowledge is concerned, and this has made me believe that the future of this knowledge will be tightly connected to the use of visual data in research. That is why, I have proposed by this project to add the visual techniques in the methodological 'kit' of the social scientists in Braşov and to spread their use in the Romanian social studies. And by this book, I try to popularize our attempts to bring Romania's visual studies to the attention of the international public, to propose novel methodological discussions on the use of visual data in social research, and to highlight the multitude and variety of research contexts where the visual can be applied.

Thus, the main objective of the project was the use of visual techniques in various social research situations. I have proposed applying new techniques, novel for Romania, with a view to show their potential and to encourage Romanian researchers to use them. After applying the visual techniques, the project aimed at analyzing the relevance of these techniques for enhancing social knowledge. We wanted to demonstrate, by comparison to the classical techniques used in social research, what kind of information generates the application of visual techniques, how this information differs from that collected by other means, in what research situations the visual techniques are better suited, and if they bring about, by their application, a significant contribution to the comprehension of the phenomena under study.

If the first objective was a new one at the national level, the second aimed at enriching international knowledge. Thus, although in the specialty Western literature there are numerous examples of social research cases where visual data were used, there are very few studies in which the results obtained after the application of the visual techniques are compared with the results obtained from the application of classical techniques in identical or similar research situations.

In order to accomplish these goals, I formed a team where each member was responsible for applying one or more visual techniques in their own research projects. Most team members applied these new techniques in their field of interest and expertise, in projects they had previously worked on with techniques other than the visual ones. Firstly, my colleagues became acquainted with the new techniques, then, they applied them for the first time in their research and, in the end, they compared the newly obtained results to previous results from identical or similar studies in which they applied classical research techniques.

Each team member had their own research objective so that a spectacular variety of situations where we applied visual techniques resulted. Therefore, we have set as objectives: to capture community dynamics in Drăguş village, to identify the specific characteristics of volunteers in the social field, to find out what the defining aspects of adolescents' identity are, to discover how elderly people's identity changes after retirement, to identify the way in which preschoolers and early schoolers represent divinity, to discover the manner in which the partner is perceived at different stages of the family life cycle by social workers, and to find out in what contexts bound to school activities students experiment moral emotions – shame, embarrassment, and guilt. None of these objectives has ever been addressed from a visual perspective, either in Romania or abroad (it is only the one referring to adolescent identity that might have approximate correspondence in the specialty international literature).

From a methodological point of view, the plan was that each member of the team should choose (depending on the research objectives, participants' availability, ethical, deontological limitations, etc.) and should apply one or more of the existing visual methods and techniques of data collection. For example, to capture in images the studied 'object' – namely, to take photos, to film or, in the impossibility of using the cameras, to draw what they see; to collect already available or provoked visual documents; to perform visual elicitation interviews, etc.

Then, each member of the team had to process and analyze the collected data, for example, by classification (using a priori or emergent categories), by quantification, counting, etc. The processing and analysis operations of the images referred to the content of the images and to the interpretations given by the participants, without the researchers attributing meaning to some of the components of the visual representations (as psychologists usually do). For example, a drawn hollow was nothing else than a hollow or the place where the subject would hide from his/her parents (as he/she confessed in the interview), not a childhood trauma as a psychologist would interpret it. We were interested in the perspective of those under study, in the interpretations that they gave to the elements in the images; we processed and analyzed the aspects obvious to the researcher or the aspects revealed by the subjects in the interviews about images, not the unconscious aspects revealed by any psychoanalysis.

And in interpreting data, each member of the team had to show how they applied, verified, completed, modified, or grounded theories in their own visual study.

The plan, precisely accomplished, was the following: for each stage of the research I organized training meetings with the team members; there were seven school meetings that also referred to the analysis of the visual data by means of NVivo 10 software, to the use of images in presenting the results of the research, and to the observance of ethical and deontological rules specific to image research. After each training session, each member of the team put into practice, in their own research project, what they learnt – they collected visual data, analyzed them, and interpreted them under my direct supervision. The last session was a workshop when we analyzed the relevance of visual data for each piece of research (by comparison to the results obtained in previous similar studies where other types of data were collected by using techniques other than the visual ones). The end of the project was dedicated to writing a chapter in a collective volume by each member of the team. This book includes, besides the introductory chapter, a methodological one written by me where the relevance of visual data in social research is analyzed and seven chapters, one written by each member of the team, describing the studies where they applied the visual techniques.

Subsequently, I present each chapter of the book and each of their authors. I will mention what each chapter deals with (the objectives of the study, the methodology, what it brings new, and the conclusions of the research) and what is the previous expertise of the authors in the topic under research.

The first chapter, the one about the relevance of visual data in social research, is written by me. I am an associate professor, and I have been teaching for 15 years courses on qualitative research methods and techniques. Lately, my interests have also focused on qualitative visual data. Consequently, I also teach a course on Visual Sociology in Communication and Public Relations Program, and I am preparing one course on Techniques for Image Analysis and Interpretation for the Digital Media Program. As I have stated at the beginning of this introduction, in 2016, I wrote the first book in Romania on visual research: *Visual Data in Social Research* published by Cluj University Press Publishing House. I also published in internationally recognized journals – an article on the visual representation of the social structure in Romania and a visual essay by which I tried to describe in images what it means to live with an incurable disease. In the first study, the participants were asked to draw the representatives of the social classes ('Acceptable and Unacceptable Sources of Inequality in Romania, A Visual Study,' published in *TRAMES - A Journal of Humanities and Social Sciences*, vol. 19, no. 4, 2015), and, in the second study the participants were asked to take photos of aspects of their everyday lives ('Photovoice: Adult Patients of Hospice Braşov (Romania) on What it Means to Live with Cancer', published in *Visual Communication*, vol. 16, No. 2, 2017). I also participated in international conferences organized in Romania and Canada where I presented the results obtained in the studies where I collected, analyzed and interpreted visual data.

I showed in the first chapter – 'The relevance of visual data in social research' why visual data are valuable in research. I tried to prove that they are not less important than the textual or numerical data, that sometimes they are even indispensable in social research, that they have amazing features that in many situations make them superior to other types of data; that they offer various and less complicated ways of collecting them by applying innovative, creative data collection techniques, that they can be subject to the same processing, analysis and interpretation methods and techniques that are used for textual data without the necessity of adapting or inventing new ones; that visual data can be used not only in descriptive studies but also in explicative ones either for testing hypotheses or for generating hypotheses (or even theories); that they make the presentation of research results more accessible, easier to understand, and that they allow access not only to scientific knowledge but also to other types of knowledge. I tried not to overlook the difficulties inherent in the use of visual data in research, and each of the advantages and disadvantages presented was exemplified with images or descriptions of real visual research situations (most of the examples come from the very studies presented in the other chapters of this book).

The second chapter, the one about the study of change in a rural community in Romania, is written by Codrina Csesznek. Codrina has been an associate professor since 2008; she is interested in studying (local and ethnic) communities and their community development mechanisms. She teaches courses on the Sociology of Community Development, Community Development Strategies, and Sociology of Interethnic Relations. She defended her PhD thesis entitled 'Social Networks of Local Elite in Harghita and Covasna Counties' in 2006 at Bucharest University, and she defines herself as a qualitative sociologist. She had her book *Ethnic Communities and Local Elites* published in 2007 at 'Transylvania' University Publishing House in Braşov and two illustrated volumes related to the rural community that became the subject of study for this book, too: 'Drăguş. Images of a Romanian Village' at C2 Design Publishing House in Braşov and 'Studies and Confessions about Contemporary Drăguş' at Cluj University Press Publishing House. Equally, in the book *Italy-Romania. L'esperienza completa della migrazione*, published in 2014 in Italy at Kurumuny Publishing House, Codrina presented the results of studying the return migration phenomenon to Drăguş community. She had articles published on the civic engagement in local communities, on the role of the ethnic economy in local development, on the assessment of needs in these communities, on the experiences of foreign tourists in Transylvania's rural area and others. Similarly, Codrina also participated in several international conferences in Italy and Romania where she talked about rural communities and social change.

In Chapter II, 'Studying social change through the re-photography technique in a rural Romanian community', Codrina describes social change within a typical rural Romanian community. The chapter presents, with the help of photos taken by the researcher herself, comparative aspects of social life specific to this community in two moments: 2004 and 2017. Codrina intended to show whether significant changes occurred over a period of 13 years and to what extent, the orientation, amplitude, and even the mechanisms of change can be identified in photographs. Her chapter is full of mirrored images of places, participants and activities/functions/processes, descriptions, and explanations of change. It demonstrates the value of photography and of the technique of re-photography in rendering social dynamics and it reveals their critical function – activating community consciousness and stimulating the elaboration of local development policies.

Chapter III is written by Marinela Şimon. She is a lecturer, and one of her major research interests is volunteering; her doctoral thesis refers to "Implications of Cost-Benefit Theory in Volunteering in the Social Field" and her latest book published at the European Institute Publishing House – *Volunteering in the Social Field. Motivation and Management*, and some of her papers published in specialized journals and volumes of conferences similarly deal with volunteering issues (e.g., general aspects of volunteering in Romania and of volunteering in the social field, volunteer management, students' opinions on volunteers and volunteering, the role of motivation in volunteering, altruism as a form of prosocial behavior, etc.). Equally, Marinela is currently working on the courses Volunteering and Social Responsibility and Social Responsibility of the Organizations that she is about to teach at specialties in the domain of human resources at bachelor and master level, and she is keen on promoting volunteering among students. Thus, in 2014, she coordinated an event where the students volunteered to create objects to offer on celebrations to the elderly in residential centers in Braşov, and in 2016 she organized the event 'Chance for Change' where representatives of the public and nongovernmental institutions in Brasov were invited and who presented to students the role of volunteering in their personal and professional training, as well as in the life of social service beneficiaries and of the community in general.

Chapter III, 'Are the volunteers different from non-volunteers? A comparative analysis based on visual data (drawings)', attempts at exploring the specific characteristics of volunteers and non-volunteers. Twenty-five subjects of different ages and levels of schooling, women and men, volunteers or not, were asked to represent in drawing a person who volunteers in the social field and one who does not. What Chapter III brings new is not only the presentation of the results obtained by using this novel technique, but also the attempt at comparing these results with those obtained by the author in previous studies on the topic of volunteering (studies where she used the semi-structured interview and the questionnaire). The characteristics of the volunteers in the social field (as they emerged from the analysis and interpretation of the drawings) matched the theoretical model of the altruistic personality, but the visual data also allowed the identification of some factors that could complement this theory (for example, those referring to the training and education of volunteers).

Chapter IV is written by Ada Dobrescu. She is a university lecturer with serious insights in psychology. As early as her doctoral work she focused on studying identity in adolescents, she participated in international conferences in Romania, Bulgaria, and Italy where she presented papers on the identity profile of adolescents, focusing on different personal or social components of their identity – for example, gender identity, vocational identity, etc. Ada published in 2016 a book on adolescent identity: *Adolescence Today. Psycho-Social Aspects* at

Cluj University Press Publishing House, and she has been teaching for several years a course on the Sociology of Identity and one on the Psychology of Small Groups.

In Chapter IV, 'A visual perspective on adolescent identity', Ada attempted at comparing the verbal identity descriptions of adolescents obtained by semi-structured interviews (within the doctoral program) with visual identity descriptions. So, she asked her subjects to draw their adolescence and illustrate it with photos from their own albums. The results contain, among others, the adolescent social network, the favorite loisir activities, adolescent models, the defining elements of this life stage (not only the major ones from the point of view of researchers such as the beginning of sexual life, the baccalaureate, etc., but also some major elements from the point of view of teenagers, such as the appearance of the pimples or the first hair dyeing), and the way in which they deal with important life experiences (from the onset of a vice to peer discrimination or the death of someone dear). Ada demonstrates that the images, unlike the text, better capture context-bound or nonverbal communication aspects and they describe more suggestively states of mind, feelings, or relationships.

Chapter V is written by Diana-Cristina Bódi. She is a lecturer and the most important of her scientific concerns is the study of the elderly. Connected to this topic are the two research projects funded by national and international organizations she was member of (one referring to the elderly and volunteering and the other referring to the cultural and informational opportunities specific to this age group), the course on Elderly Assistance that she teaches at the Social Assistance Program, her PhD thesis: 'The Elderly as a Resource in Family and Society', her book published in 2017 at European Institute Publishing House: 'The Elderly People. An Important Resource in Family and Society' and the many articles she published in specialized journals and in volumes of international conferences. Diana's publications refer to the identity and lifestyle of elderly people, to identity transformations and to the old-age identity crisis, to the role of social services in changing the identity of the elderly, to spending their free time at this stage of life, to the role of these people in the contemporary family, to the problems and risks the elderly are confronted with, to their social integration, etc.

Chapter V – 'Using the drawing to identify post-retirement identity transformations' – reveals how the elderly's life has changed after retirement. When in interviews Diana obtained in a previous piece of research on the same subject, answers of the type 'Before retirement it used to be better', she tried to find out what was the 'good' that the pensioners did not manage to satisfactorily describe it in words. Thus, she used a visual technique to complement the information she had previously obtained, but also to show, comparatively, what type of data drawing technique facilitates access to. Twenty-six seniors aged between 60 and 84, women and men with different levels of schooling and living in urban and rural areas, were asked to draw themselves as they were before retirement and how they are now as retirees. By comparing the two drawings – the active period and the passive period in the life of each subject – Diana discovered both identity changes related to roles, feelings and desires, passions and leisure time, and some sort of identity completions with specific matters related to age issues, disengagement, disruption of the social network, and ageism. The technique of drawing seems to provide information that contradicts the theories that advocate the restriction of activities after retirement. Diana has discovered a diversification of the elderly's activities; even if they no longer have professional activities, they seem to use more intensively their free extended time.

Chapter VI is written by Daniela Sorea. She is a lecturer and she teaches General Logic, Epistemology and Sociology of Religions at the Sociology Program. She considers this combination of subjects exciting, challenging. She elaborated a PhD thesis entitled 'Paradigmatic Dimensions of C. G. Jung's Thinking' (2006); she has been a member of CRIFST (Romanian Committee for the History and Philosophy of Science and Technology of the Romanian Academy) since 2017 and a member of EASA (European Association of Social Anthropologists). She had the volume *Epistemology of the Socio-human* published at the 'Transilvania' University Publishing House in 2006 and studies in the collective volumes *The Christian Family. Anthropological Fundamentals, Love and Sexuality in Celibacy and Marriage* (2015), *Church and Society* (2016), *Spe Salvi. Faith, Trust and Hope: History and Forecasts* (2017) all published at Cluj University Press Publishing House. She participated in numerous conferences in Romania, Hungary, Bulgaria, and France; she has recently published articles on the generosity of Jung's religiosity, on the religiosity of Romanian students, on neo-paganism, on the future of secularization, and on the epistemological implications of Brexit.

Chapter VI – 'God, as the children of Romania draw It' – reveals how Romanian children represent God and how the Romanian children's religiosity is related to the evolutionary trends of contemporary Western religiosity. A total of 186 children (101 aged 6 years and 85 aged 7 years) were asked to draw God in 2004 and 2016; they were then invited, while or after drawing, to explain what they drew and to tell what they know about God. The chapter includes a pertinent analysis of God's characteristics – as perceived by the children (e.g., God is happy, human, but at the same time from another world and It communicates by the Church, etc.) and interesting comparative findings related to the representation of divinity with the children of 2004, respectively with those from after

12 years (the 2016 children are being told about God more by parents rather than by grandparents, the church dimension is more common in children's drawings in 2004, etc.) or related to the representation of God with Orthodox and Protestant children. Noticing the ease with which the children drew and the coherence of their representations, Daniela demonstrates that her subjects are not atheists and neither are their parents, as long as they are the ones who tell their children about God. Then, the comparisons between the generations of children made the author claim that the children's parents are less anchored in the Christian religion (from which they allow themselves liberty) than their grandparents. The tendency associated to this finding seems to be the expansion of spirituality in contemporary times. Some of the children's representations exemplify spectacularly this tendency: God is a woman or an angel, God is all that surrounds us, It is the wisdom that helps people build blocks, etc.

Chapter VII is written by Mihaela Gotea. She is a lecturer, and for the last 15 years while teaching at university, her concerns have been related to the study of family and to the training of social workers. Mihaela teaches a course on Family Sociology and one on Family and Child Assistance. She defended her doctorate in sociology in 2012, at the Babes-Bolyai University of Cluj-Napoca. She had the book *The Social Network and Marital Conflict: Constraints and Opportunities* published in 2014 at the Cluj University Press Publishing House; she has also published numerous articles on intra-familial relationships, on determinants of marital satisfaction, on the causes of couple conflict, on the attitudes to marital conflict, or on various types of families at social risk. She participated in different conferences where she presented papers on the cost-benefit paradigm in family study, on the marital market in contemporary society and on family – cause and solution for children's behavioral problems. Mihaela has got tight relationships with practitioners in the social field, and she is involved in various community programs meant to prevent and combat domestic violence. In this context, she has moderated for three years in a row the Annual Campaign for the Prevention of Domestic Violence organized by the Reformed Christian Center 'House of Hope' Braşov and a meeting of the Inter-professional Network for the Prevention and Control of Domestic Violence in Braşov.

In Chapter VII – 'Exploring social workers' perceptions of their marital partners in different family life stages, using visual methodology' – Mihaela presents the elements specific to each stage of family life trying to establish a connection between them and the perception of the social assistants about the couple partner. She highlighted a relationship between the perception of the couple partner, the perceived quality of the marital relationship, and the characteristics of the profession of social assistant. The visual data she worked with are provided by 22 social workers who were asked to draw, to take photos, or to film the way their marriage partner currently is. The chapter also provides an interesting analysis of how the subjects responded to the visual techniques, of how they worked with them, and of the effects they had on the participants.

Chapter VIII is written by Ioana Anisa Atudorei. She is a lecturer, she defended her doctorate in sociology in 2014 at the University of Bucharest. The dissertation included an exhaustive research where she used both qualitative and quantitative techniques in an attempt at capturing the moral emotions experienced in various contexts by the students enrolled in the bachelor cycle at Transylvania University in Braşov. The results she obtained are described in the book *Moral Emotions in the Context of the Crisis in Romania* published in 2016 at Cluj University Press Publishing House. Equally, Ioana published and presented at conferences papers on the effects of social solidarity on moral emotions and morality and on the integration of moral emotions and education in the context of the economic crisis in Romania.

In Chapter VIII – 'Studying students' moral emotions by visual techniques' – the author presents situations when moral emotions appear in this category of people. Ioana asked her subjects (39 students from the technical-engineering, vocational, socio-human profiles at 'Transilvania' University of Braşov) to draw contexts related to their school activities when they felt embarrassed, ashamed, and guilty. The analysis inspected different variations, depending, for example, on the gender of participants, on their residence or on their material well-being. There are analyses of the diversity of moral emotions reflected in drawings and of the diversity of the situations where they occur, as well as analyses of the factors that are associated with each separate emotion. Similarly, as the author considers that emotions should be analyzed in close correlation with the socio-cultural experience of those who experiment them, the chapter clarifies the similarities and differences of the ways in which moral emotions are defined in the Romanian context compared to other contexts. What is equally spectacular in this chapter is the attempt at comparing the results obtained now by applying the visual technique with previous results obtained by applying the questionnaire (Ioana worked then with a much larger sample of students which allowed her to statistically analyze the data).

After we wrote the book, I felt it lacked a proper ending. Therefore, I asked a researcher who has already used visual data in her studies and who is not Romanian to evaluate our work and to complete our book by writing a closing chapter.

Thus, Chapter IX – 'Concluding notes: Applications and developments of visual techniques' – is written by Giuseppina Cersosimo. She is an associate professor at the University of Salerno (Italy), she wrote various essays and articles about the importance of the images in social research, and she participated in international seminars and conferences where she addressed visual topics (in Italy, United Kingdom, Poland, Spain, and USA). Recently she even organized an international conference about visual sociology: 'Visual research in Sociology: Applications and Development' (2018, University of Salerno). Giuseppina applied visual research techniques in the field of health and disease (see 'Images, Perceptions and Representations of Choosing Where, How and When to Die', published in *Salute e Società*, vol. 1, 2011; 'Improving Health Communication through Renewed and Enlarged Social and Technological Interactions', published in *Sociologia e Ricerca Sociale*, vol. 114, 2017; and 'Health and Illness: Interpretations and Meanings through the Photograph', in press now), but her interest in image is larger than that (see her book chapter 'Everett C. Hughes: The Gaze and the Imagination', published at Kurumuny Publishing House in 2018 or her article 'The Urban Imagination of Anselm Strauss', published in *Sociologia e Ricerca Sociale*, Vol. 106, 2015).

Chapter IX is the concluding chapter in which Giuseppina tried to briefly evaluate previous chapters and to add other research situations where visual techniques could be applied; she tried also to introduce other visual techniques that we did not use in this project and which are not presented in this book. The chapter also contains a look into the future of the visual research; it discusses some development directions in the use of the images in social research and mentions some new and creative visual research techniques that probably will be used more and more in research.

As this is a book on the use of the visual in research, each of the ideas and each of the results presented here is exemplified in images. This makes the volume attractive, interesting, and very easy to follow and understand. I believe the presence of images in the book is of great help, by providing useful examples to those who want to use visual techniques in their social research.

The book addresses current methodological issues related to the use of visual data in research, and it illustrates the variety of social topics that can be visually addressed; it discusses the methodological elements that are thoroughly debated in the literature, but also some novel ones that appeared in the visual pieces of research described in this book; the types of information that are generated by the application of visual techniques are presented in each chapter of the book, as well as the way they can confirm, complete, modify, or even contradict the knowledge obtained by analyzing textual or numerical data. I consider that a book that contains methodological debates and examples of visual research conducted in entirely new contexts is never superfluous.

I consider that it is an interesting volume by the diversity of research situations presented. Both sociologists and social assistants can find interesting topics as the themes that are addressed are not only methodological, but there are also some that deal with worthy aspects related to community change, to identity, to perceptions and representations, and to emotions. By the variety of the knowledge and scientific interests of the authors, the chapters introduce the reader into the sociology of religion, rural community development, self-development, identity transformation, and moral emotions. The participants the studies presented in this book deal with also vary, depending on research, from preschoolers and adolescents, to adults and the elderly.

The methodological diversity can also be an attraction of the book. Visual data were collected by the researcher directly in the field, but images were equally produced by participants at the request of the researcher, both drawings and photographs were collected, visual elicitation interviews were taken, etc. But, what is even more important is that in the attempt at solving the same research objectives, the results obtained by analyzing and interpreting the images were compared with the results obtained by interviewing (in-depth and semi-structured) or from questionnaire.

Then, each chapter is written differently. I do not know whether this is a limitation of the book or whether it is rather a part of its charm. The chapters resemble each other by the fact that they all deal with the use of a visual technique in research, but they are written in different styles, by very different authors. Some have a formal and sober writing, others have a playful or critical style; with some it feels like their writing 'suffer' from a philosophical 'deformation', with others it feels like 'the deformation' is statistical or psychological; some prove an extraordinary ethnographic spirit, others, a solid culture, and others a devout methodological passion.

One of the important limitations of the book is the fact that we could not work with the film, that we could not include in our chapters even a study where filming should have been applied. Although we have tried in some situations to use it, making films does not seem to be the first option of the participants when they have a choice between filming and drawing or taking photos. Another limitation is that we did not intend to work with the innovative techniques that the visual approach allows of (e.g., making objects, collages, lego constructions, sandboxing). And finally, none of the studies made use of quantitative analysis of images, of statistical sampling, and in any of the studies we did not test a priori formulated hypotheses.

Then there were some methodological objectives that have not been touched upon and which, along with the use of the research techniques mentioned in the previous paragraph, remain a desideratum for our future projects. For example, most of the research presented in this book assumes the use of a single visual technique (as more techniques could not be used, as the subjects would not work with more, etc.). I wish we were able to provide more conclusions on possible differences in content among the images obtained with different techniques (drawing, photographing, and filming) to solve the same objectives. Then it would have been interesting, but it proved impossible to do in this project (because, for example, the students of the past years are no longer students today, because the Third-Aged people a few years ago are no longer alive today, etc.) to collect visual data from the same subjects that previously offered (for the same purposes) textual or numeric data. I wish we could discuss more about the differences between visual data and other types of data, obtained from the same subjects, applying different collection methods and techniques within the same research.

I have designed this project and I have coordinated this team in the hope of bringing the visual closer to my colleagues and to the Romanian researchers in general. I have coordinated this book with the intention of persuading as many social scientists as possible that visual data is relevant and it deserves to be used in their research. After I had had the opportunity to see how my colleagues introduced the images for the first time in their research, how they processed and analyzed the visual data for the first time with the NVivo software, etc., I was very happy to notice their curiosity about visual techniques, their passion in working with images, the happiness generated by the amazing findings they have reached. Now I hope that this book will cause similar experiences in its readers.

Florentina Scârneci-Domnişoru

I The relevance of visual data in social research

Abstract: The chapter shows how valuable images are in social research. It firstly describes what the status of images is within research methodology and then what their potential contributions to social knowledge are, by presenting their characteristics and their role in each of the stages of the research. The chapter answers questions like: What social research objectives can be solved by means of visual data? Why collect visual data in social research? What does visual data processing and analysis mean? How can visual data be interpreted? Why make a visual presentation of the research results? The chapter demonstrates that visual data are very easy to collect, they facilitate interviewing, they efficiently and unexpectedly complement information collected in the form of numbers and texts, they have great potential in describing and explaining social phenomena, and they are both scientifically and artistically relevant. The chapter concludes that visual data are significant, they deserve to be placed next to the other social research data – the textual and the numerical ones – and they deserve to be used to the same degree and with the same trust by social scientists. The examples brought in support of the ideas presented are taken mostly from the visual pieces of research in the other chapters of this book.

Keywords: visual data, photographs, drawings, films, visual research, visual sociology

1 What is the status of visual data in social research?

In a bizarre way, visual data have been forgotten for a long time by most social researchers in the social field, and if they were not forgotten then, they were long avoided. Schnettler and Raab (2008) consider that visual sociology exists in its own right only since 1970. Many authors concerned with visuals claim that before photographs had been used more decoratively by sociologists, as illustrations in their professional texts. Between 1920 and 1960, photographs almost disappeared from the sociological scientific materials, being gradually replaced by graphics and statistical tables.

It is true that, in many places in the world, since the 1990s onwards, things have changed significantly, that the visual has had an ever more consistent and important presence in social research. Rose, in 2014, defined this situation as being the most striking development in social sciences in the last decade, and other authors speak, referring to the early 21st century, about a 'visual turn' recorded in these sciences. But this situation does not occur everywhere, and in any scientific or professional environment. In Romania, for example, at least in sociology, it seems that visual data do not exist.

I have written above that in a 'bizarre' way, visual data were avoided because I had discovered in Becker (1995) an idea that remained in my mind as a great wonder. The author shows how natural sciences use visual materials as something indispensable and that no one can imagine how biology, physics or astronomy would look without photographic evidence. Recently, an anonymous reviewer of an article where I have presented many images has also expressed his/her opinion that 'the strength of this paper lies in the face validity of the photographs presented, not just as 'illustration' but as actual evidence'. But this is not a unanimously accepted opinion among the specialists in the social field. That is why my amazement remains: How did it happen for images to be categorized as 'unscientific' in social sciences?

The academia tends to be the most resistant to the idea of introducing visual materials in the study of the social. It seems that for this medium the image is a too naive reproducer of reality (see Kolb, 2008). And from here another amazement of mine: Don't some reliable data have to do this? Namely, should not they be as simple and ingenuous as possible and should not they reproduce reality as reliable as possible?

Henny (1986) considers that visual data have been discredited because they have been used in social sciences to illustrate the obvious. Perhaps this is the reason why anthropology and history are less blasphemed when using images – because their subject matter is not really evident. But again my amazement: Should visual data be discredited or those who used the images to illustrate obviousness? Similarly, I would also interpret Becker's (1995) idea that the loss of influence of visual data was due to the use of images that compromised a research report or of some that, by their strong impact, shadowed some questionable results. Again: Should the researchers who did this have been defamed for the idea of using images in research?

An easier to understand cause for the discreditation of visual data would be the idea that they were used more decoratively with a view to maintain the interest and attention of the readers (Henny, 1986). I do not see anything wrong in trying to make more interesting the results of research by images, but their exclusive use in this manner can indeed minimize their value.

Whatever the cause, the fact remains: visual data have long been used inconsistently with their importance and relevance. In my opinion, visual data can and should be treated in the same way as the other types of data (textual and numerical data) are treated in social research. I consider that their status in research can and must be identical to that of the other types of data.

Actually, maybe I should talk about the status of data in general. And maybe this would be the right place to express another amazement of mine: Why is there so little talk in the methodological treaties about the type and character of the data? Data are collected, data are processed, data are analysed and they are interpreted; thus, data are the most important elements of any research and depending on their characteristics, we have to adapt our collection techniques, the processing methods, the types of analysis, etc. Nevertheless, there are no chapters in books dedicated to them; sometimes you run into difficulties even when you try to identify some elementary classifications of data, some simple data typologies.

I think that any methodological discussion should begin with the data and that it is high time we should put the images where they belong, that is, within data; we should talk about methods and techniques for collecting images, about how we should process and analyse them, about how they should be interpreted, about their role in presenting the results of research, etc. Namely, we should integrate them into the social research methodology. I divide the data into qualitative (textual and visual) and quantitative (numerical), and I claim that in any type of research and with any of the methods and techniques of data collection both textual and numerical data (see Rotariu, 2016) as well as visual data can be obtained. For example, observation can provide numerical data, such as, how many people enter a store, how much time they spend there, etc.; textual data, such as, what they wear, what questions they ask the shop assistant, etc.; and visual data, such as, photographs of the store, of the shop assistants, etc. Or, by means of the questionnaire, you can collect numerical data such as age, income; textual data such as genre, civil status; and even visual data when subjects are asked to choose one of a range of images.

All sorts of methods and techniques for collecting, processing and analysing numerical and textual data have been perfected over time. For example, the questionnaire survey and the interview are largely discussed in the literature, statistical processing of numerical or textual quantified data has spectacularly developed, the coding of textual data is now done by using all sorts of techniques in continuous diversification, etc. I believe it is high time we showed the same consideration (methodologically speaking) to visual data which, as I have demonstrated, as early as the 1990s, have begun to grow in popularity among social scientists. They are used more, more is written about them, solutions for the problems that their use in research might bring about are being looked for and so on. I join, by this chapter (but also by coordinating this book) the authors who strive to integrate images among the data relevant to social knowledge.

I will thus try to demonstrate that visual data deserve the same attention, that they are equally relevant in social research as the other types of data. In my opinion, the relevance of visual data, as well as the relevance of textual and numerical ones, comes from both their intrinsic characteristics (see the advantages of taking photographs in social research in Flick, 1998 and the characteristics of visual data in Weber, 2008) and from their specific contribution to a piece of research (see Banks, 2001; Emmison and Smith, 2002; Banks, 2007; Van Leeuwen and Jewitt, 2008; Mitchell, 2011; Margolis and Pauwels, 2011; Harper, 2012 and Pauwels, 2015b). Numeric data are relevant because they allow, for example, advanced statistical processing and establishing some sophisticated statistical relationships between variables. Textual data are relevant because they allow, for example, access to intensive meanings of experiences and a deep understanding of the phenomena under study. I will not insist further on the significance of textual and numerical data, but I will try to illustrate the importance of visual data (of photographs, drawings and films) by describing their characteristics and potential contribution to every stage of social research.

2 What social research objectives can be solved by means of visual data?

There are many social research objectives for whose resolution the image is more appropriate, not to say indispensable. For example, just as a study on the distribution of wage earnings in a population asks for the collection of numerical data, similarly, a study on the configuration of a human settlement asks for the collection of visual data (see the structure of a rural household in Transylvania in Chapter II of this book). Sure enough, most types of social research do not exclusively collect data of a certain type; in fact, most of the research collects both textual and numerical data. But I am convinced that there are also many situations when the visual may add to these two types of data. This is either because some information about the phenomena under study can only be obtained in a visual form or because it is good to visually complete and check the information obtained in textual or numerical form. This is the case, for example, of some perceptual or representation studies, of some change studies or of some related to social impact.

For example, you can definitely ask your subjects to describe the representatives of the lower and upper classes in Romania today (asking for information about how they are, what they consume, how much they earn, etc.), but may be the identification of the way in which the representatives of the two social classes are perceived would be more precise and complete if you asked them to draw them as well (see Fig. 1).

The images reveal information that, normally, is not provided by language-based methods. For example, it is very likely that, in a discussion about social

Fig. 1: 'Typical Romanians from the Upper and Lower Class in today's Romania', drawn by a 21-year-old woman, 2012 (author's archive)

class representatives, subjects do not largely refer to the way they dress, to the accessories they wear, to the language of their bodies, etc. When drawing them, however, it seems inevitable that the subjects should include such elements in the images they produce (e.g. they mention car or bag brands owned by the upper-class representatives, they highlight hairdressings or bowing and knelt postures of the lower-class representatives, etc.).

In this volume, you can find many other examples dedicated to the study of the representation, change or impact that show the abundancy of information brought by images and the major contribution of this type of data to solving various research objectives. Visual data can also be used in studies related to the everyday life of people from different contemporary communities (e.g. Roma

Fig. 2: 'God', drawn by a 7-year-old girl, 2016 (with permission of Daniela Sorea)

communities, gay communities); social interactions (e.g. in organizations, in groups of children); reconstruction of events; relationships; rituals (e.g. wedding traditions); of human settlements and so on.

Because I started writing this chapter wondering, I wonder again why we should not collect visual data when, obviously, the objectives refer to images (e.g. what is someone's self-image or how someone imagines God – see Fig. 2) or when the objectives can be solved more easily and precisely with images (e.g. by taking photographs of how much and to what degree the appearance of a building changed or by filming the effect of a new rule on the behaviour of some workers, etc.).

This is not the place to describe the importance of the symbols in the lives of those who are our object of inquiry, but I claim that by means of images we can have easy access to this side of human life. Sometimes, the numbers and the texts are not enough to symbolize a reality, and the images can complement the need of expression of the subjects and the need of understanding of the researchers. For example, a teenager may find it easier to describe in images than in words how his/her life will be if s/he gets to be taken care of by his/her alcoholic father (see Fig. 3). On the other hand, researchers and the public may find it easier to understand how, for example, poverty or old age are if they see them.

Fig. 3: 'A life full of mistakes and garbage', photograph taken by a 16-year-old boy, 2012 (with permission of Noemi Bernad)

If social research aims at understanding the various phenomena related to humanity, then the feelings as specific human affective processes cannot be neglected. You can ask your subjects to choose a figure from 1 to 10 to show how nervous they were in a certain context, you can ask them to describe what they felt when they underwent a particular experience, but, for an easy and complete access to feelings, I think it would be appropriate to retort to images, as well. It is quite often impossible to reduce to numbers, and it is difficult to express in words a state, a feeling, an impression, a sensation; it is hard to make the others understand, by words, what you felt in a certain context, or how much a certain gesture touched you. The image seems to express emotions better, transmitting emotions. For example, to really understand what a cancer patient feels like having this disease, it may not be enough to have an interview. An image similar to the one in Fig. 4, explained in a few words, may be more telling.

Fig. 4: 'I have a whole collection of watches, but now … they count my hours …', photograph taken by a 50-year-old man, 2013 (with the permission of Hospice Casa Speranţei Braşov)

The tasks of image production seem to induce in subjects, better than other research techniques, all sorts of emotional revelations. For example, in Chapter VII of this book there is a study on the perception of the marital partner. Participants have revealed how the task of producing the images about husband/wife has induced a strong emotional state. They have looked better at the partners, they have remembered (trying to show others) who their spouses were, why they were together, what keeps them together, why they appreciate them, etc. The production of visual documents has made them ponder over it, has made them aware of their feelings towards their partner and has made them share those feelings (thus, they reached the researcher more easily, in an intensive, profound form). The author of the study shows how the subjects have insisted, unprovoked, to show her how much they were touched by their participation in the study, how clear the feelings for the partner have become, for a few days. When you look at the images produced by these subjects, you can also feel the love they felt when they took photographs and when they made the photograph collages: the tenderness they put in rendering even elements that disturb them – the tics of their partners, their frivolity, the things they left unfinished, their lack of reaction, the fact that they are forgetful or untidy, etc.

Thus, images facilitate access to information indispensable to any social scientist. I consider that solving many of the research objectives is complicated and incomplete when not approached from the visual point of view, as well.

3 Why collect visual data in social research?

Moving on to the data collection stage, I do not understand why we always talk about textual data when it comes to putting into practice the observation. In the chapters dedicated to this method, the methodology textbooks indicate to us how to make 'observation notes', that is to say, to collect texts. This is a further wonder of mine as to why in the age of gadgets, when almost every device records images, there is not more talk about taking photographs or filming.

The images, compared to the observation notes, give a bird's eye view of the studied object and not a sequential one generated by a verbal description of the same object (see Schnettler and Raab, 2008); visual data can capture the studied object in more detail, they can record things that happen too fast to be observed (see Flick, 1998), elements that the observer fails to notice in the field can be identified at a closer or repeated analysis of the image (it is also possible to enlarge the image and to examine the images in slow-motion in case of filming). For example, in Chapter II of this book, the author confesses that, when looking at the photographs taken in the field, she discovered elements she had not noticed as an observer. She considers that the photograph worked as a stimulus in the identification of the details of change (she discovered, by comparing the photographs taken of the same places and from the same angles, after a period of 13 years, all sorts of details that could be easily overlooked, e.g. the pavement, roofing, etc.).

It is true that when collecting textual or visual data using the observation method, the suspicion referring to the selectivity of the information gathered always exists. There are always questions like: isn't it that the researcher wrote or captured in images the things that seemed important to him, wasn't s/he rather subjective in choosing what is to be noted or photographed and filmed? But capturing images in collaborative or participative research eliminates this criticism. The collection of visual data in collaboration with the participants or their production by the participants themselves allows of a change in the power relationship between the researcher and the subjects, an emic approach of the studied phenomena, but also the access to what is inaccessible to the researcher. For example, it is one thing to take photographs of how poor your subjects are and it is another thing to ask them to show this by taking photographs.

My wonder is equally stirred by interviewing. I wonder why we force it in cases where it is unproductive. It is often easier to use visual techniques when it comes to collecting data from more special subjects such as children, people with poorer linguistic abilities, emotional persons, the subjects coming from other cultures or speaking languages other than the researcher; equally, it is easier to apply visual techniques than interviewing techniques when it comes to collecting information on sensitive issues about which it is more difficult to talk, such as illness, direct boss, death, religion, etc. For example, it is one thing to ask the employees to list their direct boss defects, and it is another thing to ask them to make a caricature of him or her (possibly as a group task).

If visual techniques are not chosen to replace the interview, they could at least be given the chance to potentiate it – as it happens in visual elicitation studies. This technique is used to encourage interviewees to say more, to remember past events or to allow access to forgotten information, but it can equally reveal participants' hidden values and opinions (Holm, 2008). Thus, visual data not only facilitate interviewing, they actually complement and check the information gathered during the interview. Harper (2002) adds the fact that word exchange uses less of brain capacity than the situations when the brain processes both words and images and that this may be one of the causes for which the visual elicitation interview is not just an interview where more information is gathered, but it is rather one that provides a different kind of information.

The technique can become indispensable when the question-response context is intimidating for respondents or when there is an evident power relationship between the interviewer and the interviewee (Clark-Ibáñez, 2004). The same author claims that images can detense the relationship between the researcher and the interviewees; they can reduce the strangeness of the interview because they offer something to those involved to focus on (direct visual contact between the researcher and the participant must not be maintained, as the two can look at the images; similarly, the embarrassing silences can be masked by looking at the images – see also Collier, apud Banks, 2001).

Visual elicitation interview exploits some characteristics of images – the fact that they have a great potential in eliminating language and cultural barriers and that they are evocative. For example, it is one thing to ask children to talk about God, and it is another thing to ask them to draw Him and then to tell what they have drawn about (see Chapter VI of this book). It is one thing to ask people to tell you about their life and another to ask them to do it in their parent's home where they 'see' their past or with a photo album in front of them.

A great advantage of image-based interviewing technique is the variety of visual data that can be used: from drawings and photographs to objects and films, from images belonging to subjects to images belonging to the researcher, from images resulting from data processing and analysis to images from the public space, from images produced by subjects to images captured by researcher in the field and so on.

It is worth collecting images because there are different possibilities of collecting visual data in a social research. Besides the camera- or video camera-mediated observations, social visual documents can be collected. The great advantage of this data collection method is that it requires minimal effort on the part of the researcher. This is the case of already available visual documents, that is, of the numerous pre-existing image collections waiting to be processed, analysed and interpreted (collections of drawings, photographs or films found in subjects' houses, in institutions, on the Internet; in addition, there are the images collected by other researchers with a view to solving the same or similar objectives – see secondary analysis), but also the case of provoked visual documents where the participants are asked to produce images related to various themes (e.g. to draw the ideal teacher, to take photographs of what makes him/her proud of his/her job or to film the difficulties they encounter when using a particular product).

Besides the fact that the spontaneous visual documents found in collections are fairly easy to obtain (see online collections of visual materials), their great advantage is that they are non-reactive (there are very rare data collection situations in social research where we are not confronted with the issue of reactivity). The production of visual documents has also got advantages: subjects can be given time to think about what to capture in the images and how to produce them (thus, they can meditate on what they want to transmit), they are alone when they do all this, unstressed by the researcher's presence, and they can change anytime and as many times they want the produced images; on the other hand, researchers have the participants at their disposal to explain the significance of the visual data produced and they know exactly who produced the visual data, for what purpose and in what context.

These ways of collecting visual documents, which have already become classic, are accompanied by the possibility of inventing new creative visual data collection techniques. The visual offers the chance for some spectacular methodological developments (see mapping with Powell (2010) and Clark (2011), or the constructions using objects symbolically laid out in boxes and the Lego parts constructions with Gauntlett (2007) or sandboxing with Mannay (2016)).

The greatest merit of images at the data collection stage is that they can assure an important type of triangulation. Why should not we complete and check

Fig. 5: 'A volunteering/A non-volunteering person', drawn by a 24-year-old woman, 2017 (with the permission of Marinela Simon)

reciprocally not only the textual and numerical data, but also the former with the visual data? As I have already pointed out, visual techniques generate hardly accessible information through interviews or questionnaires. For example, if you ask your subjects to describe a volunteer, interviewing will probably give you information related to different specific characteristics and actions, and rarely, if ever, information related to the volunteer's physical aspect, to what s/he communicates non-verbally and other similar data provided by drawings made upon the request of the researcher (see Fig. 5).

Chapter V of this volume shows how visual data provide for more information than interviews on the same topic. Moreover, the author describes how visual data contradicted some of the previous findings obtained as a result of interviews and questionnaires. And in line with the idea of triangulation, it is possible that two different visual techniques complement the data obtained to solve the same objectives. Within the study presented in the aforementioned chapter, the subjects were asked, for exploratory purposes, not only to produce drawings representing them before and after retirement, but also to present pictures illustrating the same situations. Although only three of the subjects provided photographs, they revealed new themes that had not appeared in their drawings. See, for example, the emerging theme of friends that was revealed only in the photographs that represented the subjects before retirement, not in the drawings on the same theme. I therefore consider that triangulation between visual techniques is equally valuable. It is highly likely that the drawings should elicit certain information, the photographs should elicit other information and the films other information about one and the same subject.

It is not always that the photographs are more offering than the drawings. For example, in Chapter IV of this volume, the author shows that there are many more categories and codes extracted from the drawings rather than from the photographs in the case of her study on adolescent identity. Coming back to triangulation, a combination, within the same project, of the already available visual documents with elicited visual documents can prove precious. Even though she did not make such a combination in her project, the aforementioned researcher attempted at comparing the information provided by the provoked documents (drawings and photographs made at her request) with that provided by the pre-existing imagery (see the identity studies carried out by various researchers who used the photographs spontaneously posted on adolescent Facebook pages). It seems that, in this case, there are considerable differences between the visual documents usually posted by teenagers on the Internet and the photographs (but especially the drawings) that some teenagers have provided my colleague with in her research. The publicly posted images are rather directed when the adolescents present themselves favourably; on the Internet, there are even modified images with the intention of correcting some defects; apparently, they reflect what teenagers would like to be rather than what they really are.

There are, of course, problems with the collection of visual data. If they are collected by the researcher, there is always the question of access to the field (legal, ethical or technical restrictions) and the issue of getting permission to take photographs or film or the ethical and deontological dilemmas related to the covered collection of images. By collecting visual data within the project that was the data source for writing this book, I have noticed that there are situations when the images captured by the researcher may not bring into discussion major issues. For example, in Chapter II it is shown that there is nothing strange in the application of visual techniques for a regular community to be in the limelight. If the researcher is also well known to the community, they accept gladly, openly and interestingly to be photographed over and over again. Not only do they accept the method, but they consider it useful because it helps them to be known, to show to the world how and who they are. Similar situations are reported by other researchers who consider that the subjects want to be seen, to get out of anonymity, to transmit a message through images (see Wiles et al., 2010).

There is also the great problem of reactivity, of naturalness in the participants surprised in the images when they know they are photographed or filmed (see other issues generated by field photographing at Holm, 2008). The study mentioned above, presented in Chapter II of this book, describes subjects' attempts to groom themselves for the photograph. In front of a camcorder, it often happens that the participants try to arrange their hair, to smile, to be surprised in situations that reflect the normality, well-being, harmony, etc., they try to sweep the yard, to arrange the house and the objects to be captured in photographs, etc. But all methods and techniques for collecting data from human subjects suffer from the problem of reactivity. Surely, this problem has its specificity when it comes to capturing subjects in images but, I emphasize again, reactivity characterizes any data collection in the social domain as long as we do not talk about applying covered techniques or collecting pre-existing documents.

There are also authors who consider exaggerated the question of human reactivity to the devices that capture images. For example, Heath et al. (2010) deems that there is little evidence that the devices would change the way the participants act, and Knoblauch (2012) claims that the presence of an observer among the studied ones may produce more distorted reactions than the presence of video cameras.

In the case of collecting already available visual documents, that is, of existing image collections, there are some problems that the researcher should face. First of all, the researcher needs to identify the data collections and to obtain permission to use them. Then, if the collections are not accompanied by information about who caught the images, in what context and for what purpose, it is very difficult for them to be processed, analysed and interpreted without significant errors. One of the studies in this volume (see Chapter VI) refers to the situation when the researcher processed and analysed collections of drawings she had been collecting over time. Even in this happy context when she knew exactly whom the data was collected from and to what end, there were some challenges she had to deal with. For example, it was impossible for her to go back to the participants to clarify matters related to the classification of images or to verify together with the subjects the conclusions she drew (the children who drew 12 years ago are no longer children today, and it is highly unlikely that they recalled having drawn God once, and it is even less likely that they knew what they wanted to represent then by the elements in the drawing).

In my opinion, the pre-existing visual documents are fairly useful in visual elicitation study type when they facilitate confessions, revelations and memories. In the case of a visual research carried out exclusively on spontaneous visual data collections, it is necessary to adapt the objectives to the characteristics of the collection; in these situations, one cannot research whatever, one does not have much freedom, one's objectives depend less on what one wants to find out than on what one has at one's disposal. The research described in Chapter V of this volume attempted at collecting existing photographs in the collections of the elderly to illustrate how they were before retirement and how they are now after retirement. The existing images, however, captured people's lives incompletely because they took photographs (especially in the past, when photographs were neither easy nor cheap to take) only in certain situations – usually at important and happy events of life such as wedding or baptism, holidays or trips, etc.

If the visual documents collected in the research are elicited, there is the problem of convincing the participants to capture the images and the problem of their minimal influence in the process of image capturing. The broad descriptions of these problems and the ways of solving them can be found in Scârneci-Domnişoru, 2016. In short, I mention the fact that it is possible that the task of producing visual data may seem bizarre, if not unreasonable, to adult subjects; it must be presented in such a way as to be attractive and to convince them that they will be able to do it successfully irrespective of how experienced they are in using the coloured pencil, the camera or the camcorder. Then, the production of images must be presented clearly enough to obtain useful data, but at the same time vague enough to obtain data consistent with what the subjects rather than the researchers believe, feel, think, etc. I will further present some observations referring to the collection of the provoked visual documents that I have made while collecting images within the project underlying this book.

When asked to produce images, the subjects react differently. The studies described in this book seem to indicate that the older they are, the more reluctant the people are to visual techniques. For example, the seniors refuse drawing more often, they look for reasons not to draw (e.g. because their hand shakes) or they draw very schematically (see Fig. 6). In Chapter V, where the study this image is taken from is presented, it is even concluded that the expressiveness of the drawing is lost with age. The comparison of the drawing in Fig. 6 (drawn by an elderly person) with that in Fig. 7 (drawn by a teenager – see Chapter IV of this book for details) backs up this conclusion. Neither taking photographs nor filming seems to be an elderly specific activity. In the research in Chapter V, the attempt to collect from the elderly pre-retirement and post-retirement photographs resulted in a failure after several elderly people claimed that they 'do not have post-retirement photos.'

In my opinion, the refusals to participate in some visual research are not more numerous than those in studies that collect data with other methods and techniques. Chapter VII of this book shows that one-third (11 out of 34) from

Fig. 6: 'Me before retirement/Me after retirement', drawn by a 81-year-old man, 2017 (with the permission of Diana Bódi)

Fig. 7: 'Me in adolescence', drawn by a 19-year-old girl, 2017 (with the permission of Ada Dobrescu)

those asked to participate refused to participate in the research; I do not consider it's a scary proportion.

It is possible that the drawing technique may be more suitable for women than for men. I have come to this conclusion by comparing the number of refusals to participate in visual research on the criterion of gender (see Chapter VIII which shows how more male students rather than female students refused to draw); similarly, I have found out that women's drawings, unlike men's, contain more often more elements that are more detailed. I think a similar claim could be made in the case of education level and in the case of residency: the drawing technique may be more suitable for people with high level of education and that come from urban areas than for people with low education level and coming from rural areas.

The subject's reactions to the request of producing images may be surprising in a different way. For example, it is highly likely that they do not want to produce visuals, but that they find easier ways to get them. For instance, they may choose to bring images from the Internet, as it happened in the case of the study described in Chapter VII. In such situations, it is possible for the subjects to consider the images found on the Internet more beautiful, more suggestive, more appropriate, or simply to consider that it saves more time and it is handier to retort to them. When you allow the subjects to decide how many images to produce, you may have other surprises – for example, they could bring only one. In the study presented in the same chapter, there were social workers who described their marital partner in a single image – 6 out of 23, but also a subject that provided 17 images for the same request.

The entire above-mentioned study showed that, when adult subjects have a choice among different visual techniques, they prefer photography (all 23 social assistants chose to describe their partner through photographs, not through drawings or films). Photography may be a more familiar, an almost daily activity for adults as opposed to drawing (an activity that stopped when graduating the secondary school) and filming (which requires more training, direction, favourable context, etc.). I believe that it can be asserted that photography is the most appropriate means of visual expression for adults. It is highly probable that the lack of drawing skills will lead to a visual product that is considered insufficiently expressive; on the other hand, filming seems to be far too expressive and explicit; it can capture much more than the adult subjects would want to reveal.

If you ask your subjects to produce images related to unfortunate things or situations, you might cause cognitive dissonances in them. The photographs or the films are taken or made in happy contexts everyday; to ask your subjects to capture illness, suffering, death, dismissal, incarceration, etc. may be a task not well received. Then, it is possible that the drawing task generates confusion. For example, the more educated subjects who have heard about the 'tree test' can associate the task of drawing and its role with psychological testing. Problems may also occur when the participants are asked permission so that the researcher could publish the images they have captured; they may happen to be more reserved when taking photographs or filming. For example, in the same research described in Chapter VII, it has been found out that many of the social workers have avoided to explicitly take photographs of their partners even if the study referred exactly to who and how they are. The researcher's amazement when faced with this aspect was all the more so, as most of her subjects were social network users and they would constantly post on the Internet (therefore, highly public) explicit images of their life partners.

As to the issue of the minimal influence of subjects in their task of capturing images, we have also tried to avoid anything that might have sounded as an indication or suggestion. For instance, in the study presented in Chapter III of this book, the participants were asked to draw a person who volunteers and one who does not. If we had asked them to draw these two types of people directly, we would have suggested that there are or there should be differences between them, and the subjects could have even invented differences between the two categories just to please us. In order not to transmit from the start the idea that there are differences between those volunteering and those not volunteering, we did as follows: we asked them if they consider that there are differences between these two types of persons and only if they claimed that they existed, they were asked to draw the differences.

Another issue related to the collection of visual data would be the one referring to the context where the subjects produce the images. There are situations described in the literature where the time, the place and the activities performed by subjects before or after the production of images have had a great impact on their content (see Kuhn, 2003, Banks, 2007 or Pauwels, 2010). In one of the studies presented in this volume (where the children were asked to draw God, see Chapter VI), the researcher noticed that some of the images were very similar to the religious icons, which signalled that in these situations the children were guided to the icons or they have had some at their disposal. Those who capture images can be seriously influenced by other people when they produce them even if the researcher does his/her best to avoid this error (e.g. s/he asks them to produce them themselves, without getting inspired, without getting any counselling, etc.). In this project as well we have encountered issues of parental influences in children's drawings (e.g. a mother has narrated how, while her son was drawing God, his father asked him why he was not drawing that too, why had not you drawn that, too, etc.) or of the grandchildren in the drawings of the elderly (e.g. the seniors without inspiration were advised by their grandchildren to draw themselves as they were walking together).

One of the most commonly cited problems related to the collection of visual data in social research is that not everything can be captured in images (see Holm, 2008 or Pauwels, 2010). Examples of abstract things or concepts that have no visual material references are often given. We have shown that this is not really the case. For example, in Chapter VIII a study where the participants have been able to draw emotions – shame, embarrassment and guilt is described (see Fig. 8); and in Chapter VI the ease with which children have been able to draw God is claimed.

Fig. 8: Drawing by a medical student, 2017 (with the permission of Ioana Atudorei)

I have enumerated some of the difficulties that researchers may encounter when collecting images. I am convinced that other justifications exist or can be invented for not using images in research. But all these and whatever else can be imagined are nothing but common difficulties inherent in the application of any instrument and in the collection of any kind of data in social research. Are there no refusals when it comes to interviewing or questioning the subjects? Are not there all sorts of errors generated by field operators, the order and the content of the questions in the questionnaire, by the context of the interview, and so on and so forth? Each method, technique or research tool applied in social studies has its advantages, problems and difficulties, its sensitivities, etc. Each of them generates errors – some identical to those produced by the other instruments, others specific. Visual data collection is not special. Their collection does not give rise to more problems or more serious problems than the collection of other data types and, as with textual and numerical data collection, there are solutions to eliminate or reduce the errors specific to the collection of visual data.

And, to end this section, I would say that the application of visual techniques in social studies is a salutary getaway from the common and monotonous questioning and interviewing. After the surprise and even the initial lack of confidence in these techniques, both researchers and subjects react positively to them. They are a pleasant surprise, and they represent a relaxing activity; capturing images, even to a scientific end, is, more than interviewing or questioning, natural, normal and agreeable. This causes that both researchers and subjects give more time and more attention to collecting or producing visual data.

4 What does visual data processing and analysis mean?

For the processing and analysis of visual data, the same methods and techniques are applied as in the case of textual data. I mean the general methods and techniques for processing and analysing visual data used in common, regular social studies, not specific approaches generated by special knowledge interests (as it happens, for example, in the semiotic approach of images). In the same line, Pauwels (2015b) shows that researchers have used over time some theoretical frameworks that they have adapted to visual analysis (e.g. sociosemiotics, rhetoric, psychoanalysis, cultural studies, post-colonial theory, feminist theory), and he claims that 'some of these frameworks offer concrete methodological tools, while others do not seem to suggest any method of investigation and leave it to the researcher to incorporate their views into a more or less systematic, qualitative and/or quantitative type of content analysis' (page 28). Thus, we do not need to invent and to develop specific processing and analysis techniques because visual data can be subject to all the procedures used for other qualitative data. Image processing and analysis are allowed by specialized software, as well.

Therefore, visual data can be categorized by a priori categories (see content analysis) or by emerging categories (see coding). Thus, for classifying images, content analysis grids can be used resulting from the operationalization of concepts defined in various theories. Similarly, images can be coded; any of the invented procedures for text classification can be applied to images, as well (see the thematic coding or coding procedures in grounded theory studies – open coding, axial coding and selective coding). Then, visual data can be quantified; they are suitable for counting and even measuring, and different relationships can be established among the visual data categories, just as they are established among other types of qualitative data. I have shown, with examples, each of the procedures listed above in Scârneci-Domnişoru, 2016.

I presented, at the beginning of this section, the idea of using the same processing and analysis procedures for the image as used in the text as an advantage. I considered that, if there are no specific methods and techniques for image processing and analysis, then, they can be used, without major problems in any study, by any social scientist who knows how to work with qualitative data. Yet, it is still possible that images require special treatment. While showing to my colleagues how to code the images, we have come to discussions that might make us ponder over it a little. Thus, with one of the participants in this project, I had long polemics about extracting the codes from children's drawings. Don't we spoil the image if we bring it to pieces? If the image still has a major advantage over the text by showing it all at once, don't we annihilate its superiority by cutting some fragments out of it? It remains to be seen if large-scale use of images in research will also bring about the development of specific methods and techniques for processing and analysing them.

Even if we use in most cases the same procedures as in the case of texts, it is known that a researcher, when in front of images, faces more processing and analysis problems than one faced with texts. Therefore, it happens quite often that images are harder than texts to process and analyse. I will try to further show why.

The first major problem is the complexity of visual data analysis. The image is more complex than the text; it simultaneously reveals much detailed information. Among the visual data, the most complex are the films. They contain not only an image but more, they are not static, but in motion and in a meaningful sequence, they can contain both text and sound, these being in their turn significant, etc.

Thus, the big problem with the images seems to be that they offer a lot of information, much more complex and harder to process than the one offered by texts and numbers. Wolcott, Hammersley and Atkinson (see Banks, 2001, p. 176) consider, for example, that video recordings can produce 'more data than anyone can use'. Consequently, the researcher may be completely overwhelmed by the task of processing and analysing images; I consider that it is actually the only serious reason that can be invoked in the decision of not using visual data in research – you risk getting lost in data, you risk not coping with them.

We have also encountered this problem in the project research underlying this book. For example, in front of hundreds of God's drawings made by children of different ages between 5 and 11 years, gathered in two different time periods from girls and boys, having different confessions, the researcher felt overwhelmed. She had to divide the database into a few smaller parts and she tried to process on less overwhelming drawing categories. And by reducing the number of drawings and by narrowing down the category of children to only 6 and 7 year olds, the researcher was extremely strained while data processing and analysing due to the multitude of variations she had to follow (see Chapter VI of this book).

A clear idea of how complex the processing and analysis of some images are is also given in Chapters III and V. The researchers succeeded in writing fairly long and extremely dense chapters after processing only 25 or 26 rather schematic and simple drawings; they managed to make a lot of interesting ideas out of nothing. In brackets, once I noticed what my colleagues did, I thought if it would not be correct to say that, although the drawing is less complex than the photograph (technically, chromatically speaking and in terms of capturing the details and the context, etc.), the drawing generates a higher complexity of the data processing and analysing than the photography. I think that researchers tend to consider the smallest details of the drawing as relevant because – 'As long as they are there, surely the subject wanted to transmit something by them'. On the other hand, it is possible for researchers to treat photographs more superficially (perhaps justly!), considering that many of the context elements s/he had caught were irrelevant. For example, I can think it was an accident that someone was dressed in black on the day of filming, that a passer-by happened to appear in the background or that the person being photographed was wearing an umbrella because rain was forecast that day. Yet, in the drawing nothing can be considered chance! Would a researcher neglect the fact that the drawn man wears black clothes? Would anyone draw people in the background if they did not want to suggest people around or a public context?

Many times the researcher feels the complexity of visual data and especially the pressure that s/he may not manage. I consider that every serious scientist gets to wonder, uncertainly, when facing the visual data: Did I code everything that was significant in an image? My belief is that we cannot really manage the wealth of visual data, but, paradoxically, this is not really a major issue as to the results we obtain. Surely, it is very possible to leave many components of drawings, photographs or films uncoded, but, because in most studies we analyse not one, but more images, the error does not become significant. It may happen that a tiny element in a drawing, for example, could escape the analysis, but if the same tiny element appeared in several drawings, I am convinced that it would pop into researcher's eyes and it would not remain unanalysed. And repetition often makes it not only visible, but also significant.

On the other hand, in most visual pieces of research, participants speak about images presented or produced either in visual elicitation interviews, or by the words or explanatory sentences they add to the images. In this way, I consider that many errors and the uncertainty of the analysis generated by the complexity of the images are annihilated: the most important information that the subjects wanted to transmit visually will be mentioned either verbally or textually. In addition, in any research, when we have at our disposal those who produced the images, we can always go back to them and ask them if we analysed everything that was significant in them, if there are any overlooked elements that could complete our understanding.

The second big problem related to the processing and analysis of visual data is that they are symbolic, that one and the same image or element can mean something in a certain context, something else in another, something for a particular person, something else for another, etc. In the literature, this problem is frequently described. For example, Schirato and Webb (apud Sligo and Tilley, 2011) show that one image can be read in a thousand ways, Flusser (2003) speaks about the connotative symbolic complex of the image (with more meanings) that provides space for multiple interpretations and Banks (2007) argues that 'images are multivoiced and they 'speak' in different ways to different people and in different contexts' (p. 94). For exemplification, see Kearney and Hyle (2004) who show how an image can be mistakenly classified and interpreted in the absence of some verbal explanations of the drawer or Literat (2013) who describes the difficulties of cross-cultural interpretation of graphic representations.

Chapter III of this book describes the rather common situation in which the researcher would classify the image differently than the subject would do. Thus, a tree with gifts under is considered by the researcher appropriate to be classified in the category of 'giving'. However, the explanations of the subject of what the tree represents reveal entirely other categories or subcategories it can fall into: the fir represents the volunteer's 'strength, verticality, energy, physical and psychological strength'.

However, this issue related to processing and analysing visual data has solutions. One of them has already been suggested: visual data collection must be accompanied by explanations given by subjects for the images presented or produced. This is why there is no purely visual research, and verbal presentations of collected visual data are needed (interviews can be taken based on images, or the participants can be asked to write some words or some clarifying sentences near the images). We have complied with this requirement in each of the studies presented in this book; in each chapter the authors show how the subjects were asked to explain the images provided. Another way to deal with the aforementioned difficulty is to carry out in parallel classifications by several researchers. It is thus possible to check to what extent the images have been classified identically or similarly and which are the visual elements that generate coding errors.

Of all the visual techniques, the one that creates the biggest problems with classification is drawing. This happens because drawings are also symbolic, but also because not all people are very expressive and explicit in their drawings. Chapter V provides a suggestive example. A drawing (reproduced in the aforementioned chapter), which seemed to represent a woman in the office, was initially interpreted by the researcher as representing a professional role in the active life of the drawer. The verbal clarifications of the participant revealed that in fact there was a little child drawn in a crib and that the role the drawing hinted at was the familial one.

Of all categories of subjects, children's drawings are the most difficult to decipher and classify correctly. Chapter VI of this book indicates how difficult it is, without explanations, to realize what the children intended to suggest when they drew God. The researcher did the right thing and obtained explanations from the children about their drawings. But, within this context, she struggled with a new and interesting problem: she discovered that it is faster to reach saturation in the analysis of images than in analysing the verbal explanations of children. In other words, one and the same element in the drawings is explained in many different ways. The extremely rich imagination of children can make us believe that, if we were to interview them again, repeatedly, about their drawings, they would have always found another explanation for what they represented, another characteristic of God, another situation in which He exists and manifests, etc.

An aspect that is not much talked about in the literature should be mentioned. In order not to confuse what the social researcher does in analysing and interpreting the images (drawings, in particular) with what the clinical psychologist does, I have always claimed that the researcher is interested in what is obvious in images and not in their hidden, unconscious meanings. The problem is that it happens quite often to realize, as a researcher, that in the drawings there are elements that the designer himself/herself is not aware of, that s/he does not choose to explain them, whose meaning s/he may not even be aware of and that you really do not know what to do in this situation. Pauwels (2015a), for example, mentions this difficulty tangentially. The author claims that sometimes even the subjects are unaware of the significance of some aspects captured in the images, when the visual data are produced, that it is only the verbal clarification of the participants and the questions of the researchers that reveal certain meanings. I really think that there are situations when the subjects do not realize what some of the drawn elements represent and why they chose to sketch them. It is possible, for example, that the drawing representing a rich man is an unconscious copy of a stereotyped image that circulates in the mass-media.

In order to further clarify this issue, I provide more examples. In one of my previous visual projects I discovered open doors to the houses owned by the drawn lower-class representatives of Romania. Not only one, but more drawings contained this item, and none of the subjects spoke about this aspect during the interview. At the first data analysis, I did not even notice this pattern. When I no longer had access to my subjects, this element popped into my eyes, and I do not know yet whether to explain it by the opening that characterizes the lower class, by the idea that there is nothing valuable in their house, by the fact that in the rural area of Romania (where the lower class is often represented in drawings) it is still common not to close the doors of the houses, etc. Then it seems that, in the perception of those who have been my subjects, the higher the hat, the higher the social status (see Scârneci-Domnişoru, 2015). Have my subjects drawn this with awareness? Do they have any explanation for drawing the hat and especially for the height of the hat? Is it that the high hat is a sign of wealth in films, in literature and in history? And besides that I wonder: Should a researcher consider these visual elements? How should they manage them?

In conclusion, if we were to look for issues related to the use of visual data in research, I think that at this stage of research they can be easily found. Just as many visual studies have shown so far, these issues do not represent sufficient reasons to abandon the use of images in research. In my opinion, the complexity of the ones we study justifies a rather complex data handling than the more or less rough simplifications of human subjects. I consider we need to look for and manage complex data if we want to get into the complexity of the ones studied. Then, as I have already shown, there are solutions for some of the issues raised by image processing and analysis, and for the unsolved issues and for those that will be discovered in the future, solutions will be, similarly, found.

I do not consider that my optimism is exaggerated. The evidence has been the extraordinary evolution of the use of visual data in research since the 1990s. The rhythm and the extent of this use is surprising, the number of articles and books written in this area is by far increasing and the number of those who study and discuss different aspects of the use of visual data in research begin to be considerable. All these are supplemented by technical elements that facilitate the introduction of visual data into research and its management. It has become extremely easy and inexpensive to take photographs and to shoot, and the software processing and analysing the qualitative data undergoes spectacular and promising improvements every year. For example, NVivo, up to version 10, released on the market a few years ago, did not allow of visual data analysis. Starting with this version, the program can also be used for static image analysis and motion image analysis; it now allows to even work with images captured on the internet.

5 How can visual data be interpreted?

In order to return to the methodological wondering that characterized the beginning of this chapter, I wonder again, confusedly, why the chapter dedicated to 'data interpretation' is absent from the methodology books. It has been immensely written on how data are collected, fairly much about how data are analysed and almost nothing about how they are interpreted. I profoundly wonder how the most important of the research stages is so indifferently treated.

In my opinion, at this stage you have to show how you have completed the knowledge so far. This previous knowledge is articulated in theories. Consequently, you have to show what your contribution to this field is: Have you produced new scientific knowledge? Have you applied or verified a theory or parts of it in a new context? Have you completed or modified a theory or parts of it? Have you produced a new theory?

All sorts of theories can be applied and verified in visual studies, even if they have resulted from pieces of research where only textual and numerical data have been collected and analysed. Thus, theories or parts of them can be applied or verified in entirely new research contexts where a visual data approach is predominant. For example, in a study on the perception of inequality carried out a few years ago, I first applied the theory of status beliefs in visual research. The subjective social hierarchies had been previously researched exclusively by processing and analysing textual or numerical data resulting from questionnaires or interviews. Therefore, in Scârneci-Domnişoru (2015) I presented Romanians' beliefs of status as they resulted from the interpretation of some unusual data used in studying the perception of social inequality – drawings representing the social classes in Romania made by the subjects at my request. In this book, there are many other examples of applying theories to visual research done by my colleagues (each chapter refers to at least one such theory) – see the development theory as modernization applied in the study on social changes in Chapter II, the model of the five personality factors applied in the study on the characteristics of volunteers and non-volunteers in Chapter III, the theory of disengagement and the theory of continuity in the research on the identity changes suffered after retirement in Chapter V, the theory of desacralization in the interpretation of God's representations in Chapter VI, family development theory applied in the study on perception of life partners in Chapter VII or the theory of blushing applied in the study of moral emotions in Chapter VIII.

In the visual study presented in Chapter V, even more competing theories are applied, indicating which of them or what parts of them apply where and under what conditions. Then, the author of Chapter VI highlights another interesting aspect related to the application of theories in visual research. Some of the theoretical statements referred to in her study belong to fields other than sociology (e.g. from the phenomenology of religion and from theology), which reveals the interdisciplinary potential of visual studies.

As I mentioned before, checking hypotheses and theories is also possible in visual studies. Even though this book does not provide such examples, the literature provides numerous descriptions of visual studies made on large volumes of visual data (e.g. TV or magazine images, newspaper, school textbooks), by using probabilistic samples that validate or invalidate hypotheses (see quantitative content analysis of images).

It often happens that the application of theories in contexts of visual studies reveals the need to modify existing theories. Thus, there is the possibility that existing theories in visual research can be completed with new dimensions or indicators, sometimes with new concepts or with sentences describing unusual relations between concepts. For example, in the visual study referring to status beliefs, I have discovered, besides the classical dimensions of perceived inequality mentioned by most theories (e.g. income inequality, age, education, background inequality), a new dimension, which does not appear in the results of studies based exclusively on textual and numerical data: the inequality of relational capital (see Scârneci-Domnişoru, 2015). Another example can be found in Chapter II of this book, where the author shows how she completed the methodological scheme of re-photography (identified in the literature) with sub-dimensions and indicators specific to the project she worked on.

It is also possible that visual research suggests contradictions of existing theories. For example, previous studies on the legitimacy of social inequality claimed that 'people may believe the level of inequality that exists is legitimate because they underestimate the degree of inequality in the society' (Kerbo, 2009, p. 448). As a consequence of my study on the legitimacy of inequality, I have proposed a hypothesis that contradicts Kerbo's idea: the perceived level of inequality determines its acceptability, but in the sense that the higher the perceived level of inequality, the more acceptable it becomes (Scârneci-Domnişoru, 2015, p. 397). Chapter V of this book provides other examples of contradicting some theories – for example, the principle of universality in the disengagement theory is contradicted by the researcher's discoveries showing that this principle does not apply to her female subjects.

I will try to explain why I have said above that it often happens to change the existing theories by visual research. Most of the visual studies that we do are absolutely new; given the fact that the full involvement of visual data in social science research is relatively recent, whatever visual study you aim at is highly likely to be the first in the field (see only in this volume: the first visual research on God's representation with children, the first visual study related to identity change after retirement, the first visual study of the differences between the characteristics of volunteers and non-volunteers, etc.). The novelty brought about by the use of visual data in social research, and especially the features of these data that offer entirely new perspectives on the phenomena studied, make it quite often that existing theories before the implication of images in their production undergo changes. I have already shown in the preceding sections of this chapter that images yield another type of information than that provided by the textual and numerical data which have hitherto been the basis of theory formulation; this is why it is very likely that the new knowledge gained from the visual studies will complement, modify and even contradict the old theories.

I think it is equally possible to propose new theories resulting from visual studies. It is especially the case of research topics that have not been previously dealt with in textual or numerical terms, but not only in their case. I consider that visual data are not less valuable than other types of data, that they can provide the same types of results as those offered by qualitative textual data. If the texts allow of the grounding of theories, I do not see why images would not do it. For example, in Scârneci-Domnişoru (2015), in the study on the perception of social inequality, I attempted at proposing a theory based exclusively on the processing and analysis of drawings representing the social classes in Romania and Italy. Thus, I forwarded the idea that the sources of inequality are hierarchically perceived. Therefore, if in a society the perceived inequalities are significant in the economic (basic, 'inferior') dimension, then perceiving the other sources of inequality ('superior', higher in the hierarchy) is obstructed (e.g. cultural, political sources, etc.); and if the perceived economic inequalities are low, then people tend to perceive 'higher' inequalities.

Thus, the images allow hypotheses or theories to be tested, as well as they allow hypotheses or theories to be generated. Then, even if visual data are rather used in descriptive studies, it is not excluded that they allow of the formulation of explanatory conclusions. As far as the descriptive sentences are concerned, the chapters in this book provide numerous examples. Thus, as a result of the visual research, descriptive sentences are presented as illustrating community changes or identity changes occurring after retirement, adolescent self-identification and heteroidentification of the life partner, representations of God, of the volunteer in the social field or of the contexts when some emotions have been experienced.

Explanatory sentences resulting from visual studies are less common. From the research on social inequality that I have mentioned above, more explanatory propositions have resulted. Here is one of them: the higher the perceived level of inequality, the more acceptable it becomes. Another example can be found in Chapter V of this book, which explains how diminishing the social network after retirement is dependent on the level of instruction of the subjects. In other words, if the elderly have a low level of instruction, then they are more likely to diminish their social network after retirement. In Chapter VII the author discusses the idea that the perception multiplexity of the couple partner is determined by the perceived level of marital satisfaction and by the duration of couple relationship.

I had the pleasant surprise to discover in one of the visual studies presented in this book some results of the type – predictive sentences. The analysis of children's drawings from two different generations has made the author of Chapter VI think of a change over time related to the representation of God; the drawings were farther away from the classical conception of Christian religiosity, they resembled less traditional religious representations, they depicted less Christian scenes and themes; instead, there were more drawings with nonconformist representations like: God is a woman, It is in everything around us, It is wisdom, etc. These observations have made the researcher formulate a predictive proposition: there is a tendency to enlarge spirituality in contemporary Romania. It remains to be seen whether the drawings or other types of data collected in a few years will confirm or infirm this proposition.

Even if, in my opinion, images do not represent a drawback by comparison to the other qualitative data when it comes to interpretation, it is yet possible that this stage will generate some frustration in visual researchers. It is a great pleasure to work with visual data, they are interesting, they awaken many ideas and emotions, etc., but when you get to the results, you have to transform everything you have found out from images into words. So far, scientific knowledge has been text and number, it has stored in sentences that contain terms and links between terms; that is why, at least for the time being, we can only contribute to it by textual additions. Therefore, what you found out from images becomes scientifically relevant only if it is expressed verbally and/or numerically.

Even though visual scientists have to abandon in frustration the images at the interpretation stage in order to bring extra scientific knowledge, there is also a compensation for them. The good part of the interpretation in the studies where work is done on images is that they also allow access to another type of knowledge – the artistic one. For the skilled and art-loving researchers, the option of forwarding research results in a less conventional form is a great challenge. When research is conducted in a context where, besides scientific knowledge, other activities such as promotion, awareness, social criticism, communication, etc. are important, images can be transformed into convincing artistic products. We can include here posters, collages, visual essays, films, etc. – fairly easy to achieve and to expose publicly. The texts (the other qualitative type of data) also allow access to artistic knowledge in various literary forms that research results can take (e.g. stories, poems, plays), but the images, as I will demonstrate in the next paragraph, have a superior expressive potential. That is why, in my opinion, ignoring this variant of data interpretation and public exposure of research results generates a great waste of information, ideas, knowledge, and implicitly, of understanding, attitude, change and progress.

Given the data presented in this section, I believe that I can assert without failing that visual data add significant value to social knowledge and that neglecting them is not only unjustified but also counterproductive.

6 Why make a visual presentation of the research results?

The presentation of research results in a visual form brings along many advantages. Either by using primary visual data (e.g. drawings, photographs or films collected directly in the field or produced by subjects at the request of the researcher) or by using secondary visual data (e.g. graphs, tables, networks resulting from data analysis), they make the research report easier to understand and they have a greater effect on the reader.

Even when scientific results are expected from visual research, the information, the descriptive, explanatory or predictive sentences can and should be accompanied by images. The situations when the results of sociological surveys are greatly illustrated are common; ideas are quite often accompanied by tables and graphs resulting from statistical processing and analysis. The more suggestive the drawings, the photographs or the films would be, their presence in the research reports does not diminish the scientific character of the results if the images presented are well chosen and if they do not suffocate, by quantity, the communication of the results. Not to mention the situation of an artistic communication of the research results; in this case, the value of the images is obvious and undisputed.

Images are much more expressive than texts and numbers. If you want to get through to the public, to convince, to sensitize or just to inform, images are the perfect means. For example, the audience will understand poverty in a community much better by images than by enumerating some objective numerical indicators. In Chapter II of this book, we can see how the image greatly enhances the information about the change that is textually offered.

The great success of images when they appear in research result reports is due to a few characteristics they have. Weber (2008) shows that visual data capture the ineffable. There are things that can be much better described in images than by any sequence and combination of words and numbers (e.g. extreme phenomena like war or natural catastrophes, but also common social-human issues such as emotions or discrimination). The same author demonstrates that the visual has a greater impact on the public, that the images are memorable and that they facilitate empathetic understanding (e.g. those that capture the effects of some illnesses or the difficulties faced by people with disabilities). Then, image is more accessible than language: it facilitates the communication of ideas and the access to the non-specialized public.

Consequently, a research report containing images has a greater influence on the reader: it is more spectacular, richer, more complete and more complex, less monotonous, less difficult to read and easier to understand. Each of the chapters of this book is proof of this claim; in fact, I think that much of the value of this volume is given precisely by the illustrated ideas. Then, a visual communication of research results allows the results of the research to reach a wide audience, even untrained, it can awaken any kind of feelings, it can last, maybe haunt, it can trigger actions.

In the previous section, I have shown that visual research also gives way to the artistic presentation of the results. The characteristics of the images enumerated above make them extremely useful and suggestive in artistic projects like collages, films, visual essays, etc. For example, in 2014, in a project of Hospice Casa Speranței in Brașov, we planned to identify the difficulties faced by patients with a limited life expectancy that this foundation looks after. We interviewed these people then, but we also asked them to take photographs of 'what it means to live with an incurable disease'. We wanted the research results to be handier for the authorities and for the general public, and we have organized, besides a formal report of the research results, an exhibition of the highly emotional photographs taken by the subjects. To the same end, I also made, by the help of the same photographs, disturbing visual essays (one was published in Scârneci-Domnişoru, 2017).

The visual presentation of research results also raises disputes, for example, the image interpretation by the public. In the literature, there is a concern about what they transmit, how the images presented get to audiences. Do they mean what was meant or is the meaning distorted by the ability of understanding of those who watch, by what they evoke or by the context in which they are presented? Holm (2008) mentions the 'intentions' of those who watch, the personal experiences that can sketch different interpretations of one and the same image. That is why, Wiles et al. (2008) recommend minimizing the risk of misinterpreting the image by adding texts that make the intended meaning explicit. Consequently, it is very important to make sure that what you want to transmit through the images you present is as such perceived by those who look at them. Generally, in research reports the images are presented as exemplifications, as evidence of the sustained ideas, and the problem mentioned above is not very common. It is possible, however, that what we want to transmit is shaded by collateral strongly evocative visual elements. For example, from an image that should illustrate the accomplishment of house chores, someone's bizarre attire from the foreground may catch someone's eye. In this case, the viewer may be so fascinated by this element, s/he can imagine so many things about him/her that the originally intended message of the image is lost.

Then, when publishing images where people can be explicitly identified researchers face many ethical and deontological problems. Ensuring anonymity is a major challenge in the case of images, and their obscuration is not always a desirable practice (see Wiles et al., 2008 and Wiles et al., 2010). The important issue in this case is to not harm those who get exposed to the public through images. Certainly, all respected researchers capture images, and they use them publicly only after obtaining the informed consent of their subjects or of their caregivers. But this protects us, the researchers and the institutions we represent, rather than the participants (Wiles et al., 2008).

Pauwels (2010) shows that both researchers and participants are often unable to predict all the risks for the subjects when they appear in images or when they can be identified as image producers. Unpleasant consequences can unexpectedly occur even after many years after research completion and result publication. Important issues can also appear when images with subjects or made by them become accessible from websites and different archives; they may be used by others for purposes other than the ones they were collected for or the ones involved agreed to (Wiles et al., 2010).

In the situation of children subjects, their protection poses even more serious problems. Therefore, you will have to try, as much as possible, to anticipate the effects of publishing visual materials that reveal your subjects and use them with caution even when the participants give you total freedom in using the images where they appear or that they have produced.

Moreover, there is also the issue of copyright if the researcher wants to publish images that do not belong to him. It may happen that the identification of the copyright holder of the images that someone wants to publish becomes very complicated and time-consuming. The question then arises as to whether the copyright holder grants permission to use and publish the images in research, and sometimes it may happen to pay some money in the account of this permission being given.

These problems are still debated in the literature, and although the ethics committees of the various national and international organizations have imposed extremely tough rules on the use of images in research and in relation to their subsequent publication, my conviction is that things will become less complicated in terms of subject protection. Researchers have already made pressure to relax ethical and deontological codes, showing that participants are most often little concerned about their exposure and demonstrating the rarity of situations when subjects are really threatened by the publication of visual materials that represent them.

It has become an ordinary thing for the subjects to be dissatisfied with the attempts of researchers to anonymize their images; because there are participants who really want to be seen – to be identified is for them a desire and a right they claim; their participation in research is thanks to their belief that they will be identified and that they will be proud to be involved in a study (Wiles et al., 2010). The same author also points out that the identification of subjects is not just a matter of being seen, but it is also related to having a message or a viewpoint to be seen and heard. The latter is really important in the case of stigmatized groups for whom being seen is a way to get out of anonymity. Then, the authors claim, in the 21st century, the use of visual materials with such great care contrasts to the way people choose to show themselves to the public on the internet (see social networks that have changed people's attitudes about public image use, including images which represent children or young people).

In my opinion, scientific articles, for example, circulate in such a small circle of professionals that the risks taken by the participants that can be identified in the images are much less significant than the advantages of using images to complement the scientific knowledge of the social.

7 Conclusions

Until recently, the images have not benefitted from a privileged status in social research. They have been rather avoided, categorized as unscientific or used exclusively for decorative purposes. Even though things began to change fundamentally after the 1990s, I have anyway felt the need to write a methodological chapter that would demonstrate the relevance of visual data. I have the feeling that they still need to be pleaded for, that they still need to show their value and potential.

In each section of this chapter, I have tried to illustrate this relevance and to draw conclusions about the importance of including images in social studies. I have shown, among others, that visual data are very easy to collect, that they facilitate interviewing, that they efficiently and unexpectedly complement information collected in the form of numbers and texts, that they have great potential in describing and explaining social phenomena and that they are both scientifically and artistically relevant. I have also shown that there are difficulties, problems, challenges and limitations regarding the use of visual data in research, and that most of them can be overcome.

I hope that I have been able to convincingly present the idea that visual data are significant and that they deserve to be placed next to the other social research data – the textual and the numerical ones – and that they deserve to be used to the same degree and with the same trust by social scientists. I believe that visual data have not revealed (yet) but a small part of what they can bring to the domain of social knowledge and that the future of this knowledge will be closely related to the collection, analysis and interpretation of visual data.

Bibliography

Banks, M. (2001). *Visual Methods in Social Research*. London: Sage Publication.

Banks, M. (2007). *Using Visual Data in Qualitative Research*. London: Sage Publication.

Becker, H. (1995). Visual Sociology, Documentary Photography, and Photojournalism: It's (Almost) All a Matter of Context. *Visual Studies*, 10(1), 5–14.

Clark, A. (2011). Multimodal Map Making with Young Children: Exploring Ethnographic and Participatory Methods. *Qualitative Research*, 11(3), 311–330. Retrieved from: http://qrj.sagepub.com/content/11/3/311.

Clark-Ibáñez, M. (2004). Framing the Social World with Photo-Elicitation Interviews. *The American Behavioral Scientist*, 47(12), 1507–1527.

Emmison, M., Smith, P. (2002). *Researching the Visual: Images, Objects, Contexts and Interactions in Social and Cultural Inquiry*. London: Sage Publications.

Flick, U. (1998). *An Introduction to Qualitative Research*. London: Sage Publications.

Flusser, V. (2003). *Pentru o filosofie a fotografiei*. Cluj: Idea Design & Print.

Gauntlett, D. (2007). *Creative Explorations: New Approaches to Identities and Audiences*. Abingdon: Routledge.

Harper, D. (2002). Talking about pictures: A case for photo elicitatio. *Visual Studies*, 17(1), 13–26.

Harper, D. (2012). *Visual Sociology*. New York: Routledge.

Heath, C., Hindmarsh, J. & Luff, P. (2010). *Video in Qualitative Research: Analysing Social Interaction in Everyday Life*. London: Sage Publication.

Henny, L. (1986). Trend Report: Theory and Practice of Visual Sociology. *Current Sociology*, 34(3), 1–76.

Holm, G. (2008). Photography as a Performance [34 paragraphs]. *Forum Qualitative Sozialforschung/Forum: Qualitative Social Research*, 9(2), Art. 38. Retrieved from http://nbn-resolving.de/urn:nbn:de:0114-fqs0802380.

Kearney, K. & Hyle, A. (2004). Drawing out emotions: the use of participant – produces drawings in qualitative inquiry. Qualitative Research, 4(3), 361–382.

Kerbo, H. R. (2009). *Social Stratification and Inequality: Class Conflict in Historical, Comparative, and Global Perspective*. Boston: McGraw-Hill.

Knoblauch, H. (2012). Videography. Focused Ethnography and Video Analysis. In H. Knoblauch, B. Schnettler, J. Raab, & H.G. Soeffner (Eds.), *Video Analysis: Methodology and Methods. Qualitative Audiovisual Data Analysis in Sociology* (pp. 69–85), Frankfurt am Main: Peter Lang.

Kolb, B. (2008). Involving, Sharing, Analysing—Potential of the Participatory Photo Interview [37 paragraphs]. *Forum Qualitative Sozialforschung/ Forum: Qualitative Social Research*, 9(3), Art. 12. Retrieved from http://nbn-resolving.de/urn:nbn:de:0114-fqs0803127.

Kuhn, P. (2003). Thematic Drawing and Focused, Episodic Interview upon the Drawing—A Method in Order to Approach to the Children's Point of View on Movement, Play and Sports at School [50 paragraphs]. *Forum Qualitative Sozialforschung/Forum: Qualitative Social Research*, 4(1), Art. 8. Retrieved from http://nbn-resolving.de/urn:nbn:de:0114-fqs030187.

Literat, I. (2013). 'A Pencil for Your Thoughts': Participatory Drawing as a Visual Research Method with Children and Youth. *International Journal of Qualitative Methods*, 12, 84–98.

Mannay, D. (2016). *Visual, Narrative and Creative Research Methods. Application, Reflection and Ethics*. Abingdon: Routledge.

Margolis, E. & Pauwels, L. (Eds.). (2011). *The Sage Handbook of Visual Research Methods*. London: Sage Publication.

Mitchell, C. (2011). *Doing Visual Research*. London: Sage Publications.

Pauwels, L. (2010). Visual Sociology Reframed: An Analytical Synthesis and Discussion of Visual Methods in Social and Cultural Research. *Sociological Methods & Research*, 38(4), 545–581.

Pauwels, L. (2015a). 'Participatory' Visual Research Revisited: A Critical-Constructive Assessment of Epistemological, Methodological and Social Activist Tenets. *Ethnography*, 16(1), 95–117.

Pauwels, L. (2015b). *Reframing Visual Social Science. Towards a More Visual Sociology and Anthropology*. Cambridge: Cambridge University Press.

Powell, K. (2010). Making Sense of Place: Mapping as a Multisensory Research Method. *Qualitative Inquiry*, 16(7), 539–555, Retrieved from: http://qix.sagepub.com/content/16/7/539.

Rose, G. (2014). On the Relation Between 'Visual Research Methods' and Contemporary Visual Culture. *The Sociological Review*, 62, 24–46.

Rotariu, T. (2016). *Fundamente metodologice ale ştiinţelor sociale*. Iaşi: Polirom.

Scârneci-Domnişoru, F. (2015). Acceptable and Unacceptable Sources of Inequality in Romania. A Visual Study. *TRAMES - A Journal of the Humanities and Social Sciences*, 19(4), 367–402.

Scârneci-Domnişoru, F. (2016). *Datele vizuale în cercetarea social*. Cluj-Napoca: Presa Universitară Clujeană.

Scârneci-Domnişoru, F. (2017). Photovoice: Adult Patients of Hospice Brasov (Romania) on What It Means to Live with Cancer. *Visual Communication*, 16(2), 195–208.

Schnettler, B. & Raab, J. (2008). Interpretative Visual Analysis. Developments, State of the Art and Pending Problems [45 paragraphs]. *Forum Qualitative Sozialforschung/Forum: Qualitative Social Research*, 9(3), Art. 31. Retrieved from http://nbn-resolving.de/urn:nbn:de:0114-fqs0803314.

Sligo, F. & Tilley, E. (2011). When Words Fail Us: Using Visual Composites in Research Reporting. *Visual Communication*, 10(1), 63–85. Retrieved from http://vcj.sagepub.com/content/10/1/63.

Van Leeuwen, T. & Jewitt, C. (Eds.). (2008). *Handbook of Visual Analysis*. London: Sage Publication.

Weber, S. (2008). Visual Images in Research. In G. Knowles & A. Cole (Eds.), *Handbook of the Arts in Qualitative Research: Perspectives, Methodologies, Examples, and Issues* (pp. 41–54). London: Sage Press.

Wiles, R., Coffey, A., Robison, J. & Heath, S. (2010). *Anonymisation and Visual Images: Issues of Respect, 'Voice' and Protection*. ESRC National Centre for Research Methods, NCRM Working Paper Series, 7. Retrieved from http://eprints.ncrm.ac.uk/1804/1/anonymisation_and_visual_methods_working_paper.pdf.

Wiles, R., Prosser, J., Bagnoli, A., Clark, A., Davies, K., Holland, S. & Renold, E. (2008). *Visual Ethics: Ethical Issues in Visual Research*. ESRC National Centre for Research Methods Review Paper, 11. Retrieved from http://eprints.ncrm.ac.uk/421/1/MethodsReviewPaperNCRM-011.pdf.

Codrina Csesznek

II Studying social change through the *re-photography technique* in a rural Romanian community

Abstract: The research presented in this chapter, based on visual data, has the objective to illustrate social change in a typical Romanian rural community through photographs. Thus, I compared and contrasted some aspects specific to the social life of this community in two moments in time: 2004 and 2017. I chose a community that had been a privileged subject of sociological studies during the interwar period, due to the monographic research conducted by the Bucharest School of Sociology. I used a methodological framework based on three dimensions (Places, Participants, and Activities) and ten sub-dimensions. In interpreting the visual data collected, I highlighted the elements illustrating the development, modernization, improvement of various aspects of the socio-economic life or, on the contrary, those showing backwardness or incongruity with the values of development and modernity. In many cases, the photographs speak for themselves, clearly illustrating the change. The main contribution of this research to visual sociology is the confirmation that producing sets of photographs using the repetition technique is an efficient method to document social change.

Keywords: social change, rural community, visual data, re-photography

1 Introduction

Thirteen years ago, I initiated a project of visual sociology for which I had both a professional and personal motivation. The rural community I was born in – Drăguş, from Braşov County, Romania – had been a privileged subject of sociological studies during the interwar period, due to the monographic research conducted by the Bucharest School of Sociology. In 1929, Drăguş was the subject of the largest monographic research campaign in Romania, carried out by more than 80 scholars grouped in multidisciplinary teams. They published numerous works describing the structures and phenomena specific to this rural community, based on the theory of social frames and manifestations, elaborated by Dimitrie Gusti (Larionescu, 1996). The year 1929 was also when Drăguş became the set for the first sociological documentary film in Romania, *Drăguş. The Life of a Romanian Village*. The aim of this documentary was to re-enact a day in the life of this village, in the first part, and to present various local customs and rituals, in the second part.

Studies regarding the social changes of this community continued in the 1930s as well, since the village social life was a matter of interest for researchers (Stahl, 1981). But at the beginning of the 21st century, village life seemed to get less attention and emphasis. Not only has there been no research conducted to illustrate social transformations, but the village itself has appeared deprived of the force of a living and attractive rural community: an important part of the young population had migrated to work abroad, demographic indicators showed accentuated ageing of the population, rural subsistence economy was mainly based on domestic production, the infrastructure was not developed and no significant investment had been made in agriculture, tourism or other sectors of the local economy (Şandru, 2009).

In 1996, I performed a research study focused on the changes undergone by the economic elite of Drăguş village in the transition process from socialism to capitalism (Şandru, 2009). But I endeavoured to do more in order to bring this rural community back to the attention of sociological interest. In 1999, while being in Italy on a research fellowship, I discovered visual sociology and understood that photography can be a very clear mirror of reality, but also an instrument which has the power to transform reality, through the inherent cultural meanings assigned to any interpretation of an image (Valli, 1993). Consequently, I contemplated a way of bringing Drăguş back to attention by means of a book that could reveal interesting aspects of social life through pictures and photographs. This plan was based on the idea that photography has a powerful reflexive force (Purcell, 2007), that it could raise awareness about community development (Şandru, 2005), that it could make community members, especially leaders, see and think critically about their community and about methods to improve various aspects of it. Furthermore, I aspired to a book with a public relations value, addressed to foreigners in countries where young people from Drăguş were working – Italy, Spain and Germany – these young people having the role of communicators, or promoters, beyond the country's borders, of the real image, unaltered by ethnic prejudices, of what they called "home".

The book *Drăguş. Images of a Romanian Village* (2005) emerged from this aspiration. The book was created in collaboration with my former sociology student, Romulus Oprica, and my father, then the mayor of Drăguş Commune. In over 75 photos, we illustrated various aspects of social life in the community, organized in five chapters, in accordance with a system that we developed at that time and which we called TIMOG – acronym from the Romanian words *tradiţii* (traditions), *instituţii* (institutions), *muncă* (work), *oameni* (people) and *gospodării* (households). In addition, the first part of the book also included several panoramic photos which provided an overview of the village. Each photo was accompanied by a description in three languages: Romanian, English and Italian.

In 2017, within the project "Applying Visual Techniques in Social Research", coordinated by my colleague, Florentina Scârneci-Domnişoru, and described in the Introduction, I decided to study the social changes in Drăguş through "repeat photography" or "re-photography". I used as theoretical background the methods and approaches formulated by Rieger (2011): re-photographing places, participants and activities/functions/processes.

2 Theoretical framework. The use of photography in the analysis and the making of social change

Visual data can be a valid and consistent material for the study of social change. According to Rieger (2011), sociologists have recently discovered that the usage of photography in the analysis of change processes is a highly valuable methodological approach. Although photography and sociology emerged at about the same time, photography was long neglected by sociologists as they were developing a discipline based mainly on numerical data (Harper, 1988).

Between 1896 and 1916, a certain interest towards the use of photography as "evidence and illustration" existed (Staszapud Harper, 1988), but after 1920, photography – according to Harper – disappeared for many years from sociological publications. It is noteworthy that the Bucharest School of Sociology used photography in its monographic studies from the interwar period, as is the case with the illustrative photographs revealing the social life of the village of Drăguş in 1929 (Stahl, 1981, and http://www.cooperativag.ro/?s=dragus)

Starting with the 1930s, photography became increasingly important in American sociology, being used as "systematic photographic documentation" in community studies, as well as being used extensively in anthropology and visual ethnology (Harper, 1988).

The popularity of visual methods has recently risen considerably. Some authors have tried to systematize and to find coherence in the vast field of approaches and methods of visual sociology. Harper (1988) suggested a classification of "photographical methods" into four categories or methods: scientific, narrative, reflexive and phenomenological. Following the scientific method, sociologists collect and analyse visual data in the same way as numerical or verbal data, creating categories, establishing relationships between them, and producing scientific explanations. But instead of numbers or words, photographs are taken or collected. Using the narrative method, the images are collected and presented in order to illustrate social processes. Following the reflexive method, it is the subject of the research who chooses the images or proposes interpretations of the images; and according to the phenomenological approach, the researcher is at the core of the knowledge process, using his/her own experience in order to illustrate or understand certain situations and social phenomena based on visual data.

Faccioli (1993) noted that research using photographic or video material can be classified into two large groups: 1) research using images along with other materials for descriptive or clarifying purposes and 2) research conducted primarily around images, seen as an essential part of the research process itself. In the former case, images have a hermeneutical role: they are able to produce a higher degree of empathy and understanding of various social situations. In the latter case, the images have a communicative function: the representations, symbols, signs, gestures, facial expressions, etc. are themselves objects of research through visual techniques.

Pauwels (2010) proposed an interesting integrative model of visual social research based on three dimensions: 1) origin and nature of visual, 2) research focus and design and 3) format and purpose. The model is rather a methodological map comprising the fundamental milestones needed to conduct sociological research based on visual data, from selecting the types of information used to the final result and the areas where this result can be capitalized.

Karpov and Kryuchkov (2015) propose the concept of *analytical photography* with "clear, scientifically formulated goals, objectives, methods, and topics" (p. 679) as a useful research tool in social sciences and interdisciplinary studies.

Recently, in the first Romanian book addressing the use of visual data in social research (Scârneci-Domnişoru, 2016), the author emphasizes the fundamental methodological elements necessary for processing visual data and shows the numerous possibilities through which visual sociology can generate knowledge.

Many authors assert that photographs can provide a considerable amount of interesting information about places and about realities or phenomena related to social change and to community development. Harper (1988) used aerial photographs to highlight "housing patterns, farming practices, and field conditions in an agriculture neighbourhood" (p. 61). Rose (2008) states that photographs have a great illustrative power in the field of human geography. According to Pauwels (2010), the main objects of social research through visual methods are *material culture* and *human behaviour*. Material culture comprises objects and artefacts (chambers, halls, art objects, etc.) and visible social structures (urban centres, cemeteries, etc.).

Rieger (2011) argues that there are various ways to use photographs in "documenting social change" (p. 132): photographs as sociological evidence, the use of repeat photography, retrospective studies, cross-sectional studies, etc. "The most reliable way we can use photography to study social change is through the systematic visual measurement technique of repeat photography or, simply, re-photography" (p.133), which implies re-photographing the same social group, place, or phenomenon after a certain period of time. Methodologically, re-photographing requires the researcher to compare "the content of the photographs, looking for evidence of change in a manner similar to survey data in panel studies. The change, or lack of change, that the photographs reveal we then interpret in accordance with our theoretical expectations" (p. 133). The author outlines five steps to studying social change based on visual data: 1) selecting a subject, in base of a theory or without any theory, but on the basis of the researcher interests; 2) identifying visual indicators to be recorded, for example, in research on the development or decline of a community, the first visual indicator should be "the build environment"; 3) finding "existing documentation or creating such documentation for the initial (Time 1) measurement" (Rieger, op. cit., p. 148); 4) "carrying out the follow-up (Time 2) documentation when appropriate" (idem); and 5) "analyzing the accumulated evidence" (idem).

Rieger (op.cit.) also proposed a methodological framework for re-photography projects, focusing on three dimensions or strategies: 1) re-photographing places; 2) re-photographing participants; and 3) re-photographing activities, processes, or functions. "The most basic strategy we can use in studying social change visually is to re-photograph sites or things that we (or others) have previously documented" (p. 133) in order to "systematically document the build environment" (idem): streets, schools, businesses and residences.

Afterwards, "a second strategy of re-photography exploits the continuity provided, not by a specific site of a photograph, but by the experience of the human participants in the social change process. In this approach, our objective is to track the witnesses. The participants' biographies and experiences become the linkage between temporally ordered contexts and events" (p. 134), as, for example, "the evolution of a *core* family" (p. 135) in a community.

Last but not least, "sometimes the link between successive points in time lies not in a specific site or object, nor in the lives of individuals, but in some particular process, activity, or function. We might want to track an institutional process, such as education, or trace people's changing levels of living, as shown, for example, in the kinds of houses they live in. Or we might follow the evolution of a group's leisure activities. Such phenomena are quite basic in social life, and photography offers a means for documenting both their persistence and their changing incarnations over time. Here the camera is an especially powerful tool of measurement" (p. 137). A relevant example of documenting change through this strategy can be, Rieger says, working in a certain field: What differences occur over time when that activity takes place, which are its tools, its procedures, etc.?

According to Harper (1988), photography reproduces a moment in time. When someone re-photographs the same thing or something similar after a certain period of time, this means to "measure change", therefore an archive of earlier photographs is necessary to this end. Harper indicates that several projects have already used this strategy, most of them documenting the changes occurring in the physical environment or illustrating the social life of particular groups in different historical periods.

For example, in 1982 Garry Rogers used re-photography to show changes in the natural environment of the Great Basin Desert of Utah after 100 years. In 1984, Mark Klett re-photographed a number of places in the American West that had been photographed in the 19th century by Timothy O'Sullivan. The photographs showed "the effects of human habitation in buildings, roadside signs, roads, erosion, and different vegetation patterns" (Harper, 1988, p. 62).

Bill Ganzel also re-photographed in 1984, after fifty years, a series of people and households in the USA. Ganzel used two techniques: re-photographing the same people or scenes and re-photographing the same people in new locations and life settings, thus illustrating certain consequences of social mobility and socioeconomic changes, such as remaining in poverty or reaching prosperity. In 1987, Jon Rieger photographed exactly the same settings after ten or fifteen years in the Upper Peninsula of Michigan to document social change. "Rieger's photographs, even aside from text, show the devolution of community in rural areas in which industries shut down or leave" (Harper, 1988, p.62).

Harper considers that the re-photography method has great potential for studying social change: "In the case of studying social change of the material environment or the social lives of a group in different historical periods and circumstances, the re-photographic survey does what no other social method can" (Harper, 1988, p. 62).

The specialized literature also highlights the power of visual communication in relation to different types of audience: community members, sponsors, or policy makers. Photographs present information in an accessible, easy-to-understand manner (Sanchez, 2015) and "could be used to present a particular issue in a photo essay or an exhibition in the community" (Hinds, 2017).

I would also mention an interesting research direction through visual methods – developed in the field of community development – where photography is seen as a tool for producing positive change, stimulating critical thinking and motivating people to act. Wang and Burris (1997) argue that photographs are a very powerful means of assessing needs in a community context, and Hinds

(2017) adds that photography can be used in assessing needs and assets of a community, as well as in investigating how the notion of "community" is understood and experienced.

Purcell (2007) shows that techniques such as photo-elicitation, photo-novella and photovoice used in "critical photographic practice" are very useful for the "development of individuals and communities"; photography, as "community-based practice", becomes in this context "a developmental tool" (p. 114). The photograph acquires a reflexive function. The challenge of taking photographs or interpreting photographs develops critical thinking and produces *empowerment*. The mechanism is explained by Rod Purcell: photographic approaches could "facilitate local people reflecting on their life situation, developing their vision of a better life that leads to action for change, then photographic approaches have much to offer for effective community development practice" (p. 120). I consider it to be an interesting approach, easily applicable to research and community intervention projects, and I intend to explore the crucial role of photography and to promote it in the research projects focused on the Romanian communities.

3 A brief description of the community of Drăguş

Drăguş Commune is located in the centre of Romania, in the county of Braşov, in a depression bounded to the South by the Southern Carpathians range and to the North by the Transylvanian Plateau.

According to the data received from the National Institute of Statistics – County Directorate for Statistics Braşov[1], in 2017, Drăguş had a population of 1092 inhabitants living in 427 households.

Drăguş was present in a series of socio-demographic data from the first half of the 20th century, included in the monographic works made by the members of the Bucharest School of Sociology. In 1910, Drăguş had 1414 inhabitants, and in 1938 – 1459 inhabitants, mostly farmers (Georgescu, 1945). During the socialist era, the local economy was organized within the Agricultural Production Cooperative, but many people, especially males, also worked in the industrial sector, in factories in neighbouring towns. After 1989, the socio-economic life of the village entered the process of post-communist change. In 1995, the village had a population of 1170 people living in 325 households. Evolution in the population structure at that time indicated ageing processes, unemployment rise, as well as an increasing migration rate abroad (Şandru, 2009).

1 Data are extracted from the TEMPO database of the National Institute of Statistics (http://statistici.insse.ro).

Drăguş Commune is still currently facing population ageing, as is the case with the general Romanian population. According to the latest census, conducted in Romania in 2011[2], the population of Drăguş Commune was counted to 1162 inhabitants living in 423 households. Data regarding the level of housing modernization show that all households have their own kitchen and 328 of them have a bathroom in the dwelling, and most are connected to the water and sewerage network; all dwellings have electricity and most of them are connected to the public gas network.

Modern telecommunications networks can also be noticed on site in Drăguş: cable and wireless internet, cable television and mobile telephony networks. Moreover, the city's web pages feature Drăguş as a modern community with a developing infrastructure which, at the same time, preserves and valorizes its own cultural heritage (http://primariadragus.ro/prezentare_locala and http://www.comunadragus.ro/).

Recently, Drăguş won the title of Cultural Village of Romania in 2016 at the third edition of the National Cultural Competition of Romania. Additionally, Drăguş City Hall, in collaboration with other local and county institutions, organizes cultural events every year, which are also promoted online (on the Facebook page of the institution).

Regarding local institutions, the commune has its own administration coordinated by a mayor and a local council consisting of nine members (http://www.comunadragus.ro/). In the village, there is a secondary school, a kindergarten, an Orthodox church and a Greek-Catholic church, a clinic where a general practitioner and a nurse provide medical care, a cultural centre and 26 companies (ibidem).

4 Methodology

The objective of my research is to illustrate social change in a typical Romanian rural community through photographs. Thus, I will compare and contrast some aspects specific to the social life of this community in two moments in time: 2004 and 2017.

In this re-photography project, I collected digital photos for a visual database between July and December 2017. I tried to photograph, after 13 years, approximately the same scenes or situations in order to make a comparison, precisely

2 The data from the 2011 census were provided by the County Directorate for Statistics in Braşov. I thank sociologist Anca Dogar for the professional support throughout the project.

Tab. 1: Visual dimensions and sub-dimensions of the research

Places	Participants	Activities
Panoramic views	People in public spaces	Work activities in local institutions
Households' exteriors	People at home	Work activities in household
Households' interiors	People on holidays	Community events
Public buildings		

to identify any significant changes and to what extent we can determine the meaning, measure, or even mechanisms of change in these photographs.

The framework for documenting social change through photographs, elaborated in 2004, has been modified in order to allow the achievement of greater theoretical relevance. I opted for redefining the framework proposed by Rieger in 2011, resulting in three dimensions instead of five (including panoramic images). *Institutions, houses* and *panoramic photographs* from the previous framework are now included in the chapter *Places*. Photos about *people, work* and *traditions* are now encompassed in the chapters *Participants* and *Activities*. Within each dimension, I set a series of *visual indicators*, as Rieger suggests (op. cit.), termed "sub-dimensions". Based on these dimensions and sub-dimensions, I reorganized the 2004 visual data (Time 1) and collected the new 2017 visual data (Time 2). Tab. 1 presents the methodological framework based on dimensions and sub-dimensions.

In some situations, re-photographing the same scenes as in 2004 was impossible because the "object" of the photograph was no longer there or it had been profoundly altered. I am referring to people who died, activities which were no longer practised, or places which had been significantly transformed. In these situations, I tried to find a substitute: people, places, or activities which could replace them or were similar to those photographed 13 years before.

During the process of data gathering, I lived in this community for a few days and, besides photographing, I tried to engage in informal conversations with *privileged witnesses* (Laumann & Pappi, 1995) – mayor, former mayor, other employees of local administration, priest, etc. – in order to find relevant information to my research topic. Thus, each set of photographs will be accompanied by a description meant to facilitate the understanding of the social change reflected in various aspects of the community life. The texts accompanying each photo are also important for understanding change as they contribute to the visual information by putting it in a wider context. This approach is supported by Rieger (2011), who states that "pictures alone, like other indices, are hazardous to interpret without the contextual reinforcement of other information gathered in the field situation" (p. 143). Many photographs are described based on the personal information I obtained, as I know the community well, I am familiarized with all its inhabitants, I often visit Drăguş, and I am interested to know how this community is changing.

The re-photographing activity on site was very enjoyable, as my request to be allowed to take pictures was always received with openness, even with interest and joy by the locals. There were some situations where people who were being photographed needed some clarifying explanations, since they were sometimes tempted to change something in their aspect to "look good" in photos; they wanted to change their clothes with "more beautiful" ones, to improve something in the scenes where we were about to take photos or even to pose in a rigid, unnatural position. In these cases, I explained that the photographs were for ethnographic purposes, and therefore I intended to capture the people's life in its natural course.

In order to capture traditions and events better, I needed to attend certain ceremonies in the community on several occasions: a wedding, a funeral, Christmas Day, etc.

The descriptions follow below each set of photographs, explaining what they represent, the differences between the two images and other relevant information about the subject illustrated by that set of photos. In the visual monograph from 2004, I published 72 photos. In 2017, I re-photographed 65 scenes, but in this study I will only use 37 of them. I consider that the 37 photographs are sufficient to illustrate the change – or its absence – on the three dimensions considered relevant, according to the above-mentioned theoretical model.

An important distinction to be made here is that the *Activities* dimension, including the sub-dimensions *Work activities in local institutions* and *Work activities in the household*, will only feature my comments regarding the changes, but will not be illustrated by the sets of photographs, since they are included in a visual essay (Cseszneк and Scârneci-Domnişoru, 2019).

With respect to the other sub-dimensions studied here, each compares and contrasts a minimum of two sets of photographs, that is, two taken in 2004 and two taken in 2017. I relinquished certain photos for several reasons: 1) Some aspects did not seem relevant to the research topic (for example, a photo of the graves in the cemetery or a picture showing the village cattle in the field); 2) In order to avoid redundancy: in 2004 I photographed several aspects illustrating the same scene, for example, the same street or groups of women on the street, therefore I decided to eliminate the photographs showing similar contexts; and 3) Some scenes no longer existed in 2017, for example, the tradition of the

Troupe of Lads, some people from 2004, such as my grandmother, as well as some spaces, for example, the workshop of the village blacksmith.

5 Social change in Drăguş Commune, illustrated through photographs

The concept of *social change* refers to "the transition of a social system or its components from one state to another qualitatively and/or quantitatively different state" (Vlăsceanu, 1993, p. 529). In sociology, there are many approaches to social change, from the classical macrosocial theories (Comte, Spencer, Durkheim, Marx, Weber, Parsons) to more recent studies based on longitudinal analysis techniques, causal or interactive patterns, and they often have a microsocial dimension. These studies look at changes in different social subsystems (family, work, education, political systems, etc.) and aim to "describe, explain and predict change" (idem), but analyses of social change are often "limited to description" (Durrheim, 2014, p. 1768). More specifically, social change describes "fundamental alterations in how people live, what they do, and the whole social and psychological infrastructure that makes social life possible, including the laws, technologies, forms of exchange, and subjectivities" (Durrheim, 2014, p. 1767).

According to Rieger (2011), in sociology photographs can be a very good instrument for documenting change in re-photography-based research, where the camera becomes "an especially powerful tool of measurement" (137). Although he uses the term "measurement", Rieger does not describe methods, procedures or indicators for measuring. He only suggests to the researchers to choose their own visual indicators and to describe the aspects illustrating the change of the subject captured in the pictures. Starting from Rieger's methodological guidelines, previously set forth in the *Methodology* chapter, I produced a corpus of photographs and their written interpretations forming "a comprehensive photographic record" on social change in a Romanian rural community since the beginning of the 21st century. In interpreting the photographs, my theoretical reference point was the meaning of social change as *development* and *modernization*.

The concept of *development* – as defined by the United Nations – refers to processes which create better social and economic conditions: economic growth, equitable distribution of income and social development. These objectives translate into goals such as poverty reduction, universal primary education, promoting gender equality, health improvement, etc., each goal having specific indicators for measuring progress. The European Union's approach towards the concept of *development* is based on a series of criteria (employment, poverty and inequality, education, health and housing), change being measured by structural indicators for social inclusion (Popescu, Vârdol and Briciu, 2006).

Modernization – closely related to development – is described "as a double process: 1. international acculturation emanating from the initial modernization of the West; 2. indigenous adaptative change in each society" (Schifirneţ, 2016, p. 42). Often used as synonyms, both concepts – *development* and *modernization* – refer to change towards a desirable state of a social system. Emerged in the Western civilization, the two concepts designate "obtaining great economic, scientific and cultural performances" (Schifirneţ, 2016, p. 128) and comprise several aspects: technical-economic development or modernization (introducing new means of production or new technologies); development or modernization of the workforce structure and planning (increase in the level of education, emergence of new professions); modernization of organizational and leadership structures or political modernization in the sense of democratization and division of power among social groups (Mihăilescu, 1993).

In interpreting the visual data collected in Drăguş, I will highlight the elements illustrating the development, modernization, improvement of various aspects of the socio-economic life or, on the contrary, those showing backwardness or incongruity with the values of development and modernity. In many cases, the photographs speak for themselves, clearly illustrating the change. However, by combining the images with the descriptions, extra knowledge is gained. Each set of photos is accompanied by information which underlines the meaning of the noticeable change. The purpose of providing the additional information is to describe what could not be captured in the photographs in order to create a coherent depiction of the social change in Drăguş Commune over the past 13 years.

6 Places

6.1 Panoramic views

The photograph in Fig. 1.1 was taken at the foot of the Făgăraş Mountains, from a place at approximately 9 kilometres to the South from the village. In 2004, when the photograph was taken, I wanted to illustrate the natural depressed setting in which Drăguş is situated. At the same spot, in 2017 I found a completely changed landscape, an example of the economic development of the community and of the area (Fig. 1.2). On the land where, 12 years before, there was an unused meadow, today there is an entertainment area – Aventura Park Drăguş – offering tree-top climbing courses, next to which, in 2015, a restaurant was recently open

Fig. 1.1: Drăguş – view from the South, 2004 (author's archive)

Fig. 1.2: Pizza Drăguş – restaurant, 2017 (author's archive)

Fig. 2.1: Luţeanu family house, 2004 (author's archive)

under a new brand name: *Pizza Drăguş*. The owners are locals: two families that are closely related. The entire area where the restaurant is located – now called Drăguş Touristic Area – is under touristic development, being in the proximity of a well-known monastery and an access road to the Făgăraş Mountains. The land in this area belongs traditionally to locals from Drăguş, many of whom have invested here in the past years, opening guest houses, restaurants or other tourism-related businesses such as a ski slope and a craftsmanship centre.

The photographs (Figs. 2.1 and 2.2) were taken from the steeple of the Orthodox Church. They represent a view of the village towards the North, where one can see the hills of the Transylvanian Plateau in the background. We notice the structure of a typical Drăguş household, organized almost as a fortress, with construction, walls and gates that clearly delimitate it from the neighbouring households. Most of the households in Drăguş consist of three distinct spaces: 1) the courtyard of the main house; 2) a yard for animals, annexes and agricultural equipment and 3) a garden where fruit and vegetables are grown. Most of the houses have been renovated and modernized in the recent years – the new, cleaner look making them more pleasing to the eye: the facades have been repaired and painted, the wooden gates replaced by new, more durable metallic ones, in some cases the roof tiles have been changed and the old, wooden window frames replaced with modern double-glazing windows. In the first decades of

Fig. 2.2: Luțeanu family house, 2017 (author's archive)

the socialist regime, Drăguș suffered significant architectural changes: most old, wooden houses were demolished and new, concrete houses were built instead – such as the house in Figs. 2.1 and 2.2 – but with a similar structure: two front chambers, not permanently occupied, and several other chambers in the back of the house with a functional purpose: kitchen, bedroom, pantry and outdoor (or summer) kitchen. The photographs show that in front of the houses, along the road there is a new pedestrian pavement made of concrete plates, separated from the road by a strip of grass or by a ditch for collecting rainwater. In the right-side image from 2017, I have intentionally zoomed out in order to include the roof of the neighbouring house, which is fitted with a solar panel – a modern and novelty element in Drăguș, not yet very common.

In these photographs (Figs. 3.1 and 3.2), also taken from the steeple of the Orthodox Church, we have an image of the village towards the South, the Făgăraș Mountains. One can notice the integration of the houses in the natural surroundings: each household is in a green environment with grass and fruit trees – the household's garden. The foreground shows us a change in the construction in the churchyard: the small hut from 2004 was replaced in 2017 by a larger, modern building (Fig. 3.2). It is the new "cold chamber" or the mortuary of the community – the place where, according to the new EU regulations and Romanian law no. 102/2014, each family has to depose the bodies of their deceased an

Fig. 3.1: Panoramic view towards the South, 2004 (author's archive)

Fig. 3.2: Panoramic view towards the South, 2017 (author's archive)

Fig. 4.1: Ulița Mare, 2004 (author's archive)

hour after their death (www.dreptonline.ro). From my personal observations in Drăguș and from conversations with the members of the community, this regulation is mostly ignored and the mortuary is, at this point, an investment with no real utility. The community follows the traditional rituals when it comes to funerals. According to tradition, the body of the deceased is placed in the house where they lived and kept there for three days. This is an interesting case of both modernity and resistance to modernity: the local administration built the necessary infrastructure to comply with the new regulations (the mortuary), but the social norm based on tradition is stronger within the community than the legal requirements. Further in this paper I will illustrate other elements related to the funerary rituals as I captured them in images in 2017.

The images (Figs. 4.1 and 4.2) show a typical Drăguș street. It is one of the many similar streets in the village. This one is called Ulița Mare (Grand street) – *uliță* is an archaic word for street – and in 2004, I photographed it in December, as I liked its hibernal aspect. The photograph from 2017 is from the same angle, but in the summertime. There are several new elements in the photograph from Fig. 4.2. In the first place, the houses have renovated facades. In 2004, the facades were the original ones, thus being 40–50 years old. The house on the right side has a new roof. In the second place, in 2017 the street has asphalt pavement, which in 2004 did not exist (I can confirm this in writing, since it is not visible

Fig. 4.2: Ulița Mare, 2017 (author's archive)

in the photograph) and the sidewalks are paved. In the 2017 image, we notice more cables hanging from the street posts; in 2004 there were significantly fewer. These are electricity and internet cables which, on the one hand, are a sign of modernity and, on the other hand, create an unaesthetic view of the village – in modern communities today, the trend is to install these cables underground. It is an aspect that indicates delays in modernization, delays shown also by the manure one can still find on the asphalt in 2017, another weak spot of the community. The explanation is that from early spring until late autumn, the cattle from each household (cow and buffalo) are herded every day – an old way of organization of the local economy – to various pastures at the edge of the village. The dirty streets are the effect of the cattle's passage on the streets in the mornings and evenings, and Drăguș does not have a public service for street cleaning. The cleaning of the streets is the responsibility of the villagers, each cleaning in front of their own property, without any regulation from the local authorities. There is, though, an informal, traditional authority that monitors this activity: the *neighbourhood*, led by a *head of neighbourhood* – an old form of social organization structured by streets, still active today and observed also by the researchers of the Bucharest School of Sociology (Stahl, 1981). The *head of the neighbourhood* is elected by the inhabitants of a neighbourhood (generally one street) and has the task of coordinating the participation of the members

Fig. 5.1: Dineti family house, 2004 (author's archive)

of that neighbourhood to all public activities and events of interest. Another noticeable difference between the two photographs is that in the latest image the trees in front of the house on the left have been cut down. Usually, people cut down trees for more sunlight. In Drăguş, each household manages the space in front of their house: they decide whether to plant flowers or cut down trees, they clean the ditch, and they install protection railings for animals or a bench. I will exemplify below elements related to the organizing of this private space that contributes significantly to the image of the village.

6.2 Households' exteriors

The house from the images (Figs. 5.1 and 5.2) is a typical Drăguş house. In 2004, this house had already been renovated. The original facades from the second half of the last century did not have colours such as this one, as grey, white and green prevailed. In that same era, most of the front windows had similarly designed wooden shutters. Their role was protective but they also indicated that, generally, the front rooms were not occupied. The shutters were lifted and the rooms used if guests were received or if an important event took place: baptism, marriage or funeral. The front of the house in Fig. 5.2 has been renovated again, judging by the different colour. The old tiles on the roof were changed, the windows are new, with double glazing, and there are flower pots at the windows. This aesthetic detail

Fig. 5.2: Dineti family house, 2017 (author's archive)

is new in Drăguş. In 2004, no one had flowers at the windows whereas today we see many houses with flowers, either on the ground in front or at the windows. I believe it is a novelty element brought from Western Europe by the migrants of Drăguş who return home on holidays or have returned for good (Şandru, Scârneci, 2014; Scârneci-Domnişoru, Cseszne, 2017). We notice a metal railing in front of the house. This railing is mainly to protect the house from the herded cattle, but I have noticed that it also has a social function: neighbours lean on them while chatting in front of the house or children playing use them for "gymnastics". In the 2004 photograph, the trees are also protected against cattle with a wooden fence. In 2017 they are already fully grown and do not require protection from cattle anymore, but their trunks are whitewashed for protection against pests. A creek runs in front of the house. Most streets in Drăguş that are on the North-South direction have similar creeks coming down from the mountains across the village. I consider them to add more aesthetic value of the village. They are beautiful, picturesque and they bring freshness to the streets although they are not always clean. Sometimes, these creeks contain waste specific to consumerism such as plastic bags, wraps or bottles. Liquid waste from the household's animals (pigs, sheep, or cattle) is sometimes discharged in the creeks. I feel as if these small environmental resources were not sufficiently taken care of and valued in Drăguş.

Fig. 6.1: Old house, 2004 (author's archive)

In 2004 in Drăguş, there were only three houses left that were built out of wood in the traditional, early 20th-century style. All others had been demolished in the 1960s and 1970s and replaced with new, brick and mortar houses, larger and more comfortable. The three remaining houses were uninhabited in 2004. I photographed one of them (Fig. 6.1) which was later demolished by its owners since it was deteriorated beyond the possibility of repair. Another one of the three, found in the vicinity of the town hall, was transformed by the local authorities into an Ethnographic Museum with the help of European funding (Fig. 6.2). The museum is organized as a traditional household, with two rooms where local items are on display: traditional costumes and textiles, wooden pots, and agricultural tools. It belongs to the community, and it is available for various cultural events. The museum is named *Dimitrie Gusti* in the memory of the professor and sociologist who led the monographic research in this community in the interwar period. In the 2017 photograph, one can see the identification elements on the facade of the building: the name of the museum and of the project through which European funding was acquired. The well-groomed aspect of the house is noticeable with its renovated facade, roof and woodwork as well as the not so aesthetically pleasing cables hanging across the front of it. This photograph was taken in 2017 during the month of October at the event called "Traditional Drăguş wedding", as children dressed in traditional costumes were waiting outside of the museum for the event to begin.

Fig. 6.2: Ethnographic museum, 2017 (author's archive)

6.3 Households' interiors

Figures 7.1 and 7.2 illustrate the courtyard of a Drăguş household. As mentioned earlier, the typical household has, generally, three distinct spaces. Here we see the first of these spaces, the courtyard, which has an entrance straight from the street. In this space, the protagonists are the people. Beyond the fence, in the second space, the animals are kept and in the third space the main "actors" are the cultivated plants: fruit trees, vegetables, etc. The house usually has two entrances from the courtyard: one for access to the "good" or "front" rooms and the other for the day-to-day living areas: kitchen, bedrooms, etc. In 2004, in the house pictured (Fig. 7.1), Livia Sucaciu, a septuagenarian, lived alone. In 2017 her daughter-in-law, Mariana Sucaciu, lives there (Fig. 7.2). These photographs of the courtyard show many elements of development: the doors and windows are new, the living space has been enlarged and renovated and the courtyard itself is full of flowers and flower pots. The fence that separates the first courtyard from the animal space is also covered with ornamental plants. Overall, the courtyard looks nice, modern and clean.

In these photographs (Figs. 8.1 and 8.2) we see another typical Drăguş household where lives an extended family, with three generations. They have separate sleeping quarters but a shared kitchen. The elders, Viorica and Nicolae Jurcovan,

Fig. 7.1: Ms. Sucaciu's courtyard, 2004 (author's archive)

Fig. 7.2: Ms. Sucaciu's courtyard, 2017 (author's archive)

Fig. 8.1: Jurcovan's family courtyard, 2004 (author's archive)

Fig. 8.2: Jurcovan's family courtyard, 2017 (author's archive)

Fig. 9.1: Racu's family courtyard, 2004 (author's archive)

live in the smaller house in the back where the kitchen is also located. To the right is the entrance of the main house, with two rooms facing the street where the Jurcovans' son, daughter-in-law and their boy live. Both houses have been recently renovated. The concrete stairs were covered in floor tiles, the walls painted, wooden windows replaced with double-glazing windows and the left entrance door was also changed (with PVC instead of wood). Grape vine and flowers are an aesthetic element of the courtyard and have multiplied since 2004 along the stairs and the sidewalk.

The yard for animals in the Racu family household has been significantly transformed. In 2004 it was a space for farm animals and storage (Fig. 9.1). The chickens were left free in this area and because of this, grass never grew here. On the left side of the image we notice the pit for manure, the chicken coop and the toilet (the leftmost white wooden shack). On the right side there is the shed for storing hay and in the back, there is the fire wood. In 2017 the courtyard looks neater and cleaner. The main courtyard has been extended over parts of the animals' section, and on the left side they planted vegetables and grape vine. The two courtyards are separated by the metal gate which has a typical design for Drăguş. In the animals' section, trees were planted but the wooden constructions are still there, even though they do not serve any purpose anymore, as is the case of the wooden toilet.

Fig. 9.2: Racu's family courtyard, 2017 (author's archive)

The modernisation of the living space above is obvious. A traditionally decorated living room (Fig. 10.1) with a rustic bed filled with pillows was transformed into a different space with new elements: laminated floors, walls painted in a modern style, without the old patterns, new furniture, a gas stove in the corner of the room and a new carpet. Also, the room itself was enlarged; in 2017 I changed the angle of the camera slightly to capture this aspect. In 2004 the traditional pillows were in use, as seen on the bed (Fig. 10.2), but in 2017 they told me that they put these decorative pillows in a chest with traditional items. They felt that the modern aspect of the house is more important.

The modernization of the living space is also obvious in the above photographs depicting another living room (Figs. 11.1 and 11.2): the wooden windows are replaced with double-glazing windows and the curtain is changed; the painting on the walls has no more patterns as it was the 1970s and 1980s style, it is in one colour; new furniture replaces a traditionally decorated bed and the woven carpets on the wall have been removed; the table cloth is new, bought and not homemade as was the case in 2004; the rug is new; there's a religious painting on the wall, but without the traditional decorative elements that used to hang above icons before. Some new elements, common to both interiors, presented are the flower vases and the porcelain figurines (Fig. 11.2). It is noteworthy that these rooms are empty most of the year. They are used to receive guests or for special family events.

Fig. 10.1: Poparad's family living room, 2004 (author's archive)

Fig. 10.2: Poparad's family living room, 2017 (author's archive)

Fig. 11.1: Bobeica's family living room, 2004 (author's archive)

Fig. 11.2: Bobeica's family living room, 2017 (author's archive)

Fig. 12.1: Jurcovan's family kitchen, 2004 (author's archive)

This kitchen from Figs. 12.1 and 12.2 was already refurbished in 2004, not much has changed between then and 2017. Wall tiles on the kitchen walls were a new element in Drăguş, appearing in the 1990s and were associated with well-being and hygiene. The L-shaped kitchen bench is another element of modernity that was also very popular in this community during the 1990s.

In many of the households of Drăguş there is a summer kitchen, usually found in the first courtyard, with its own entrance directly from the courtyard. It is being used from spring until autumn for practical reasons, that is, to avoid steam and odours from the cooking to spread in the living areas of the house. We can see in Figs. 13.1 and 13.2 that the Potinteu's family summer kitchen has changed a lot since 2004: over the dirt floor they fitted a wooden one, a new terracotta brick stove was built, they purchased a gas cooker with a gas tank so as to have both wood and gas cooking options, a running water sink was installed and new kitchen furniture fitted – the suspended cabinets (Fig. 13.2) for storing the dishes and saving space, another modern element of recent interior design in Drăguş.

6.4 Public buildings

We start the description of the public institutions with the town hall (Figs. 14.1 and 14.2), the seat of the local public administration. During the socialist era

Fig. 12.2: Jurcovan's family kitchen, 2017 (author's archive)

Fig. 13.1: Potinteu's family summer kitchen, 2004 (author's archive)

Fig. 13.2: Potinteu's family summer kitchen, 2017 (author's archive)

Fig. 14.1: Drăguş Commune Town Hall, 2004 (author's archive)

Fig. 14.2: Drăguş Commune Town Hall, 2017 (author's archive)

when the village of Drăguş was ascribed to another commune, the building was used as a pub and later abandoned. It was renovated with the village's own funds in the 2000s. It was continuously modernized after 2004, each new mayor trying to improve its condition and to make it more modern and more functional. We notice in Fig. 14.2 that the building has both a modern and rustic look: plastic and metal were replaced by wood, there is a rustic wooden plaque in front with the name of the building, the front ditch has been repaired, trash bins installed and flowers planted. The building was extended in the back where an interior yard was created for parking purposes. The tall and old spruce trees, visible in the 2004 photograph, have disappeared. In this case modernization, reflected in the planning of the public spaces around the building, can be associated with changes in the natural environment.

This is the school (Figs. 15.1 and 15.2) where the children of Drăguş study from the first until the eighth grade. Lately, children from neighbouring communities come to this school for two reasons: first, some of them only have primary schools, and second, in the past years the secondary school of Drăguş has developed an attractive offer of educational and extracurricular programs such as German language classes, after-school activities or summer school. The building was entirely renovated both on the inside and on the outside (Fig. 15.2). The wood heating was replaced with a gas central heating system, the classrooms

Fig. 15.1: Secondary school, 2004 (author's archive)

Fig. 15.2: Secondary school, 2017 (author's archive)

Fig. 16.1: The nursery school, 2004 (author's archive)

and laboratories were renovated, toilets were installed inside, replacing the outdoor ones, and the courtyard was renewed with a sports field and a playground. In the after-school programme, children are provided with a hot meal by a local catering company.

The other educational institution of the commune is the nursery school (Figs. 16.1 and 16.2) for children from 3 to 6 years old. We can see the positive changes in the images above, as the building has been completely renovated. The roof and windows were replaced, the building painted and the alleys reconstructed (Fig. 16.2). This change is visible on the inside, too, where the spaces for children and educators are renovated. The grounds are well taken care of and, although not visible in the images, there is another element of novelty and modernity in the community: on the grounds of the nursery school there is a playground at European standards. An adjacent building belonging to the nursery school, but not in use because of the reduced number of children, was leased by the administration to two private companies who operate a pharmacy and a dentist's practice, services that were not present in 2004 in Drăguş.

The Community centre has changed a lot in the past 13 years (Figs. 17.1 and 17.2). The building was constructed at the end of the 1970s as a cultural and events centre for the community. During the socialist era, shows were organized

Fig. 16.2: The nursery school, 2017 (author's archive)

Fig. 17.1: Community centre, 2004 (author's archive)

Fig. 17.2: Community centre, 2017 (author's archive)

here, film screenings, weddings or balls. Today, in the big hall of the Community centre, wedding ceremonies are no longer organized but shows and other cultural events, balls and, in the past several years, wakes take place here. The building has been renovated both inside and outside: the facade is new as well as the doors, windows and roof. It has a modern central heating system and indoor toilets (in 2004 they were outdoors) and a modern equipped kitchen for community events. The building also hosts a local association for development by attracting European funds: The Local Action Group "Valea Sâmbetei". The grounds around the building have also been renewed. A slightly visible metal fence in the 2004 photograph has been replaced with a well-kept kept hedge and parking spaces have been set up. As a novelty, we can see in Fig. 17.2 that there are new informative signposts about the touristic area that I mentioned earlier, close to the Făgăraş Mountains, at about 9 kilometres from Drăguş.

The clinic is the place where the medical practice is. The building (Figs. 18.1 and 18.2) was constructed in the 1970s by the local administration, and it was designed with a triple function: medical practice, pharmacy and living quarters for the physician and their family. With a design similar to that of other houses of the village, the clinic is comprised of the doctor's office, the nurse's office, a waiting room, a storage area (which used to be the pharmacy in the 1980s) and a separate wing where the doctor's family living quarters are. The building is

Fig. 18.1: Clinic, 2004 (author's archive)

Fig. 18.2: Clinic, 2017 (author's archive)

Fig. 19.1: The Orthodox Church, 2004 (author's archive)

surrounded by a courtyard and garden. The clinic is well-maintained, being periodically renovated both inside and out. In the 13 years since 2004 the gate was replaced (Fig. 18.2) and the doctor's office was provided with modern medical equipment (I will present a photo of the interior further on). The clinic was a clean and well-maintained facility in 2004 and so it is in 2017.

In Drăguş most people are of Christian Orthodox faith. There are two churches in the village: Orthodox and Greek Catholic. The orthodox church (Figs. 19.1 and 19.2) was built in 1896. In the 13 years between 2004 and 2017 it was repaired and renovated: the staircase leading to the tower was consolidated, the windows replaced and the wooden floors replaced with floor tiles. In the images we notice new, decorative trees in front of the church as well as a new roof on the right side of Fig. 19.2 – this is the roof of a new parking space for agricultural machinery that was built in the middle of a private garden, which, during

Fig. 19.2: The Orthodox Church, 2017 (author's archive)

the socialist era, belonged to the church. We can see the new sidewalk as well as the pedestrian crossing sign – many traffic signs have been installed in the village in order to comply with European norms of traffic safety.

The Greek Catholic church was closed during the communist regime, the cult being forbidden between 1948 and 1989. Immediately after the 1989 revolution, the Greek Catholic communities began renovating and to reclaim their properties and their churches. It is the case of Drăguş where the Greek Catholic was reborn (Figs. 20.1 and 20.2), but with a very small number of families; today there are less than 10 members of this faith in the village. Unlike the orthodox priest who lives in the parish house in the centre of the village, the Greek Catholic priest travels to Drăguş only for Sunday service or for any special events that might require religious service. Although it is a small church and it has only a few parishioners, the church has been renovated and it is in a very good condition

Fig. 20.1: Greek Catholic church, 2004 (author's archive)

(Fig. 20.2). The facades have been renovated, woodwork repaired, a new fence and gate installed, a new pavement in front of the church and the roof renovated.

The pub as a social institution was the object of social research in Drăguş in the interwar period, during the monographic research. A place for spending leisure time and socializing, the pub was, for a long time, a male-only space where women were not allowed (Fig. 21.1). Even in the last decades of the communist regime, the pub was dominated by groups of men meeting for a chat over a drink. Today the idea of pub in Drăguş has been replaced with that of a bar, and there are several bars now in the village. In the place of the old pub the space is completely transformed, modernized and refurbished to create the atmosphere of an urban bar, with new furniture and artificial lighting (Fig. 21.2). The bar has a new name, in English – *The Brothers* – and women are allowed in, too.

Fig. 20.2: Greek Catholic church, 2017 (author's archive)

7 Participants

7.1 People in public spaces

Small groups of old women sitting in front of their houses are a common sight in Drăguş (Figs. 22.1 and 22.2). Many houses have a small bench in front, where the neighbours (women as well as men) gather to chat and to "watch who is passing by". Images like the two above are very common in the summer mornings and evenings. Of the three women I photographed in 2004, only the one on the right, Olimpia, is still alive in 2017. She has an infirmity now, and she walks with the help of a walker that we can see on the left of Fig. 22.2. She comes out to sit on the bench every day, in front of her neighbours' house, where she chats with her friends. Women's outfits are always the same: a skirt with an apron over it, a simple blouse and, if it is not very hot, a vest. The headscarf is a mandatory

Fig. 21.1: The pub, 2004 (author's archive)

Fig. 21.2: The bar "The Brothers", 2017 (author's archive)

Fig. 22.1: Old women on the bench (lăicioară), 2004 (author's archive)

Fig. 22.2: Old women on the bench (lăicioară), 2017 (author's archive)

element for the older women of Drăguş, especially for widows. They wear black, grey or brown stockings. The house pictured is used mostly during the summer and weekends when the heirs that inherited it from their parents come over from Braşov. It is a clean renovated house, a holiday home.

The elders of Drăguş seldom go out for leisure walks. Generally, they go out with a specific purpose in mind. The concept of strolling is not part of their life, but it is increasingly so for children and young people. The young often go out for walks, as the elders have always something to attend to. The couple in Fig. 23.1, Sofia and Vichente Sucaciu, were walking home, coming from the post office where they had a parcel to send. They were walking slowly, as the lady had mobility problems. They passed away since, so in 2017 I took a picture of someone else to illustrate this social category of people. I noticed Mr. Vasile Nichiu (Fig. 23.2) on the street on a mobility scooter – a modern locomotion means, battery powered with an autonomy of several hours. He was also out with a specific purpose: visiting his wife's grave in the cemetery. He goes there every day, and for this he attached a small stool to the scooter for when he needs to sit near at her grave.

People who clean in front of their houses, especially on Saturday evenings, are a common sight in Drăguş. They clean the streams or ditches, sweep the dust or clean the manure from the asphalt. It is an unwritten old convention which has

Fig. 23.1: Old couple on the street, 2004 (author's archive)

Fig. 23.2: Old man on the street, 2017 (author's archive)

been respected through the decades and political regimes. The tools used are simple: shovels, hoes, rakes and brooms. In Fig. 24.1 I captured the image of a family with children and grandchildren, in the middle of which, in a green vest, was the mayor of the village helping out. In Fig. 24.2 there were two women, neighbours who were cleaning the street after the herd had passed. The next day was a holiday and someone on their street had recently passed away, so the street had to look good, as they said to me.

In 2004 I took many photographs of children playing in the street. In 2017 I saw quite fewer children out playing. One explanation might be that the number of children has decreased significantly but also that other ways of playing indoors have appeared with the advent of technology.

In this place, for example, I saw children at play every day in 2004 (Fig. 25.1). The bridge over the stream was a place for meeting and playing for them. Today, most of the children in that image are adults. In the neighbouring houses there are no more children, only adults, many already old, and the street is lively only during the summer holidays when the elders' grandchildren come to visit from the city or from abroad. The photograph in Fig. 25.2 is valuable though, since it reveals a series of significant details of the changes in the community: asphalt on the street, renovated houses, a concrete sidewalk, gas piping and traffic signs.

Fig. 24.1: Cleaning in front of the houses, 2004 (author's archive)

Fig. 24.2: Cleaning in front of the houses, 2017 (author's archive)

Fig. 25.1: Children on Nicheşti street, 2004 (author's archive)

Fig. 25.2: Nicheşti street without children, 2017 (author's archive)

The children in Fig. 26.1 were given a ride by this lady with her horse-drawn cart. She was going to work on her fields and, for a portion of the route there, she was giving the children a very enjoyable ride. In 2017 I saw considerably fewer children in horse-drawn carts and more and more children in carts pulled by tractors. The rural households in Drăguş have progressed as the traditional horse and cart has been replaced by tractors and modern agricultural machinery. In the image in Fig. 26.2 we can see a group of children who get together on the summer or winter holidays when they visit their grandparents in Drăguş. The father of a local girl is giving them a ride with the tractor. The children in this image live in Drăguş, Bucharest and Belgium.

7.2 People at home

Viorica and Solomon Trâmbiţaş (Fig. 27.1) were part of the economic elite of the village (Şandru 2009) both in the socialist period as well as after, in the capitalism of the 1990s. They administered and owned the mill from Drăguş – a very useful installation for the local economy – being the place where cereals were ground and turned into flour. Working at the mill kept them busy from dawn until dusk which is why they had set up a little room at the mill where they felt like home. In 2004, I met them in a moment of respite, at lunchtime, in their

Fig. 26.1: Children in cart, 2004 (author's archive)

Fig. 26.2: Children on a tractor, 2017 (author's archive)

Fig. 27.1: The Trâmbiţaş family – the millers of the village, 2004 (author's archive)

Fig. 27.2: Viorica Trâmbiţaş, 2017 (author's archive)

room at the mill. Their clothes had the signs of their work, being white with flower. In 2017 Viorica is alone. Solomon passed away in 2016. At home, even though her house has several rooms, she only uses one of them and the summer kitchen in the warmer months. She has decorated her room with many religious icons (Fig. 27.2) and with photos of her deceased husband. She wears only black, as all Drăguş widows do for many years after the death of their life partner.

Zoriţa Poparad is one of the oldest women in the village. She is 86 years old and yet still very active (Figs. 28.1 and 28.2). She has been a widow for almost twenty years and she lives in the household with her son and daughter-in-law. She works alongside them in the household and in the fields, and in her spare time she weaves traditional costumes at her loom. For the photograph, she insisted to be dressed in a traditional costume, not in regular clothes. She loves flowers and every year she strives to have her courtyard full of them. The house is modernized and renovated; new elements are visible in Fig. 28.2 (PVC door, new stairs with floor tiles, new plastered and painted exterior walls).

In the 1990s and the beginning of the 2000s an ample phenomenon of migration was recorded in Drăguş. People left abroad to work, mainly to Italy and Spain. As in many other cases, in the Roştioru family the husband, Constantin, was the first to leave and a few years later, the wife and the three daughters joined him. Every summer they return home on holidays. In Fig. 29.1 there is Mariana,

Fig. 28.1: Zorița Poparad, 2004 (with permission of Ovidiu Poparad)

Fig. 28.2: Zorița Poparad, 2017 (with permission of Ovidiu Poparad)

the mother, and Simona, the youngest daughter of the Roștioru family in the courtyard of the family house in Drăguș where Mariana's mother lives and is looking after the household. In 2017 I found Constantin at the house after having renovated, over the years, the house and yard (Fig. 29.2). The family's life project is to return to Drăguș at their retirement, or even earlier because, in their

Fig. 29.1: Emigrants from Spain, visiting home, 2004 (author's archive)

Fig. 29.2: Emigrants from Spain, visiting home, 2017 (author's archive)

opinion, it is getting increasingly harder to find work in Spain. We notice several important changes in the courtyard: a pathway has been built with floor tiles, the pavement has been renewed and a grape vine-covered pergola made. Constantin still works on the house in order to transform and give it the most recent amenities.

7.3 People on holidays

Drăguş has several holidays when some of the locals dress up in traditional costumes, especially the women and children. The holidays are religious, such as Easter or Christmas, or important moments in the cycle of life like weddings or baptisms or simply days when important events in the community take place. In the past years, the number of such events was on the rise and the traditional costumes are used by the locals and promoted by the local leaders as cultural patrimony.

Figure 30.1 was a staged photograph. At the beginning of the 1990s in Drăguş, the interest for tradition and wearing the traditional attire seemed to fade. In order for me to illustrate this cultural heritage, one Sunday evening I asked the women and girls in the image to wear the traditional costumes just for this photograph. In 2004, the mayor in office started a campaign of promoting the local

Fig. 30.1: Women in traditional costumes, 2004 (author's archive)

Fig. 30.2: Women in traditional costumes, 2017 (author's archive)

traditions by creating community events and by the participation of the Drăguş women's choir in national festivals. This initiative was continued by those elected in office afterwards and so Drăguş benefits from a series of events in which the traditional attire and local customs are put forward. An example of such an event is the project "Traditional Drăguş Wedding", an annual event organized with the help of the County Council of Braşov in which there is a staged wedding as it was organized in 1930. Figure 30.2 was taken in the yard of the *Dimitrie Gusti* museum from Drăguş, when the suite of the traditional wedding was arriving at "the house of the bride".

The girls in Fig. 31.1 were featured on the cover of the book I coordinated in 2005. They are now women and mothers; they have children of their own. That photograph was also staged. In 2017 though, it was very easy for me to spontaneously find little girls dressed like this (Fig. 31.2). During summer and autumn there are multiple community events where children wear traditional costumes. Most of them involve the school, which means that both pupils and teachers take part in these cultural community events.

Christmas in Drăguş is strongly connected with the tradition of the "Herods" – a group of 13–14-year-old boys who on Christmas Eve go from house to house, sing Christmas carols and play out a nativity scene. Their name comes from Herod, the Roman emperor that ordered the massacre of the innocents at the

Fig. 31.1: Little girls' costumes, 2004 (author's archive)

Fig. 31.2: Little girls' costumes, 2017 (author's archive)

Fig. 32.1: Herods, 2004 (with permission of Ovidiu Poparad)

time of Jesus Christ's birth. The Herods (Figs. 32.1 and 32.2) are dressed in traditional costumes, they wear handmade coloured cardboard crowns decorated with shiny paper and religious images and they bear wooden swords. From the houses where they sing and play they receive money and ritual foodstuffs (white braided bread and smoked pork meat). This custom is unchanged since 2004 and is still supported by the parents and the school. Another Drăguş custom is the Troupe of Lads (*Ceata de feciori*) – young, bachelor men who sing Christmas carols organize the dance during the winter holidays and live together for two weeks. In 2017 the Troupe of Lads was not organized in Drăguş.

8 Activities

8.1 Work in local institutions[3]

Work in local socio-economic institutions has generally become more specialized and is largely based on the use of new technologies. I took pictures of the mayor's office, the family physician's office, the accounting office of the largest

3 As mentioned in the *Methodology* chapter, work-related changes are described in a visual essay (Csesznek, and Scârneci-Domnişoru, 2019).

Fig. 32.2: Herods, 2017 (author's archive)

agricultural and zootechnical farm in the commune, the bakery and a wood-processing company which replaced the traditional craftsmanship of carpentry. In all of these cases, re-photography documents change in the sense of modernization, technological upgrading, renovation of the premises and work efficiency in the local institutions.

8.2 Work in households

Within the households, some of the activities are still done manually, without major changes in the way they are performed or in terms of the tools used. Other work is done with the help of technology. For example, milking cows or buffaloes, mowing, cooking or cleaning the courtyards and the exterior of the houses are done as before, manually, according to traditional techniques and with simple instruments. Other activities, however, are carried out with the help of modern technologies, such as washing clothes or preparing food for various community events. There are also activities that have disappeared from the local community, such as the craftsmanship of smithery or carpentry. In other cases, the disappearance of a traditional role such as that of the village cook is now replaced by the existence of a very modern kitchen set up within the cultural centre where meals are prepared for local events (memorial services, celebrations, commemorations,

Fig. 33.1: Bride and groom exiting the church, 2004 (with permission of Ovidiu Poparad)

etc.) as well as for pupils from the village school who are enrolled in the after-school program.

8.3 Community events

Weddings (Figs. 33.1 and 33.2) are events which attract the attention of the members of the Drăguş community, as the ceremony has several spectacular stages taking place in the public space. A lot of people go out in front of their gates or go to church to see the wedding ceremony. The exit of the newly wedded couple from the church is followed by the "bride's dance". Not only are the wedding guests taking part in this custom, but also many onlookers do. The ritual has remained unchanged over the years. In 2017, I noticed the presence of many cars in front of the church. This is where the element of change appears: the wedding reception does not take place at the cultural centre as before, but the people drive their cars, which are decorated with ribbons and flowers, to a restaurant outside the village.

On the way from the church to the party venue, the wedding cortege is stopped in front of a ritual "gate" – a symbol of the transition to another stage of life (Figs. 34.1 and 34.2). The gate opens after the "guards" are paid by the godfather. In 2017, the ritualistic gate was not part of a real wedding, but of an event

Fig. 33.2: Bride and groom exiting the church, 2017 (author's archive)

Fig. 34.1: Ritualistic wedding gate, 2004 (author's archive)

Fig. 34.2: Ritualistic wedding gate, 2017 (author's archive)

created by the local government: Re-enactment of the traditional wedding. This cultural event, into its fourth edition in 2017, attracts several hundred visitors annually. Local and county institutions (city hall, school, Orthodox church, county council, etc.) are engaged in organizing the event, sustained financially by local firms, and several press agencies are invited.

In Drăguş, the death of a person is not regarded as a private, family event, but as one involving a large part of the community. For three days, the deceased is kept at home in one of the front rooms of the house, while assisted day and night by the family, relatives, neighbours and friends (Figs. 35.1 and 35.2). It is a period called watch, and it lasts until the day when the deceased is buried in the village cemetery. People who attend the funeral bring candles, flowers, food and, optionally, money. In recent years, funeral homes, which are based in nearby towns, have been asked to perform the embalming. Until the year 2000, embalming was done by the relatives and friends of the deceased. In most cases, the dead, especially the elderly, lie in a coffin dressed in a traditional costume.

The burial is the most emotionally charged moment of the funeral ritual in Drăguş (Figs. 36.1 and 36.2). Every family has their own plot in the cemetery, generally a companion plot. After the funeral procession moves through the village, the priest officiates the funeral service which takes about 20 minutes,

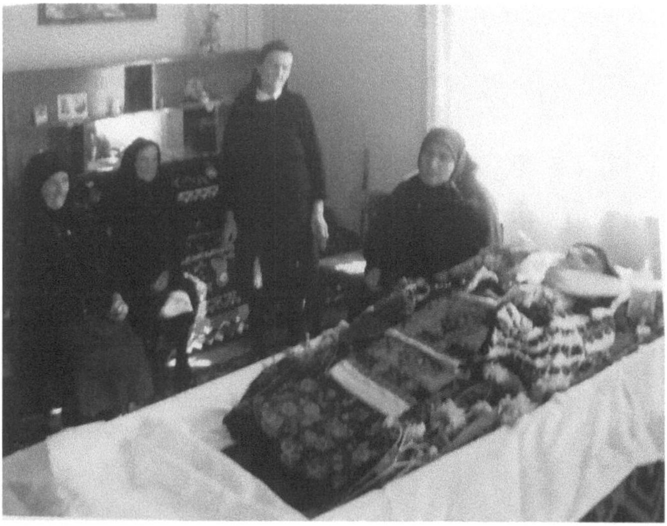

Fig. 35.1: Wake held in the house of the deceased, 2004 (author's archive)

Fig. 35.2: Wake held in the house of the deceased, 2017 (author's archive)

Fig. 36.1: In the cemetery, 2004 (author's archive)

Fig. 36.2: In the cemetery, 2017 (author's archive)

then all the participants are invited for the post-funeral meal – the so-called alms (*pomană*).

For many years, post-funeral receptions have been organized in the main hall of the community centre (Figs. 37.1 and 37.2). Until the 1990s, they were held in the yard of the deceased. The alms always include at least a hundred participants: family, relatives, friends, priest and other people who work or volunteer for the church, such as the village's women choir present at each funeral, but underprivileged people can attend as well, especially widowed people. It is a costly meal: three courses and drinks are served. Food is prepared at the community centre, in the new kitchen previously mentioned, or ordered from catering companies or restaurants in the area. The tables, chairs and utensils are available at the community centre, as a common property of the community members. The 2017 photo shows that the hall was renovated and modernized over the past 13 years: the painting was restored, the heating and lighting systems were upgraded, the furniture was changed (the upholstered chairs replaced the old wooden benches) and the entrance to the kitchen can be noticed to the right. It is a modern and comfortable space for organizing community events.

Fig. 37.1: Alms, 2004 (author's archive)

Fig. 37.2: Alms, 2017 (author's archive)

9 Conclusions and further discussion

Re-photography proves to be a useful technique for studying social change in a community, as it gives prominence to visually recorded realities at different times. This means illustrating indisputable aspects which document various dimensions of the social life change. Three decades ago, Harper noted a growing tendency to integrate re-photography techniques into the study of community change (1988). Creating a temporal order where the same reality is photographed at a time T1 and at a time T2 (Rieger 2011) provides valuable information about social dynamics, because important dimensions of transformations can be captured in images and then interpreted by the researcher. Moreover, these photographs can also serve a critical purpose: set in the context of community awareness, they can become stimuli for elaborating local development policies.

Producing sets of photographs using the repetition technique is an efficient method to document change even in the absence of commentary. Images are powerful in themselves. They "isolate and freeze a fragment of reality, which, immovable, is subject to detailed successive analyses" (Secondulfo, 1993). As a result of my field experience, I think that the best way to illustrate and study change is by adding some relevant descriptions to the pictures. In this way, one can briefly tell the story of change and can identify the mechanisms and meanings of social change processes.

I agree with Rieger (2011) who argues that documenting social change is best performed when the researcher has the possibility to use other techniques: observing processes, interviewing participants, producing new images and collecting other "evidence" essential to understanding change. Thus, the purpose of a visual-based research study is described by Rieger: "In implementing the visual approach, our objective must be to build up a comprehensive photographic record, buttressed by interviews and field notes" (p. 143).

Visual techniques seem to open a vast array of methodological creativity. In 1988, Harper argued that "not all sociological data can be photographed, of course, but in studies of social or environmental ecology and social interaction, the camera can gather information that cannot be gathered with the human eye or other recording devices" (p. 62). This is only partially true. I think that almost any social phenomenon can also be studied using visual techniques, if not directly, at least through the subjects' perception and representations of that phenomenon. It is true that you cannot photograph the "feeling of belonging to a community" – a research topic which requires a complex methodology, based on verbal or written techniques and on measuring instruments. But one can use, for example, the photovoice technique in order to capture those images in which the subjects express their belonging to a community and their attachment to it. Similarly, there are tools developed to study the values of a community or the matter of identity, but visual techniques (photo-elicitation, photovoice, photonovella) can be used to reflect people's perception of value and identity in their lives at a certain moment. Furthermore, any attempt to repeat such a study over a certain period of time will provide abundant information on change, on individual and collective metamorphoses. These are arguments meant to reinforce the efficacy of visual techniques in social research in general, and in the study of social change in particular.

Drăguş village, re-photographed after 13 years, is the picture of a dynamic community undergoing profound transformations. The photographs are witnesses of these transformations taking place in Drăguş: the aspect of the houses and streets is changing, public buildings look well maintained or even completely renovated, events are organized here, new services appear, etc. In terms of the previous definitions, change as development and modernization is present in most of the aspects photographed in Drăguş. Numerous new elements have been imported to Drăguş through migration processes. Migrants send or bring home not only material resources but also new ideas, adopting superior life quality standards.

Other changes, especially at the institutional level, have been and are currently made through European financial mechanisms. The European and national financing lines for economic and social development stimulate the creation of modern infrastructure or the rehabilitation of the existing one, but also revitalize traditions by reorganizing cultural events. I believe that the mechanism of social imitation should not be ignored, as I perceived the local people's increased motivation to adapt to the changes proposed by their neighbours or relatives. Conservatism is manifested in the approach to certain household chores and to traditional, ritualistic activities. Nevertheless, these also feature an innovative dimension: the renovation of spaces for traditional community events, the use of new facilities and technologies and the creation of events as forms of cultural marketing; all these illustrate the socio-economic development of the community. And as far as the values of modernization are concerned, I also noticed some insanitary public spaces and unalluring aspects which create an impression of neglect within the village.

I think there are a number of advantages in using photographs in order to illustrate change:

Firstly, comparative photographs depicting the same aspect of social life contain great evidence of change. This evidence is easily noticeable in the photographs and stimulates the interpretation process. The images exert a powerful stimulus effect on me as well on the members of this community, evoking the "story of change". Furthermore, the photographs enhanced the people's awareness of change. Frequently, both I and especially the subjects would look at the photographs and comment on them, exclaiming: "So many things have changed around here! In real life, they don't seem so many…" or "I haven't even realised that there are so many renovated houses and buildings!"

Secondly, the photographs illustrate those elements of change which could prove to be rather dull in written form. For example, I explained the structure of a typical house in Drăguş, but the photograph of the household seen from the church's steeple is more revealing than the description. In addition, while looking at the photograph, even I noticed elements of modernization that would have eluded me otherwise: concrete pavements or solar panels installed on the rooftop. Therefore, photographs concentrate a lot of information, which is provided to the viewer in an attractive and easy-to-understand form.

Thirdly, data are easy to collect and can be interpreted in various ways: based either on the researcher's knowledge or on photo-elicitation, requesting interpretations from community members in order to discover the story of change and to revive relevant aspects of the community dynamics. Photo-elicitation may also require opinions from neutral observers who previously did not know the community; without revealing the purpose of their study in order not to induce answers, researchers can ask these observers to interpret what they see – i.e. the sets of comparative photographs illustrating the community in the two moments. I intend to apply this method with a group of students who have the role of neutral observers – not involved in community life and without prior knowledge of the community. The aim is to see to what extent pictures suggest the idea of change seen as development and modernization.

The positive reaction of community members was significantly helpful in the field research in Drăguş Village. For each photograph, I asked for the subjects' consent for taking and publishing the respective images. I did not encounter any problems or refusals. Sometimes the duration of the meeting with the photographed subjects was considerably prolonged, because people wanted to give me explanations and they were interested in my project. In many cases, my request for taking photographs triggered positive emotional responses: people were impressed and flattered by the fact that their life was interesting enough to become the object of research. Some even cried with excitement!

Also, taking photographs is easy and cheap. Cameras have become accessible and, as pictures can now be taken with smart phones, it is very easy nowadays to capture various aspects of the community life in high-quality digital pictures and to create electronic archives.

Working with photographs also has its drawbacks:

You cannot capture a series of data which are fundamental to understanding change, such as socio-demographic indicators. Although researchers can quantify change (they can count how many new elements appear in the picture at time T2 compared to T1, for example), the function of the pictures remains illustrative. A rigorous explanation of change also requires the use of statistical data.

In addition, some realities no longer exist. Here the researcher must look for a substitute, if it exists, or specify that the respective element has disappeared. It can sometimes be quite difficult to decide.

Another inconvenience is the quality of the photographs taken prior to the digital age. In my project, the quality of the 2017 pictures is very different to that of the photographs taken 13 years before. In 2004 I used a camera borrowed from a friend. The digital cameras were still very expensive, and I had to do my field research in a fairly short time. In 2017 I used two of my own digital cameras and the photo archive was easy to manage.

Bibliography

Cseszneck, C., Scârneci-Domnişoru, F. (2019). Changes in Working Practices in a Rural Community of Romania Community. *Visual Communication*, 18(2), 189–204.

Durrheim, K. (2014). Social Change. In Teo, T. (Ed.), *Encyclopedia of Critical Psychology* (pp. 1767–1771). New York: Springer.

Faccioli, P. (1993). La sociologia visuale. Tecniche e campi d'applicazione. In Cipolla, C., Faccioli, P. (Eds.), *Introduzione alla sociologia visuale* (pp. 49–69). Milano: Franco Angelli.

Georgescu, D.C. (1945). *Drăguş. Un sat din ţara Oltului. Demografia şi igiena populaţiei*. Bucureşti: Institutul Social Român.

Harper, D. (1988). Visual Sociology: Expanding Sociological Vision. *The American Sociologist*, 19(1), Spring, 54–70.

Hinds, G. (2017). Photography and Teaching in Community Development. In Halsall, J.P., Snowden, M. (Eds.), *The Pedagogy of the Social Sciences Curriculum, International Perspectives on Social Policy, Administration, and Practice* (pp. 85–92). Cham: Springer International Publishing Switzerland. DOI 10.1007/978-3-319-33868-2_7.

Karpov, D., Kryuchov, Y. (2015). Analytical Photography as a New Tool for the Representations of Reality. *Procedia – Social and Behavioral Sciences*, 166 (2015), 675–679. Retrieved from https://www-sciencedirect-com.am.e-nformation.ro/science/article/pii/S1877042814067330

Larionescu, M. (1996). Dimitrie Gusti. Fondatorul Şcolii Sociologice de la Bucureşti. In Larionescu, M. (Ed.), *Şcoala Sociologică de la Bucureşti. Tradiţie şi actualitate* (pp. 10–48). Bucureşti: Editura Metropol.

Laumann, E.O., Pappi, F.U. (1995). Reti di azione collettiva. In Piselli, F. (Ed.), *Reti. L'analisi di network nelle scienze sociali* (pp. 227–249). Roma: Donizelli Editore.

Mihăilescu, I. (1993). Modernizare. In Zamfir, C., Vlăsecanu, L. (Eds.), *Dicţionar de Sociologie* (p. 368). Bucureşti: Editura Babel.

Pauwels, L. (2010). Visual Sociology Reframed: An Analytical Synthesis and Discussion of Visual Methods in Social and Cultural Research. *Sociological Methods & Research* 38: 545. DOI: 10.1177/0049124110366233.

Popescu, R., Vârdol, A., Briciu, C. (2006). Măsurarea dezvoltării sociale. In Zamfir, C., Stoica, L. (Eds.), *O nouă provocare: Dezvoltarea Socială* (pp. 313–330). Iaşi: Polirom.

Purcell, R. (2007). Images for change: community development, community arts and photography. *Community Development Journal*, 44(1), 111–122.

Rieger, J.H. (2011). Re-photography for Documenting Social Change. In: Margolis, E., Pauwels, L. (Eds.), *The Sage Handbook of Visual Research Methods* (pp. 132–149). London: Sage.

Rose, G. (2008). Using Photographs as Illustrations in Human Geography. *Journal of Geography in Higher Education*, 32(1), 151–160.

Sanchez, L. (2015). Students as Photo Activists: Using Cameras in the Classroom for Social Change. *Theory Into Practise*, DOI: 10.1080/00405841.2015.1010838.

Secondulfo, D. (1993). Un'immagine vale più di mille parole? Alcune notazioni in margine all'uso sociologico della fotografia. In Cipolla, C., Faccioli, P. (Eds.), *Introduzione alla sociologia visuale* (pp. 159–172). Milano: Franco Angelli.

Scârneci-Domnişoru, F. (2016). *Datele vizuale în cercetarea socială*. Cluj-Napoca: Presa Universitară Clujeană.

Scârneci-Domnişoru, F., Csesznek, C. (2017). Ethnographic Reflections of Return Migration in a Romanian Rural Community. *DVE domovini - TWO homelands*, 46, 89–102.

Schifirneţ, C. (2016). *Modernitatea tendenţială. Reflecţii despre evoluţia modernă a societăţii*. Bucureşti: Tritonic.

Stahl, H.H. (1981). *Amintiri şi gânduri din vechea şcoală a monografiilor sociologice*. Bucureşti: Editura Minerva.

Şandru, C. (2009). *Studii şi confesiuni despre Drăguşul contemporan*. Cluj-Napoca: Editura Presa Universitară Clujeană.

Şandru, C. (2005). Reţele sociale şi forme asociative comunitare ca bază a dezvoltării durabile. *Sociologie Românească*, 4, 160–172.

Şandru, C., Scârneci, F. (2014). *Italia-Romania. L'esperienza della migrazione completa*. Calimera: Edizioni Kurumuny.

Şandru, C., Oprica, R., Pop, V. (2005). *Drăguş. Imaginile unui sat românesc*. Braşov: Editura C2 Design.

Valli, B. (1993). Dalla fotografia come indice alla sua utilizzazione nella ricerca sociologica. In Cipolla, C., Faccioli, P. (Eds.), *Introduzione alla sociologia visuale* (pp. 141–157). Milano: Franco Angelli.

Vlăsceanu, L. (1993). Schimbare socială. In Zamfir, C., Vlăsceanu, L. (Eds.), *Dicţionar de Sociologie* (pp. 529–533). Bucureşti: Editura Babel.

Wang, C., Burris, M.A. (1997). Photovoice: Concept, Methodology, and the Use for Participatory Needs Assessment. *Health Education and Behaviour*, 24(3), 369–387. Retrieved from http://heb.sagepub.com/content/24/3/369

Webography

http://www.cooperativag.ro/?s=dragus Accessed: 15.01.2018

https://www.facebook.com/search/events/?q=primaria%20dragus Accessed: 16.01.2018

http://primariadragus.ro/prezentare_locala Accessed: 16.01.2018

http://www.comunadragus.ro/ Accessed: 16.01.2018

http://economie.hotnews.ro Accessed: 16.01.2018

http://www.dreptonline.ro/legislatie/legea_102_2014_cimitirele_crematoriile_umane_serviciile_funerare.php. Accessed: 31.01.2018.

Marinela-Cristina Şimon

III Are the volunteers different from non-volunteers? A comparative analysis based on visual data (drawings)

Abstract: This chapter aims to show how volunteers and non-volunteers are perceived by others using a comparative analysis based on visual data (drawings). It also aims to show the relevance of drawing as a visual method of collecting data in social research, in general, and in volunteering research, in particular. First, the chapter presents the theoretical models found in the literature review on the differences between volunteers and non-volunteers, and then presents the characteristics of volunteers and non-volunteers as perceived by participants. Through a visual research methodology, the study confirms that there are differences between volunteers and non-volunteers, especially in terms of their personality, but also that there is a link between personality and the willingness to volunteer. Also, the chapter emphasises that drawings are highlighted not only by the richness of the data obtained, but also by the fact that they are extremely valuable and can support the results obtained through other types of data, being them quantitative or qualitative.

Keywords: volunteers, non-volunteers, visual data, drawings

1 Introduction

Volunteering has always been a topic of wide interest not only among researchers and practitioners, but also politics makers because, along the time, it has proven its multiple benefits which can be brought both to the person who gets involved in the unpaid activities and to the organisation, community and, in a larger sense, to the society.

Generically, the volunteer can be seen as that person who, out of his/her own initiative, pays services to the benefit of other persons without expecting any paid rewards in return. However, it is well known that not all people display such a desire to offer time and energy to the others, which enables us to believe that volunteers are, in a certain way, different from the others.

Exploring those qualities specific to volunteers, in general, and to volunteers active in the social area, in particular, represents for me an important research topic, which is reflected in my entire academic activity, both in the didactic field (by means of the courses) and in the scientific research field (by means of my Ph.D. thesis, a book and numerous articles published and/or defended on the occasion of some national or international conferences). How volunteers think that they are perceived by the others, what their own perception is about themselves and what the characteristics of volunteering in the social field are represent some of the questions which found their answers in the studies I have undertaken until now (Şimon, 2017; Şimon, 2013; Şimon, 2010).

In the present chapter, I intend to present the theoretical and methodological approach and the results obtained in my last study on the topic of volunteering, in which I aimed at exploring the characteristics specific to volunteers and non-volunteers, using, this time, a visual method for collecting the data, a method novel to me as a researcher, i.e. drawing. Thus, I tried to catch the representations of the people over volunteers and non-volunteers, the subjects under focus being asked to sketch the two categories by drawing.

2 Theoretical framework

The interest of the researchers in the study of the differences between volunteers and non-volunteers in different contexts arises just before the 1950s. The oldest study on this topic is linked to the name of Norman (*apud* Kerschner, 1975), who acknowledged the fact that the volunteer respondents of a questionnaire sent by mail proved to be more interested in the topic under investigation, more intelligent, better educated and, more likely, members of medium-income groups than the ones who did not respond (non-volunteers).

The numerous studies which followed on this topic confirmed the conclusions reached by Norman and proved the fact that there are notable differences between volunteers and non-volunteers from different points of view. Thus, volunteers tend to be better educated (Wallin, 1949); are more open to accept discouragement, anxieties and deficiencies (Rosen, 1951); have a high self-esteem (Efran and Boylin, 1967); prove self-acceptance (Sheridan and Shack *apud* Kerschner, 1975); display a lower level of anxiety (Scheler *apud* Kerschner, 1975); and a much higher tendency towards self-accomplishment than non-volunteers.

A particular place in literature review is occupied by the research which examines the relationship between personality and volunteering. There is evidence which supports the existence of some personality traits which characterise the persons who offer volunteer help. Omoto and Snyder (1995), for example, believe that certain personality traits predispose some people to get themselves involved in helping relationships and that attributes such as empathy, care and social responsibility characterise a person willing to help. The research which used the Sixteen Personality Factor Questionnaire (Cattel and Mead, 2008) indicated that volunteers are characterised by confidence and acceptance (Spitz and

MacKinnon, 1993), which reflect the features of an agreeable personality. The results derived from other studies (Carlo et al., 2005; Elshaug and Metzer, 2001) suggest positive associations between volunteering and extraversion, conscientiousness, acceptability and openness (Powers, 2008).

Elshaug and Metzer (2001), for example, starting from the Five-Factors Model of Personality developed by Costa and McCrae (1992), tested the hypothesis according to which there can be a constellation of traits specific to the personality of volunteers comprising: extraversion, agreeableness and openness to experience. In their approach, they applied a standardised instrument (NEO-PI-R) to measure the theoretical model on a sample of 106 subjects, volunteers and non-volunteers, and reached the conclusion that there are significant differences between volunteers and non-volunteers regarding agreeableness and extraversion. Similarly, Carlo et al. (2005), starting from the same theoretical model, applied the Big Five Inventory, a scale of 5 dimensions and 44 indicators, on a sample of 796 subjects (high school pupils), to test if volunteering is influenced by personality traits and by motivation. The results showed that each of the personality traits (extraversion, openness to experience, agreeableness and conscientiousness) was positively associated to volunteering, except for neuroticism. Agreeableness was the closest related to volunteering, followed by extraversion, conscientiousness and openness.

After considering several theoretical models regarding human personality developed along the time, I chose to present and to use for analysing and interpreting the data in the present study, the Five-Factors Model of Personality, belonging to Costa and McCrae (1992), because it is considered the most comprehensive framework of understanding human personality, also encompassing aspects which were not measured by other models. Moreover, this model has been translated into several languages and applied in tens of cultures resulting into a model which not only confirms its validity as a theory of personality, but it also establishes its validity at an international level.

According to this theory, the five personality factors are: neuroticism or the emotional instability versus emotional stability, extraversion versus introversion, openness to experience, agreeableness and conscientiousness.

Neuroticism (or low emotional stability) refers to the degree to which an individual is uncertain, anxious, depressed or emotional versus being calm and self-confident (Salgado, 1997). Persons with a high level of emotional instability provide a weak response to the stress in the environment, perceive normal situations as being threatening and can experiment with minor frustrations as being overwhelming, hopeless (Widiger and Oltmanns, 2017). In the article in which McCrae and Costa (1987) want to validate the theoretical model developed, they mention that "persons with a high level of emotional instability can use inadequate coping responses more frequently, such as hostile reactions, because they have to face disturbing feelings more often. Neuroticism seems to include not only negative feelings, but also disturbing thoughts and types of behaviour which accompany emotional suffering" (p. 87).

Extraversion, the second personality factor, refers to the degree to which individuals are assertive and sociable, as compared to the antisocial, shy and quiet ones (Salgado, 1997). The extroverts are predisposed to experiment with positive feelings (Judge, Heller and Mount, 2002). Extraversion means positivism, vigour, intimateness and courageousness (Jabari, Boroujerdi, Ghaeini, Naghshbandi and Karimi, 2013).

Openness to experience defines individuals who are creative, curious and educated as opposed to those who have limited interests (Salgado, 1997). The ones with openness to experience are also characterised by appreciating variety and by the desire to try diverse activities (Elshaug and Metzer, 2001). Openness to experience maintains curiosity, love of art, artistry flexibility and wisdom (Jabari et al., 2013). McCrae and Costa (1987) consider that this trait is best characterised by original, imaginative, wide and daring interests. Nevertheless, persons open to experience tend to be perceived by themselves, as well as by the others, as, somehow, more intelligent.

Agreeableness refers to the degree to which individuals are cooperative, warm and tolerant as compared to the cold, disagreeable and hostile ones (Salgado, 1997). Agreeableness is compassion, mercy, sympathy, generosity, philanthropy and trust (Jabari et al., 2013). McCrae and Costa (1987) consider that, from a cognitive point of view, the persons who are not agreeable are distrustful and sceptical, from an emotional point of view, are anguished and lack sympathy, and behaviourally, are non-cooperative, stubborn and impolite.

Conscientiousness measures the degree to which individuals are hardworking, organised, reliable and perseverant as compared to the lazy, disorganised and incorrect ones, and the ones with more limited interests (Salgado, 1997). Conscientiousness includes the characteristics of order, efficiency, self-organisation, progress orientation, logic and calm (Jabari et al., 2013). The conscientious is that person governed by conscientiousness, being attentive and minute. The conscientious is, also, the hardworking, ambitious, energetic and perseverant individual, according to McCrae and Costa (1987).

In order to supplement the results of my previous studies on the topic of volunteering in the social field, as well as to expand the type of data used until now by me or by the other researchers interested in this topic, I aimed at discovering by means of drawing, as a visual method of research, if people consider that there are notable differences between volunteers and non-volunteers, from the point of view of their personalities and not only.

3 Methodological aspects

While the research methods based on language – both written and oral – dominated the research spectrum on communication for a long time, a new set of non-textual strategies has been developing progressively, as an alternative and very versatile means of exploration. More precisely, "participatory visual communications, such as drawing, photography, and video, hold the inherent potential of painting a more nuanced depiction of lived realities, while simultaneously empowering the research participants" (Literat, 2013, p. 85).

Historically, researchers who have used visual methodologies have been anthropologists, engaged in ethnographic studies, or individuals working in media studies (Emmison and Smith *apud* Woodhouse, 2012). Beyond the fields of anthropology and sociology, the visual research methods – and, especially, drawing – have been used extensively also in psychology and psychotherapy (Reavey *apud* Literat, 2013).

Technically speaking, **drawing**, as different from photography or video, is listed in the category of primary visual data and of non-mechanical, non-digital instruments.

Participative drawing, as a visual research method, certifies "the non-textual means of exploration" by activating "the interpretative dimensions" of the images (Singhal and Rattine-Flaherty *apud* Literat, 2013). Drawings have the power to communicate complex messages in simple, but rich manners. They are considered long-term artefacts which can be used to express the messages of the participants. Compared to other methods of collecting visual data, drawing distinguishes itself by simplicity, concreteness and tangibility ("while watching a drawing you can touch it"). Drawings "talk". All you need is "a piece of paper and a pencil" (Theron et al., 2011, p. 2). Moreover, when using this method there is no restriction regarding the characteristics or the profile of the participants, drawing being allowed to be used for studies with subject "belonging to all socio-demographic categories" (Scârneci, 2016, p. 46).

"According to Freire's pedagogy, the drawing technique discourages the feeling of a hierarchy between the researcher and the subject" compared to textual strategies (*apud* Literat, 2013, p. 88). Another advantage of this method is that, as different from interviews or group discussion sessions, where an instantaneous answer is expected, the participants are given time to reflect upon their answers, active conceptualisation and contemplation being encouraged (Gauntlett *apud* Literat, 2013).

However, mention should be made that, if in the case of drawings simplicity is involved when collecting the data, there is always complexity when the interpretative process follows. Using drawing as a research method presupposes more than engaging the participants in designing the drawings and then having these artefacts analysed by the researcher. The word *drawing* is both a noun and a verb; it is both a product and a process. The symbolic interactionist Dewey (*apud* Guillemin 2004, p. 51) highlighted this "linguistic accident": It is no linguistic accident that "building", "construction" and "work" designate both a process and its finished product. Without the meaning of the verb that of the noun remains blank.

When drawing is used as a method of collecting data, it is likely that the researcher will involve the participants "in activities using varied forms of a 'draw-and-write' or 'draw-and-talk' technique that have facilitated the rich exploration of children's and adults' reflections, perceptions, and views on multiple topics and phenomena" (Mitchell et al., 2011, p. 19). As such, drawing as a research tool is often complemented by verbal research methods that encourage collaborative meaning-making that allows the drawer to give voice to what the drawing was intended to convey (Guillemin, 2004).

In my research, I used drawing as a means of collecting data out of my desire to complement and validate, first of all, the results of my previous studies on the topic of volunteering, in which I had used other types of qualitative data (the semi-structured interview) and quantitative data (the questionnaire). Second of all, I wanted to use the visual method of drawing because I could not identify in the literature review that I read any other studies on the topic of volunteering to have used drawing as a method of collecting data. Thus, to enrich the already existing results on this topic, I planned to rely on a method meant to capture and to render in a unique manner the way in which people perceive the ones who get involved in volunteering activities, especially in the social field.

For collecting the data, I offered the subjects some paper (A4 sheets containing two quadrants) and diverse writing tools, so that they could choose from coloured pencils, ball pens or simple pencils. In order not to induce the idea regarding the existence of differences between volunteers and non-volunteers, the participants in the study were asked beforehand if, from their point of view, they considered that the persons who do volunteering are different form the ones who do not get themselves involved in volunteering activities. Thus, all subjects who answered affirmatively to this question were asked to sketch by means of drawing, in the first quadrant, a person who does volunteering in the social field, and in the second, a person who does not do any volunteering, so that they could catch the specific characteristics of each of them. To avoid possible rejections of the subjects to participate in the study, which could have been caused by being asked to make a drawing, it was useful to mention to them that the aesthetic aspect was of no importance, and that it was not their creativity or artistic sense that were under evaluation, but the content of the drawing.

After the subjects finished their drawings, they were asked to describe and to interpret what they had drawn. Consequently, each drawing was accompanied by a text meant to explain as detailed as possible what the participants had drawn and wanted to convey through their drawings. Thus, I made sure that I would not be the one to associate meaning to the drawings afterwards, an endeavour which could have proved wrong sometimes. One of the subjects, for example, drew a Christmas tree and some presents underneath it to represent the volunteer (Fig. 1). This could have been interpreted in many ways, but what I personally considered was the willingness of the volunteer to make gifts. However, in reality, the significance was completely different and the description made by the subject to the drawing confirms and clarifies this thing: just like the Christmas tree, the volunteers prove "strength, verticality, energy, physical and mental force to fight different health, social or age-related issues" (of the people).

To select the subjects investigated, I relied on the **theoretical sampling** used, in general, for collecting generated visual documents when "the selection criteria are permanently provisional" – until the theoretical saturation is attained – depending on data processing, analysis and interpretation (Scârneci, 2016, p. 84). A first selection criterion was that related to previous experience as a volunteer, trying to include in my sample both persons who had been volunteers and persons who had not been. A second criterion was the age of the respondents. I wanted to investigate both youngsters, adults and persons of age. Subsequently, the sample was made of 25 subjects, females and males, of different ages and educational backgrounds, who did not necessarily have to have experienced volunteering before (Tab. 1).

The fact that my sample was not made up of volunteers exclusively and that it included subjects of different ages and educational backgrounds allowed me to reach the next level of my research on volunteering in the social field, because all my previous papers had focused either on students or only on volunteers in the social field.

The image processing and analysis operations referred to the content of the images and to the interpretations rendered by the subjects to them, using the drawing-writing technique.

For classifying the data collected, I relied on **emergent categories**, discovered while coding the visual data. For coding the material, I used the NVivo 10 soft, specially created for analysing qualitative data. On the collected data, I applied

Fig. 1: The symbolic representation of the volunteer in the social field (drawing made by a person of feminine gender, aged 66) (author's archive)

coding procedures (open, axial and selective coding). In the next section, I will present the findings of my study, as they resulted from processing and analysing the data.

4 Findings and discussions

4.1 Representations of volunteers and non-volunteers

The drawing method allowed the subjects investigated to choose the way in which to visually represent the volunteers, either by drawing people or, symbolically, by drawing different other things (an open door, a heart, a house, a tree, a sun, a pair of wings, a smile, a flower, etc.). Of all the symbols, as it can very well be seen in the picture below (Fig. 2), *the heart* is the only recurrent symbol, appearing in three different drawings, and in one of them the contour of the heart is made up, in its turn, of hearts, representing "the echo of kindness, smaller or bigger feelings breaking through".

Tab. 1: The matrix of the sample

Subjects	Gender	Studies	Age	Volunteered
1	feminine	faculty	31–50	No
2	masculine	faculty	31–50	Yes
3	feminine	faculty	18–30	Yes
4	feminine	faculty	18–30	No
5	feminine	faculty	18–30	No
6	masculine	high school	31–50	No
7	feminine	faculty	18–30	Yes
8	feminine	faculty	31–50	No
9	feminine	faculty	18–30	Yes
10	feminine	faculty	18–30	Yes
11	feminine	faculty	18–30	No
12	feminine	high school	31–50	No
13	feminine	faculty	31–50	No
14	feminine	faculty	18–30	Yes
15	feminine	faculty	31–50	No
16	feminine	faculty	18–30	No
17	masculine	high school	18–30	No
18	masculine	faculty	18–30	No
19	masculine	faculty	31–50	No
20	masculine	high school	over 51	No
21	feminine	faculty	31–50	No
22	feminine	high school	over 51	No
23	feminine	high school	over 51	No
24	feminine	vocational	over 51	No
25	feminine	gymnasium	over 51	No

On the other hand, the non-volunteer is represented by means of an empty cup "which has nothing to offer", a closed door, a bench from which we can passively watch "the problems of the ones around us", a tree with a few branches and roots "strictly necessary to stay alive", a cloud pouring raindrops and an apple.

An interesting aspect identified when analysing the drawings was the fact that, while the subjects under 30 years represented the volunteer and the non-volunteer by drawing people, (Fig. 3), the ones **over 30 years** preferred to rely on **symbols**, with the exception of two out of 15 subjects questioned, who included people in their drawings. In their case, the explanation can reside in the fact that they had graduated from a pedagogical high school, an institution which

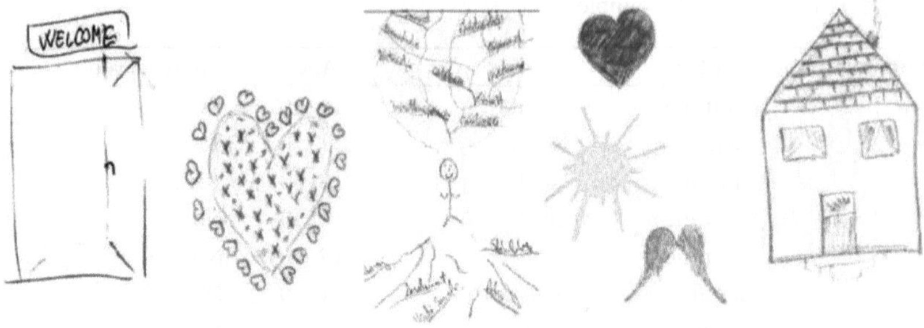

Fig. 2: Clippings of drawings (symbolic representations of the volunteer in the social field) (author's archive)

Fig. 3: Representations of volunteers drawn by subjects under 30 years. Drawings sketched by a 21-year-old man, a 23-year-old man and 29-year-old woman *(from left to right)* (author's archive)

evaluates, upon admission, the artistic skills and which favours along the study years the development of the aesthetic sense.

Also, from the point of view of the composition, the subjects under 30 years drew much more complex representations, which contain many details. For example, in all the drawings picturing volunteers there are either some other persons present (in 7 out of 9 drawings) or other elements meant to render a more complete image of the context in which the volunteer can develop his/her activity (e.g. sun, ball, tables, trees, buildings, hearts, books, flowers, presents). The same thing can be observed in the case of the drawings picturing non-volunteers. Even if the drawings are not filled with details, they contain elements (computer, closed heart, house, clouds, alcohol bottle) which manage to tell a story about the ones under representation.

Regardless of the way in which the subjects chose to render their drawings (in pencil, ball pen or in coloured pencils) and to represent the volunteer and the non-volunteer (by means of people or symbols), mention should be made that the majority considered that there are differences between volunteers and non-volunteers. As a matter of fact, with the exception of one subject, all the others captured these differences in their drawings. The suspicion that there might be some other subjects who may consider that there are no differences between volunteers and non-volunteers determined me to check this aspect in all the subjects belonging to the sample. However, this suspicion did not confirm until the end of the collecting data stage, the fact which allowed me to conclude that we were talking about an isolated case.

In the following, I will present, one at a time, the main differences between volunteers and non-volunteers, as they were depicted by the subjects investigated.

Generically speaking, the volunteers in the social field were positively evaluated by all 24 persons in the sample, of the fact that they had done any previous volunteering activities or not.

4.2 Psychological differences between volunteers and non-volunteers

From an emotional point of view, the volunteer in the social field experiments with positive feelings, being a "sensitive", "cheerful" person, "in a good mood" and with a smile on his/her face, the drawings capturing these aspects very well by the way the subjects drew the mouth of the volunteers (Fig. 4). Starting from Judge, Heller and Mount's opinion (2002), according to which the extroverts are more predisposed to experiment with positive feelings, it can be derived the fact that the volunteers in the social field are **extrovert persons**, meaning "assertive and sociable" (Salgado, 1997).

In the present study, the extraversion of the volunteers in the social field is also emphasised by the explanations the subjects rendered to their drawings. From their point of view, volunteers are "active persons", "open", "surrounded by many friends", "by people and crowded places" and "sociable, cheerful, who spend their time with their groups of friends".

This fact comes as a confirmation of the results of the studies which showed that volunteers, in general, seem to be friendlier in a higher degree than

Fig. 4: Clippings of drawings – Portraits of volunteers/non-volunteers (author's archive)

non-volunteers, enjoy the connections established with the others and experiment with lots of positive feelings (Elshaug and Metzer, 2001).

Non-volunteers, on the other hand, are, from an emotional point of view, sad persons or "not necessarily cheerful". To emphasise this, the subjects chose to represent their mouth in their drawings either through a straight line or through a curved one, but pointing downwards (Fig. 4). Contrary to the extrovert, the non-volunteer is described as being rather "a monotonous person", "having no one to talk to", "alone" and "apathetic". Loneliness, as a matter of fact, is the most mentioned characteristic of the non-volunteer.

From the analysed data, it can be derived that the most common trait of volunteers in the social field is **the desire to help**. Fifteen of the subjects under study mentioned this, considering that volunteers are characterised by: kindness and "the desire to support and to help". The ones who activate as volunteers in the social field are persons "available anytime", "kind", "big-hearted", "willing to help", "willing to offer help and support" and who "can always offer something". This availability to offer is also rendered graphically by the way the hands of the volunteers are drawn: pointing upwards, indicating an open attitude, holding hands with other persons, arms wide open or away from the body, with their palms in plain view (Fig. 5). The desire to help of the volunteer is also underlined by the frequent mention of the verb "to offer". Almost half of the respondents (10) use this verb, when they characterise the volunteer. These data confirm the results of a study made by me on the students in the Social Assistance programme, according to which "people's empathy and willingness to help others are the most important elements that characterize the volunteer from social field" (Şimon, 2010).

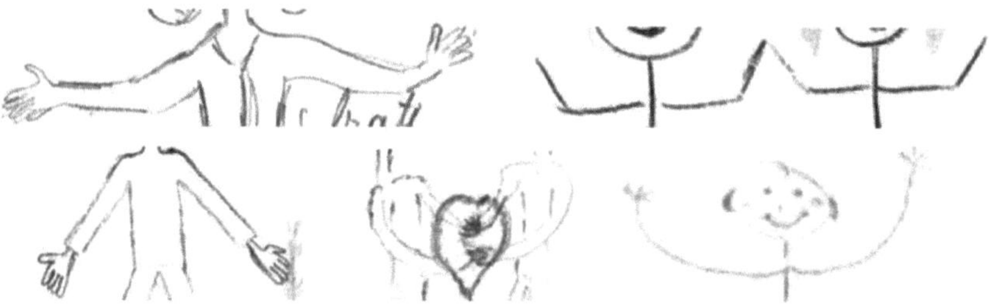

Fig. 5: Clippings of drawings – The availability of volunteers to help (author's archive)

In the literature review, this desire to help represents an indicator of *agreeableness* (*agreeable character*), which, in its turn, is a trait of the altruistic personality. Agreeableness, as mentioned at the beginning of the chapter, encompasses sympathy, generosity, compassion and philanthropy (Jabari et al., 2013).

From the point of view of agreeableness, the visual data collected within the framework of the present study confirm the results of other studies (Elshaug and Metzer, 2001; Musick and Wilson, 2008) which show that volunteers, as different from non-volunteers, are more interested in the well-being of the ones around them and display sympathy and empathy for the ones in need.

As opposed to the volunteer, the non-volunteer is considered to be a person "less open to empathy and help", "selfish", "indifferent", "mean", "acting to his/her own interest", "passive to the problems of the ones around", who "does not want to help", "cannot offer" and who "is not so much interested in contributing to the well-being of the ones in need".

The lack of involvement and passiveness (non-agreeableness) are very clearly depicted by means of the visual data, regardless of the choice the subjects made when expressing themselves either through people or though symbols for drawing non-volunteers (Fig. 6). In the case of the drawings with people, the non-agreeableness is suggested by the position of the hands of the non-volunteers, these being drawn pointing downwards or crossed. Regarding this, Pease (1992) reminds that crossing the arms represents, almost everywhere, a defensive or negative attitude. In the case of the drawings containing symbols, this characteristic is expressed either by "an empty heart", a closed door, a clock indicating the lack of time or by "hands and legs with which (the non-volunteer) does not know what to do".

If we were to analyse the reasons why people do not get themselves involved in volunteering activities, from the data collected we could identify two categories of non-volunteers: the ones who do not want to get involved and the ones who want,

Fig. 6: Clippings of drawings – Representation of non-volunteers (author's archive)

but cannot. The majority of them belong to the first category and are the ones who prefer to do other types of activities (at work, in bars, in front of the TV, in the virtual medium), while the second category is filled with persons who either do not have time (2) or do not know how to help (4), because they "are not trained enough to cater for the needs of the people" or "do not know" where they could bring their contribution. "The organisations do not come to say that they need volunteers".

Another important trait of the volunteers, as depicted from the visual data collected, is **openness to experience**, characterised by Elshaug and Metzer (2001) as the desire to look for diverse activities and appreciation of variety. Consequently, the volunteer is a person "active in different domains and who wants this", who "looks for something new all the time", "always willing to know" and who "is not frustrated by, but happy about his/her daily experiences".

Although mentioned by only three subjects, *the lack of openness to experience* appears as one of the traits of non-volunteers. These "do not desire to explore and to escape, to experiment", "do not want to get out of their comfort zone" and "are satisfied with the minimum required".

Even though it cannot be named a main trait of personality, because it was mentioned by only few subjects, ***conscientiousness*** seems to also characterise the volunteers in the social field. According to the data, they are persons full of "energy", "hard-working" and "diligent". Conscientiousness, as a trait of volunteers, was also tackled by the students who participated in the study from 2010. According to their opinion, "the volunteer in the social field 'must' be a person with a sense of responsibility" (…) (Şimon, 2010).

Socio-demographic differences between volunteers and non-volunteers

From a socio-demographic point of view, according to the visual data collected, no conclusion can be drawn regarding any potential difference between volunteers and non-volunteers based on **age or gender**. Actually, the subjects made no reference whatsoever to this aspect, for either of the two categories. This fact highlights that anyone, regardless of age or gender, can get involved in volunteering activities in the social field, even if the studies which collect socio-demographic data of volunteers prove that, in reality, just certain age categories and persons of a certain gender get themselves more involved in volunteering activities. In Romania, for example, the volunteers are rather young people, persons over 65 years of age being rarely involved in formal volunteering, institutionally organised (McCloughan et al., 2011, p. 16). Even the persons over 60 years, from Braşov county, Romania, participants in 2014 in a study funded by Braşov County Council on the topic of volunteering, think that volunteering is an activity that is specific to young age: *it's for young people; a work young people do; volunteering is a good thing nowadays especially for young people because it teaches them to be more responsible; volunteering means the help young people offer to elders* (Scârneci-Domnişoru and Şimon, 2019)

However, when it comes to **social status**, things are not the same. Even though there were not many participants in the present study who referred to such differences, the ones who did it said that only the persons who have "an affordable standard of living" can do volunteering, "if you work by the day, you cannot".

Another difference between volunteers and non-volunteers, which can be depicted from the references made by the ones who drew (used drawing), consists of the quantity of free time that each of the two categories has, the volunteer being the one who enjoys this resource to a higher degree. Actually, the lack of time is mentioned by only one respondent, the majority of them considering that the problem would not reside in the lack of time, but rather in **the way in which time is used**. The non-volunteer "has other interests, mostly related to the virtual medium", preferring to spend his/her time "sitting on a couch or on a bench in the park".

Fig. 7: Educational differences between volunteers and non-volunteers. *Drawings made by a 22-year-old woman (to the left) and a 21-year-old woman (to the right)* (author's archive)

Moreover, according to the vision of the same subjects, volunteers, as different from non-volunteers, are "much better documented, educated" persons, because, "to do volunteering a person must have graduated from an educational institution". The volunteer "has more knowledge in the field" and "can meet the needs of the people". Visually, the subjects captured this difference by drawing some books or several books in the image depicting the volunteer than in the one picturing the non-volunteer (Fig. 7).

Volunteers are also characterised by the subjects under analysis as being persons full of "courage", "physical and psychological strength" and who "do not emphasise the financial aspect".

4.3 Costs and benefits of the volunteering

Besides the idea that volunteers have an altruistic personality, the visual data also revealed other elements meant to complete the portrait describing volunteering in the social field and the volunteers who activate in this domain, and one of these elements refers to the benefits of volunteering. It is known the fact that the volunteering activity can offer a wide range of benefits, both on short and medium term, and on long term (Wilson and Musick, 2000). The authors of numerous studies on this topic (Clark and Wilson, 1961; Olson *apud* Chinmann and Wandersman, 1999; Omoto and Snyder *apud* Chinmann and Wandersman, 1999) have tried to catalogue and to sort into different categories the costs and benefits involved in the volunteering activity, generating, thus, models containing one factor (one single category encompassing several items) or models which contain even 5–6 factors (categories) (Tab. 2).

In the table above, it can be seen that the benefits differ according to the field the volunteers activate in or to the type of organisation. Considering the fact that I focused on the volunteers in the social field, it was difficult for me to use, in the present study, any of the pre-existing models so, consequently, I designed a model of my own.

In my previous studies I also designed specific typologies, derived from the data analysed. For example, in the study focused on the students enrolled in the Social Assistance programme – entitled *What do the students think about*

Tab. 2: The empirical evaluation of the benefits of volunteering (Chinman and Wandersman, 1999, p. 52)

Authors of the study	Name of the factors	Examples of items	Type of organisation
Butterfoss (1993)	One factor which comprises all items	1. Learning new skills 2. Support from the other members of the group 3. Satisfaction of being involved in an important project	Organisation fighting against alcohol or other drug consumption
Friedmann, Wandersman and Meier (1988)	1. Personal benefits 2. Helping the others	1. Improving status or prestige 2. Increasing the sense of responsibility	Tenants association
Knoke (1988)	1. Normative 2. Social 3. Occupational 4. Lobby 5. Informational 6. Material	1. Boosting the prestige of the organisation 2. Offering some social activities 3. Help to find a job 4. Influencing legislation 5. Publishing some articles 6. Offering some insurance policies	Women associations and clubs for spending free time
Snyder and Omoto (1993)	1. Values 2. Understanding 3. Community care 4. Personal development 5. Self-esteem	1. The moral obligation to help the others 2. Learn how people cope with difficult situations 3. Community care 4. Personal challenge 5. To feel oneself better	Associations fighting HIV/AIDS

volunteers and volunteering? – I built a model which contained two categories of benefits: those which **regard the beneficiaries** ("helping the under-privileged persons", "activity run for the sake of the community", "to help those who need it") and those which **regard the volunteers** ("aiming to gain new knowledge, developing abilities already gained or build up through experience", "aiming to offer personal satisfaction") (Şimon, 2010, p. 105).

Considering the data collected as a result of the interview method, in another study of mine focused exclusively on the volunteers in the social field, I designed a model with three categories: **personal benefits** (e.g. acquiring information, knowledge and experience in the social field); **social benefits** (e.g. "you make new friends", "you get acquainted with new people, you make new relationships, you are in other environments") and **psychological benefits** ("more self-trust and credit to your own strengths", "you get more spiritual satisfaction") (Şimon, 2017, p. 110).

As different from the classification of benefits used in my previous studies, I considered more appropriate that for the present paper I should rely on a more complex one, derived from the analysis of the data collected. Subsequently, instead of two (benefits for the beneficiaries of the volunteering activity and benefits for the volunteers) or three categories (personal, social and psychological benefits), this time I grouped the benefits into five categories (personal development, social benefits, professional fulfilment, self-esteem and care for the community), being thus able to obtain a more complex image over the benefits of volunteering in social field.

A first category of benefits depicted by means of the visual data would be the one which addresses **personal development**. According to the opinion of the subjects investigated, the volunteers "can develop themselves through each activity they participate in", "they develop their communication skills" and "they learn how to face new situations". Even the respondents who mentioned that they were or still are volunteers admitted that through volunteering "we can develop ourselves" and "we can learn new skills". The data confirm the results obtained in other studies as well. Epure (2013), for example, concluded that the participants perceived a real upgrade of their skills and they agreed upon the fact that it was a useful experience that may boost their personal development.

The social benefits include, from the perspective of the participants in the study, all those aspects which refer to social interaction or socialising: "A volunteer benefits from... beautiful experiences", "(volunteers) spend a lot of time in groups of friends", "... (volunteering) favours the exchange of good practices" and "(the volunteer) makes new friends, acquaintances, becomes more sociable".

Through volunteering one can satisfy the need to belong and the need to have friends (Bussell and Forbes, 2003).

The fact that volunteering offers one the opportunity to socialise, regardless of the age one chooses to get involved at as a volunteer, was confirmed by the elder ones, as well: "I enjoy socializing very much, very, very much"; "we can get energized from one another, we talk, we share opinions about this and that, we get a little more involved, we talk"; "I'll do anything to get away from home and come here to socialize" (Scârneci-Domnişoru and Şimon, 2019).

Professional fulfilment or the prospective of a career can represent a benefit and, at the same time, a reason why people choose to do volunteering. In the present study, according to the opinion of the subjects investigated, "the persons who do volunteering enter the labour market, enter the field", "have much more knowledge about this (social) field", "are better documented, more knowledgeable", "it is an opportunity for them to learn in a practical way" and "they benefit from future collaborations". In general, the young (14–22 years old) are the ones interested in this benefit, because they do not have a job and volunteering "can offer them the opportunity to get hired or they can improve different skills which will help them in their future professional career" (Şimon, 2017, p. 135).

Still in the view of the elders, volunteers are, in the majority of the cases, young people who participate in certain activities because of **personal interest** (most of the time this interest is to acquire professional experience); "young people who get involved in these volunteering activities will gain the necessary experience and find a job faster"; "there are also many students who during university do volunteer work to gain experience in the field they are specializing in"; "it's a good start to be able to really get a good job" (Scârneci-Domnişoru and Şimon, 2019).

Another benefit is **self-esteem**, volunteering being considered a means or a strategy through which a person can end up feeling useful, wholesome and important (Okun, 1994). In this way, the results of numerous studies have demonstrated the fact that volunteers have a high self-esteem or that the self-esteem of the volunteers is higher than the one of the non-volunteers (Andam, Rajabi, Benar and Hosseini, 2013; Omoto, Snyder and Martino, 2000). The participants in the current study are also of the opinion that volunteering boosts self-esteem because the activities one gets involved in (as a volunteer) make one feel "spiritually satisfied". "A volunteer benefits from colour in his/her life and …from spiritual fulfilment".

The care for the community could be incorporated in the category named benefits of volunteering for the others, for the beneficiaries and for the ones

Fig. 8: Social interactions of the volunteers. Drawings made by a 23-year-old man, a 28-year-old woman and a 24-year-old woman (author's archive)

the volunteers dedicate their time and energy to. This care can take different shapes: "presents (that the volunteer) brought to the children", "meets the needs of the people", "offers moral support", "offers and teaches the other" and "is willing to help the persons around him/her".

Another element of novelty that the present study brings consists of the fact that the drawings enabled the subjects to also catch in an eloquent manner the benefits of volunteering on long term, such as **physical and mental health** (Wilson and Clack, 1961), a thing which was impossible to depict in my previous research by means of the data collected using the questionnaire or the interview guide as research instruments. Even if the subjects did not make overt reference to these benefits, by using words, the portraits of the volunteers managed to visually catch these benefits, the joy, the happiness and the smile on their faces being prone to be considered indicators of the physical and mental health.

Moreover, the idea of benefits of volunteering on long term is visually captured by the participants in the present study also through the fact that in the majority of the drawings the volunteer is surrounded by other people (Fig. 8). This thing allows us to consider that the volunteer, as opposed to the non-volunteer, is involved in social interactions to a higher degree, and the high number of social relationships has positive effects on his/her mental health, while social isolation triggers depression (Wilson and Musick, 2000).

From the category of costs, the only one mentioned is **time**, considered the most precious resource offered by the volunteer and, at the same time, the biggest impediment in the way of those who would like to get involved as volunteers but cannot due to lack of time.

Fig. 9: Beneficiaries of volunteering in the social field. Drawings made by a 67-year-old woman, a 29-year-old woman and a 21-year-old man (author's archive)

4.4 Categories of volunteering beneficiaries

From the visual data collected (Fig. 9), it can be derived the fact that the beneficiaries of the help provided by volunteers in the social field are, in general, "the ones with problems", "the disabled persons, the aged ones", "the ones in difficulty", "all those asking for help", "children" and "the ones finding themselves in a disadvantaged situation".

4.5 Types of help offered by volunteers

Another important element captured by the subjects of the study by means of drawings and which completes the image of volunteering in the social field refers to the ways in which the volunteer can help. Thus, the **help** offered by volunteers can be diverse, from a material one (presents, time) to an emotional one (brings a smile and happiness on the face of a person, can offer moral support, offers listening, empathy and love) or psycho-social (helps the person to develop). Nevertheless, the word *help* and its derivatives (to help, helps and helping) is one of the most frequently used words (10 times) by the subjects when they refer to volunteers.

5 Conclusions

Considering the aims that it started from, the present study completes the findings of my previous research which was more focused on identifying the type of motivation specific to volunteers in the social field and on the costs and benefits that the volunteering activity involves, but less on the characteristics of the volunteer. In the study presented in this chapter, I intended to examine the differences between the volunteers in the social field and non-volunteers, both from the perspective of volunteers and from the one of non-volunteers.

In general, the results show that there are considerable differences between volunteers and non-volunteers, especially from the point of view of their personality. The volunteers in the social field are, in turn, those persons *willing to offer help* to the disadvantaged persons, are more interested in the well-being of the persons around them and display sympathy and empathy for the ones in need. Volunteers, as different from non-volunteers, have a **prosocial personality**, in the way in which Pennel et al. (*apud* Powers, 2008)consider that this concept includes two dimensions: empathy oriented towards the others and helping others. These dimensions place volunteers among those through which Christian love is recovered in a post-secular context as charity (Sorea, 2015).

Moreover, there are *extrovert* persons who like being in the company of someone and who actively look for social stimulation. Volunteers manifest openness to experience, appreciating diversity and being characterised by the desire to look for and get involved in different activities. Not the least, volunteers in the social field are characterised by conscientiousness, being hardworking, diligent and energetic persons.

Thus, the outcomes of the present study confirm the fact that there is an interdependence between personality (McRae and Costa, 1987) and volunteering. Nonetheless, what is also confirmed is the fact that the most important personality factors of volunteers in the social field are the ones validated by Eishaug and Metzer (2001), namely: agreeableness and extraversion. However, the visual data reveal the fact that the volunteers in the social field are also characterised by openness to experience and conscientiousness, thus the findings of the study belonging to Carlo et al. (2005) being also confirmed. According to these results, each of the personality factors can be significantly positively associated to volunteering, with the exception of neuroticism.

In my study, the only factor from the theoretical model developed by McRae and Costa which could not be verified and validated is neuroticism. None of the subjects investigated made any direct reference to the emotional stability or instability of the volunteers, but from the interviews with the volunteers in the social field (Şimon, 2017) it could result that "none of the volunteers should lack patience and calm", characteristics which could prove the emotional stability rather than instability.

In the same study, from 2017, some other traits of the volunteers in the social field were identified, but back then I limited myself to simply listing them (e.g. communicativeness, perseverance, patience, the desire to help the others, courage and optimism). According to those results "the self of the volunteer is interdependent, his/her attributes being valued and used only in relation to the others" (Şimon, 2017, p. 111). In the present study, using the visual data enabled not only the simple enumeration of these traits, but also the more in-depth analysis of the psychological profile of the volunteer in the social field, through the lenses of a theoretical model.

If, from the point of view of the personality, it can be said that the volunteer in the social field has specific traits, from a demographic point of view there is no such profile. To be a volunteer in the social field you do not have to be a woman or a man, or to be of a certain age. Not even the place where you live seems to be of any importance. Something which is altogether valid for the non-volunteer, as well. However, differences between the two categories do appear, but from a social point of view. The volunteer needs to be in the possession of "some knowledge" and to have source of income, because "if he/she works on a daily basis he/she cannot think of volunteering".

The volunteer in the social field offers help to all the ones in need, to the ones who find themselves in a disadvantaged situation, being them elderly people, disabled persons or children. The help offered by volunteers, even though also a material one (presents for children), usually is an emotional, affective and psychological one (e.g. a smile, love, listening, empathy and moral support). The benefits of volunteering, in exchange, cover different layers, from the social- and community-related ones to the ones regarding self-esteem and personal and professional development.

The disclosure of the way in which the subjects perceive volunteers and non-volunteers make the present study not only complete and clarify the results obtained in my previous studies on the same topic, but also confirm the relevance of a theoretical model for studying volunteering.

Another element of novelty brought about by this study consists of the research methodology used. Unlike the methods and instruments implemented so far, both in my previous studies (the questionnaire and the semi-structured interview) and in the studies found in literature review (questionnaire, brainstorming, scale and interview), in the present research I chose to use, for the first time, one of the visual methods of collecting the data, i.e. the drawing.

Drawing got itself noticed, in the first place, through the richness of the material collected, offering to me information not only about the psychological and social characteristics of volunteers and non-volunteers, but also tangent data about categories of beneficiaries, types of help offered, costs and benefits of volunteering, reason for non-volunteers' involvement and activities preferred by non-volunteers. Suggestive in this way, can be the scheme below in which I caught the richness of the information offered by drawing regarding the characteristics of volunteering in the social field (Fig. 10).

In the second place, drawing as a research method stood out through its easy way of implementation once I managed to convince the subjects to participate. The ones over 30 were the most difficult to convince, the reason mentioned, with no exception, being related to the lack of talent for drawing, the lack of drawing skills. However, after they drew, it came very easy to them to talk about what they had drawn and about the significance of their drawings.

Also, I would add that the visual data are extremely valuable and can support the results obtained through other types of data, being them quantitative or qualitative.

The limitation of this study consists of the fact that it explores the perception of people concerning the characteristics of volunteers only in the social field. What would also be interesting to check is whether the traits of the volunteers

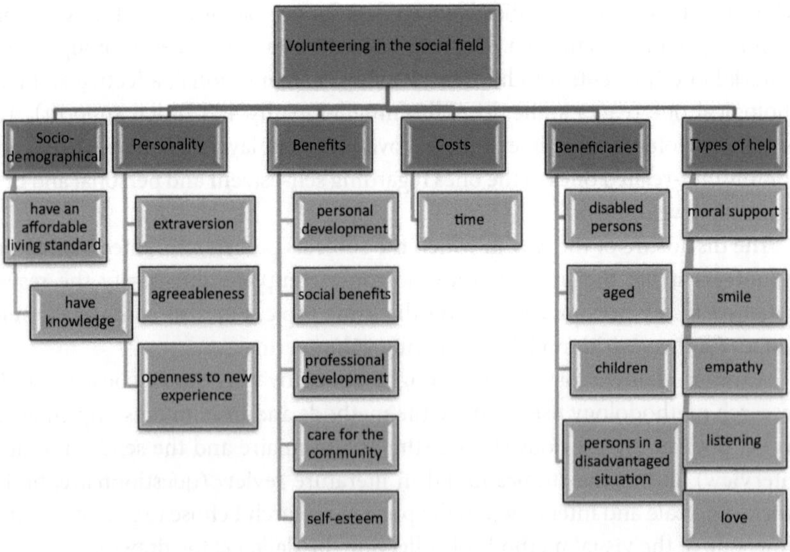

Fig. 10: The visual representation of the data concerning the characteristics of the volunteer in the social field (author's archive)

who activate in other fields (environment protection, education, health, sport, etc.) are the same or different.

But beyond these limitations, mention should be made that the results of the study, besides the theoretical and methodological implications mentioned above, also have practical implications which can be implemented not only by the ones who directly work with volunteers or want to work with them, but also by the ones who desire to increase the involvement of the Romanians in volunteering activities. Starting from the fact that a certain type of behaviour is initially determined by the perception an individual has over the situation or the context (Fazio, 1986), it can be said that the positive perception that we detected people have regarding volunteering and volunteers can be a factor favouring or triggering the decision to become a volunteer. Being known that there is a relation between perception – attitude – behaviour and the results of the present study, viable strategies of attracting volunteers can be built and campaigns promoting volunteering can be developed in order to determine people to adopt a proactive position and to take action (to enable the involvement in volunteering activities).

Bibliography

Andam, R., Rajabi, A. G., Benar, N., & Hosseini, S. S. (2013). The study of self esteem among volunteer and non volunteer in sport. *International Research Journal of Applied and Basic Sciences*, 4(2), 286–290.

Bussell, H., & Forbes, D. (2003). The volunteer life cycle: A marketing model for volunteering. *Voluntary Action*, 5(3), 61–79.

Carlo, G., Okun, M. A., Knight, G. P., & Guzman, M. R. T. (2005). The interplay of traits and motives on volunteering: Agreeableness, extraversion and prosocial value motivation. *Personality and Individual Differences*, 38, 1293–1305.

Cattell, E. P., & Mead, A. D. (2008). 16PF Fifth Edition Questionnaire. In G. J., Boyle, G., Matthews & D. H., Saklofske (Eds.), *The Sage Handbook of Personality Theory and Assessment* (pp. 135–159). Thousand Oaks: Sage Publications.

Chinman, J., & Wandersman, A. (1999). The benefits and costs of volunteering in Community Organizations. *Nonprofit and Voluntary Sector Quarterly*, 28(1), 46–64.

Clark, P. B., & Wilson, J. Q. (1961). Incentive system: A theory of organization. *Administrative Science Quarterly*, 6(2), 129–166.

Costa, P. T., & McCrae, R. R. (1992). Normal personality assessment in clinical practice: The NEO Personality Inventory. *Psychological Assessment*, 4(1), 5–13. doi: 10.1037/1040-3590.4.1.5

Efran, J. S., & Boylin, E. R. (1967). Social desirability and willingness to participate in a group discussion. *Psychological Reports*, 20(2), 402. doi: 10.2466/pr0.1967.20.2.402

Eishaug, C., & Metzer, J. (2001). Personality attributes of volunteers and paid workers engaged in similar occupational tasks. *Journal of Social Psychology*, 141(6), 752–763. doi: 10.1080/00224540109600586

Epure, M. (2013). Learning about volunteering – A path to personal development. *Review of Applied Socio-Economic Research*, 5(1), 61–68.

Fazio, R. H. (1986). How do attitude guide behavior. In R. M., Sorrentino & E. T., Higgins (Eds.), *Handbook of Motivation and Cognition: Foundations of Social Behavior* (pp. 204–243). New York: Guilford Press.

Guillemin, M. (2004). Understanding illness: Using drawings as a research method. *Qualitative Health Research*, 14(2), 272–289.

Jabari, N., Boroujerdi, S., Ghaeini, S., Naghshbandi, S., & Karimi, G. (2013). Big-five personality traits predict Sport Volunteer Satisfaction. *Middle-East Journal of Scientific Research*, 13(1), 49–54. doi: 10.5829/idosi.mejsr.2013.13.1.1168

Judge, T. A., Heller, D., & Mount, M. (2002). Five-factor model of personality and job satisfaction: A meta-analysis. *Journal of Applied Psychology*, 87(3), 530–541.

Kerschner, J. (1975). *A Comparison of Volunteers vs. Non-volunteers and the Effects of the Volunteer Experience on Self-Actualization and Social Intelligence*. Master's Theses, Paper 2704. Retrieved from http://ecommons.luc.edu/luc_theses/2704

Literat, I. (2013). A pencil for your thoughts: Participatory drawing as a visual research method with children and youth. *International Journal of Qualitative Methods*, 12, 84–98. doi: 10.1177/160940691301200143

McCrae, R. R., & Costa, P. T. (1987). Validation of the five-factor model of personality across instruments and observers. *Journal of Personality and Social Psychology*, 52(1), 81–90.

McCloughan, P., Batt, W. H., Costine, M., & Scully, D. (2011). *Participation in Volunteering and Unpaid Work*. Dublin: European Foundation for the Improvement of Living and Working Conditions. Retrieved from http://projekte.bagso.de/fileadmin/user_upload/redaktion/WeDO/Downloads/Participation_in_volunteering.pdf.

Mitchell, C., Theron, L., Stuart, J., Smith, A., & Campbell, Z. (2011). Drawings as research method. In L., Theron, C., Mitchell, A., Smith & J., Stuart. (Eds). *Picturing Research Drawing as Visual Methodology* (pp. 19–37). Rotterdam: Sense Publishers.

Musick, M., & Wilson, J. (2008). *Volunteers: A Social Profile*. Bloomington: Indiana University Press.

Okun, M. (1994). The relation between motives for organizational volunteering and frequency of volunteering by elders. *Journal of Applied Gerontology*, 13(2), 115–126. doi: 10.1177/073346489401300201

Omoto, A. M., & Snyder, M. (1995). Sustained helping without obligation: Motivation, longevity of service, and perceived attitude change among AIDS volunteers. *Journal of Personality and Social Psychology*, 68(4), 671–686.

Omoto, A. M., Snyder, M., & Martino, S. C. (2000). Volunteerism and the life course: Investigating age-related agendas for action. *Basic and Applied Social Psychology*, 22(3), 181–197. doi: 10.1207/S15324834BASP2203_6

Pease, A. (1992). *Limbajul trupului. Cum pot fi citite gândurile altora din gesturile lor*. Bucuresti: Editura Polimark.

Powers, K. W. (2008). *Who Do I Want to Help? An Examination of Characteristics Distinguishing Groups of Volunteers*. A Dissertation Submitted in Partial Fulfilment of the Requirements for the Degree of Doctor of Philosophy in the field of Clinical Psychology. Retrieved from https://search.proquest.com/openview/0e90e1e2a66dcab5c282575ba3812db9/1?pq-origsite=gscholar&cbl=18750&diss=y

Rosen, E. (1951). Differences between volunteers and non-volunteers for psychological studies. *Journal of Applied Psychology*, 35(3), 185–193. doi: 10.1037/h0061411

Salgado, J. F. (1997). The five factor model of personality and job performance in the European community. *Journal of Applied Psychology*, 82(1), 30–43. doi: 10.1037/0021-9010.82.1.30

Scârneci-Domnişoru, F. (2016). *Datele vizuale în cercetarea socială*. Cluj-Napoca: Presa Universitară Clujeană.

Scârneci-Domnişoru, F., & Şimon, M. C. (2019). Significances of Volunteer Work for the Senior Citizens of Braşov (Romania), *Social Work*, 17(1), 21–44. doi: 10.13165/SD-19-17-1-02

Sorea, D. (2015). Dreptate şi caritate. Cinci demersuri post-seculare valorizând iubirea aproapelui [Justice and charity. Five post-secular approaches that value neighbor's love]. In G. Răţulea (Ed.), *Justiţie şi coeziune socială* (pp. 207–226). Iaşi: Editura Institutul European.

Spitz, R. T., & MacKinnon, J. R. (1993). Predicting success in volunteer community service. *Psychological Reports*, 73, 815–818. doi: 10.2466/pr0.1993.73.3.815

Şimon, M. C. (2010). What do the students think about volunteers and volunteering? *Review of the Air Force Academy*, 2, 103–106.

Şimon, M. C. (2013). Theoretical aspects concerning the management of volunteers. *Bulletin of the Transilvania University of Brasov*, 6(55), 247–254.

Şimon, M. C. (2017). *Voluntariatul în domeniul social. Motivaţie şi management.* Iaşi: Institutul European.

Theron, L., Mitchell, C., Smith, A., & Stuart, J. (2011). *Picturing Research Drawing as Visual Methodology*. Rotterdam: Sense Publishers.

Wallin, P. (1949). Volunteer subjects as a source of sampling bias. *American Journal of Sociology*, 54(6), 539–544. doi: 10.1086/220418

Widiger, T. A., & Oltmanns, J. R. (2017). Neuroticism is a fundamental domain of personality with enormous public health implications. *World Psychiatry*, 16(2), 144–145. doi: 10.1002%2Fwps.20411

Wilson, J., & Musick, M. (2000). The effects of volunteering on the volunteer. *Law and Contemporary Problems*, 62(4), 141–168.

Woodhouse, J. (2012). The use of visual methodology in nursing. *Nurse Researcher*, 19(3), 20–25. doi: 10.7748/nr2012.04.19.3.20.c9055

Ada Ioana Dobrescu

IV A visual perspective on adolescent identity

Abstract: The chapter shows how identity is described from teenagers' view. This is done through the photographs and drawings made by them. The chapter answers the following questions: In what way is the adolescent period portrayed through images? How do adolescents describe and picture themselves in photographs and drawings? The chapter includes the description of adolescence as an age stage, the adolescent identity definition and other visual researches related to adolescent identity. It demonstrates that there are specific aspects that portray the teenage identity like relationship with friends, family, colleagues, teachers, partner, God, particular definitions and symbols of adolescence, school and professional achievements, hobbies and negative experiences. The chapter concludes that the tools used in this research – photographs and drawings – describe in detail the elements of teenage identity.

Keywords: identity, adolescence, drawings, photographs

1 Introduction

Nowadays, the topic of adolescence is a subject currently identified in socio-humanistic research because the challenging contemporary society, with all its multiple alternatives, generates a series of lifestyles specific to the young, different from the ones in the past. Excessive digitisation and the alternative means of communication among these age categories have changed their description, as a group.

The idea of this chapter arose when our colleague, Florentina Scârneci-Domnişoru, suggested that we should work together in a project visually displaying our topics of a sociological interest.

The identity of adolescents was the topic chosen by me, this one also being the subject of my Ph.D. thesis. In this chapter, I tried to describe the identity characteristics of the adolescents using visual techniques: drawing and photography. Afterwards, I drew a comparison with the findings in my Ph.D. thesis and the ones derived from my previous research on the same topic, making use of the classic instruments specific to sociology: the questionnaire (applied to 350 young respondents) and the semi-structured interview (which I had with approximately 50 adolescents).

As I mentioned before, in my Ph.D. thesis and in my previous research, I tried to configure, relying on quantitative investigations, followed by a qualitative study, a description of the adolescents' identity and of its sub-behaviours. I focused on the description of the beginning of adolescence (when the events that the young classify as being important at the beginning of this life stage occur), on designing an identity profile of the adolescents and on measuring some indicators such as social and personal identity, gender identity, ethnic identity and vocational identity. Moreover, I wanted to capture certain identity coordinates, such as self-esteem, the identity crisis during adolescence and the description of the lifestyle of an adolescent.

In this article, I tried to answer several general questions: *In what way is the adolescent period portrayed through images? How do the adolescents describe and picture themselves in photographs and drawings?*

2 Theoretical framework

Adolescence is a life stage which means a change, a transition stage from childhood to adulthood, during which many fundamental questions are asked regarding existence: *Who am I? What is my purpose in this world? Who do I look like? Who loves me? Who understands me? What are my interests? What do I like?* and so on.

Stanley Hall is the first person who initiated the scientific study of adolescence in the USA. He considers that adolescence is a period of storm and stress, of universal and inevitable change (*apud* Steinberg & Lerner, 2004).

Where the adolescents are concerned, during this period of life there are changes which occur both at a biological level and at a psychological and social one.

The stages of adolescence, identified by the literature review with an impact over identity are as follows:

- ✓ *The puberty stage (between 10 and 14 years old)* with the associated biological changes;
- ✓ *The stage of adolescence properly (between 14 and 18/20 years old)* dominated by the adaptation to the stage of adulthood, developing one's own identity and abstract thinking;
- ✓ *The stage of prolonged adolescence or early adulthood (between 18/20 and 24/25 years old)* – based on financial independence by starting work (today, more and more difficult to gain) and/or marital option by matrimonial engagement (Şchiopu, 2008).

Nowadays, the young extend their adolescence period, not turning to maturity until later, due to the extension of the period of time spent in school – faculty and master. Previously, during Communist times, this stage ended around the age of 18–20 years, after graduating from high school the young being offered working places, with no financial dependence on the parents.

The literature review presents identity under the form of one's well-defined conception regarding one's own person and the world, consisting of values, beliefs and aims which the individual dedicated himself/herself to (Harwood, 2010).

The construction of identity is continuous and complex and lasts all our life. The social roles that we play while we turn to maturity determine continuous changes of our identity. We engage in different tasks, especially during adolescence and adulthood, both at a personal and at a professional level, which will configure the different traits of our identity. Exploring new roles and opportunities, we interact with new persons, we gain new responsibilities and thus our identity is in a continuous change (Marcia *apud* Harwood, 2010).

Each individual has only one self, but several identities, these differentiations depending on the relational contexts, such as the family, the group of friends or the school. Adolescence is characterised by an increase in the number of identities, the aim being the building of an integrated self. Adolescents want to find answers to fundamental questions regarding life, at the same time experimenting with diverse roles which will create their identity afterwards. These developmental transitions have at their basis puberty changes, cognitive development and the change of social expectations. All these contexts can develop a coherent sense of life aiming at shaping identity or generating the lack of it; and then, identity confusion occurs, or *identity crisis* (Demir et al., 2010).

In the case when adolescents meet a crisis generated by some significant events in their lives, some overcome them successfully, without major efforts, while some others cannot deal with these problems without the help of the others.

The different instances of socialisation – family, school and the group of friends – play an important role in the construction of values, attitudes and behaviours of the young. These can be found as outlines of the social and personal identity of adolescence.

At a social level, the adolescent wants to manifest his/her independence in relation to his/her parents, the family having alternative requirements (sometimes, the young person is considered a child and treated as such: "you have to come back by X hour"; some other times, he/she is considered an adult: "you don't have to fool around, you're not a child anymore"). During this period, the influence of the group of friends (peer-group influence) is highlighted, the adolescent desiring to spend his/her free time with the ones of his/her age.

Socially speaking, adolescence coincides with: the first romantic meeting, entering a new cycle of schooling with new demands and requirements (the contact with different role models: teachers, colleagues; the experience of competitions – contests, championships), the right to vote, the right to drink alcoholic beverages and the right to take one's driving license. All these aspects are changes which can shape identity elements or which can lead to identity crises.

Being such an important life stage from the point of view of challenges, an adolescent has to face (drugs, tobacco, alcohol, anorexia, bulimia, exams – baccalaureate, driving license, etc.), I consider that a type of visual research would round up the data obtained in my Ph.D. thesis regarding the important dimensions which characterise the identity of adolescence.

In the following, I will refer to a series of theories which explain a part of the dimensions present in the data analysis and interpretation.

The social network theory (Boudon et al., 1996) mentions that there is a set of links which reunite the members of a group, some of these individuals having multiple connections, some others being isolated. The network represents the configuration of the connections observed, focusing on the means of accessing the resources and the information. The structure of the network is conceived as a constraint which stresses upon the behaviours. The first person to mention this theory is Bott (*apud* Boudon et al., 1996), who studied the enlarged family of the English urban workers as a network. Subsequent approaches belonged to Galaskiewicz (*apud* Boudon et al., 1996), according to who the notion of network meant the modality to function as a group in a place. Nevertheless, Granovetter (*apud* Boudon et al., 1996) defines the network as a way by means of which an unemployed person can find work. This theory explains the influence different social networks can have in shaping the identity of adolescents. Thus, the family, the group of friends and colleagues or the neighbours can influence the development of the young's personality.

In his book *Stigma: Notes on the Management of Spoiled Identity* (1963), Goffman talks about the fact that social identity can comprise anticipations and expectancies of the others which make the rest discriminate (kinsmen who discredit you, physical deformities, labelling triggered by race or religion, stigma generated by the social identity of the group). The discriminated ones make special efforts to compensate for their stigma because they do not have complete social acceptance: they draw the attention to some other areas, they use their stigma as an excuse for their lack of success or have skills which impress (https://www.thoughtco.com/stigma-notes-on-the-management-of-spoiled-identity-3026757). This theory explains why the adolescents discriminated by their colleagues receive a negative label which influences their subsequent development of identity.

In the psychosocial development theory, Erikson (1968) uses the term "identity crisis" for the first time, a term also applied at the level of adolescence because during this period a lot of transformations take place which require the management of two states: *identity vs. confusion*. The variety of options the adolescent has to choose from, the fundamental questions regarding life that he has to find answers to, the significant events from this period – all this can influence the adolescent, thus creating role confusion. In opposition, if the young person overcomes all this with success, if there is a coherent sense of his/her life, this one can have a shaped identity.

The role identity theory reminds of the fact that each of us is a sum of multiple identities associated to each role that we take on. In the literature review, different types of identity can be mentioned: of gender (regarding the attributes of masculinity and femininity), ethnic (regarding group belonging, lifestyle associated to clothing, nourishment and traditions) and vocational (regarding the educational and professional options).

Moreover, **the social identity theory** belonging to Turner and Tajfel (1979–1986) stipulates that there is a continuum between *personal identity* (which involves physical characteristics and personality traits) and *social identity* (which involves characteristics related to the state of being a member in a group). Someone's identity, at a certain moment, is a dot from a continuum. Depending on the contexts in which the individual finds himself/herself, one of the two types of identity is more prominent than the other (Scârneci, 2009). This theory suggests terms used in research to explain the types of identity specific to adolescents, such as personal and social identity.

3 Visual research of identity with adolescents

During my documentation process, I discovered articles focused on the visual field regarding adolescents. These contain research in which images posted on the Internet by the young were studied. Many of them refer to the digital (online) activity connected to the socialising sites (Facebook, Instagram and Twitter) that are accessed by adolescents. The young use digital resources more and more, such as laptop, tablets and mobile phones – all influencing the development of their identity. One of the major research questions in this area is whether the online and the offline identities really match in the context of school and outside it (Hughes et al., 2017).

It seems that the presence on these socialising sites creates values, beliefs, backgrounds and experiences that they share with the others. Self-identity is seen as a repertoire of social and cultural resources, as well as of technological experiences (Anstey and Bull *apud.* Hughes et al., 2017).

Internet consumption modifies the relationship with the others – friends, family and colleagues. If in the past, interpersonal relations happened only face-to-face and were based on trust, mutual help and respect, today friendships on the Internet do not always involve one's physical presence, only a virtual one, within which you are not necessarily who you are, but someone you would like to be. In this way, authenticity disappears, adolescents become more courageous and experiment with things they would not normally do in reality, due to rules and shyness (e.g. sexual experiences).

Through socialising networks, they have fun, relax, are more creative and colourful in the language they use and do not become nervous as when they stand in front of the class for the lessons; but, at the same time, they lack real social skills – they cannot generate life solutions, they use interfaces as substitutes of the real world, at school or in their everyday life are shier and take more time to reflect before they answer questions (Hughes et al., 2017).

Moreover, the adolescents who experiment with the Internet have as a main reason to access it the exploration of the self – to investigate how the others react, to facilitate social relations. It has been discovered that they communicate more frequently with people of different ages and of diverse cultural backgrounds than they would in real-life situations (Valkenburg et al., 2005, 2008).

By means of Internet consumption, adolescents satisfy their need for audience (someone to listen to them, to watch them) and, at the same time, they only display to the others that much of their privacy as they want, having their own degree of freedom and decision (Stern, 2010).

Much rarer are the studies on adolescents regarding their activities described using visual instruments, besides the ones related to Internet consumption. For example, I found a study belonging to Sibeoni et al. (2017) based on the photo-elicitation technique in which adolescents were asked to talk about their family experiences connected to food and meal times. Narrative interviews were carried out focused on a picture. The photo was considered as having a mediating role during the interview. By taking pictures, adolescents get themselves involved in research. Photography represents a favourable means of expression of the adolescent, considering the modern vocabulary and the present means of expression of the adolescents, useful in research interviews.

The ones passionate about photography can express their points of view much better; they feel pleasure in taking photographs because they choose them, they share from their experience with the others, they talk about them and they have fun collecting the data.

Thus, photo-elicitation can be used as a technique for identifying and exploring dynamic examples of the concept of the self and of identity construction (Sibeoni et al., 2017).

4 Methodological framework

In my chapter, I will describe the qualitative, exploratory research that I have undertaken. This consists of: "studying people in their natural environment, in their everyday life. It aims at knowing the way in which people live, talk, and behave, as well as the things that make them happy and sad… Its main target is to comprehend what the people's own words and behaviours mean to them" (Tutti et al. *apud.* Scârneci, 2006, p. 64).

Because in my previous studies dedicated to describing adolescent identity I used only textual data, I would like to mention that, beyond words, communication involves feelings and emotions which can be easily identified in images than in texts. The advantages of the research using visual techniques are described by Weber (*apud.* Scârneci-Domnişoru, 2016): "images are more accessible than the majority of the academic discourse forms, are more memorable than the text, can catch everything that words cannot render, facilitate understanding, and catch feelings which cannot be verbally expressed" (p. 64).

I used the drawing and photography technique, one filling in for the other, because I consider that through photography some aspects could be captured, while through drawing some additional clarifications could be brought regarding the description of the adolescence stage.

In the first instance of my research, I used photographs. The researchers in the social field use photographs in their different studies due to the major potential these have to describe and to explain the phenomena under study (Scârneci-Domnişoru, 2016).

"Photography presents the certain interpersonal relationship between the subjects. Images talk, create details, have an impact, and have a voice" (Powels *apud.* Scârneci - Domnişoru, 2016, p. 44).

In the literature review, the *photo-novella* term is also used when asking the subjects to arrange the photos under the form of meaningful successions and to add short texts to them to make the message more intelligible (for example, stories of the young's relations in which the topic of friendship is placed on top position on their scale of preferences). Considering all these aspects, I believe that photography is a useful instrument in my research.

The adolescents were asked to give me a photo which they considered representative for their life stage, irrespective of the context it had been taken in. At the same time, I asked them to assign a significant title to the photo for a better understanding of its meaning. During the period of August 2017–January 2018, I collected approximately 40 photographs and drawings from adolescents.

As I said before, the participants in my study, adolescents with ages ranging from 16 to 20 years, girls and boys, were asked to draw who they were at that moment of their life, and to add people, things and social contexts that they considered important for their life stage. Also, on the back of the page, they had to explain what they had drawn, how they characterised the stage of adolescence and how they self-defined.

I used both photography and drawing because I considered that the two visual techniques could compensate for each other, and that only through photography I could not gather sufficient information to be able to do relevant research. Drawing filled in for photography, in what both the richness of information was concerned and the complexity of the dimensions presented when analysing and interpreting the data.

Drawing is a metaphor of the important elements which define youth's identity, being used in studies which aim at describing different experiences that the subjects experiment with (for example, identity crisis in adolescence). It is used to complement the text, to explore different perceptions regarding adolescents' education and their relationship with their family, friends and school.

In the literature review, Bagnoli mentions that adolescents use self-portrait as an instrument to describe their identity. Moreover, Galman and McCloud state that, when using *photo-novella*, the subjects create a succession of drawings, placed in deliberate sequences, in which they include texts to explain different experiences that they live and which refer to their identity (*apud.* Scârneci-Domnişoru, 2016).

For coding, I used the NVivo 10 soft, specially created to analyse and interpret qualitative data. I identified topics which are recurrent in the drawings, photos and texts and which will be displayed in the next part of my article. The analysis and processing of the data was carried out based both on the content of the images and on the interpretations that the subjects rendered to them.

5 Findings and discussions

As a result of analysing the drawings and the photos received from the adolescents, I identified a series of topics which capture elements related to the identity of the young. These were organised according to their frequency and importance that the adolescents attributed to each (from the most frequent to the rarest topic encountered in drawings and photos).

Fig. 1: The representation of the relation with friends, in photographs, featuring adolescents: The trip with friends without parents (author's archive)

5.1 Social relations – the relationship with friends

The most frequently encountered topic, both in photos and in drawings, is the one of friendship. Friends support and develop the networking skills of the adolescent, creating social identity. They are the ones with whom adolescents share the same passions (theatre, library reading and dances).

According to the photographs, friends are the ones adolescents usually have fun with (going out, taking trips): "I also had fun, I used to spend my free time with my friends, going to a movie, swimming, playing billiards", a male adolescent says. It can be understood that smile triggers pleasure when they interact (symbol of the state of good disposition, specific to this life stage) (Fig. 1).

From the photos, it can be seen that the friends are similar to the adolescents questioned (they are represented as looking alike). It can be derived that they choose their friends on account of the similarity of the free time activities.

Moreover, as observed in my previous research, friends are important persons for the young, who support and develop the social skills of the adolescent;

Fig. 2: The representation of the friendship relations with adolescents (author's archive)

friendship relations substantiate common values and beliefs, such as altruism, reciprocity and solidarity (Fig. 2).

Furthermore, according to the drawings, some female adolescents who have as a behavioural pattern the tendency for solitude or introversion have only one girlfriend, who is their confidant in case of deception caused by love, and whom they talk everything with: "Alexandra is my best friend who helped me and always listened to me when I had a problem". In drawings, the friend appears next to the adolescent or is pictured alone, being positively labelled as "the best friend". This aspect is encountered in my previous research, as well, the friends being seen as important persons who satisfy the emotional needs of the adolescents, these ones confiding in their friends when they have conflictual relationships with their parents (Fig. 3).

5.2 Social relations – The relationship with the family

A frequently identified element in images is the relationship with the family, an important component in supporting the identity development with adolescents. There is a category of adolescents who have amiable relationships with their parents and consider that the adolescence period was beautiful because of this relationship: "The most beautiful period of my life was adolescence because I had my family close to me".

From the sample drawings, it can be depicted that the nuclear family is present in certain situations: parents and children, united, close both physically and emotionally. In the photographs collected by me, the family as a social network defining adolescents does not appear. This is to be found only in drawings (Fig. 4).

Fig. 3: The representation of the relationship with the girlfriend by female adolescents (author's archive)

Fig. 4: The representation of the nuclear family, as envisioned by adolescents (author's archive)

As a result of analysing the images, it can be derived that the family is associated to home or to the activities performed by its members (the parents who love each other – the father bringing flowers to the mother, the children performing different activities: photography, reading and swinging); there is also a pet who is viewed as a member of the family (Fig. 5).

Fig. 5: The representation of family and of home, as envisioned by adolescents (author's archive)

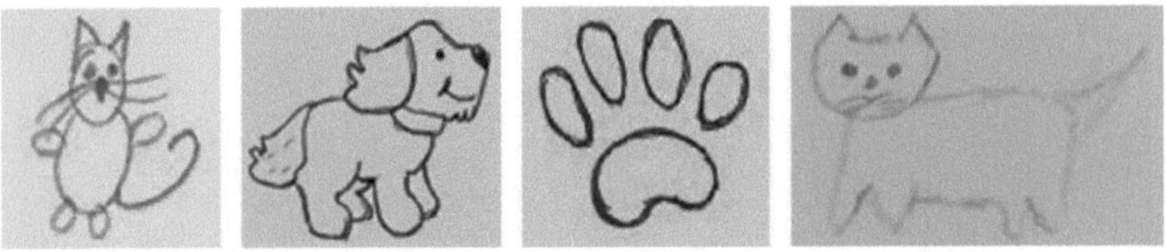

Fig. 6: The representation of pets as friends of adolescents (author's archive)

According to the drawings, the pets – dogs or cats – are seen as real friends to the adolescent. They are part of the family, are integrated members of it and, at the same time, make adolescents more responsible because these have to take care of them (to ensure their daily comfort: food, water, walking, cleaning and doctor): "In my early adolescence, I found a little cat which I still have; I consider it a member of my family who helped me become more responsible", a female adolescent says (Fig. 6).

Moreover, if the social relations have shortcomings (they do not have friends, have suffered from a deception caused by love) adolescents substitute this socialisation need with animals who offer them support and unconditioned presence.

In some drawings, only the nuclear family is represented (mother, father and children), while in others, the extended one (uncles, grandparents, great-grandparents and cousins included) (Fig. 7). This aspect depicted from drawings

Fig. 7: The representation of the extended family of adolescents (author's archive)

supports the social network theory, the family representing an assembly of connections among the members of the group which creates a network in which the observed relationships exist.

As it can be derived from my previous research, the presence and the support of the parents, as well as the amiable relationships with them, involve feelings of equilibrium and trust when constructing the positive social identity of the adolescents. Family is seen as a supportive pillar in developing the young, if the time spent with these ones is of quality.

The pleasant events spent together with the family (such as trips and other spare time activities) make the adolescents develop a positive self-identity: "My adolescence is based on my trips with my family, in which we are all happy and we relaxed as we wished. We are a united family which makes me happy", a female adolescent says.

5.3 Social relations – The positive relationship with the colleagues

Another frequently met topic in defining social identity is the positive relationship with the colleagues. This is represented in the drawings belonging to adolescents by picturing the high school where they studied. The building is the symbol of the socialising context in which the adolescent can make acquaintances (Fig. 8).

What can be seen in the pictures is that the relationship with the colleagues is presented under diverse social contexts, such as: the end of high school, the state of waiting before one of the most important exams in life – the baccalaureate, certain team projects where the cohesion of the adolescents is visible or certain activities such as beauty contests or those in which the adolescents made a presentation of their own culture. All these contexts generate for the adolescent

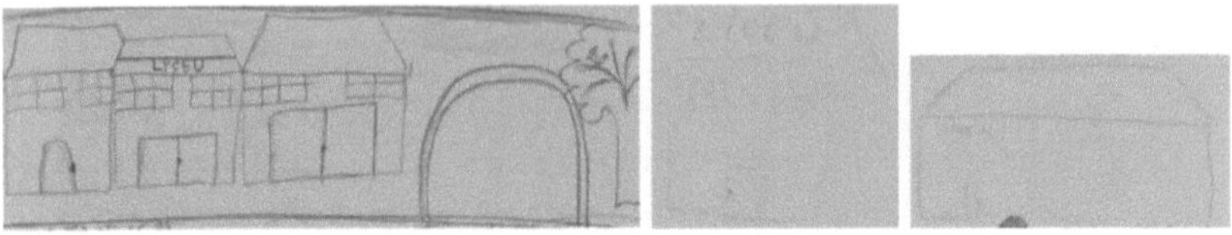

Fig. 8: The representation of the high school where the adolescents studied (author's archive)

Fig. 9: The representation of the relationship with the adolescents' colleagues, in photographs: End of high school – Waiting for the final exam (author's archive)

relational skills and pleasant memories which lay the foundation of their own social identity: "I liked the high school period because I had the chance to meet moral and beautiful people", a female adolescent says.

Just like in my Ph.D. thesis, the photographs implicitly render some skills that the adolescents form by means of the interaction they have with the group of colleagues for the school projects, such as: organisational, verbal and counselling skills (Fig. 9). The multiple roles that the adolescents have within the group, such

Fig. 10: The representation of the significant events in adolescence: The sweet 18th party (author's archive)

as the group leader, the party entertainer and so on, enable the young to discover new characteristics of their vocational or social identity.

As observed in the literature review as well (Marcia *apud.* Harwood, 2010), these roles make adolescents grow up and, implicitly, determine their identity be under change. Exploring new roles creates new opportunities and new responsibilities for the young which can emphasise their capacities and skills.

Just like in my Ph.D. thesis, the leitmotif associated to free time is represented by parties. Awaited with enthusiasm, these are real sources of formation, consolidation and development of the social network.

Consequently, the significant events from adolescence are connected to the relationship with colleagues and friends. From the photographs, it can be seen that the sweet 18th party, the banquet, the graduation festivities and awards ceremonies – all are life moments committed to the long-term memory of the adolescents (Fig. 10).

5.4 Social relations – The negative relationships with colleagues

Another element identified in the images refers to the fact that, for the introvert youngsters, the ones with tendencies seeking solitude, the period of adolescence represented a trauma due to the fact that the other colleagues discriminated, labelled and marginalised them: "During that period I felt degraded, marginalised, laughed at, I can say that even scorn was reached. I used to go to school with a frozen heart, waiting for all this routine which had got generated to be reiterated, accepting my role as 'the jester' of the class", a male adolescent says.

From the drawings, it can be depicted that discrimination is stigma for the adolescent, which can generate inferiority complexes. The negative label is suggested by the non-verbal behaviours of the colleagues (some have the forefinger pointed at the adolescent, others laugh at him/her and throw themselves on the floor). The face of the discriminated youngster is sad, delineated in black, and there are tears represented as a sign of the associated suffering (Fig. 11). This aspect confirms what Goffman (1968) mentioned about stigma – certain signs, physical deformities or labelling lead to exclusion and isolation, the social identity being a negative one.

Fig. 11: The representation of adolescents' discrimination by their colleagues (author's archive)

Furthermore, Erikson (1968) was of the opinion that negative events lay stress on the young person generating role confusion (the adolescent does not know what is good and what is bad, does not have correct guiding marks and is ambivalent regarding his/her behaviour).

This conclusion was also identified in my Ph.D. thesis: the marginalisation generated by the colleagues imprints the adolescents' self-esteem, and school becomes an element of stress due to the collective which is divided into subgroups and implicitly due to the conflicts arisen for gaining popularity or power within the group.

Moreover, the group of colleagues or friends may influence the formation of some deviant behaviours, such as smoking or alcohol consumption. Breaking the rules represents a normal attempt in adolescence, certain colleagues or friends having an evil influence over the young. As a result of analysing the images, it became obvious that, in what adolescents' vices are concerned, they started smoking because they saw this behaviour as an element of popularity in front of their colleagues and friends: "I started smoking because it seemed to me that it was super cool to smoke and that I looked elegant while smoking and drinking coffee (now I know that I don't)", a female adolescent says. This aspect became clear in my previous research as well, the influence of friends and colleagues coming first in what the antisocial behaviours of the young are concerned (Fig. 12).

5.5 Social relations – The relationships with teachers

Both from the drawings and from my previous research, it can be noticed that, among the socialising instances which create identity with adolescents, teachers can be listed too: "I consider that the teachers were also important and contributed

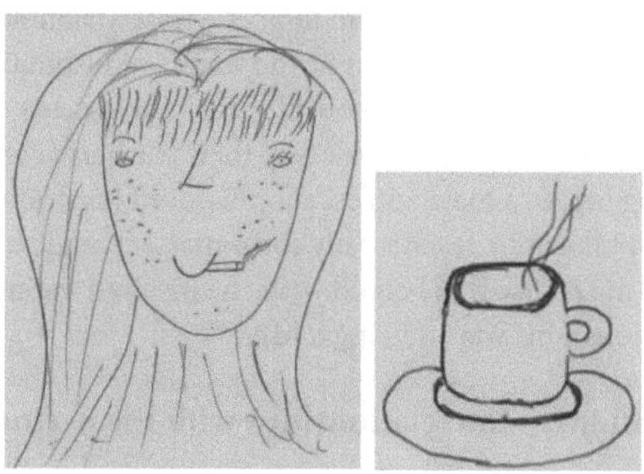

Fig. 12: Representation of adolescents' vices (author's archive)

Fig. 13: The representation of some role models such as teachers or form masters, as envisioned by adolescents (author's archive)

to my formation". In the majority of the cases, these are role models for the pupils; they can encourage the development of some of their skills or they can discover some potential elements in them (the preference or the pleasure to learn for a certain subject, or the pleasure to study a field is inoculated by the teacher, as well).

From my previous studies, it can be derived that teachers and form masters implicitly (because they have a closer relationship with them) can be real mentors for adolescents – emblematic figures whose vision about life, traits of personality and professional skills can be the source of inspiration for an adolescent. Adams and Berzonsky (2009) consider that adolescents will have positive results if they are appropriately rewarded by their teachers (Fig 13).

In the drawing below, a male adolescent portrayed his favourite teacher: "My psychology and philosophy teacher (my form master) made a great impression on me. He made me realise that I could write, he inspired me and he still inspires me every day through his way of being a MAN".

5.6 Social relations – The relationships with the partner

Love experiences represent another important chapter in defining adolescent identity. Starting sexual life, creating relationships based on trust, mutual

Fig. 14: The representation of the relationship with the partner, as envisioned by adolescents (author's archive)

support and respect are just a few elements which shape adolescent personality. Some events are positive. Others have as repercussions disillusionment and lack of trust in the others: "I have an ex-relationship which helped me realise that I don't have to be too good all the time", a male adolescent says.

The relationship with the partner is portrayed, in drawings, through symbols such as hearts, flowers and the presence of the couple (the girl holding hands with the boy), elements which define love (Fig. 14).

Both from my previous research and from the drawings, it can be seen that girls have a more idealised vision of the relationship with the partner: "I fell in love… and yes, we are still together. And now we both dearly remember the beautiful moments in adolescence, browsing through the photo album", a female adolescent says. Boys, on the other hand, have a more pragmatic view over the couple relationship; love is seen as pleasure, involving playing and sexuality.

5.7 Social relations – the relationships with God

In my previous studies, the memorable events in adolescence (the death of a parent, friend or of a close grandparent, the leaving abroad of a parent or of both parents) influence the identity development of the young. When describing adolescence, girls mention these events and rely on divinity as their support for solving the identity crisis occurred. The symbol of the cross, of the angles, of the church and of God are just a few of the elements recurrent in the female adolescents' drawings.

As depicted from my previous research, the religious identity comprises a behavioural pattern which is formed inside the family. Religion is seen as a solution, a way of dealing with destructive emotions and problems, a remedy for the

Fig. 15: The representation of divinity, as envisioned by adolescents (author's archive)

instability in the lives of the young (Adams and Berzonsky, 2009). The relationship with God renders feelings of respect and trust to the adolescents towards the adults (Fig. 15).

God is seen by adolescents as a solution to their conflictual moods of tension, experienced as a result of both their hormonal changes from inside the body and their conflictual relationships with their parents, colleagues or friends: "And, most importantly, God changed my life, and I live through Him every day and I grow and I fathom deeper into my relationship with Him. It was only in this way that I found peace and complete happiness, through the recurrent anxiety generated by adolescence", a female adolescent says.

5.8 Defining adolescence

Another frequently met topic both in drawings and in photographs is that in which adolescents define this stage in their life. From the drawing below, it can be noticed that the period of adolescence is seen as a stage of intense happiness, well-being and optimism: "The drawing represents my way of being, my optimism and the happiness of life. You never have to regret anything you have done, as long as you did it with an aim in mind or for someone dear (to make the one next to you laugh, then when he/she is sad)" (Fig. 16).

After analysing the photos, similarly to the drawings, it can be observed that adolescence is a period in which elation is predominant, as well as the pleasure of living life to the maximum without considering the consequences, freedom being seen as an ace, the memories with the colleagues and the "foolishness" of those moments being deeply rooted in the identity structure of the young (Fig. 17). Smile can be a symbol of the good mood in adolescence, and it is to be found both in drawings and in photos. The above-mentioned aspects, regarding the role of colleague, friend and daughter/son support the role identity theory

Fig. 16: The representation of the adolescence period (author's archive)

which specifies the fact that each of us has multiple identities, associated to each role we assume. The role of friend, in adolescence, is the one which leads to satisfaction at a social level and creates the social identity of the young.

As different from my Ph.D. thesis, in which the definition of adolescence highlighted important events such as the beginning of high school, the start of sexual life, the occurrence of pimples, the dyeing of the hair for the first time or the receiving of the identity card; in the present study the stress is laid more on the exploration of the self through different experiences, initiations and pursuits in the company of friends.

5.9 Symbols of adolescence

Another topic present in the drawings of the young is that in which they represent some typical elements associated to adolescence. After analysing the images, it can be seen that, in what the symbols connected to adolescence are concerned, girls mention elements related more to the environment, such as butterflies or flowers, associated to their delicacy, tenderness and femininity. Their special beauty, which cannot be rendered through words, but which is full of expressivity due to the colours, shapes and perfumes, is an analogy to the unicity of this life stage, which some consider to be the most beautiful: "Flowers are very perfumed and delicate, and even though not obvious, I identify myself to them very well" and "I consider that butterflies characterise me, besides the fact that I like them very much" (Fig. 18).

Fig. 17: The representation of the adolescence stage through photographs: Freedom in adolescence – no worries or problems (author's archive)

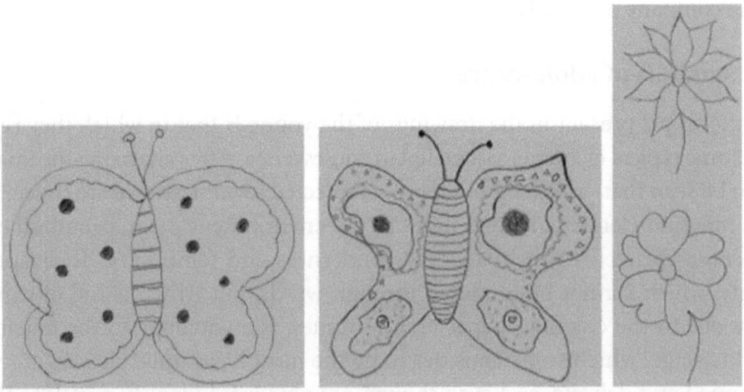

Fig. 18: The representation of the symbols associated to the period of adolescence by girls (author's archive)

Fig. 19: The representation of some symbols associated to the period of adolescence by girls (author's archive)

From the drawings, as well as from my previous research, it can be derived that the hourglass girl represents a standard of beauty (for example, 90-60-90), so frequently advertised by the media sources and taken as a benchmark by female adolescents, as explained in one of the texts which accompany the drawings: "In the drawing, I am the hourglass girl because in adolescence I observed how much importance girls in my school gave to the shape of the body and this got stuck in my mind" (Fig. 19).

The cube, as a symbol of semitransparency and perfection, could indicate some sort of a mystery that female adolescents display. They do not let themselves be completely revealed to the others: "The cube is of thick glass, so that you could see though the glass, but distortedly. As much as I like sharing about me, I am still called mysterious, many times", a female adolescent says.

5.10 School and professional accomplishments

As a source of self-esteem, another topic met in both drawings and photographs is that of school and professional accomplishments. As a result of analysing the images, it could be seen that among the targets aimed at in adolescence there is also the driving license: "I drew the day when I took my driving license. On that day I was the most nervous. It was my first big accomplishment of this type and the first time I was proud of myself", a female adolescent says. This type of success makes adolescents trust themselves: "The driving license was another target of mine that I wanted to hit, and I succeeded in getting it, which made me more ambitious and determined", a female adolescent says. The drawings portray either a car driven by an adolescent, the policemen acknowledging the results or a heart framing a driving license and a car (Fig. 20).

Fig. 20: Taking the driving license as an accomplishment of the adolescents (author's archive)

Both from the drawings and from my previous research, it can be noticed that these events in the life of adolescents are significant both at a personal level and at a social one, because they involve assuming responsibility. They represent important stages in life which imprint the shaping of identity.

School accomplishments such as high school admission, school contests or passing the baccalaureate exam are important events in the evolution from childhood to maturity and validate the self-trust of the adolescent: "The baccalaureate was an important event to me, I realised I had great responsibility", a male adolescent says.

Moreover, from the photographs it can be observed that, for some adolescent girls, an accomplishment can be that of practising modelling for a period of time or participating in and winning some beauty contests. This type of activity validates self-trust and represents a confirmation of the attractiveness potential specific to gender identity with female adolescents (Fig. 21).

5.11 Hobbies of adolescents (activities to pass their free time)

An important topic for the young is represented by spending their free time and doing some preferred activities. From the drawings, it can be observed that one of the most encountered spare time activities with adolescents is photography (the adolescent represents himself/herself holding a camera in his/her hand, framed by a heart): "I was and still am passionate about photography. I love playing with effects", a female adolescent says.

Fig. 21: The representation of accomplishments with female adolescents, in photos: I was a model for a time (author's archive)

Fig. 22: The representation of hobbies with adolescents through drawings (author's archive)

Nature lovers are offered the feeling of freedom by photography: "In adolescence, I liked to take pictures, I had a lot of freedom, but I was very shy. I loved nature very much and I was away very much", a male adolescent says.

Hobbies create positive self-esteem with adolescents because they are activities done with pleasure by the young, configuring in this way their role identity (Erikson, 1968) (Fig. 22).

Fig. 23: The representation of hobbies with adolescents through photos: Trip to Bran, Moeciu (author's archive)

From the photos, it can be noticed that one of the main hobbies of adolescents is represented by trips: "I used to like visiting new places, I always liked walking", a female adolescent says. These take place together with the family or with the friends and are occasions to explore the surrounding environment and to make pleasant memories, which will constitute the basis of the identity of the young as future adult. When these take place for the first time in a certain place, they can also have initiating implications (Fig. 23).

After analysing the images, it could be derived that artistic activities are also preferred by adolescents. They listen to music and compose both songs and poems. Furthermore, reading is also one of the pleasant activities to adolescents. Through these, they discover a series of interesting things and ask themselves fundamental questions regarding life: "I experienced powerful emotions in adolescence, a deep interior torment fed by books" or "I learnt to read very much and even to start writing poetry. I also participated in some contests with them", two female adolescents say. This aspect was also evident in my Ph.D. thesis,

Fig. 24: The representation of the artistic activities of adolescents as hobbies (author's archive)

Fig. 25: The representation of free time activities of adolescents as hobbies (author's archive)

reading being a spare time activity which involves self-discovery and knowing, an escape from the real, mundane space which projects the adolescent into the sphere of creativity (Fig. 24).

There is a category of adolescents who experimented with folk dances and theatre, as activities. These made them get rid of nervousness, socialise more and trust themselves more: "I started for a period with theatre. I loved what I did there. I both made new friends there and gained experience. Step by step, I managed to get rid of the fear to speak in public", a male adolescent says.

Moreover, another element identified in the images is represented by the activities outside the house, with friends, which are preferred by adolescents to the detriment of the computer, tablet or phone games, which generate isolation, the lack of socialising, sedentarism and sometimes obesity (Fig. 25). These generate beautiful memories and satisfy the need for socialising with adolescents: "I used to spend all my time with my friends in the street playing different games, such as: volleyball, hopscotch, thick milk. Through these games I promoted recreation in a pleasant manner (walks in nature, going out with friends) instead of playing phone games isolated, inside the house, being sedentary and later on ending up being obese", a female adolescent says.

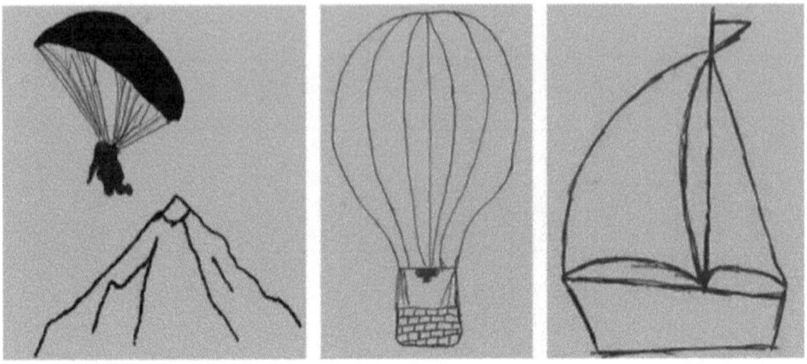

Fig. 26: The representation of sports as hobbies with adolescents (author's archive)

The literature review brings forth again the fact that the activities in fresh air are much better alternatives to spending time in front of the computer (Fig. 26). The Internet is but a good source of ambivalence regarding self-knowing. Socialising sites and the connection to different information lead to an extension of one's self image, some being virtual, others being real and valid (Modrea, 2006).

Still from the drawings of the adolescents, it can be seen that playing sports is among the preferred activities by adolescents, especially boys. They experience the utmost freedom when they get involved in activities which generate adrenaline: "I like paragliding, it is an extreme sport which makes me feel in my world", a male adolescent says.

Just like in my Ph.D. thesis, popularity among boys is rendered also by the sports played. Sports disciplines, creates responsibility, ambition and is a source of self-esteem when the adolescent is successful.

5.13 Negative experiences in adolescence

From my previous research and as well as from the present study, it can be noted from the drawings that the significant experiences in the young's life (such as: the death of one or both parents, of a grandparent the young person feels attached to, the divorce of the parents, the emigration of the parents to another country to ensure a better life or an incurable illness) mark the identity development of the young: "In my adolescence I experienced many things which influenced my life and which will never get right. The loss of both my parents in the same week touched me very much, I couldn't make any decision without thinking about them, to what they would have told me", a female adolescent says (Fig. 27).

These events, as resulted from my Ph.D. thesis as well, can generate identity crises or a loss of the fundamental guiding marks, which crash adolescent dreams and trigger self-depreciation and the loss of one's own self (Clerget, 2008).

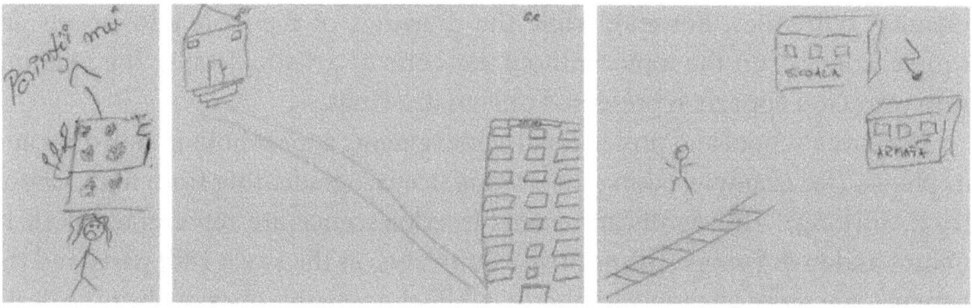

Fig. 27: The representation of significant experiences in adolescence (author's archive)

This fact is also maintained by Erickson (1968) in his psychosocial development theory where he states that, during adolescence, the shocking events can lead to identity crisis or confusion, the adolescent not knowing what way to go, what guiding marks to have.

Furthermore, for boys, serving their first military service, which presupposes rules and undebatable orders, is an event which seems to hurry the process of their maturity "My adolescence was marked by strict rules during military service, considered many times absurd, away from my family. I had to observe the rules and I had the biggest deceptions regarding the concept of military service", a male adolescent says.

6 Conclusions

The present research is an extension of my study on adolescents' identity, a topic which made the interest of my analysis over the time both in my Ph.D. thesis and in my previous research. It is a normal continuation of my preoccupations, but using other instruments than the classic ones – the questionnaire and the semi-structured interview – i.e. the visual techniques – drawing and photography.

The images, as different from the text, capture the context and the non-verbal communication better and describe the moods, the emotions and the relationships of the adolescents more suggestively.

Regarding the topics which occurred when analysing and interpreting the data during research, I can mention that through photos adolescents represent their relationship with their friends and colleagues more often while the relationship with their family is completely absent. This one occurs more frequently depicted in drawings, both the nuclear family and the extended one being portrayed.

In what the female adolescents are concerned, the drawings are complex, full of details and symbols (for example, the ones related to feminine identity: butterflies, flowers); while the drawings of the male adolescents are simple, concise, on the topic, without aesthetic or artistic details. The relationship with God appears represented only in drawings.

Moreover, school and professional achievements appear both in drawings and in photos (for example, taking the driving license, graduating from high school, team working). The significant events in adolescence are represented both in photos and in drawings. The positive events, such as the sweet 18th party and the banquet, are more often met in photos, while the negative ones, such as the death of the parents and discrimination by colleagues, appear more often in drawings. Adolescents' hobbies, as an element of defining adolescent identity, are more often represented in drawings than in photos.

In what the literature review is concerned, I remind of the fact that the majority of the articles on the topic of visual identity with adolescents presented in documentaries comprise research which involves images and texts regarding the young's activity on the Internet. In these articles, what appears as obvious is the fact that the relationship with friends is a virtual one, unreal, sometimes dissimulated (for example, the young display desirable behaviours to be accepted or the shy ones are much more disinhibited in the virtual medium than in the real one in what their sexual activity is concerned). As different from these articles, my research shows that in photos, the relationships among friends are genuine (the smile can be read on their faces).

This visual research comes to complete my Ph.D. thesis, exhibiting much better, through photos and drawings, certain topics and dimensions which can be found in both instances (for example, the relationship with family, friends and the hobbies).

As a limitation of my research, I would mention that I cannot pretend to have completed with this study the problematics of visual identity with adolescents, considering the reduced number of adolescents, and, more than that, that in my sample group there were more girls than boys.

I liked working for this book chapter – I consider that it was a new type of experience which completed the knowledge previously gathered; it was a challenge which generated unsuspected satisfactions.

Bibliography

Adams, G., & Berzonsky, M. (2009). *Psihologia adolescenței. Manualul Blackwell*. Iași: Polirom.

Boudon, R., Besnard, P., Cherkaoui, M., & Lecuyer, B-P. (1996). *Dicționar de sociologie Larousse*. București: Univers Enciclopedic.

Clerget, S. (2008). *Criza adolescenței. Căi de a o depăși cu success.* București: Trei.

Demir, B., Demir, H.K., & Sönmez, E.I. (2010). Sense of Identity and Depression in Adolescents. *The Turkish Journal of Pediatrics*, 52, 68–72.

Erikson, E. (1968). *Identity. Youth and Crisis.* New York: Norton Company Inc.

Goffman, E. (1968). *Stigma and Social Identity.* London: Penguin.

Harwood, R., Miller, S., & Vasta, R. (2010). *Psihologia copilului.* Iași: Polirom.

Hughes, J., Morrison, L., & Thompson, S. (2017). Who Do You Think You Are? Examining the Off/On-Line Identities of Adolescents Using a Social Networking Site. *Youth: Social Media and Adolescence*, 20, 3–19.

Modrea, M. (2006). *Imagine de sine și personalitate în adolescență.* Focșani: Aliter.

Scârneci, F. (2006). *Îndrumar de cercetare calitativă în științele socio-umane.* Brașov: Editura Universității Transilvania.

Scârneci, F. (2009). *Introducere în sociologia identității.* Brașov: Editura Universității Transilvania.

Scârneci-Domnișoru, F. (2016). *Datele vizuale în cercetarea socialului.* Brașov: Presa Universitară Clujeană.

Sibeoni, J., Costa-Drolon, E., Poulmare'h, L., Colin, S., Valentin, M., Pradere, J., & Revah-Leroy, A. (2017). Photo-Elicitation with Adolescents in Qualitative Research: An Example of Its Use in Exploring Family Interactions in Adolescent Psychiatry. *Child and Adolescent Psychiatry and Mental Health*, 33, 120–127.

Steinberg, L., & Lerner, R.M. (2004). The Scientific Study of Adolescence: A Brief History. *The Journal of Early Adolescence*, 24, 45–56.

Stern, S. (2010). Features and Gender Differences in Adolescents' World Wide Web Home Pages. *Journal of Broadcasting & Electronic Media*, 48, 218–243.

Șchiopu, U. (2008). *Psihologia modernă. Psihologia vârstelor.* București: România Press.

Valkenburg, P.M., & Jochen, P. (2008). Adolescents' Identity Experiments on the Internet, Consequences for Social Competence and Self-Concept Unity. *Communication Research*, 21, 111–120. https://www.thoughtco.com/stigma-notes-on-the-management-of-spoiled-identity-3026757. Accessed: 11.08.2019

Valkenburg, P.M., Schouten, P.A., & Jochen, P. (2005). Adolescents' Identity Experiments on the Internet. *New Media & Society*, 18, 186–197.

Diana-Cristina Bódi

V Using the drawing to identify post-retirement identity transformations

Abstract: The demographic changes – an increase of life expectancy, the decline of birth rates, and a greater increase of the population over the age 65 in the West – have stimulated a moral panic and a new interest regarding consumption and the social and cultural potential of elderly people. The chapter submits the results of a visual research on the identity transformations of elderly people and their roles as pensioners. The data were collected by means of drawings, an uncommon method used in studies concerned with the ageing phenomenon. The analysis was applied to 26 drawings of elderly people from Braşov, Romania, both from urban and rural areas. The results refer to the perception upon identity after retirement compared to pre-retirement identity. Moreover, the present chapter highlights the roles before and after retirement and how the elderly adapted to their roles, depending on the new period, after retirement. This research confirms the need for qualitative research with alternative methods, such as visuals, on older people in addition to quantitative research, as it can bring up new questions, new hypotheses, and new approaches to this target group.

Keywords: elderly people, visual research, continuity theory, identity transformations at the Third Age

1 Introduction

Although the sociology of ageing is a relatively new field, the studies on the ageing phenomenon started to increase at the beginning of the 20th century, as a consequence of the alarm signals highlighted by demographers with regard to demographic ageing. Most of the studies in the field describe the lifestyles of the elderly, the way in which they relate to social evolution as well as aspects concerning the relation between generations.

My preoccupation with the sociology of ageing started in my student years, during my Master's program, when the research for my dissertation focused on the quality of life of the institutionalized elderly. Later on, I developed a few studies on the life and needs of the elderly, also investigating their roles within society and family in my PhD thesis.

In this chapter, I will present the results of my latest study which centred on identity transformations of the elderly. I have tried to capture the implications of the transition from an active lifestyle to a passive period in order to reveal the differences between life before and after retirement. I have also tried to discover how the elderly perceive life before retirement in comparison with life after retirement. The research aims to complete and even contradict some of my own conclusions from previous studies concerning the role and identity of the elderly. It was quite an ambitious challenge as the methodology used for this study was altogether new to me. My approach features visual and drawing techniques in order to identify the identity transformation underwent by the subjects of the research through the transition from an active phase to something that is usually thought to be a passive period in a person's life.

In the present study, I have tried to explore the life of the subjects before retirement in contrast with their life after retirement. I also wanted to identify the identity changes that interfere in an individual's life after retirement. What are the main roles that define a person before retirement? What are the roles that define a person after retirement, and how are these roles perceived by subjects? What did retirement bring into their lives?

In the following chapter, I will present the stage of the current research in the field as well as the concepts I will use in analysing and processing data.

2 Theoretical framework

To define an elderly person today can be quite challenging. Aside from the classifications found in the literature which deal with terms like elderly people, old people, Third Age, Fourth Age, young elders, middle elders, or old elders (Bucur & Maciovan, 2003), a clear and generally accepted definition of ageing has yet to be established by the scientific community. This situation is mostly the consequence of the diversity of scientific perspectives that capture many new definitions of this phenomenon. Moreover, each person, as a part of a certain culture, defines and perceives the process of ageing differently, as suggested by the Special Eurobarometer 378 (2012). According to the data, the medium age of "old age" in Europe is 63,9 years, although the answers of the participating subjects vary according to their geographical area, to their age, and to the local perceptions and stereotypes. For instance, in Holland, people see themselves as "old" when they reach 70,4, while in Slovakia, people who are 47,7 fall into the elderly category. Romania – along with other European countries (Hungary, Ukraine, and Germany) – adopts a pessimistic view, believing that the Third Age begins at 60,5. In addition, women think that old age begins slightly later than men do (65 years versus 62,7 years).

This data can provide us with clues on what retirement actually means for an individual. On the one hand, there are people who consider themselves young and physically capable, and whose identity can be affected by mandatory retirement. On the other hand, there are people, especially those who had routine-based jobs, without any responsibilities, who cannot wait to retire in order to have more free time for the activities they could not perform during their active life (Bódi, 2017).

Although the concept of "identity" has a long history, it gained exposure in everyday language only in the 20th century, along with the increasing interest towards psychology and sociology. Identity, as a psychosocial reality, is linked to the problem of the self-defined as "the totality of thoughts and feelings of an individual that refers to himself as to an object" (Rosenberg, apud Marshall, 2003, p. 523).

The concept of the self in a modern society is dealt with by Giddens (1997) and May and Copper (1995) who claim that the processes of identity are not identical, as they differ according to the historical background, to the social segment of a person, and to the events in an individual's life. The authors maintain that the functioning of the modern society has led to the fragmentation of the self in the sense that the individual, who finds himself overwhelmed by the burden of external pressure and a plurality of social roles to fill, has a wider range of attitudinal and behavioural possibilities to choose from. Therefore, in order to better express himself, the individual adapts the socially acquired attitude and behaviour according to his life goals, while at the same time inventing new ones, according to social contexts.

The psychologist Erik Erikson described identity as a process which takes place both in the inner space of the individual, but also in his exterior, in the culture of his community. This approach has led to establishing a connection between the individual and the environment. Moreover, Erikson developed the idea of "identity crisis", which was later on generalized with old aged people. In this period, these identity transformations which occur imply the management of the states in which the elderly person might be: personal integrity or despair (Fontaine, 2008; Gideon, 2008; Iluţ, 2009).

Other identity transformations undergone by elderly people are related to the shift from high self-esteem, once enhanced by fulfilling professional roles during the active period, to low self-esteem and stigma associated to retirement years, when individuals no longer engage in paid activities. They could experience the "Hemingway" Syndrome (Iluţ, 2009), which deals with regret caused by the passage of time. Furthermore, the issues which affect the elderly, doubled by health problems, can be influenced in a positive or negative way by the elderly person's family and social care services.

Retirement can trigger minor and major "crises", and thus, they require resources meant to help people adapt to changes in point of acquiring new skills and habits (Dubar, 2003).

The changes which accompany retirement – the "empty nest" syndrome (Gotea, 2014), lack of social support, disease, disability, and fear of dying – appear to be difficult to manage for the elderly, as they have to redefine their identity according to the new status. The parent who is faced with the "empty nest" syndrome has to rethink family identity by means of other life goals. A study on elderly people in Europe and Israel points out that people redefined their post-retirement identity after an initial phase of despair and that a very important part was played by social and community networks (Tummala & Hernandez, 2008).

Retirement crises also develop because the individual's identity is strongly linked to his or her profession (Muntean, 2006). These crises which become visible during retirement interfere with the normal course of life and cause material and relational damage, ultimately activating subjectivity shifts. These identity crises alter the image and self-esteem of the individual (Bódi, 2012).

All these identity shifts are subject to many theories, starting with the functionalist paradigm, with the disengagement theory, activity theory, continuity theory, and symbolic interactionism.

The disengagement theory was developed in 1961 by the functionalist sociologists Elaine Cumming and William Henry (Marina, 2003; Quadagno, 1999; Diggs, 2008a), who illustrated the manner in which elderly people start distancing themselves from their work roles, thus preparing more for their death. The authors claim that the gradual withdrawal of the elderly from professional and social spheres is a natural and inevitable process. Therefore, disengagement is the process of withdrawal from society, by decreasing the social roles played by an individual and by diminishing social interactions which, in time, tend to become more preoccupied with affection rather than functional solidarity. The disengagement process bears four characteristics: reciprocity, between the elder people and society; functionality, in the sense that the labour market is freed from a poorly productive workforce; irreversibility, which suggests that disengagement is not prone to cycles; and universality, in the sense that disengagement is to be found in all contemporary societies (Marina, 2003).

The activity theory emphasizes the fact that old people have the same psychological and social needs as young individuals and that the process of disengagement is not a natural or normal process for those who isolate themselves from their social life (Diggs, 2008a). The person who best manages his/her age remains active and resistant to the "narrowing" of his/her social world. This implies maintaining middle age activities as long as possible and finding some "substitutes" for work, for friends, and even for late partners. Successful ageing is active ageing, and this involves productive roles destined for elderly people engaged in different organizations, volunteering, and other social activities.

The continuity theory suggests that an individual's development is a constant and complex process that has not been grasped completely, according to some authors (Dolinar, 2008). This theory, which was mentioned for the first time in 1968 by George Maddox (apud Diggs, 2008b), focused on the fact that Third Age people tend to turn to a lifestyle similar to the one they had before retirement. Atchley (1989) speaks about continuity as a strategy for successful ageing. Personality continuance means that changes can be incorporated in the unique conserved traits of one's individuality. The continuous performing of activities allows people to prevent, compensate, and minimize ageing effects. The continuity of relationships preserves the social support system of the individual. Feminist theories have criticized the continuity theory by stating that it defines normal ageing with reference to the male model only.

The ageing process can be studied through the analysis of the identity transformations in daily interaction. Sociologists approach the concept of identity by finding inspiration in **symbolic interactionism** and its relational component. The conceptual articulation of two transactions which alter identity seem to be relevant here: the biographical transaction or self-negotiation (the reflexive attitude of thinking about what you are now in relation to what you were in the past and what you can become in the future) and relational transaction (the reaction of our own self mirrored in another person) (Marina, 2003). Researchers use terms coined by Cooley and Mead (apud Manea, 2000), such as "social self" or "looking glass-self" and think that if we want to understand what people do, we have to study the meaning they attach to themselves, to their situation, and to their actions. The key concepts are *mind, self* (as a symbolic representation of a person, built in the midst of social interaction), *socialization, role, and defining a situation* (Băran-Pescaru, 2004).

In one of his studies concerning daily interactions of the elderly, Minichiello, Browne, and Kendig (2000) identify a few simple, yet effective actions which contribute to the ageing sensation: people's remarks on slower movement, the drivers' horns that sanction a way of driving too cautiously, people's distrust regarding the ability to perform certain tasks, the doctors' lack of understanding and lack of attention, protective attitudes in certain situations (priority seats in public transport), etc. Moreover, these daily interactions take place in public spaces which cannot be avoided by the elderly, thus highlighting their consequences. This way, the elderly feel constantly followed and labelled. The repercussions are direct; by assuming their label, they face the confrontation with a new image of the self: the image of an old person, no longer capable of handling things and being a burden to others.

Symbolic interactionism suggests that the roles associated to the status of an old person are built by means of social interactions, not by placing that person in a certain age layer (as functionalists believe). Studies that confirm this relationship have been made by MacRae (2011), who captured the importance of social interactions and relations for those who suffer from Alzheimer's disease, at an early stage, through the perspective of symbolic interaction. Therefore, among many other things, real support, cooperation, encouraging the patient to create his or her own life, and to sustain his or her identity in these new conditions are issues of great importance.

To my knowledge, in Romania there are not many studies performed on the elderly and even less research concerning the identity of the elderly and their way of coping with retirement. In my previous research, I have identified a few elements of their identity and the roles that can be fulfilled by the elderly within society and their families, which I am going to refer to in the final subchapter.

The present study aims to complete previous data on this topic through a new qualitative research method – the drawing technique.

3 Methodological framework

Qualitative research implies studying people in their natural habitat in order to determine how they live, how they speak and act, and how they deal with the more or less fortunate events in their life (Emerson apud Tutty, Rothery, & Grinnell, 2005). Moreover, it captures elements of daily social life, which cannot be measured by quantitative research (Sumner, 2006).

Gerontologists learn about old age by means of qualitative research. Unlike quantitative research, which is used to look at the relationship among generations (children – adults – elderly people) (Ionescu & Bunescu, 2007; Tîrhaş, 2007; Costaforu, 2005), qualitative research attempts to achieve a better understanding of people and their lives (Quadagno, 1999), their beliefs, and their attitudes (Scârneci, 2006). The techniques used in qualitative research of the elderly have mostly been: the unstructured interview (life story or narrative research) (Lieblich, Tuval-Mashiach, & Zilber, 2006; Atkinson, 2006), to the detriment of other types of interviews such as the structured or semi-structured type. Visual techniques have proven to be useful as well, both because of their ability to overcome language and cultural barriers (Flick, apud Scârneci-Domnişoru, 2016) and for the fact that usually, elderly people tend to face difficulties in expressing their thoughts because of the biological processes of the Third Age stage and because they somehow feel nervous while being in the position of research subjects.

The advantages of a research with visual techniques are described by Weber (apud Scârneci-Domnişoru, 2016): images are more accessible than academic discourses, and they are easier to remember than texts, they can also capture everything that cannot be said through words by facilitating empathy as well. These features are quite important because communication involves feelings and emotions which cannot always be conveyed through words. Images have the capacity to complete verbal communication and to capture feelings which cannot be otherwise expressed.

The research on the elderly by means of visual techniques has developed over the last few years, and studies have concentrated on the image of elderly people's bodies, on life-course aspects, and residential care (Pilcher, Martin, & Williams, 2015). Also, the theme of identity with mature bodybuilders has been addressed by Phoenix (2010). Some of the visual techniques used in these studies are photography, videos, and photo-elicitation.

The present study comes with a new perspective on the identity of the elderly that has yet to be explored in other studies, from my documentation. This paper features the drawing technique which was used with the subjects of my research. I initially wanted to combine multiple visual techniques. Thus, aside from drawing, I intended to use photography as well (one representative photo for the life before and after retirement). However, as a research instrument, photography has its limits. The respondents found it difficult to search for old photos located in less accessible places. In addition, the photos would not be relevant for the present research since they did not express their state of mind before retirement as in the past, pictures were taken only during happy events (wedding, baptize, and anniversary). Also, the respondents did not have recent photos of themselves after retirement, because few elderly people were able to use smart phones to take photos, and even if they had been photographed by the people around them, they would not have been able to print those photos.

As Bagnoli (2009) sustains, drawings are used by subjects when they find it hard to verbally express themselves. In my qualitative research performed for my PhD thesis by using semi-structured interviews, the elderly would often mention that it was better before retirement, without being able to clearly describe and develop the word "better". Some of them recalled material aspects and only a few others talked about friendship and appreciation. This is why I believe that the drawing technique can complete these data for the simple fact that one can freely express thoughts and ideas with a white sheet of paper at hand. It is what Bagnoli calls the evocative nature of an image which generates memories and entertains acts of remembrance.

I have chosen the drawing technique also because retirement is not subject to frequent discussion in terms of feelings and emotions. Generally, people express themselves better by drawing than verbally. Retirement is the most frequent psycho-social phenomenon, aside from entering kindergarten, school, marriage, and getting a job. Its significance is overwhelming for all those who were accustomed to define their usefulness through their profession. The workplace offers a lot of social interaction, and this represents the most important loss. By losing contact with their co-workers, pensioners experience isolation, marginalization, and social uselessness.

Retirement is an attribute of the modern era. After they retire, people become poorer and less prone to social prestige. It is a moment of passage to a new stage which is not easy to cope with, given the fact that there is no other life stage after this. It is as if these people were writing the final chapter of their lives. Researches (Chelcea A., & Chelcea S., 1986) have shown that, in the stories they share, the elderly have the tendency to constantly go back to their youth, to the times of activity and social usefulness. The fact that they are not prepared for their retirement period complicates things and makes them even more difficult to perceive and understand. There are feelings that can be described through the drawing technique, the retiree having the possibility to draw third-life emotions and feelings unknown to others, every discussion focusing on the health chapter. How about you, retiree? How do you perceive your new life as a pensioner? Stuart and Smith (2011, apud Scârneci-Domnişoru, 2016) underline the idea that drawing can be used to explore values and beliefs regarding a variety of aspects, themes, and topics.

Therefore, the aim of the present study is to explore identity transformations of the elderly, by choosing retirement as a point of reference. The research was conducted in Braşov County and the data have been collected from July to October, 2017. The principle was *theoretical sampling*, which allowed me to discover several aspects of the same issue regarding identity transformations triggered by retirement.

To collect the data, I did the following: I split a page in half, on the left side I wrote "me, before retirement" and on the right I wrote "me, after retirement". Paper, pens, and coloured pencils were offered to the participants as they were encouraged to use them in their drawings. It is noticeable that only four subjects drew using coloured pencils, while the rest of them chose crayons or pens. The subjects were told what they had to do, and during the activity there was no outside intervention. Upon finishing, they were asked to describe and interpret their drawings.

They were told about the aim of the research, and all participants gave their verbal consent for their drawings to be used for scientific purposes.

I collected 26 drawings from people ranging from 60 to 84 years old, among which 7 young pensioners were up to 64 years old, 13 people with ages between 65 and 74, and 6 people with ages between 75 and 84. I have taken into account that the current legislation on the status of the elderly (Law 19/2000 updated annually) provides that the standard retirement age is 60 years for women and 65 for men (Law no. 263/2010).

In the sample, I had 9 men and 17 women, 20 of them being married and living with their life partner, and 6 people living alone. Six people live in the rural area and 20 people live in the urban area (Tab. 1).

I introduced more variables in the socio-demographic data to see if they determine identity transformations along with retirement. The most relevant differences were in point of gender, and I shall present them in the following subchapter. I will also highlight a few difficulties that I encountered during the data collection process.

Elderly people are not accustomed to being asked about their lives; much less to being asked to draw them. Thus, my request was met with some sort of resistance. They all stated that they would provide me with any information as long as I did not ask them to draw. They all referred to their lack of talent although they were told from the very beginning that talent was not important as the study did not focus on their artistic abilities. Some of them apologized for their drawings by mentioning a certain medical condition (shaky hands, for instance). In order to better understand their drawing, I asked them to provide extra information about the drawing on the back of the paper. Indeed, I noticed that elderly people express themselves better in writing and in speech than through drawing.

The receptivity of the subjects in point of representing their lives and feelings through drawings was different from one person to another. The reactions generally ranged from participation and active involvement to initial refuse followed by sceptical acceptance. From what I noticed, the desire to participate was stronger in women than in men.

During the data collection, I introduced the data in the NVivo 11 software, performing a primary analysis to identify the maximum number of subjects necessary for my research on several criteria that I found interesting: rural/urban areas of residence and education. I analysed and processed the data relating to the content of the images and also to the interpretations given by their authors. In analysing the collected data, I used both categories described and identified in the literature as well as categories obtained during the process of coding the

Tab. 1: Matrix of socio-demographic data

Subjects	Gender	Living with	Area	Social status	Most recent qualification	Age group
1	Female	Alone	Urban	Other	Faculty	65–74
2	Female	With their life partner	Urban	Married	High school	55–64
3	Female	With their life partner	Urban	Married	Post-high school education	65–74
4	Male	With their life partner	Urban	Married	Post- high school education	65–74
5	Female	With their life partner	Rural	Married	Faculty	65–74
6	Male	With their life partner	Rural	Married	Faculty	65–74
7	Male	With their life partner	Urban	Married	Vocational school	65–74
8	Female	With their life partner	Urban	Married	Post-high school education	65–74
9	Male	With their life partner	Urban	Married	Faculty	65–74
10	Female	Alone	Urban	Widowed	Post-high school education	55–64
11	Female	With their life partner	Urban	Married	Faculty	55–64
12	Female	Alone	Urban	Other	Faculty	65–74
13	Female	Alone	Urban	Widowed	High school	55–64
14	Male	With their life partner	Urban	Married	Vocational school	75–84
15	Female	With their life partner	Urban	Married	High school	75–84
16	Female	Alone	Urban	Widowed	Vocational school	75–84
17	Female	Alone	Urban	Widowed	High school	75–84
18	Male	With their life partner	Rural	Married	Vocational school	75–84
19	Female	With their life partner	Rural	Married	High school	65–74
20	Male	With their life partner	Rural	Married	Vocational school	65–74
21	Male	With their life partner	Urban	Married	Faculty	55–64

Tab. 1: (continued)

Subjects	Gender	Living with	Area	Social status	Most recent qualification	Age group
22	Male	With their life partner	Urban	Married	Vocational school	65–74
23	Female	With their life partner	Urban	Married	Vocational school	65–74
24	Female	With their life partner	Urban	Married	High school	55–64
25	Female	With their life partner	Rural	Married	Gymnasium	75–84
26	Female	With their life partner	Urban	Married	Vocational school	55–64

Fig. 1: Life before retirement. Symbols drawn by women (author's archive)

obtained data. We grouped the data sources into cases, using both drawings and explanations (texts).

When I reached theoretical saturation, I interrupted the data collection process, focusing on the analysis and interpretation of the obtained information.

4 Findings

The drawings ranged from explicit figures in different situations, at the workplace, at home, in their spare time, to symbols which hinted at various activities belonging to the two periods of time which constitute the object of my research.

A first general observation is that women, more than men, used natural symbols to illustrate their lives (trees, flowers, sun, rain, and sea) (Fig. 1 and Fig. 2).

Fig. 2: Life after retirement. Symbols drawn by women (author's archive)

Fig. 3: Me, before and after retirement (up), drawings made by women (down) (author's archive)

Moreover, women used the same symbol when they were asked to represent themselves before and after retirement, as we can see in Fig. 3.

Men also used symbols, but from different registers. They did not use natural elements (trees, flowers, etc.) but technical ones (houses, buildings, cars, and watches) as we can see in Fig. 4 and Fig. 5.

We can state that in their representation, **women are more likely to use humanist symbols, whereas men use technical symbols.**

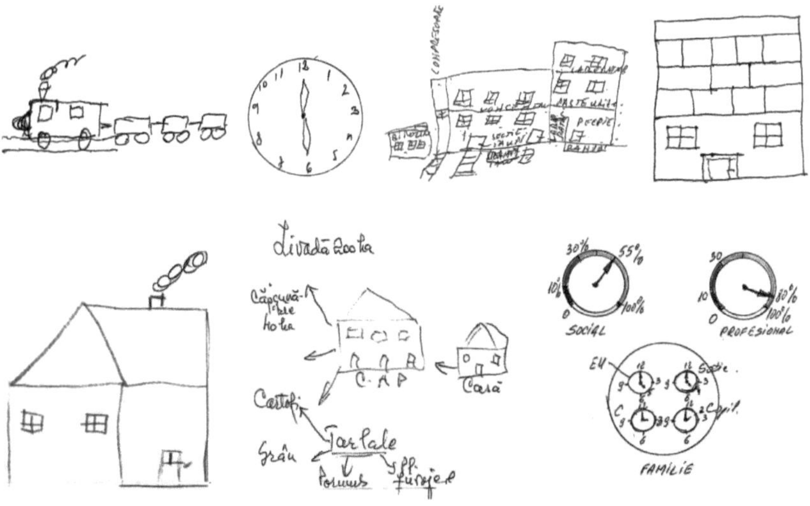

Fig. 4: Life before retirement. Symbols drawn by men (author's archive)

Fig. 5: Life after retirement. Symbols drawn by men (author's archive)

Another difference regards the educational background of the subjects. People with medium education (vocational school, high school) tend to add more details and contour to their drawings, thus making them more eloquent. As we can see in Fig. 6, thoughts are pictured in a clear manner: house, shopping, and garden.

On the other hand, people with higher education (faculty) chose sketches instead of clearly outlined pictures. In addition, they provided explanations on

Fig. 6: Drawing of subjects with medium education (author's archive)

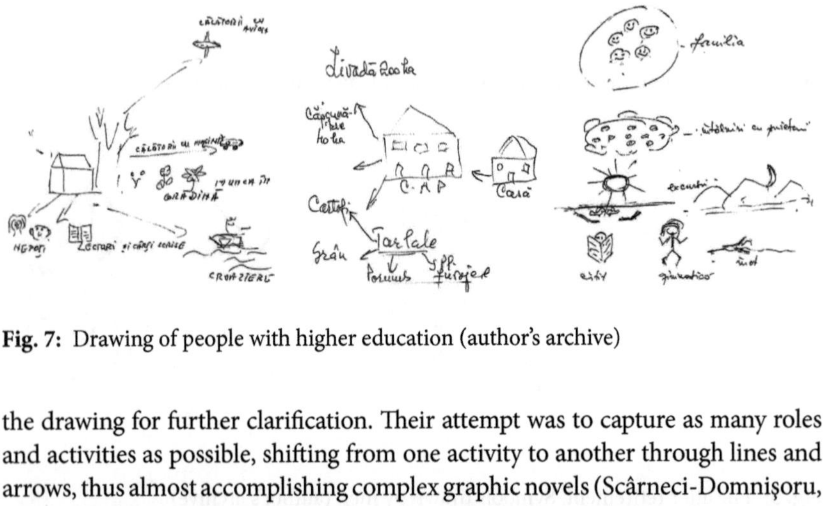

Fig. 7: Drawing of people with higher education (author's archive)

the drawing for further clarification. Their attempt was to capture as many roles and activities as possible, shifting from one activity to another through lines and arrows, thus almost accomplishing complex graphic novels (Scârneci-Domnişoru, 2016), "pictures" with activities from the two distinct periods (Fig. 7).

I also noticed certain differences in drawing according to the subjects' rural or urban area of residence. Although the study features only six people who live in a rural area, I found that all of them drew a house, as a symbol of a close connection between them and that place, as opposed to all subjects living in an urban area, with the exception of one person who drew a block, as a symbol of inactivity.

I analysed and processed the data by cutting the drawings and inserting them into categories and subcategories as they were drawn from both the drawings and their written explanations. I turned to this strategy since I did not have the

Fig. 8: Family role drawn by a woman (author's archive)

certainty that what I could grasp from the drawing coincided with the thoughts of the participants.

For instance, in Fig. 8 I thought that the woman had drawn herself at the office during her active time, which meant that this image should have been placed in the subcategory of professional roles. However, the subject specified, by means of written explanations, that the drawing pictured a baby in a cot which completely changed the subcategory.

I also named the categories and subcategories in accordance with the sociological theories of the Third Age, categories pertaining to some of my previous research based on semi-structured interviews. As I have previously mentioned, I coded the drawings according to the description made by the subjects, thus resulting in the following categories:

As we can see in Tab. 2, certain categories are applicable to both periods, among which we mention roles, leisure, hobbies, and feelings. However, for retirement I mentioned a new category: Third Age problems.

In order to identify their proportion in the drawings, we can examine the hierarchy graphic below (Fig. 9), obtained with the help of the NVivo 11 software, in which I noticed that one's activities become even more diverse after retirement. Therefore, **professional roles** are most predominant in the active period, before retirement. After retirement, these roles start to fade away and to make room for **family or household roles**, being replaced by the role reduction and the category related to "**age-specific problems**".

4.1 Roles

The first category drawn from the texts and sketches is the category of "roles". A discussion about roles implies the four dimensions mentioned in the literature (Marina, 2003; Quadagno, 1999; Diggs, 2008a) that could also be found in the

Tab. 2: Categories resulted after coding the drawings

Categories	Before retirement	After retirement
Roles	Professional Family Household Social	Role reduction Family Household Social
Leisure	Vacations	Vacations Trips Personal care Relaxation
Hobbies	Folkloric research Reading	Watching TV and listening to the radio Reading
Feelings	Positive Negative	Positive Negative
Third Age problems	-	Health problems Ageism

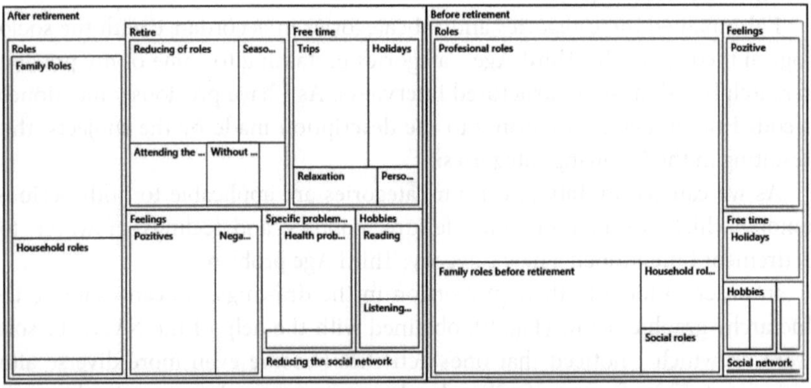

Fig. 9: Activities and roles before and after retirement (author's archive)

drawings of the participants. Thus, as we can observe in Fig. 10, we have professional roles, family roles, household roles, and social roles.

In the following lines, I shall examine each role assigned to each period, as it is illustrated by the drawings and explanations of the subjects.

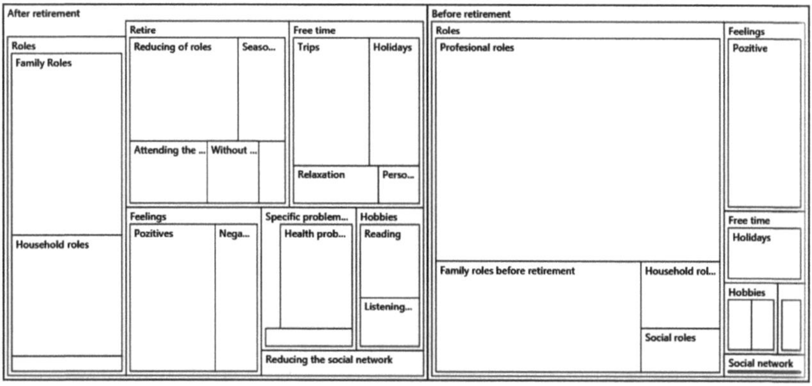

Fig. 10: The roles of the subjects before and after retirement (author's archive)

4.1.1 Professional roles

The analysis of the drawings points out that the **professional role** occupies the largest part of an individual's life before retirement. This role becomes the nucleus of a person's life, all the other roles and activities unfolding according to the time left after fulfilling the professional role. **We can state that life before retirement is focused on work, while the rest of the roles hold a secondary position.**

As expected, all the subjects of the research mention professional roles in relation to the period before retirement. In fact, when subjects began to draw the period before retirement, they first illustrated their professional role and only afterward the other roles.

Most subjects drew their professional roles and interpreted them in terms of **responsibility** towards the position they held (Fig. 11).

Responsibility is differently drawn and expressed by the subjects of the research, according to the feelings they experienced during the exercise of their profession. Women fall into two different categories as some discuss responsibility in terms of **obligation** and other in terms of **workplace usefulness**.

As we can see in Fig. 12, a part of these women drew sad faces or straight-faced figures, "hiding" behind the desk or behind the rain. "I worked in an office, I had responsibilities, and work gave me this feeling of obligation", "I did not feel comfortable with authoritative leadership", "I was stressed out after work, I was drained after commuting and I just couldn't wait to stay home and take care of the children". These are some of the explanations provided by the subjects in respect to their drawings.

Fig. 11: Professional roles before retirement (author's archive)

Fig. 12: Responsibility as obligation – professional roles described by women (author's archive)

Another part of the female respondents often mentioned the word "useful" ("I felt useful"), when discussing their professional roles and the related responsibilities (Fig. 13).

Unlike women, men unanimously described their professional roles in a positive manner, some of them mentioning the **respect** they received from others at work. In addition, they expressed their pride concerning the importance of the roles and responsibilities they had in the active period, as we can see in Fig. 14.

Pride as a feeling generated by the professional role was underlined by the subjects who added some written information as well. The text describes workplace responsibilities meant to highlight the important position the subjects held during their active period. They speak about **tasks**: "I tried to be punctual at

Fig. 13: Workplace usefulness (author's archive)

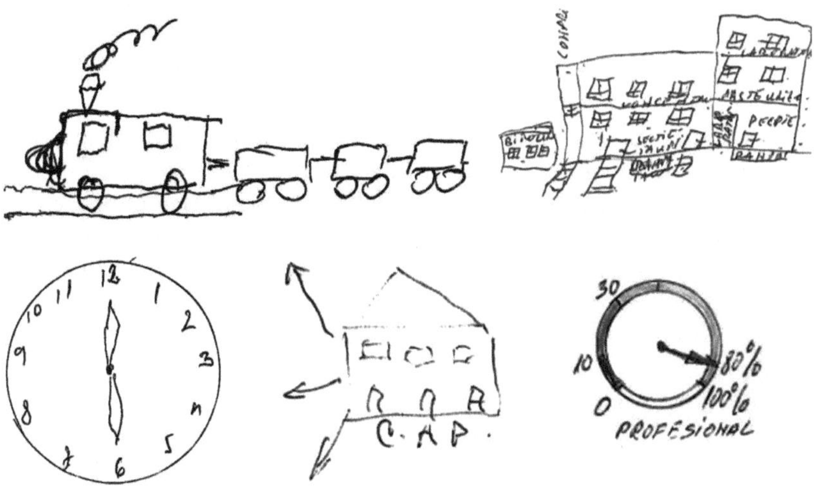

Fig. 14: Professional roles illustrated by men (author's archive)

Fig. 15: Withdrawal, drawn by men (author's archive)

work and to handle all my tasks well" and **performance**: "professional competence represents the amount of skills one possesses and uses at work and in life", "as the chief engineer of a big Agricultural Production Cooperative (CAP), I was always in the middle of things, being busy doing something day and night, even during public holidays. I developed a livestock sector; I set up 200 ha of intensive orchard, 40 ha of strawberry plantation and an industrial woodworking industry, the Agricultural Production Cooperative having its own forest. I had a lot of money and my workers were well paid".

Also, a part of the male subjects compare the two periods by providing further explanation: "As a young man I used to be a leader….now I'm being led".

For men, it seems that retirement changes everything. Men drew their active period by illustrating their professional roles which have disappeared after retirement, and this brought along the necessity to adapt to a new situation by engaging in other roles. Their drawings talk about **withdrawal**, a term which appears in the disengagement theory (Marina, 2003; Quadagno, 1999; Diggs, 2008a) (Fig. 15).

As we can see from the drawings, withdrawal seems to replace the professional role. A part of the subjects illustrated the retirement period as an involution which caused role reductions, an increased participation at church activities, or even a lack of activity on the whole.

The subjects added more information to the drawings, most of them talking about the reduction of roles and the feeling of uselessness: "During my first months as a retiree, I panicked, I felt useless" or "you just sit there and wait for your pension month after month".

One noticeable aspect is that only a few subjects represented this withdrawal in a negative manner. Most of them considered withdrawal a normal and natural stage of life.

However, taking into consideration all the other categories drawn from their sketches, we cannot state that the theory of disengagement applies to men, despite the fact that they do mention withdrawal. Yet, they embraced withdrawal from the work field, rapidly adapting to the new situation. Thus, they redefined their remaining roles, redirecting their activities towards family and household (gardening, fruit growing). This implies a reconstruction of identity during retirement, reminding more about **the theory of symbolic interactionism**.

Therefore, we can conclude that **the definition of professional roles is somehow gender-related. Women associate workplace responsibility with the concepts of obligation and usefulness, while men talk about work with pride and respect**.

4.1.2 Family roles

The following roles drawn from the sketches are family roles. The drawings are outlined before and after retirement and their proportions are fairly equal.

By analysing the drawings, I noticed that for the period before retirement, family roles are mostly drawn by women. According to Figs. 16 and 17, only one man drew family roles.

On the other hand, for the period after retirement, family roles are equally mentioned by men and women (Fig. 18).

This indicates that men tend to focus more on their families after retirement, just as I noticed in my previous research. Ionescu and Bunescu (2007) drew the same conclusion in their studies concerning the relationship between generations by showing that, for all generations, **family fulfilment** was extremely important, **especially for adults and older people**.

Thus, **family represents an important dimension for men and women, both before and after retirement, yet men seem to cast a whole new light upon their families only after retirement**.

Another aspect drawn from the sketches is the idea that women seem to experiment **a continuous course of their family roles**. In Fig. 19, they described these roles for both periods.

In my previous study, women were included in the disengagement theory. However, in the present paper, when analysing the drawings, I noticed that women do not meet the universality principle. The theory of disengagement implies that disengagement is universal and can be found in all societies. However, there are certain differences in perceiving the ageing phenomenon according to a study

Fig. 16: Family roles before retirement, drawn by women (author's archive)

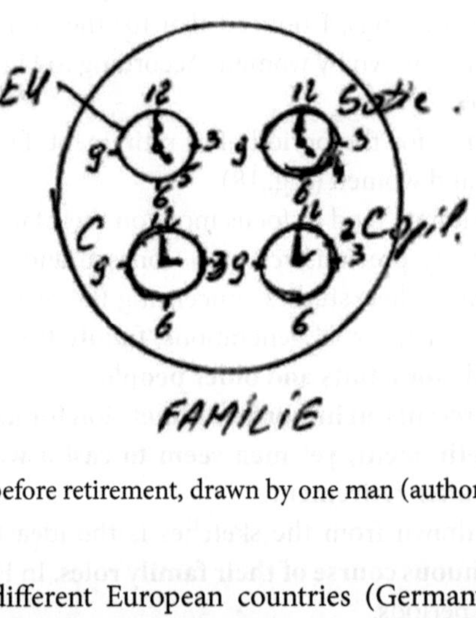

Fig. 17: Family roles before retirement, drawn by one man (author's archive)

performed in five different European countries (Germany, Hungary, Latvia, Sweden, and Great Britain). This research pursued the relationship between the social environment and Third Age health (Sixsmith et al., 2014).

The findings pointed out that gender played an important role in triggering different experiences and attitudes towards the ageing process. Consequently, for women, the household role implies providing food and maintaining an active,

Fig. 18: Family roles after retirement, drawn by men and women (author's archive)

Fig. 19: Drawings presenting the continuity of family roles with women. On the left side, before retirement. On the right, after retirement (author's archive)

social, and a family life, with the roles of wives and mothers being of great importance. For men, ageing healthily and performing activities such as gardening or decorating are part of their strategy to stay in shape, in addition to a specific diet. **The present study confirms that women experience family and household roles before and after retirement, an aspect which makes them fall into the continuity theory.**

My previous study indicated that women are more eager to retire than men, especially because of the different ways in which they perceive the status of a retiree (Bódi, 2017). Women tend to adapt easier to certain situations, being able to deal with family and household matters after retirement, just as they did during their active period.

Their adaptability can be explained by the process of role continuity from one period to another, as women tend to deal with household and family roles in both periods. If the drawings before retirement feature their life partner and children, their after-retirement drawings feature their grandchildren.

Some of the family roles which can help the elderly regain their self-esteem entails raising and educating their grandchildren. Being a grandfather or grandmother is an important source of identity for older people (Muntean, 2006). Even in countries such as the United States where the nuclear family is predominant, most elderly people live with their grandchildren and 30 % of them are responsible for the care and education of their grandsons or granddaughters (Vierck & Hodges, 2005). Studies indicate that grandparents deal with the negative effects of ageing better than old people without grandchildren (Dearborn, 2008).

In the present research, almost all subjects fulfil the roles of grandparents, and most of them drew and described activities performed with their grandchildren.

Figure 20 indicates the presence of active grandparents who are very much involved in various activities with their grandchildren. Moreover, they added texts to the drawings, revealing their desire to be an active part in their grandchildren's life: " I spend a lot of time with my elder grandson", "children and grandchildren are the symbol of God's gift to us", "taking care of grandchildren while commuting", "much happier now that I am a grandmother", "a stroll with my grandchildren", " I spend a part of my time with my children and with my beloved grandson, Matei", "I'm always around my grandson, I go to the playground with him, we're learning English together and it gives me great joy to hear him speak", or " I continued to take care of my grandchildren, to take them to and to pick them up from school".

The present research which illustrates the involvement of older people in raising and educating grandchildren supplements my prior interview-based

Fig. 20: Activities performed with grandchildren (author's archive)

Fig. 21: Household roles before and after retirement, drawn by women (author's archive)

research. Both studies show that more than a half of female respondents fall into the category of **involved grandparents** (fulfilling roles of a parental nature in some cases) and **companions** (grandparents who focus on the emotional well-being of their grandchildren, on leisure activities and friendly interaction) (Bódi, 2017).

We can therefore state that family represents an important source of identity, especially after retirement.

4.1.3 Household roles

Similar to the family roles depicted previously, **household roles are drawn for both periods only by women.** Figures 21 and 22 feature specific household

Fig. 22: Household roles after retirement, drawn by women (author's archive)

Fig. 23: Household roles drawn by men, after retirement (author's archive)

elements such as a house, a kitchen table, groceries, hangers, gardens, and flowers.

Unlike women, **men drew household roles only for the after-retirement period** (Fig. 23).

One aspect worth mentioning is that men who drew household roles come from a rural environment or temporarily live in the countryside (during spring, summer, and autumn). They also added bits and pieces of additional information to their drawings: "we retreated to the countryside from April to October, in Dobârlău where we have a vacation home with a land of 2000 square meters. Here we grow vegetables, we plant flowers, we mow the lawn, we do some gardening" or "I usually keep myself busy with my vegetable garden or with fruit growing".

Similar to the family roles, we notice **a continuity of the household roles with women**. On the other hand, **for men, household roles are present only after retirement and only for those living in the countryside.**

Fig. 24: The decrease of the social network in the view of one of the subjects (author's archive)

4.1.4 Social roles

I shall now further discuss about one of the important dimensions which defines identity, namely social roles, in close connection with the social relationships of the elderly.

My previous research showed that social roles do not necessarily decrease, but reconfigure, as the people with whom the elderly interact change over time. Thus, we do not speak about a reduction of social relationships but a change in the social network, as elderly people engage more in interactions with family members, neighbours, doctors, and the postman.

By analysing their drawings, I could see that, with a few exceptions, all subjects failed to mention this particular aspect of their life.

After interpreting the drawings of the subjects who depicted their social roles, I noticed a decrease in their social network after retirement.

According to Fig. 24, we can observe a decrease in the social sphere (in the drawing on the right there are fewer trees), an aspect confirmed by the additional text which conveys sadness triggered by the "empty nest" stage (children becoming adults): "the number of people I interact with significantly decreased since the children got married. We are getting lonelier by the day". Other subjects mentioned the difficulty of making new friends at the Third Age stage: "it is difficult to make new acquaintances late in life".

On the other hand, the decrease of the social network is perceived by one of the subjects as a natural and normal act: "the relationship with society (…) evolves differently but normally for the usual course of life".

Fig. 25: Social roles, before (left) and after retirement (right) (author's archive)

The literature in the field indicates that elderly people who experience "the empty nest" syndrome should redefine their family identity by pursuing new goals in their life, such as establishing **social and community networks** (Tummala & Hernandez, 2008). In addition, several studies point out that there is a strong link between health, social support, and social interaction in the lives of the elderly (Cloutier-Fisher, Kobayashi, & Smith, 2011; Hawton et al., 2011; MacRae, 2011).

Although some of the subjects lived alone, in the present study I did not encounter cases of social isolation as predictable risk for the elderly. Moreover, all drawings indicated that social relationships have been kept throughout the two stages (Fig. 25).

Corelating these data with socio-demographic data, we noticed that those who illustrated their social networks for the two analysed periods have a higher level of education (faculty), unlike those who talk about diminishing the social network and who hold a level of medium education (vocational school or high school).

Therefore, we can conclude that for people with medium education, social interaction tends to fade away over time after retirement, while people with higher education maintain their relationships and their social roles.

4.2 Leisure

The second category of my analysis is represented by leisure. Leisure is a dimension which appears in the literature as being specific to elderly people, most discussions revolving around the term "loisir".

Leisure is illustrated by the respondents in respect to both periods. However, free time for the period before retirement was only drawn by three female subjects, in remembrance of their holidays (Fig. 26).

Fig. 26: Leisure activities before retirement (author's archive)

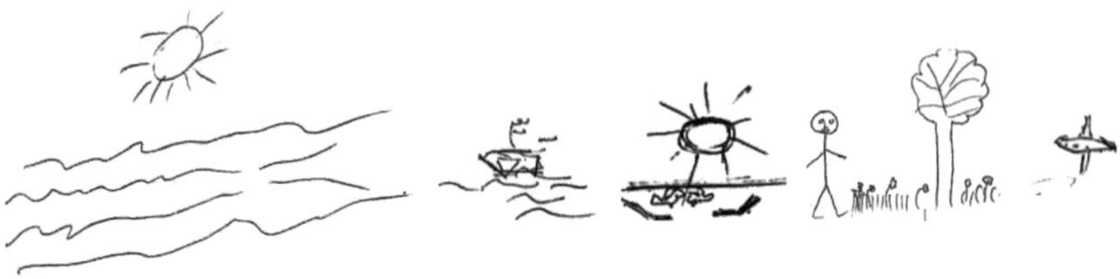

Fig. 27: Leisure activities after retirement (author's archive)

For the period after retirement, half the subjects (13) illustrated their leisure activities, which is normal since retirement brings more free time with it. The subjects illustrated their free time through various relaxation activities such as trips, vacations, and journeys (Fig. 27).

The respondents talked about the increase in their spare time after retirement, in a positive way, thus having "the possibility to have more time for me", as one female subject stated. Leisure time gains an entire new perspective after retirement, being improved by numerous relaxation activities.

Another leisure time after retirement from the subjects' drawings is watching TV shows.

As we can see in Fig. 28, this activity was mentioned by people who live alone and try to spend their free time by watching TV shows.

Guillemard (apud Fontaine, 2008) conceived a typology of retirement styles and pensioners, taking into account the degree of social engagement and types of activities. The results were as follows:

Fig. 28: Watching TV, as a leisure activity after retirement (author's archive)

- Retirement-pension characterized by: the narrowing of the social sphere and space of the individual, lack of projects, social relations, and activities;
- Third Age-pension characterized by the fact that the pensioner has a wide social network with productive activities;
- Leisure/family-pension, in which the retiree engages in family activities bearing an important role in sustaining the family structure and also developing many leisure activities regarding culture, sports, and trips;
- Claim-pension with the following elements: the pensioner disputes the status of the elderly in modern society which contributes to the feeling of social and political exclusion; the retiree prefers to establish relationships with other pensioners;
- Participation-pension: the individual permeates society by television consumption.

Taking the aforementioned family roles into consideration, we notice that the subjects of the present research fall into two retirement styles: those who have a family fall into the category of leisure/family-pension and single people fall into the category of participation-pension.

The conclusions of the present study overlap with those of my previous research as far as leisure is concerned. Therefore, **leisure is a specific category of the after-retirement period, and it implies recreation by taking trips, going on vacations, or watching TV**.

4.3 Hobbies

Another category revealed by data processing is the one related to hobbies. Hobbies were illustrated only by three subjects and, as we can see in Figs. 29 and 30, reading is one of them: "I used to love books, they were my best friends and

Fig. 29: Reading as hobby, before retirement (author's archive)

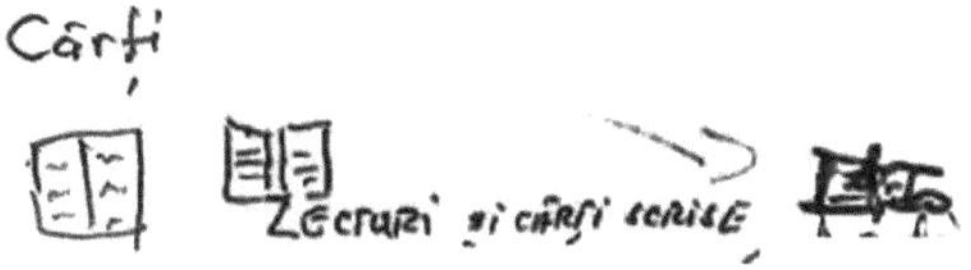

Fig. 30: Reading as passion, after retirement (author's archive)

I used to spend a fortune on them", stated one of the subjects. Also, one of the subjects mentioned folkloric research as a hobby.

By analysing the drawings, we notice that hobbies are to be found before and after retirement, which implies a certain degree of continuity.

The existence of hobbies is seen as a positive aspect for the success of the ageing process described by the activity theory. Studies (Drew, 1997) show that pensioners are able to remain active by maintaining their relationships with their friends and family, and by seeking new activities and practising their hobbies. Moreover, people who prepare for the moment of retirement are better equipped for coping with it, and retirement no longer becomes a loss due to the intervention of several motivational factors such as extraprofessional activities (hobbies) (Popovici, 2001).

My previous research features more hobbies than this research. Therefore, if in my previous study I identified hobbies such as painting, sewing, sports, fishing, and volunteer work; in the present study reading is the only mentioned hobby. Both studies showed that **people who had a hobby before retirement continued to practise it after retirement.**

4.4 Feelings

Another category drawn from the sketches is the one regarding "feelings".

In most cases, the drawings mirror positive feelings related to the period before retirement, with the exception of a few subjects who perceived the professional role as an obligation.

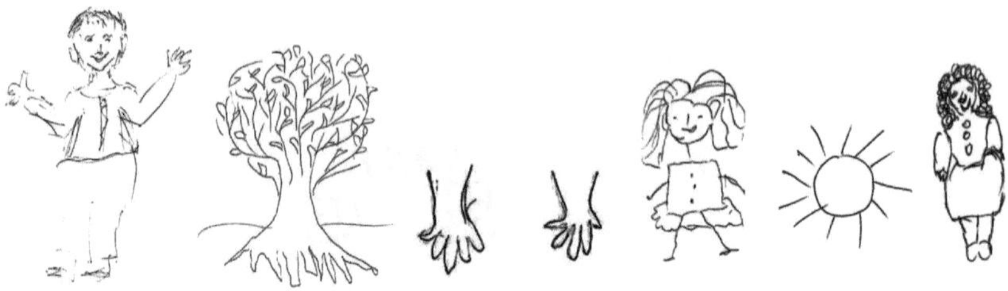

Fig. 31: Positive feelings before retirement (author's archive)

Fig. 32: Negative feelings after retirement (author's archive)

In Fig. 31 we notice trees that burst into bloom, the sun, and the smiley face, all of these conveying satisfaction in relation to the period before retirement.

However, the after-retirement period features a few negative feelings, as we can see in Fig. 32.

These negative feelings are conveyed by sad faces, leafless trees, clouds, and flowers without petals. The retirement period also brings health-related problems. As subjects point out: "old age is getting more and more difficult to bear", "there are many rainy days", or "you just can't seem to notice when time goes by".

On the other hand, there were a few subjects who just could not wait to retire and to fully enjoy their free time: "I feel like I have more free time on my hands

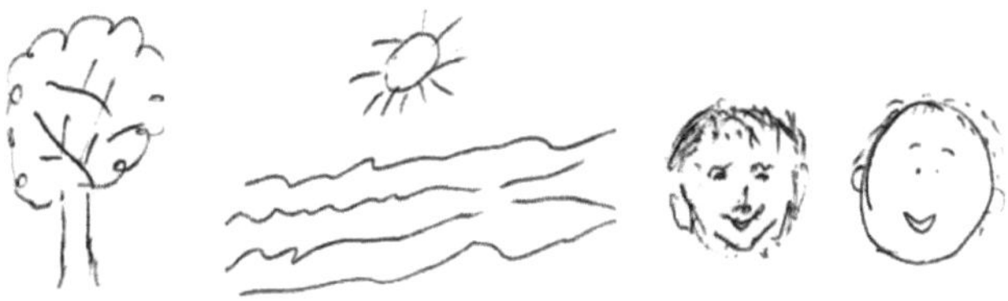

Fig. 33: Positive feelings after retirement (author's archive)

Fig. 34: Retirement period for women (author's archive)

to handle almost anything". As we can see in Fig. 33, there are happy faces, trees, the sun, the sea, and other elements which describe what the subjects also conveyed through writing: peace, satisfaction, safety, joy, freedom, and spare time.

Another mentionable aspect would be **the desire to retire** and the feeling that retirement brings.

By analysing the drawings and explanations, we can state that **women experience the need to retire more often than men.**

In Fig. 34 we see that the sun is present in most women's drawings for the after-retirement period suggesting a rapid adaptation to the new situation, as opposed to men's drawings where this element is absent. This desire is enhanced by the explanation provided by the female respondents: "I couldn't wait to stay home. Now I am calm, peaceful and secure. I'm OK".

We can conclude that the period before retirement is characterized by positive feelings, while the after-retirement period is equally characterized by positive feelings (especially in women) and negative feelings.

4.5 Third Age problems

Another distinct category emerging from my analysis is related to "Third Age problems", especially for the after-retirement period. Two problems were highlighted here, namely health problems and ageism.

Fig. 35: Third Age problems (author's archive)

Fig. 36: Ageism, drawn by a woman (author's archive)

Although I expected health issues to be mentioned more often by my subjects since ageing is marked by polypathology (more associated diseases) (Capisizu, 2014), only five respondents mentioned this aspect. This means that it is not a vital component of the present research as it does not seem to be the object of the subjects' concern, although the literature reminds us that the elderly are the largest category of medical services consumers (Rotariu, 2009).

The drawings in Fig. 35 illustrate health problems experienced after retirement. Although these drawings are suggestive, the respondents provide additional information: "health issues occurred", "old age is getting more and more difficult to bear", "there are many rainy days", or "the old tree has lost its vigour".

The literature which deals with the elderly has at least one chapter which describes health problems and yet, they were not the main focus in my research. In both my studies, health problems were mentioned by just a few subjects without insisting on them very much.

Ageism was signalled by one subject only, but it is worth remembering it since most people of old age are faced with this problem in today's society (Fig. 36).

This image features the sun with clouds, drawn by a respondent who provided additional information: "there are many rainy days (...) you are ignored most of the time".

Although research has shown that those who live in rural environments are less predisposed to ageism (Special Eurobarometer 378, 2012), the person who mentioned this phenomenon lives in the countryside.

In the literature, ageism is usually associated to older people, but studies (Anderson, 2008) indicate that other age groups are targeted as well (teenagers, for instance).

The process of stereotyping of and discrimination against individuals or groups on the basis of their age known as ageism generally leads to social marginalization and eventually social exclusion. Abell (2005) argues that more than any other discriminated group, the prejudice against old people is the most powerful force of ageism in the United States of America.

By analysing this category, we can state that for the subjects of this research health problems are Third Age problems which are not altogether very important in the view of the respondents.

5 Conclusions

The present study represents my attempt to supplement the theoretical existing data and other data from my previous research concerning identity transformations at the Third Age. One of my goals was to examine potential identity transformations triggered by retirement and to analyse the roles of an elderly person by means of the drawing technique.

The data from this research partially overlap with the conclusions of my previous studies which pointed out that the main identity source of an individual is related to the family and family roles, for the period before retirement and also for the after-retirement stage. The present study shows that **before retirement, the main identity source for men is related to work and after retirement, the main identity source is related to family**.

It is also worth mentioning that identity transformations at the Third Age are different according to socio-demographic data. Retirement is experienced differently according to age, type of environment, and education. The most important difference in perceiving the shift from an active period to a passive period is gender-related: **women perceive the ageing process differently than men**.

In addition, the results of the research contradicted some of the conclusions of my previous studies. Thus, in the present study **elderly women fall into the category of the continuity theory and men into the one of symbolic**

interactionism, as opposed to my previous research that was based on semi-structured interviews which illustrated how women belonged to the disengagement theory while men belonged to the activity theory.

We can explain these differences between the two studies by analysing the methods: semi-structured interviews versus the drawing technique, and by analysing the time of the research, as the previous study was performed nine years ago on another generation with different lifestyles.

On the other hand, the present research brings forth new aspects regarding the continuity theory which was criticized by feminist studies because it focused mostly on men. **This study demonstrates that women too are subjects to the continuity theory by fulfilling family roles and household roles before and after retirement.**

One of the limits of this study is represented by the fact that the sample did not feature the categories of the institutionalized elderly and the dependent elderly.

The present research confirms the need for qualitative research on elderly people, meant to supplement other quantitative studies. Visual methods and techniques can bring forth new aspects, questions, hypotheses, and perspectives on this target group. New techniques are, of course, needed to complete the existing data.

In my future studies, I would extend my methods in working with the elderly by using photography and film, and I would also like to further document ageism by means of visual techniques.

The present research features a few elements aimed at supplementing the current research on identity transformations triggered by retirement. It is my belief that visual methods and techniques bring elements of originality and depth which are not always revealed by interviews or questionnaires, hence the importance of studying the identity of the elderly by means of these techniques meant to unveil their untold life stories.

Bibliography

Abell, S.C. (2005). Ageism. In J.K. Roth (Ed.), *Ethics* (pp. 37–38). California: Salem Press, Inc.

Anderson, T.T. (2008). Ageism. In S. Loue & M. Sajatovic (Eds.), *Encyclopedia of Ageing and Public Health* (pp. 103–105). New York: Springer Science+Business Media.

Atchley, R. (1989). A Continuity Theory of Normal Aging. *The Gerontologist, 29*(2), 183–190. doi: 10.1093/geront/29.2.183.

Atkinson, R. (2006). *Povestea vieţii: interviul* [*The Story of Life: The Interview*]. Iaşi: Polirom.

Bagnoli, A. (2009). Beyond the Standard Interview: The Use of Graphic Elicitation and Arts-Based Methods. *Qualitative Research, 9*(5), 547–570. doi: 10.1177/1468794109343625.

Băran-Pescaru, A. (2004). *Familia azi. O perspectivă sociopedagogică* [The Family Today. A Sociopedagogical Perspective]. Bucureşti: Aramis.

Bódi, D.C. (2012). The Third Age Identity Crisis - Truth or Dare. *Bulletin of the Transilvania University of Braşov, Series VII: Social Sciences and Law*, 5(54) No. 2, 121–126.

Bódi, D.C. (2017). *Persoanele vârstnice. Resursă importantă în familie şi în societate* [*The Elderly. An Important Resource in the Family and Society*]. Iaşi: The European Institute.

Bucur, V., & Maciovan, A. (2003). "Probleme ale vârstei a treia" [Problems of the Third Age]. In G. Neamţu (Ed.), *Tratat de asistenţă socială* [*Handbook of Social Work*] (pp. 907–958). Iaşi: Polirom.

Capisizu, A. (2014). *Polipatologie şi principii terapeutice în geriatrie* [*Polypathology and Therapeutic Principles in Geriatrics*]. Bucureşti: Medical Publishing House.

Chelcea, A., & Chelcea, S. (1986). *Cunoaşterea de sine – condiţie a înţelepciunii* [*The Self-Knowledge - Condition of Wisdom*]. Bucureşti: Albatros.

Cloutier-Fisher, D., Kobayashi, K., & Smith, A. (2011). The Subjective Dimension of Social Isolation: A Qualitative Investigation of Older Adults' Experiences in Small Social Support Networks. *Journal of Aging Studies, 25*(4), 407–414. doi: 10.1016/j.jaging.2011.03.012.

Costaforu, X. (2005). *Cercetarea monografică a familiei* [*The Family Monograph Research*]. Bucureşti: Tritonic.

Dearborn, M. (2008). Family Relationships. In S. Loue & M. Sajatovic (Eds.), *Encyclopedia of Ageing and Public Health* (pp. 352–354). New York: Springer Science+Business Media.

Diggs, J. (2008a). Activity Theory of Ageing. In S. Loue & M. Sajatovic (Eds.), *Encyclopedia of Ageing and Public Health* (pp. 79–81). New York: Springer Science+Business Media.

Diggs, J. (2008b). The Continuity Theory of Ageing. In S. Loue & M. Sajatovic (Eds.), *Encyclopedia of Ageing and Public Health* (pp. 233–255). New York: Springer Science+Business Media.

Dolinar, T. (2008). Biology of Ageing. In S. Loue & M. Sajatovic (Eds.). *Encyclopedia of Ageing and Public Health* (pp. 1–10). New York: Springer Science+Business Media.

Drew, A. (1997). Recreation and Leisure Activities. In C. McMahon & R. Isaacs (Eds.), *Care of the Older Person. A Handbook for Care Assistants* (pp. 256–289). Oxford [England], Cambridge, Mass., USA: Blackwell Science.

Dubar, C. (2003). *Criza identităţilor. Interpretarea unei mutaţii* [*The Identity Crisis. Interpreting a Mutation*]. Chişinău: The Science.

Fontaine, R. (2008). *Psihologia îmbătrânirii* [*The Psychology of Aging*]. Iaşi: Polirom.

Giddens, A. (1997). *Modernity and Self-Identity*. Cambridge: Polity Press.

Gideon, C.A. (2008). Generativity. In S. Loue & M. Sajatovic (Eds.), *Encyclopedia of Ageing and Public Health* (pp. 387–388). New York: Springer Science+Business Media.

Gotea, M. (2014). *Reţeaua socială şi conflictul marital* [*The Social Network and the Marital Conflict*]. Cluj-Napoca: The Cluj University Press.

Hawton, A., Green, C., Dickens, A.P., Richards, S.H., Taylor, R.S., Edwards, R., Greaves, C.J., & Campbell, J.L. (2011). The Impact of Social Isolation on the Health Status and Health-Related Quality of Life of Older People. *Quality of Life Research, 20*(1), 57–67. doi: 10.1007/s11136-010-9717-2.

Iluţ, P. (2009). *Psihologie socială şi sociopsihologie. Teme recurente şi noi viziuni* [*Social Psychology and Sociopsychology. Recurring Themes and New Visions*]. Iaşi: Polirom.

Ionescu, M., & Bunescu, G. (Eds.) (2007). *Raporturile între generaţii. Aspecte educaţionale* [*Intergenerational Relationships. Educational Aspects*]. Bucureşti: Institute of Educational Sciences, Laboratory of Education Theory. Law no. 263/2010. Retrieved from http://www.mmuncii.ro/pub/imagemanager/images/file/Legislatie/LEGI/L263-2010.pdf

Lieblich, A., Tuval-Mashiach, R., & Zilber, T. (2006). *Cercetarea narativă: citire, analiză şi interpretare* [*The Narrative Research: Reading, Analysis and Interpretation*]. Iaşi: Polirom.

MacRae, H. (2011). Self and Other: The Importance of Social Interaction and Social Relationships in Shaping the Experience of Early-Stage Alzheimer's Disease. *Journal of Aging Studies, 25*(4), 445–456. doi: 10.1016/j.jaging.2011.06.001.

Manea, L. (2000). *Protecţia socială a persoanelor cu handicap* [*The Social Protection of the People with Disabilities*]. Bucharest: Publishing House and Press SANSA s.r.l.

Marina, L. (2003). *Rămânerea în societate-monografii ale îmbătrânirii* [*Remaining in Society – the Monographs of Aging*]. Deva: Emia.

Marshall, G. (Ed.) (2003). *Dicţionar de sociologie* [*Dictionary of Sociology*]. Bucureşti: Univers Enciclopedic.

May, C., & Cooper, A. (1995). Personal Identity and Social Change: Some Theoretical Considerations. *Acta Sociologica*, *38*(1), 75–85. doi: 10.1177/000169939503800106.

Minichiello, V., Browne, J., & Kendig, H. (2000). Perceptions and Consequences of Ageism: Views of Older People. *Ageing and Society*, *20*(3), 253–278. Retrieved from https://www.cambridge.org/core/journals/ageing-and-society/article/perceptions-and-consequences-of-ageism-views-of-older-people/0F607565509B9999B82B3A0FF4F8AADE

Muntean, A. (2006). *Psihologia dezvoltării umane* [*The Psychology of Human Development*]. Iaşi: Polirom.

Phoenix, C. (2010). Auto-Photography in Aging Studies: Exploring Issues of Identity Construction in Mature Bodybuilders. *Journal of Aging Studies*, *24*(3), 167–180. doi: 10.1016/j.jaging.2008.12.007.

Pilcher, K., Martin, W., & Williams, V. (2016). Issues of Collaboration, Representation, Meaning and Emotions: Utilising Participant-Led Visual Diaries to Capture the Everyday Lives of People in Mid to Later Life. *International Journal of Social Research Methodology*, *19*(6), 677–692. doi: 10.1080/13645579.2015.1086199.

Popovici, A. (2001). Pensionarea – pierdere sau câstig? [The Retirement - Loss or Gain?]. In D. Gal (Ed.). *Vine o zi … Eseuri pe teme gerontologice* [*One Day Comes … Essays on Gerontological Themes*] (pp.19–22). Cluj-Napoca: The Cluj University Press.

Quadagno, J. (1999). *Aging and the Life Course*. United States of America: The McGraw-Hill Companies.

Rotariu, T. (2009). *Demografie şi sociologia populaţiei* [*Demography and the Sociology of the Population*]. Iaşi: Polirom.

Scârneci, F. (2006). *Îndrumar de cercetare calitativă în ştiinţele socio-umane* [*Qualitative Research Guidance in the Socio-human Sciences*]. Braşov: Transylvania University Publishing House.

Scârneci-Domnişoru, F. (2016). *Datele vizuale în cercetarea socială* [*Visual Data in Social Research*]. Cluj-Napoca: The Cluj University Press.

Sixsmith, J., Sixsmith, A., Malmgren Fänge, A., Naumann, D., Kucsera, C., Tomsone, S., Haak, M., Dahlin-Ivanoff, S., & Woolrych, R., (2014). Healthy Ageing and Home: The Perspectives of Very Old People in Five European Countries. *Social Science & Medicine* *106*(1–9). doi: 10.1016/j.socscimed.2014.01.006.

Special Eurobarometer 378 (2012). *Active aging*. Retrieved from http://ec.europa.eu/commfrontoffice/publicopinion/archives/ebs/ebs_378_en.pdf

Sumner, M. (2006). Qualitative Research. In V. Jupp (Ed.). *The Sage Dictionary of Social Research Methods* (pp. 248–250). London: SAGE Publications Ltd.

Tîrhaş, C. (2007). Modele de schimb intergeneraţional în familia transilvană – o analiză a claselor latente în structura sociodemografică a actorilor schimbului [Intergenerational Exchange Models in the Transylvanian Family - An Analysis of the Latent Classes in the Sociodemographic Structure of the Exchange Actors]. In C. Coman (Ed.). *International Social Sciences Colloquy - ACUM 2006* (pp. 335–347). Braşov: Publishing House of "Transylvania".

Tummala, A., & Hernandez, J. (2008). Identity. In S. Loue & M. Sajatovic (Eds.), *Encyclopedia of Ageing and Public Health* (pp. 453–454). New York: Springer Science+Business Media.

Tutty, M.L., Rothery, A.M., & Grinnell, Jr. M.R. (2005). *Cercetarea calitativă în asistenţă socială* [*Qualitative Research in Social Work*]. Iaşi: Polirom.

Vierck, E., & Hodges, K. (2005). *Aging: Lifestyles, Work, and Money*. Westport: Greenwood Press.

Daniela Sorea

VI God, as the children of Romania draw It

Abstract: The chapter focuses on Romanian children's religiosity. It is about how Romanian children represent God and about the relation between this representation and evolution directions of contemporary Western religiosity. The chapter contains the results of the thematic analysis of 186 drawings (accompanied by short explanatory comments) of six- and seven-year-old children from the south-east of Transylvania. The chosen age range corresponds to the time when children in Romania start going to school, so that the results are not tainted by the way Religion is approached as a subject in school. Thus, the results also provide information on the religiosity of children's family members. The analysis has highlighted that the children who drew God are not atheist and, since those who tell them about God are their parents, nor are these. The God of children is friendly and cheerful, the drawings strengthen the status of "a religion of joy" attributed to Orthodoxy as a result of its soteriological orientation towards Resurrection. The differences between the children's approaches to the theme in 2004 and 2016 point to a widening of spirituality in the communities the drawers come from.

Keywords: children's religiosity, drawings, thematic analysis, Orthodoxy, spirituality

1 Introductory notes

References to contemporary Western religiosity revolve (approvingly or critically) around secularization. The latter intensifies atheism (Bainbridge, 2011), but it also evolves towards a post-secular stage in which good social practice models retrieve the values of Christianity (Rorty and Vattimo, 2008) and where the boundary between the sacred and the profane is flexible (Nikiforova, 2017; Pfister, 2017).

Contemporary Western religiosity is also characterized by the revitalization of some pre-Christian local faiths and practices (Rountree, 2014) and the spread of new, imported forms of spirituality (Hamberg, 2011; Heelas, 2011). In the former socialist European states, these features are interwoven with the effects of the passage from a programmatically atheist political regime.

Romania is one of these former communist states, and the majority of its people are of Orthodox confession. Its current religiosity level was deemed as very high at the European level (http://www.ucatholic.com/blog/10-revealing-maps-religion-europe), and the Romanian Orthodox Church has long ranked among the institutions that people trust. The current study focuses on Romanian children's religiosity. It is elaborated as answer of the following research questions: *How do Romanian children picture God?* and *How does Romanian children's religiosity relate to the evolution directions of contemporary Western religiosity?* The results of the research on six- and seven-year-old children, that is pre-school and very young pupils in Romania, have implicitly outlined their parents' and grandparents' religiosity, highlighting the relation between Romanian Orthodox religiosity and Western religiosity.

2 Methodological remarks

In order to accomplish the research goals (that have already been presented in the previous chapter as research questions), I employed the drawing technique. This option is mainly justified by its adequacy to children's age (Scârneci-Domnişoru, 2016), as well as by people's common reluctance to talk about their religious faith. Children draw a lot and with joy. They do not share adults' inhibitions concerning the aesthetic quality of their drawings, nor their doubts on the correct conveyance of information via elicited images. At the same time, children face difficulties answering abstract questions and when they do, they are not very eloquent since their capacity to juggle with concepts is in its developing stage. On the other hand, religion and religiosity are research topics that, generally speaking, do not lead to trustworthy results in terms of sociological enquiry. To efficiently approach those, researchers must avoid direct questions that can generate rejection (Wilson, 2000). I considered that the drawing technique as a research method employed in a study whose subjects are children is a comfortable manner to overcome all of the aforementioned difficulties and to collect data in a more efficient manner. The graphic elicitation potential of the social documents generated upon request is also appropriate in terms of drawers' age and of the topic to be drawn. In addition, the option for the drawing technique is justified by the central role played by images in religion and spirituality (Williams and Whitehouse, 2015).

I worked with 186 drawings coming from a larger database of available data obtained as a result of activities during a Sociology of Religion seminar. The drawings were made upon request in kindergartens and schools, or in a private environment (in the case of acquaintances' children) in Brasov County and in neighboring counties. While drawing, or right after finishing the activity, children were asked to succinctly explain the content and interpretation of their work. This information, along with the demographic data of the drawers (age, gender, social class, religion, the person who talks with the child about God), was separately noted. In some cases, the drawings coming from kindergartens or schools were accompanied by short comments of educators that highlighted children's readiness to accept to draw God and also the fact that some of the children made two distinct drawings arguing that, as an afterthought, they could draw better the second time. In such cases, both drawings were preserved in order to be analysed.

Out of the 186 analysed drawings, 101 come from six year olds and 85 from children of seven. A total of 140 drawings are dated 2004 and 46 are made in 2016. Concerning drawers' gender, 68 of them are male, 69 are female, and as for the remaining 51, there is no information in this respect. Seven children are Roman Catholic, eight are Protestant, and the rest of them, namely 171, are Orthodox. Thirty-one children come from rural areas and 155 from an urban environment. The time interval I chose (six to seven years of age) corresponds to the moment when children in Romania start going to school and, consequently, they attend classes of Religion (parents may choose the religious denomination that children study, and for the past three years they have had to request, in writing, their children's participation in such classes; that is the reason why the number of children attending such classes is decreasing). Until children start going to school, religious education, whether explicit or implicit, is their family's prerogative. It is my belief that the results of the research on six and seven year olds' representations of God are not tainted by the way Religion is approached as a subject in school and, hence, provide information on the religiosity of children's family members. According to genetic psychology (Piaget, 1965), the age of seven is the end of the pre-operational stage. At this age, children can use concepts, even though they do it intuitively, illogically, focusing only on one dimension of the conceptual context and ignoring the others regardless of their relevance, and they mix reality with imaginary.

I employed NVivo 10 to thematically analyse the drawings. I chose the thematic analysis because of the method's flexibility, of its independence from a predetermined theoretical framework and its applicability in the case of some under-researched area (Braun and Clarke, 2006). The drawings and explanations accompanying them were considered distinct sets of data and hence coded separately. Within the explanations, answers to questions like *Why did you draw that?* or *What do you know about God?* were parted and coded separately. False explanations, namely simple descriptions of drawings' content with no interpretation (e.g. "This is a tree, these are clouds") were not coded. The codes derived from the drawings and those coming from the explanations were then merged by themes. By comparing the amount of codes coming from different sources (drawings/explanations) within the themes, I could run a multidirectional analysis of data (transversal, in depth, and longitudinal) and thus obtain a more nuanced image of how children represent God.

I call *transversal analysis* the approach to highlighting the thematic structuring of data: classifications of codes, subordinations, and hierarchies of themes by their frequency of occurrence. The *in-depth analysis* highlights the significance of the difference between the relative frequencies of occurrence of specific themes in drawings and children's explanations. I call *longitudinal analysis* the approach to emphasizing the differences between the drawings of 2016 and those of 2004 in terms of their thematic structuring.

Next, I will present the results of multidirectional analysis. I also inserted throughout this presentation brief comments on the Orthodox correspondent of some of children's drawings in order to clarify the catechetic context in which these were made. I also inserted within brackets my own explanatory hypotheses in the case of some graphic codes for which children did not provide their own explanations. Even though the drawings and the drawers' explanations are generally presented separately, in some cases some of children's interpretations are introduced right after the drawings for a better exemplification of the arguments.

3 The way Romanian children picture God. A multidirectional analysis of their drawings and interpretations

3.1 Transversal analysis

The main themes identified as a result of research data processing are ordered decreasingly by their frequency of occurrence as presented in *Tab.1*. The numbers attached to these in the table are related to: the number of data items where the theme occurs/the number of codes related to the theme.

The main prevailing themes (in most of the data items and comprising most of the codes) are *The Church mediates the relationship with God* and *God is from another world*. I will detail the structure of the subordinated themes and of their sub-themes, staking on the fact that many of these are new.

3.1.1 The Church mediates the relationship with God

This theme includes cult-related and Christian catechetic aspects to be found in children's drawings and explanations (when answering the questions: *Why did you draw that?* and *What do you know about God?*). These are presented below.

What children drew. The codes related to the drawings were classified by the subordinated themes and sub-themes of the main theme *The Church mediates the relationship with God* as in Tab. 2.

Tab. 1: Main themes

What children drew (the content of drawings)	**Explanations**	
	Why they drew like that	**What they know about God**
-The Church mediates the relationship with God (154/313) -God is from another world (102/177) -*God's cheerfulness* (101/111)	-God is from another world (30/48) - The Church mediates the relationship with God (26/50) - God – the Protector (14/16)	- The Church mediates the relationship with God (13/17) - God – the Protector (12/17)
- *God's human appearance* (84/148) -God – the Creator (43/65) -God – the Protector (30/32)	-That's how I wanted it to be (12/16) - God – the Creator (5/6)	- God is from another world (11/16) - God – the Creator (3/6)
-God is of female gender (9/9) -God is in everything (6/6) -I do not know (3/3)	- God is in everything (4/6) - God is of female gender (3/4) - *God's cheerfulness* (3/5) - *God's human appearance* (1/1) - I do not know (1/1)	- *God's human appearance* (3/3) - *God's cheerfulness* (1/1) - God is in everything (1/1)

Thus, the children's God is wearing a halo. This is one of the most frequent canonical signs of status. Children chose different ways of drawing a halo. Some of these are reproduced in Fig. 1. In some drawings this is simple, similar to the icons representing Orthodox saints, whereas in others it either resembles the one in the Catholic religious paintings or it looks like a turban on God's head. In other drawings, the halo is that of Jesus Christ as depicted by the Orthodox iconography and bearing the acronym OWN, or it has rays. The halo is also drawn as a simple circle, a hat – probably derived from the Catholic nimbus, or surrounding God's face like a lion's mane. Sometimes the halo is meticulously decorated or it resembles an antenna above the head – possibly an original childish solution for the hard to grasp presence of the nimbus above saints' head (Fig. 1).

God, as Jesus, has long curly hair, flowing on the back up to the shoulder line, and a beard, as in the Orthodox iconography. Similar to some Orthodox saints in the icons and Christian priests, God's garment is long (through a metonymical contamination, the drawers robe God similarly to His ministers). On some

Tab. 2: Drawings. Structure of the theme "The Church mediates the relationship with God"

Subordinated themes	Sub-themes	Codes
Canonical signs of status (103/159)	God's halo (76/78)	-simple halo (28/28) -Catholic halo (10/10) -turban-shaped halo (10/10) -Jesus' Orthodox halo (8/8) -halo with rays (7/7) -halo like a simple circle (5/5) -halo like a hat (4/4) -leonine halo (3/3) -embellished halo (2/2) -halo like an antenna (1/1)
	The iconographic face of Jesus (33/40)	-long hair (19/19) -beard (21/21)
	God's special garment (26/30)	-long garment (22/22) -garment with crosses (8/8)
	God with the Bible (9/9)	
	God is old (2/2)	-beard (1/1) -glasses (1/1)
Crucifixion (44/63)	The Crucifixion scene (33/33)	
	Jesus' gloomy face (11/11)	
	Details of Crucifixion (10/15)	-Jesus' sadness (3/3) -the woman next to Crucifixion cross (3/3) -Crucifixion witnesses (2/2) -blood spilled during Crucifixion (2/2) -God next to the crucified Jesus (2/2) -rain during the Crucifixion (2/2) -the crown of thorns (1/1)
	Inside a cincture (2/2)	
	Basket with eggs under the cross (1/1)	
	Two people crucified (1/1)	

Tab. 2: (continued)

Subordinated themes	Sub-themes	Codes
Cross (30/31)	God is among crosses (9/9)	
	God is next to the cross (7/7)	
	God holds the cross in His hand (6/6)	
	Crosses in the sky (3/3)	
	Only the cross (3/3)	
	Two crosses (2/2)	
	Cross in the grave (1/1)	
Church (25/28)	From the outside (21/21)	
	Building with a cross (19/19)	
	God is inside the Church (5/5)	
	Simple House (2/2)	
Other biblical scenes (12/13)	Nativity (4/5)	-a star in the sky (3/3) -baby Jesus (1/1) -iconographic representation (1/1)
	Descent of the Holy Spirit (2/2)	
	Dormition of the Mother of God (1/1)	
	God above Noah's Ark (1/1)	
	God next to the Burning Bush (1/1)	
	Jesus, the shepherd, with a lamb (1/1)	
	Birds carrying twigs in their beak (1/1)	
	A pigeon (1/1)	
Triumph over death (9/9)	God among crosses in the cemetery (3/3)	
	Above the cemetery (2/2)	
	Above the grave (3/3)	-entirely above the grave (2/2) -head above the grave (1/1)
	Above Hell (1/1)	
God is humble (6/6)	Hands close to the body (4/4)	
	God is barefoot (1/1)	
	God is naked (1/1)	
Triangles (3/3)	God next to a triangular face (1/1)	
	God next to a triangle (1/1)	
	God with a triangular head (1/1)	

A holy martyr in a flower (1/1)

Fig. 1: God's halo (author's archive)

robes, there are also crosses. In Fig. 2 there are some such representations of God's face and garments.

The God drawn by children is holding the Holy Scripture. Shown as a book that is either open or closed, with richly embellished covers, this is one of the iconographic attributes of Jesus Christ as a Teacher, and of the Evangelists. In one of the drawings, the Scripture is in the hand of crucified Jesus. Sometimes, God is depicted as an old man.

God, as Jesus, was crucified. His face was marked with the signs of death long before the Crucifixion ("because He is dying, Jesus' skin is darker", explains one of the children). According to the drawings, during the Crucifixion, Jesus wore a crown of thorns and His blood was flowing. A woman and God (sic!) stood next to the Cross of Jesus' Crucifixion. There were a lot of spectators and it was raining. (Only) some of the drawings depicted a sad Jesus. His blood turned Easter eggs red. According to children, the scene of Crucifixion is reproduced in jewellery (they draw such status symbols that are worn by the high priests of the Orthodox Church on their garments and over their chest). In Fig. 3 there are some drawings of the Crucifixion.

The cross is God's sign. The simple cross (without the crucified Jesus) is present in representations in various contexts. God is among crosses, next to the cross or holding it in His hand. Some drawings depict crosses in the sky, others show just the cross or two crosses (a reference to the good thief

Fig. 2: God's face representation and His garments (author's archive)

Fig. 3: The Crucifixion (author's archive)

crucified next to Jesus, I believe). One of the drawings shows a cross on a pedestal in a grave.

The church belongs to God. In most of the drawings, the church, as a place of worship, is depicted from the outside, as a building with a cross on its roof or on its front, or as a simple house. Only some of the drawings show God inside the church.

God's relationship with humankind dates back long ago. In children's drawings, He stood above Noah's Ark or next to the Burning Bush, as Jesus He was born

Fig. 4: God's triangular face (author's archive)

under a star that heralded His Birth and He was a shepherd, He descended as the Holy Spirit and He was present at the Dormition of the Mother of God. Birds carrying twigs in their beak (probably an ambiguous reference to Noah's dove) and a dove (the same reference or most likely to the descent of the Holy Spirit during Baptism) are symbols of this long relation.

God rules over death. He is present among the crosses in the cemetery or flies over them, rises from the grave and Hell. God is humble (He keeps his arms close to His body, He is barefoot and naked) and He has a Trinitarian nature: in this respect, children draw God's head in the shape of a triangle or accompanied by a triangular face or a triangle, as in the drawings in Fig. 4. In one of the drawings the triangular face smiles. I believe that the triangular shapes children drew are naïve associative representations of the idea of Trinity and they are not attempts to reproduce the triangle depicting the Eye of God. The latter is present in many churches in Transylvania, even in Orthodox churches, although such a representation is considered non-canonical in Orthodoxy. Unlike the representation of the Eye of God in the shape of an isosceles triangle with its obtuse angle pointing upwards, children's triangles have an acute angle directed downwards.

God's church honours its martyrs. The inspiration source for the drawing with the Holy Martyr Leontie (identified as such based on the legend to its left) sitting in a flower might be found in the Orthodox representations of Jesse's tree that display prophets sitting in flowers, on branches. Such a theme appears on the outside walls of the painted monasteries in the North of Moldova, a tourist area in Romania. I believe that its association, as an archetypal representation, with the theme of Buddha meditating in a lotus flower is risky.

Why children drew like that (answers to the question: Why did you draw that?). Children mainly referred to God as *Jesus.* Their explanations concerning the

Crucifixion are very different emotionally speaking, from the confession "Jesus' Crucifixion impressed me" and highlighting the blood, as the sign of sacrifice, flowing from Jesus' wounds to a neutral description that is not related to the significance of the scene: "God is leaning against a cross". In one of the drawings, as the explanations indicate, God stood next to Jesus during the Crucifixion (and the drawings do represent Him next to the cross) and an angel stood on one of the arms of the cross.

God is in the church, that is in His house, and children or their family are on their way to the church. Parents go every Sunday to talk to God – "God is in the church and remains there so that people can pray to Him".

Drawers described the scene of Nativity in detail, mentioning the star that "heralds the birth of Lord Jesus Christ", the Mother of God, Jesus, and Joseph who "are like a family" and "two horses that take care of them". Children also referred to the Burning Bush scene ("To the right there is a burning bush that symbolizes the moment when God spoke to Moses. God is looking at the bush in flames") and to Jesus as a shepherd ("God is holding a rod. There is a little lamb next to Him. God is barefoot. He is wearing a long garment".). Drawers' references to canonical status signs are few and, as for the halo, they are uncertain: "there is some sort of halo around the head that shines very brightly" and "God is wearing a large yellow hat".

God is powerful and old. "God looks like an old man who can smile" say children. The source of this feature could be the references to God's power in the Old Testament conveyed by Christian catechesis, as well as to His old age ("an Elder of great age", in Daniel 7:9), a theme that is also employed by the Orthodox iconography. God's power justifies his height ("God is the one in the middle, the taller one"), the support He grants to people ("He has the power to support us all"), and His authority over them.

Concerning God's old age, apart from one explicit reference to that, one of the drawers justified the presence or pseudo-presence of old age related in his drawing: "God is wearing glasses because He is very old…" and "He is wearing a white beard that is not in the drawing because there is no such color to represent it" (sic.!).

God has statues. Children presented the context in which they saw God's statues in church as follows: "God is on a ladder (a pedestal, A/N), so that He is more visible. There is also a picture of Jesus up on the wall and light bulbs that are on". The description belongs to an Orthodox child. Similar to his drawing, his explanations show a mixture between the details characteristic of Orthodox churches' interior and God's Catholic representation (i.e., statue on a pedestal).

What children know about God (answers to the question: *What do you know about God?*). The most frequent answer is that God asks for faith. God watches over people: "He does not walk on ground, but He can see everything from high above"; "He looks after children and parents. He sees us through the window if we do wrong things" and "He even understands our thoughts". God wants us to be good, "He teaches us to be good and nice" and "We have to pray to Him to be better", that is, "we cross ourselves and think of God", since "All people should love God". Not without importance, "God does not help those people who do not believe in Him".

God is Jesus (in a children's explicit confession of Christian faith – "Jesus is God" and in a non-canonical statement – "God resembles Jesus") and "There is God and the Holy Spirit", as children also know. "Every Sunday I pray with my grandmother for my grandfather who has been with God for two years", says one of them.

3.1.2 God is from another world

The previous theme (*The Church mediates the relationship with God*) included references to familiar sides of a God, who has come into this world so that people would know Him. The theme *God is from another world* subsumes children's representations of God's nature that is different from that of people, of His strangeness.

What children drew. The subordinated themes, sub-themes, and codes from children's drawings are presented in *Tab. 3.*

Thus, God's nature is celestial. This is the most frequent subordinated theme. There are clouds close to God (I did not classify here the clouds in all the drawings, but only those related to the notion of flight, ascension, and a soaring God), God flies (as in the drawings in Fig. 5), is among the stars and levitates (close to Earth). Sometimes He is represented next to a ladder or rising rocket. One of the children only drew a rising rocket with no God around. Another drawing pictures green butterflies that, according to the child's explanation, are God's messengers (informants).

God is above people. He has a shining face; He radiates and is wearing a golden garment. He is depicted against a golden background; His hair is golden or His entire body shines. He is wearing a crown and/or a scepter and is standing on a throne. There are also other various signs indicating God's prestige: His height, ornaments, a wand just like that of a fairy, a cape, pedestal, or a monocle. Some of these features are shown in the drawings in Fig. 6.

Tab. 3: Drawings. Structure of the theme: "God is from another world"

Subordinated themes	**Sub-themes**	**Codes**
God's nature is celestial (52/72)	-Clouds (34/34)	
	-God flying (24/24)	
	-God among stars (6/6)	
	-God levitating (4/4)	
	-God next to the ladder (2/2)	
	-God next to a rising rocket (1/1)	
	-Rocket in the air (1/1)	
	-Green butterflies as messengers (1/1)	
God is above people (38/44)	God's gorgeousness (23/26)	-He has a beaming face (13/13) -He radiates (4/4) -He is wearing a golden garment (4/4)
		-He is represented against a golden background (2/2) -His hair is golden (2/2) -His whole body shines (1/1)
	God's royalty (9/10)	-the crown (8/8)
		-the throne (1/1)
		-the scepter (1/1)
	Other signs of God's prestige (8/8)	-with ornaments (2/2)
		-giant (2/2)
		-with a wand (1/1)
		-with a cape (1/1)
		-on a pedestal (1/1)
		-with a monocle (1/1)
God's angels (24/25)	-God with an angel (13/13) -God among more angels (6/6) -God with two angels (5/5) -the angels are male and female (1/1)	
God is an angel (16/16)		
God is between the worlds (9/9)	-God's body is not finished (6/6) -God on the threshold (2/2) -God in front of Heaven's Gate (1/1)	

(*continued on next page*)

Tab. 3: (continued)

Subordinated themes	Sub-themes	Codes
God's Heaven(7/11)	-the Sun (4/4) -two trees (3/3) -flowers (2/2) -angels (1/1) -the gate of Garden (1/1)	

Fig. 5: God's celestial nature (author's archive)

God is with the angels. Children drew God together with one or two angels, and among angels. In one of the drawings, angels are male and female. In Fig. 7 are some of God's angels drawn by children.

Children's God is an angel. Orthodox iconography sometimes presents Jesus as an angel. Such representations are quite rare and their source is Isaiah (9, 5) who calls Messiah "the angel of great counsel". Nonetheless, the presence for God's representations as an angel might not be too subtle from an iconographic point of view. In my opinion, there must be an overlay with the icon of the Archangels Michael and Gabriel, painted on the doors of the iconostasis in

Fig. 6: God's prestige (author's archive)

Fig. 7: God and His angels (author's archive)

most Orthodox churches and/or with the theme of the guardian angel that is so well-known to children with Orthodox parents and who are taught the prayer to their Guardian Angel at a very young age: "Angel of God, My guardian dear, To Whom His love Commits me here, Ever this day, Be at my side …".

God is between the worlds. Since God's nature is different from that of the people, His presence (manifestation) in this world is not characteristic of Him. Therefore, God's body is not finished (the drawing presenting Him does not comprise Him as a whole) or is standing on the threshold or in front of the gate.

The Heaven is God's. The representations of Heaven are identified with the help of children's explanations and depicted as a Sun shining, two trees, flowers, angels, and the gate of Heaven's Garden.

Why the children drew like that. Children provided a lot of explanations as to the celestial nature of God. "God lives in the sky in a large house", He sits on the clouds and that is probably why His eyes are like the sky ("large, blue, the color of the sky"), or lives in the space ("God is in the space. That is where His house is") and "wears little stars in His hair because He lives among the stars". "God is the symbol of peace because he can fly", explains one of the drawers by resorting to some sort of a slightly twisted logic. Another one, who shows quite an engineer's ability, mentions: "Saints wear a round halo and not a square one so that they would not inflict any harm, not even by mistake, because who knows: when they rise up to the sky they might prick a flying bird with one of the square's corners".

There is also a lot of information concerning Heaven in children's explanations. Jesus is in Heaven and two trees grow there. One of the children identifies them as "the two tree of the Good and of the Bad", a possible contamination with the theme of the trees bearing good and bad fruit in the Sermon on the Mount (Mathew 7, 17–18), or as a result of a simplifying argument like: "If Adam was not allowed to taste from the tree's fruit, than the tree was not good". One of the children describes a Heaven to his own taste: "He (God, A/N) lives by the sandy beach and there are blue fish in the water".

Children's explanations also contain indications of the reasons for which God wears royal signs such as the crown ("God is wearing a king's crown that is yellow"), the throne, and the scepter ("He has a scepter because He is powerful"); His solar attributes ("He wears yellow because this color represents the Sun rays, since without Sun, there would be no life on Earth"); and His brilliance. The children also explained God's eccentric garments in some of the drawings, which, even though it is not necessarily inadequate for people, they symbolize God's special superior status: God, standing on a pedestal so that He is more visible, is wearing a red hat and cape, as the drawer saw in cartoons. The Mother of God holding Jesus is wearing high heels, as all little girls, who idolize their stylish mothers, dream.

Some of the explanations regarding angels indicate angels' presence around God. Others, more spectacular, are non-canonical. One of the children interprets his drawing as follows: "In the upper part of the drawing there are three angels who look like fairies and who, similarly to the Mother of God, are wearing high heels". Another one explains: "In the upper part of the drawing there are angels who are girls and in the lower part angels who are boys. The girls are drawn above because they have some sort of priority".

"God is wearing wings because He is an angel", and "I picture God as a guardian angel who watches day and night", children further explained. As for God's presence in the world, one of the drawers says: "…usually you cannot see the whole body of some spirits, only half of it", whereas another states: "God has no legs; He does not walk on Earth, but He can see everything from above".

What children know about God. "God lives in the sky and fulfills all our wishes", He has a school up there ("The saints learn in a school in the sky; they live on Earth, but angels bring them homework from the sky, so that they would do it at home"). God's abode is in Heaven and "He is good and lives in a garden with a lot of flowers; this is a place that is always beautiful, peaceful and sunny".

God is above people because He is immortal, omnipotent, and great. When answering the question about what they know concerning God, children did not make any reference to any outside signs related to His status, as they did in the case of their drawings and explanations (brilliance, royalty, etc.). What they did in exchange was to state that people do not know what God looks like. "I'm a little bit afraid because I don't know how to draw Him. Nobody knows what God looks like unless they die and become angels", says one of the children. Another one claims "God is an invisible man".

The statement on the angels, who bring homework to saints, has already been mentioned. Personally, I find it amazing and consider it the sign of theological intuition.

There are numerous references to angels in the New Testament. Their role is that of messengers, Jesus' companions in various contexts, as well as assistants and companions of Apostles. Therefore, the theme related to them in children's drawings could be subsumed to the theme *The Church mediates the relationship with God* that, as I already mentioned at the beginning of this chapter, includes catechetic and cult-related references. Nonetheless, I chose not to proceed in this direction because I believe that the context in which the references to angels are made is more important than the existence of the references themselves. The theme *The Church mediates the relationship with God*, covered by children's drawings and explanations, contains Christian canonical features of God. These features are the "labels" children immediately associate with the idea of God in their attempt to integrate it in their knowledge system. These play a mediating role and assist children in getting close to God and making Him familiar to them.

On the other hand, the angels in the drawings and explanations are most often companions of God in the sky and/or when they fly, that is, they appear in contexts that are inaccessible to people, and yet they are significant for the different nature of God and people. Angels' skills signal the gap between God's world (the sky) and the world where people live. Additionally, when explaining their drawings, children assign odd non-canonical attributes to angels: they wear heels, look like fairies, and are gender differentiated.

All of the above considered, I believe that it is more appropriate to subsume the references to angels to the theme *God is from another world*. For the same reasons, namely as a result of a significant prevalence of context over its canonical legitimacy, the same theme includes the graphical and textual references to Heaven. In this respect, I believe that it is more important for the logic of data

Fig. 8: God is cheerful (author's archive)

interpretation that children place God in Heaven rather than the fact that they know about the canonical existence of Heaven.

3.1.3 God's cheerfulness and human appearance

These themes are more frequent in children's drawings than in their accompanying explanations. I will return to the significance of this imbalance in the paragraphs to follow.

Children draw God smiling (as shown in Fig. 8) and/or holding His arms above the head, but there are only a few explicit explanations that talk about a joyful God ("Both Jesus Christ and His angels smile and shine" or "God looks like an old man who can smile […]. Now He is happy because somebody said something nice about Him") as explanations for what they drew, and "Jesus, without Him there is only sorrow" as an answer to the question on what children know about God. The drawings depict a God with human appearance: arms pointed obliquely downward, slightly away from the body and/or wearing regular clothes. Only one of the drawers, whose comment has already been mentioned, explains his work by referring to God's human appearance ("God looks like an old person"), and only few of the children directly or indirectly indicate God's human appearance when they answer the question as to what they know about Him: "God is a very good person" and "God is an invisible human being". God's human appearance opens generous avenues of interpretation that lead to the very core of Christianity to unveil a God who became human (or sent His Son to incarnate) in order to lay the ground for people's redemption. However, I believe children's drawings do not take this direction. I believe that God's human features (silhouette, posture, and clothes) reflect the drawers' difficulty in operating with the concept of God. The hands slightly away from the body with the palms open to the viewer could suggest Jesus' generous sacrifice and His acceptance of that. But this posture is characteristic for how children of this age draw people in general. Therefore, in this respect, I believe that this posture is less significant than those depicting God with His arms above the Head, next to His body or spread sideways (as for the significance of this last posture, I will provide more information later). To drawers, God really looks like a human being.

3.1.4 God, the Creator

This main theme includes the graphic representations of God and His creation along with the accompanying explanations.

Children frequently drew the Sun and vegetation to represent a world created to be friendly. They also drew animals, celestial bodies, and human dwellings (God is represented as living inside these). In one particular case, the drawing depicts snowflakes with the associated explanation "He sends the snow flakes to Earth in winter", whereas in another drawing there are red hearts surrounded by vegetation, animals, and two persons (as shown in Fig. 9). The fact that the request made to children was to draw God and this last drawing does not depict His silhouette might be interpreted as a naïve and reductionist representation of the statement "God is love", from the very theological core of Christianity.
I subsumed this representation to the theme "God, the Creator" and not to the theme "The Church mediates the relationship with God" (where it would have belonged given its theological meaning), because next to the little hearts the drawing shows an abundance of the elements belonging to the created world, and due to its associated explanation: "God sends His great love to Earth so that there is love between man and woman".

In some of the drawings, the Sun is oversized, overwhelming, thus suggesting more than a truly friendly world. Spectacular codes like that are very close, in terms of their significance, to God's brilliance, which has already been mentioned before. The vegetation depicted in most of the drawings is preponderantly

Fig. 9: God as love (author's archive)

made of flowers and trees on a conventional layer of grass. In one of the drawings the flowers grow directly from the Sun. In another one, the vegetation is shown as a field uniformly colored in green. The explanations related to the presence of these elements, the Sun and the vegetation, are very few. One such explanation states: "God is also holding a flower in His hand to symbolize life".

There are birds and other animals around God. In most of the cases, these play a deliberate predetermined aesthetic role (the birds and the blue fish in the sea water are added according to the explanation "for the drawings to be beautiful") or a canonical one (the little lamb next to God, the shepherd, the horses in the Nativity scene, the dove). These roles might have prevailed in children's drawing options and hence the representation of animals as God's creations only has a secondary meaning. The representation of the sea, stars, Moon, and solar system are more clearly related to God's role of Creator. Children explain their presence and, as I previously mentioned, that of the snowflakes as creations of God. Children know that God has created people, the world and the details they provide in this respect are impressive: "God has moulded all planets, gave life to all, gave people fruit, the trees, the Red Sea, the White Sea, the Dead Sea, the

Fig. 10: God hugging the world (author's archive)

oceans, planet Earth, which He created in six days, He gathered the water of the oceans in one place, made the Sun, the moon and the Earth" and He also "created Santa Claus".

3.1.5 God, the Protector

The theme includes the references to God's watchfulness of the world, in general, and of people in particular.

In many drawings, God's arms are wide open. Some of the drawings that represent Him in this way are reproduced in Fig. 10. When referring to God's human appearance above, I stated that the drawing of the arms obliquely downward and along the body is the norm and, as a result, does not bear any special significance. Nonetheless, I believe that in the case of the arms represented horizontally, the explicit intention of the drawers is to show the beginning of a hug, namely God hugging the world.

God takes care of people and watches over them. God's large hand is represented coming from the sky to support or holding the Earth in the hollow of the hand. "It was God's hand" – a word-for-word translation of a Romanian saying, standing for the English "It was God's will" refers situations when one unexpectedly comes out of a dangerous situation, or avoids an unwanted outcome at the last minute. In my opinion, that is what children drew naively, in a reductionist and yet ingenious manner. In one of the drawings, God just like Santa Claus is carrying a large bag filled with food (according to the accompanying explanation), while in another (as shown in Fig. 11). God is a man who is taking care of His baby.

God protects love relations (graphically presented by children through the little hearts), as well as friendship among people. Sometimes He tickles top of people's heads (as the explanation of one of the drawings states) or fights for them against

Fig. 11: God as a father (author's archive)

evil. In one of the drawings, a smiling God fights with one of the dark (green) silhouettes around Him while an angel is hovering above.

Children explained that God "watches over nature and everything that surrounds us" and that "He lives in the sky in a large house and takes care of us", with the help of some "green butterflies who go to Him to announce if anything wrong happens" (sic!). They also indicate that "Animals and nature come from God so that we have resources on which to live" and, associated to some already presented drawings, there are also the explanations that "God is like a hand that helps you stand up (because every time I lose balance and fall there is always somebody to lend a helping hand and lift me up)" and that He is "like a man who takes care of His baby".

God protects the peace of the world, which He hugs ("His arms are wide open as if He hugs the whole world"; "His hands are wide open which suggests His love to people."). Children know that the God who looks after people is a good one and does good things, "inspires people's faith, and gives them confidence, emotions" and, more pragmatically, helps people build blocks of flats: "He created everything there is in the space and on Earth, but he put the blocks in people's brains". Children's God "looks after people and animals so that they reach adulthood" and brings food ("God feeds us, He is good to us"; "God looks after children and their parents, brings them bread"). The topic of food in such a context might indicate that the drawers come from families where ensuring

Fig. 12: God is of female gender (author's archive)

daily food is a challenge. Even though such a hypothesis is not ungrounded in the case of some poor communities from Romania, I believe, though, that it is rather a matter of the Lord's Prayer echoing in children's minds. In my opinion, they thought once again in a naïve and reductionist manner of "our daily bread" that Christians ask from God.

God "helps good people", "helps us when we run into difficulties and need help", "God is a very good man" (sic!), "had a good heart", and "did a lot of good things for us", children also stated.

3.1.6 God is of female gender

The theme is characterized by graphic representations of feminine features (garment, silhouette, hair style…) for God confirmed through explanations accompanying drawings, where they exist. In most of these, a God of female gender is wearing a dress or a skirt. In one of them, God resembles a fairy. In Fig. 12 are some such representations.

Children's explanations explicitly show their intentions to draw a feminine character: "God is a woman", "God is a girl in the shape of an angel", "God is like a good fairy", or "I actually wanted to represent my mother".

There are no references, though, to God's femininity in children's answers to the question concerning what they know about God.

3.1.7 God is in everything

The theme subsumes the pantheist approaches to God. The drawings included in this theme depict elements from nature, the Sun, trees, flowers, animals (as shown in Fig. 13) or, in one of the cases, an allegorical anthropomorphic representation of God's omnipresence that shows His body as the globe. This classification of

Fig. 13: God in the things of the world (author's archive)

children's work also includes an anthropomorphic representation of God who is drawn in a farm's yard, in the grass. I believe that the graphic solution chosen by the drawer is a reductionist means to express the idea that God is in the world. The idea that *God is in the things of the world* was represented as *God is among the things of the world (He is in the world).*

Children's answers to the question concerning the content of their work consolidate the latter's pantheist dimension: "God is above all and in everything, even in a spring day", "He is in everything that surrounds us [...]. We can see God in nature", He is "in everything that is beautiful", and "it is as if He represented the whole planet". In the explanation showing God's presence in the world, the enumeration of the components of the drawing suggests His intimacy with His creation: "car, street, tree, grass, house, God, Sun, clouds" in a quite impressive manner.

Among the answers to what children know about God, there is only one directly attributable to pantheism, expressed just like this: "God is everything that surrounds us".

3.1.8 I do not know how

This theme contains the expressions (only three) of the children's difficulty in drawing God. In one of the cases, the child turned in a blank sheet of paper. In another case, there is only a circle drawn on the paper. Despite the temptation to interpret the drawing symbolically (the circle is the perfect geometric shape, it is a transposition of a sphere in plane, it represents the merge of beginning and end, Parmenides' being is spherical, etc.), I believe that this particular case is only a failed attempt to represent God. The third drawing in this category is that of a car. The explanation to it, the only one actually in the case of the whole theme, is as follows: "I drew a car because I do not know how to draw God". There are no other references among children's answers concerning what they know about God that could be subsumed to this theme.

3.1.9 That's how I wanted it to be

This theme includes the answers to the *question "Why did you draw like that (namely, what does the drawing represent)?"* Simplistically interpreted, the question targets children's reasons for the content of their drawings and, as a result, the answers to it are also elliptical. Therefore, this is some sort of a meta-theme since the codes that it includes do not refer to the explicit content of the drawings, but to the intentions of the drawers.

Some of children's answers show their concern for how their drawings look: "Like this (how he drew A/N), I colored in blue so that the page is not blank" or "It is outdoors and the birdies are there to look nice". Other answers indicate what children saw in church or, unexpectedly, in cartoons. Some explanations show the drawers' will, "He is wearing yellow garments because that is how I wanted to draw Him". Another type of answer is subsumed to "That is how I imagine Him". Not without significance, one of the answers shows the drawer's nonchalant attitude: "That is how I saw God [...]. That is what God looks like".

3.1.10 Children's drawings as a reflection of their residential environment and religion

Children's residential environment (urban or rural) and their religion influence the (relative) frequency of themes in their graphic solutions. I will come back to the significance of these differences. *Tab. 4* presents the frequency of themes in decreasing order.

3.2 In-depth analysis

The decreasing order of occurrence of the main themes is quite similar to the drawings, the explanations of the drawings, and the children's answers to the question of what they know about God, with a few exceptions that I will highlight, considering them as meaningful.

3.2.1 God's cheerfulness and human appearance as implicit features

The themes *God's cheerfulness* and *God's human appearance* are more frequent in children's drawings than in their explanations (*Tab. 1*). As a result of this difference, I consider these themes as implicit: if children drew God like that, children considered it obvious that God is joyful and the human appearance fits Him.

Tab. 4: Decreasing order of themes by children's residential environment and religion

Themes by residential environment	
Urban	The Church mediates the relationship with God > God is from another world > God's human appearance > God's cheerfulness > God – the Creator > God – the Protector > God is of female gender > God is in everything > I do not know
Rural	God's human appearance > The Church mediates the relationship with God > God's cheerfulness > God is from another world > God – the Creator > God – the Protector > I do not know > God is of female gender > God is in everything
Themes by religion	
Protestant	God is from another world > The Church mediates the relationship with God > God – the Creator > God – the Protector > God's cheerfulness > God is of female gender > God is in everything
Catholic	The Church mediates the relationship with God > God's cheerfulness > God's human appearance > God is from another world > God – the Creator > God is of female gender
Orthodox	The Church mediates the relationship with God > God is from another world > God's cheerfulness > God's human appearance > God – the Creator > God – the Protector > God is of female gender > God is in everything > I do not know

Such attributes did not necessitate any distinct explanations. Children tend to draw happy human faces rather than sad ones. However, I believe that God's smile means much more than the drawers' reference to it as a nice theme (even though the relation of such a feature with children's religiosity is also important and will be discussed). Jesus has a big smile, even in many of the representations of Crucifixion. However, not all drawings picture this kind of smile in such a context, which shows that children know the meaning of smile lines and apply it in their drawings.

3.2.2 Canonical signs of status – an implicit theme

In the case of the theme *The Church mediates the relationship with God* there are very few explicative references to God's halo, even though children frequently drew it. Additionally, the references to other canonical status signs are very rare or they completely lack. Therefore, I believe that similar to the themes *God's cheerfulness* and *God's human appearance*, the subordinated theme, *Canonical signs of status*, is implicit. Children seem to consider it as implied for God to wear

Tab. 5: The Church, People find God in church, God requests faith

What children drew	Why they drew like that	What children know about God
Canonical signs of status (including the iconographic representation of Jesus' face and God with the Scripture)	Jesus The Crucifixion *People find God at church* Other biblical scenes	*God requires faith* Jesus, distinct from the Holy Spirit Grandfather is with God
The Crucifixion The Cross *The Church* Other biblical scenes	He is powerful He is old God's statue God is wearing an halo	
Triumph over death Humble Triangles A holy martyr in a flower		

such as a halo, long hair and beard, or special garments, and that it is not necessary for them to explain all that.

3.2.3 The created world is implicitly welcoming

The drawings included in the theme *God, the Creator* show frequently the Sun, flowers, and trees. These are frequent background components of children's drawings of nice themes. At the same time, the explanations of these details are very few and therefore, I deem the subordinated theme that includes them (and which I called *The created world is welcoming*) as implicit. Its codes show children's positive attitude towards the world. By drawing the Sun, flowers, and trees children rather express their state of mind than thoughts like "God has created the Sun" or "God has created the flowers, the trees". Thus, children drew the state of comfort that characterizes the world, which God, also present in their drawings, has created.

3.2.4 Clarifications through graphic elicitation: Children know that God requires faith, and Heaven as a verbal label

The components of the theme *The Church mediates the relationship with God* are shown in the decreasing order of their frequency in children's drawings and explanations, as in *Tab.5*.

I believe that the subordinated theme *The Church* in children's drawings, along with the theme *People find God in church* present in their explanations, and the

Tab. 6: God's Heaven

What children drew	**Why they drew like that**	**What children know about God**
The sky is accessible to God	The sky is accessible to God	The sky is accessible to God
God is above people	*God's Heaven*	*God's Heaven*
God's angels	God is above people	God is above people
God is an angel	God's angels	People do not know what God looks like
God between the worlds	God is an angel	God's angels
God's Heaven	God between the worlds	

theme *God requires faith* described by their references to what they know about God, indicate the drawers' attitude towards a relationship with God that is mediated by the church. The frequency of these themes is different: the Church (that is most often represented from the outside) is less frequent in children's answers to the question on what they drew than the fact that people find God in church, while the subordinated theme *God requires faith* is by far the most frequent. As for the drawings, both the explicit codes (in some of the sub-themes of *Status sign* and *The Crucifixion*) and the implicit ones (from the theme *The Cross*) referring to the Church are less frequent than those mentioning Jesus. The situation is similar concerning the theme *People find God in church*, but not regarding the theme *God requires faith*.

The drawings show what children wanted to draw; their initial explanations indicate what their thoughts were while drawing, whereas their last answers to the questions reveal what they are told about God. The questions that they answered while drawing or after that made them reassess their attitude towards God in the church, and made them more aware of what they knew (because of what they are told) about it. In the same vein, the fact that God requires faith is what children are persistently told. I dare to say that such teachings are somewhat hidebound and therefore, the children who drew God's cheerfulness know more about Him than the adults who taught them about His claims.

In the theme *God is from another world*, its components from children's drawings and explanations are presented in decreasing order by their frequency in *Tab. 6*.

The subordinated themes that are present both in the drawings and in children's explanations, and which answer the questions concerning the content of children's work and what they know about God, appear with the same frequency. The theme *God's Heaven* is an exception to the aforementioned situation because it is more frequent in the explanations than in the drawings. I believe

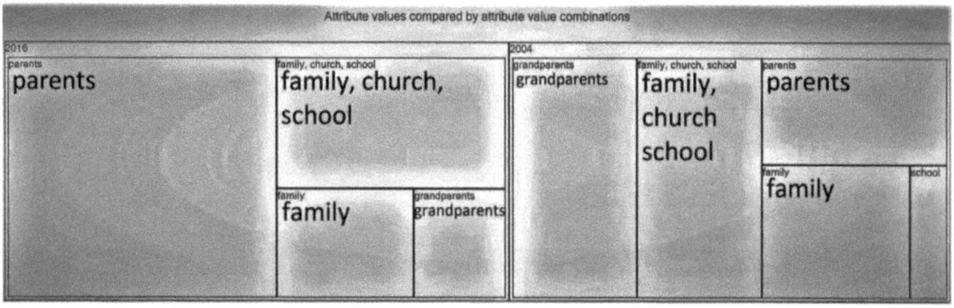

Fig. 14: Who tells children about God

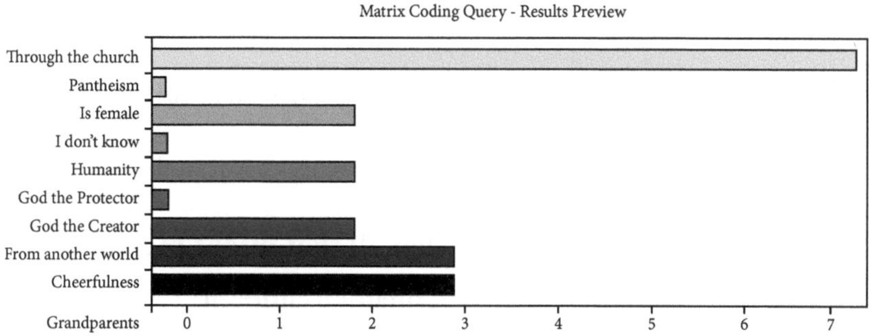

Fig. 15: What children's grandparents told them about God in 2004

the reason for that is related to the clarification on God's special place of abode brought by children's efforts to answer the question. The drawers' perception of the heterotopia of this place (Foucault, 1984), whose description may be the result of an association with the heterotopia of the ecclesiastic space, was ambiguous until they managed to clarify it through their explanations. Consequently, the linguistic label they attached to it was *Heaven.*

3.3 Longitudinal analysis

The drawings were made in 2004 and in 2016, respectively. Children's answers to the question on who tells them about God shows a significant increase in the role played by their parents (*Fig. 14*) in children's religious initiation to the detriment of grandparents' role in this area.

In the case of the children whose grandparents told them about God in 2004, the distribution of the themes identified and previously presented is by their frequency, as *Fig. 15* shows.

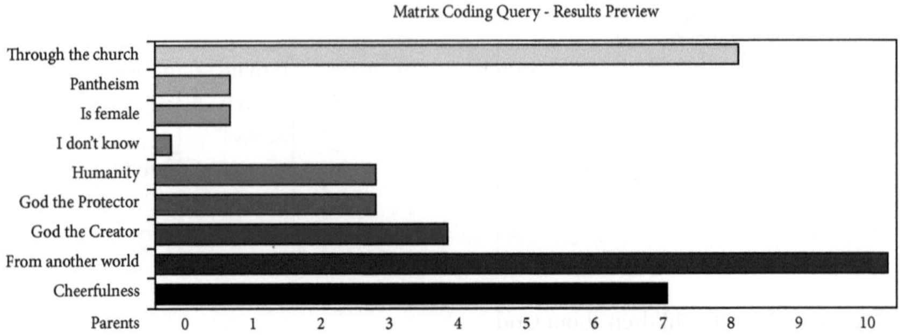

Fig. 16: What children's parents told them about God in 2016

As for the children whose parents told them about God in 2016, the distribution of the themes is presented in *Fig. 16*.

I shall come back to the meaning of the differences between the two figures.

4 Interpretation of results or what all that might mean

4.1 God, as He is represented by Romanian children

God who is known through the church is from another world, but He created this world and takes care of it. This is His representation depicted by the drawers.

Bryan Wilson (2000), taking up Durkheim's view, indicates the traditional functions of religion. Wilson separates the manifest function of religion, that is, salvation, from its latent ones. According to him, the conceptions on salvation of various religions can be categorized as spiritual or particularistic. The former are part of the higher religions, and they refer to reincarnation, Nirvana, immortality of the soul, and God's kingdom. The particularistic conceptions specific to less evolved religions envisage salvation as recovery from sickness, protection, or worldly benefits. What all these conceptions on salvation have in common is the healing connotation of suffering.

The latent functions of religion identified by Wilson are: a) social cohesion (and implicitly justification of social order and moral norms), b) interpretation of the cosmos, c) granting legitimacy to aims and actions of society, d) conferring or reinforcing individual and group identity, and e) facilitating the expression and management of emotions.

In Western contemporary society, salvation, as one of religion's manifest functions, has lost its prestige, says Wilson. Manifest religious interests are now motivated by the capacity of religion to lessen the pressure of a secular social system on individuals. At the same time, traditional latent functions are assumed as manifest functions by other institutions, organizations, and industries. Thus, in such a context, the current latent function of religion is taking shape around providing "disinterested goodwill and civic consciousness" (Wilson, 2000, p. 64) so that the present secular social system keeps working.

The identified themes derived from the analysis of children's drawings and explanations are indicative of the traditional functions of religion identified by Wilson.

4.1.1 Salvation as a manifest function in children's representations

The theme *God, the Protector* subsumes children's expectations from God and is directly associated to salvation, the traditional manifest function of religion. According to children, God takes care of people, guards them, helps them in difficult times, brings/ensures their food, and helps them build blocks of flats. The subordinated theme *The created world is welcoming* (classified under the theme *God, the Creator*) has an implicit character. The drawers see it as unequivocal. Both these themes correspond to a particularistic view of salvation rather than a spiritual one. Coming from Christian children, such a simplifying approach shows the adequacy of the representations on salvation to their age and suggests an ontogenetic resumption of the philogenesis of religiosity. It also implicitly indicates the authenticity of children's representations and that children filtered the Christian message through their own mind.

The theme *God, the Protector* does not abound in representations as far as the number of codes and frequency are concerned. Its position in the thematic hierarchy and given that even though Crucifixion is quite present in children's drawings, the references to salvation as its dimension lack, might reflect the shift of the manifest function of religion from salvation to survival in the secularized society, as mentioned by Wilson (2000). However, in the background of children's perception of God as a protector, there is the implicit theme of *God's cheerfulness* that I also consider as associated to salvation as the manifest function of religion. God's cheerfulness consolidates this function.

The theme *God's cheerfulness* expresses the joy that characterizes the core of Orthodoxy. Dumitru Stăniloaie (1991), one of the great theologians of the 20th century, considered that the Orthodox Christianity is defined by its relation with the Resurrection, the most illuminating dimension of the Gospels. For Orthodox believers, the Resurrection is more important than Calvary; it is the source of the joy characteristic of the Orthodox faith. Mutatis mutandis, this cheerfulness is reflected on the human-like God's countenance in children's drawings, a friendly and familiar one. I believe that the focus of Orthodoxy on the Resurrection also justifies the lack of explanations in the case of the salvation dimension of the Crucifixion. In the same context, it is important to mention that children's answers to what they know about God not only lack any references to this dimension, but they also make no reference to the Crucifixion.

The organic cheerfulness of Orthodoxy, which is tightly related to the salvation dimension of the Resurrection, is also discussed by Lossky in *The Mystical Theology of the Eastern Church* (2010), who calls the Easter night the "feast of faith", and closer to *Sociology* by Peter Berger, according to whom: "Orthodoxy, in contrast with the West, focuses more on Easter than on Good Friday, on the Resurrection as the focal point of the cosmic drama of redemption. Once again the dogmatic formulations may be the same or very similar, but they are animated by very different forms of piety. The West (Catholic as well as Protestant) has developed a deeply penitential piety, steeped in a gloomy consciousness of guilt and sin. By contrast, the East has been fixated on the figure of what Gustav Aulen (a Swedish Lutheran theologian) has called Christus Victor, the triumphant conqueror of both sin and death" (Berger, 2005). God's implicit cheerfulness depicted by children's drawings correlates with the absence of any reference to the salvation dimension of Crucifixion as part of a Christian faith focused on the redeeming Resurrection.

4.1.2 The latent function of social cohesion in children's representations

The multitude of codes subsumed to the theme *The Church mediates the relationship with God* indicates children's familiarity with the Christian faith, God's halo, Jesus' canonical signs of status, the Nativity, and the Crucifixion. According to their teachers, children performed the task of drawing very easily. The aforementioned theme is one of the richest main themes in terms of its subordinated themes, sub-themes, and codes. Its representations are correct catechetically speaking. The theme *Canonical signs of status* is implicit, therefore the children did not consider necessary to explain most of its content. Sharing beliefs increases social cohesion. The drawings of children, who know so many similar things about God, show the potential of religion to act as a cohesive factor in the communities where children grow.

4.1.3 The latent function of explaining the physical universe in children's representations

The theme *God, the Creator* articulates this latent function. Graphically and through their explanations children attributed the creation of universe to God.

They draw God among flowers, birds, plants, and snowflakes and explained how He has worked to create them all.

The theme *God is in everything* epitomizes the same explicative function even though the explanations are non-canonical. Christianity is not pantheist. The Christians' God has created the world, and He remains a distinct entity. The created world bears God's mark since it is His creation, but God is something else than the world. I believe the pantheist dimension from children's drawings and explanations expresses their religious intuition that comes from a distinct source from Christian religiosity, namely, in Jung's sense, from another experience of the Self.

In analytical psychology, the Self is the archetype of completeness. Its most important feature is its integrative dimension, the source of the feeling of intimacy with life, of immediate intercommunion with nature, and of the communion with the entire Cosmos (Jung, 2005b). One of the prevailing manifestations of the Self is as God's archetype. In this respect, the symbols of unity and completeness cannot be differentiated from *imago Dei*. The personal experience of the Self through its archetypal representations cannot be psychologically separated from experiencing God, shows Jung (2005a).

The Ego as the conscious dimension of the psyche gradually differentiates itself from the Self as an empirical individual acquisition, a result of individual's confrontation with the surrounding world and the inner one. The individuation process (leading to one's inner fulfilment) begins in childhood with an Ego that is not differentiated from the Self, continues with the separation of the former from the latter, and it is oriented towards the integrative reunification of these two. According to Jung, all authentic religious experiences are alternatives to this reunification.

For Christians, this redeeming reunification takes the set, specific form of the return of the believer's soul to God. In pantheism, the reunification with the Self is represented by the feeling of unification with the Cosmos. In my opinion, the six and seven year olds' pantheist intuitions are the result of these having previously experienced the Self, while still the latter was undifferentiated from the Ego, namely the consequence of a perceived continuity between themselves and a lively world.

4.1.4 The latent legitimating function of religion displayed by children's representations

The theme *God, the Protector* secondarily refers to the function of legitimating societal goals and procedures. God guards world peace and helps good people, so believe children. Some codes in the theme *The Church mediates the relationship with God* also refer secondly to the same function: God wants people to be good and He, Himself teaches them to be good and nice.

4.1.5 The latent identity function of religion in children's representations

The second main theme, in terms of its frequency in drawings, is *God is from another world*. Its content reveals the way in which children imagine and understand God. Most of the content is not canonical and even when it is (as it is the case of the representations of angels and Heaven that I have already discussed), its canonical dimension is subordinated to the awareness of differentiation between the status of people and the status of God. The former lives in the space among stars and rockets, flies, shines, gives off rays, is between two worlds, and is great. (Ordinary) people are not like that.

The assuming of status differences consolidates human identity. Thus, as a latent function of religion, conferring identity by providing complete and final answers concerning a human being's place in the world is active in the case of the drawing children ("in the cosmic space and in the eternal order", Wilson, 2000, p. 46).

Why do drawers who demonstrate enough catechetic knowledge (obvious in the representations of the theme *The Church mediates the relationship with God*) choose so many non-canonical expressions of status differences between God and people? The reason could be related to children's age and their difficulty in managing abstract concepts. As previously shown, the drawings and the explanations framing the theme *God is from another world* shape children's imagination. Their dogmatic freedom gives evidence of their permeability to unrefined religious experience that is not filtered catechistically. God is in children's mind as they draw Him. That is not the place to look for dogmatic inadequacies.

Another answer to the question above could be that children's representations picture the dogmatic freedom that Orthodox Christianity tacitly tolerates of the faithful. This broad mindedness allowed for pre-Christian beliefs to survive in the Romanian cultural space, whereas these had disappeared from Homer's Greece (Eliade, 1991). Romanian Orthodox priests often include in the cult's rites local customs and traditions in order to draw near the parishioners whom they need to guide.

Both explanations refer to a Christian faith that is slightly different from the canonical one. In the context of the explanation referring to the survival of pre-Christian beliefs, God's celestial dimension, which is well captured by children's drawings, can echo the cult of Gebeleizis, a God from Dacia whose meteorological attributes (Eliade, 1995) have been internalized by popular Christianity and ascribed to Saint Elijah. Hence, in such a case, God's celestial dimension would associate a discreet ethnic touch to the drawers' religiosity. The representations of a shining, radiating God also find their correspondence in the religiosity of the Dacians, namely in the latter's solar dimension (Surdu, 2010).

The implicit theme *God's human appearance* strengthens the identity function: God has a face and adopts human-like postures. People resemble Him, namely, according to the Bible, they are "after His image and in His likeness". The identity function of religion is also signalled by the codes of the themes *God is from another world* and *God's human appearance.* The association of these themes is somewhat paradoxical, but I believe that it does not yield any logical incongruence, or at least, it is not more logically unsettling than the dogma of the Incarnation that it captures. In any case, logical coherence is not one of the necessary attributes of religion.

The theme *God is of female gender* still displays a particular form of the identity function. God's femininity is a bold idea in a Western cultural context configured by Christianity. The Christian's God is a male. Virgin Mary is simply the Mother of God and, even though she ascended to Heaven after her Dormition, she is not part of the Trinity. She is holy but not divine. As a result of this dogmatic interpretation, men's status at church is superior to women's (and that is visible in the various interdictions for women, the place assigned to these at church or when the faithful line up for priest's blessing).

The under-appreciation of the feminine dimension of divinity generates an imbalance within Christianity and that prevents it from meeting all the needs of all the faithful, believes Jung (1997). Mary's apparitions, especially in the Catholic sphere, are a tell-tale sign of an unsolved problem related to the problem regarding the representation of the feminine element around the mystery of Trinity, shows the same psychologist. Virgin Mary's apparitions (many of them in front of children because it is easier for them to manage the relation with the collective unconscious) express the activation in the collective unconscious of the hope for a super human intervention that would restore the balance. The proclamation of the *Assumtionis Mariae* dogma in the Catholic sphere has been "the most important religious event since the Reform", claims Jung (1997, p. 302). This is the expression of a profound wish of the faithful, and it is the crowning event in the popular movement towards introducing the cult of the Virgin Mary. The proclamation of this dogma signals the time for reducing the status differences between men and women. There are other similar signs, according to Marie-Louise von Franz (2016). The increasing interest shown in Mary to the detriment of the Trinity as a masculine triad is associated with the feminist movement and debates on women's right to the priesthood. Such signals are a conscious level echo of a rising movement of the feminine principle from within the collective unconscious.

All children who declared their gender and drew God as a female are girls. First, that may mean that religious intuitions are gender dependent and that in the case of females these intuitions are later reformulated through catechesis. Despite the two millennia in the history of Christianity, girls' immediate (not mediated) religious experience is related to the archetypal image of the Great Mother. Second, if C.G. Jung (1997) is right and hence in Western religiosity, they are preparing a resurrection that is giving the feminine back its value, then that could mostly result in the affirmation (namely the imposing) of feminine religiosity. A feminine God, who is drawn (that is, confessed?) by the little girls, expresses a particular dimension of the latent identity function of religion.

The same function is also secondarily signalled as a continuity between the individual and the world in the theme *God is in everything.*

4.1.6 *The latent function of expressing and managing emotions depicted by children's representations*

This latent function of religion is present in the theme, *The Church mediates the relationship with God*, through children's references to God's dialogue with the faithful (namely those who go to church to talk to Him), and to the faith and prayers that He requests from people.

4.1.7 *Dimensions of the religious experience highlighted by children's representations*

Children's drawings and explanations indicate their relation with a religion that fulfils its traditional manifest and latent functions. The themes identified through data processing cover each of the functions described by Wilson (2000). The fulfilling of these functions associates with various dimensions of the religious experience. Rudolf Otto (1992) placed at the core of the religious experience *mysterium tremendum*, the mysterious fear generated by the encounter with the numinous, *ganz Andere*. Such an encounter gives rise in men the *creature-feeling*, a feeling of human nothingness. This feeling is highlighted by children's representations of the differences in status between God and humans.

There are several dimensions of *mysterium tremendum*, according to Otto. Out of these, in correlation with the creature-feeling, children's drawings represent the *majestas* (that is the absolute superiority of the numinous) and the *augustus* (namely, the admirable, the objective value of the numinous): God is represented as a giant because He is powerful, sits on a pedestal, shines and wears royal signs, has an halo and other canonical signs of status. The other dimensions of the *mysterium tremendum* mentioned by Otto, namely *tremendum* (the dreadful effect), *energicum* (the vital liveliness), and *fascinans* (the enchanting nature), are not captured by children's representations. The components that they picture are friendly and rather associated to serene contemplation than to religious tumult. The religious experience of which children thus indicate to have some knowledge is pleasant and relaxed. It is compatible with the joy characteristic of the core of Orthodoxy. In the case of the Protestant children, the order of the main themes by their frequency is slightly different from that of the Orthodox and Catholic children. In the case of the Protestants, the first theme (encompassing the greatest number of representations) is *God is from another world* (Tab. 4). As I have already indicated, this theme subsumes codes of a non-canonical, personalized view of God. Compared to the drawings of the Orthodox and Catholic children that are inspired mainly by the catechetic, church-specific representations of God (highlighted by the theme *The Church mediates the relationship with God*), those of the Protestants' are freer of such influences. The latter show the courage to directly and personally assume the relationship with God to a greater extent. However, on condition that a disproportionate number of sources is considered (178 Orthodox and Catholic drawers and 8 Protestant drawers), one can consider that the different hierarchies of children's options (personalized versus canonical) reiterate the distinct features of Protestantism within Christianity. The boldness displayed by the drawings could be exactly the defining feature of Protestantism that made this form of Christianity evolve from Catholic constraints. Lucian Blaga, a Romanian philosopher of culture, called this form of courage "an individuating formative aspiration" (Blaga, 1994) when referring to the Protestants from Transylvania. Also, this Christian audacity is the same that Weber (2007) placed in a formative relation with capitalism.

4.2 Romanian children's religiosity versus contemporary Western religiosity

As already mentioned, the transformations at a functional level, which Wilson (2000) considers typical of the contemporary West, do not seem to characterize the drawers' religiosity. There are also other theoretical approaches to Western religiosity, but they do not completely match children's drawings. However, in order to outline them, I will first overview, in terms of its main features, the contemporary theoretical representation of Western religiosity.

4.2.1 Secularization

The concept of secularization has been at the core of the discussions on Western religiosity. Following Weber's view on the disenchantment of the world as a result of rationality development, the term has several dimensions: loss of control over social life by religious institutions (the hard core of theories of secularization, according to David Martin, 2005), the replacement of human groups' religious organization with a profane one, and the general diminishing of society's religious character. The processes of differentiating among the social spheres, privatization of religion, and its decline (Casanova, 1994) detail and highlight these views. The latter are condensed by Dobbelaere (2011) who, in a clarifying manner, attributes two dimensions to the secularization process: the loss of religious social power and the decrease in individual piety. In the context of Weber's definition of secularization, terms like *loss, reduction, replacement, decline, and diminishing* do not acquire negative connotations. They are associated with the praise of individual religious freedom and, according to Zuckerman (2014), with its positive consequences: respect for the rights of women or sexual minorities, encouragement of independent thinking in children, and expanding the horizons of knowledge.

4.2.2 Atheism

Secularization enhances rational atheism (or, in other words, atheism resulting from scientific knowledge). This kind of atheism is not an invention of the modern West. Yet, it has found in it an environment for adequate development and manifestation (Codoban, 1996). Modern scientific knowledge has been the survival solution to the persecution of the imaginary conducted by the church (Culianu, 1994), and has gradually led (with no revanchist aim) to a representation of a world in which God is not a necessary presence. The Western *Weltanschauung* has been consolidated by the constraining claims of logical positivism dating back to the first half of the 20th century and by its hard to ignore echoes. Analytical doubts on the capacity of other disciplines than physics to own and deliver truths have supplied strong arguments against religion and have profoundly destabilized the comfort of faith. For educated Westerners, evolution towards loss of faith is logically justified and predictable, according to J. Turner (1985). Loss of faith can also be anthropologically justified: religion promotes unrealistic representations of human nature and of solutions to the great problems of humanity, and as a result it is a barrier to mankind's social and intellectual progress, a source of conflicts, wars, massacres, and a means to exploit its adepts and endanger their lives, states Bainbridge (2011).

4.2.3 *Spirituality*

At the same time, Western secularization is accompanied by an increase in spirituality. This is only an apparently paradoxical situation. The term of "spirituality" has two main definitions (Hamberg, 2011): it can refer to a superior form of piety (this is the meaning employed within a religion) or to a form of alternative religiosity (an alternative to the dominant, institutionalized religion, namely to Christianity). The coexistence of these two definitions is supported by the distinction between religion and religiosity. The process of secularization refers to dominant religions. The loss of confidence in official religion favours the development of other religious options. In this context, secularization is, as Dobbelaere (2011) claims, compatible to spirituality. Many forms of spirituality are similar to the old popular religions (Stark, Hamberg and Miller, apud. Hamberg, 2011). Besides, there is a reoccurrence of paganism in Europe (Lindquist, 1997; Sorea, 2013, 2015). Europeans' appetite for indigenous neo-pagan beliefs has been viewed as a reaction to the loss in importance of the nation state as a result of the new political configuration of Europe, within the context of globalization, technocracy, and of environmental crisis (Lindquist, 1997), and also as a consequence of the anxieties associated by Bauman (2000) to "liquid modernity" (Rountree, 2014).

The relationship between spirituality and atheism takes many forms: starting from the critical detachment from Christianity (a soft form of religious atheism), going through some rational explanations that refer to energies or fields (a form of scientific atheism), and culminating with the attempts to retrieve Christianity through the lenses of the new spiritual orientations.

4.2.4 *Secularization is neither obvious nor irreversible*

Norris and Ingelhart (2012) consider that the decrease in people's religiosity is a continuous and irreversible process in mankind's history. According to them, in former socialist European countries, after only two decades of religious resurrection, the religious reorientation is towards atheism. However, secularization is not unanimously considered obvious or unavoidable. The wide agreement of the 1960s on the Enlightenment rooted relation between modernism and the decline of religion is challenged from different directions.

In this respect, Hamberg (2011) starts from the definition of spirituality as alternative religiosity and shows that if secularization is a decline in Christian religiosity then the European countries are undergoing a process of secularization, but, according to the same author, if secularization is a decline in any form of religiosity, Europe's secularization is no longer obvious because the loss in the importance of the officially organized religion favors and is counter-balanced by thriving spiritual movements outside formal religious institutions.

Other critical views on secularization highlight clearly its local European character. The theoretical underpinnings of secularization rely on the ideas of capitalism, industrialization, individualism, and pluralism (Dueck et al., 2017), as well as on the concept of a liberal and pragmatic Europe (Nikiforova, 2017), and are tributary to a Western *Weltanschauung*. A correct approach would consider Western intellectuals (who are consolidating their position in this respect), as well Central and Western Europe's secular orientation as an exception and not a defining trait of contemporary religiosity, considers Peter Berger (2012).

Berger, one of the classics of the secularization theory (1967), has reconsidered, based on empirical findings, his position, imposing the term of "desecularization" (1999) and suggesting the coexistence of a secular implicit discourse along with a plurality of religious discourses in contemporary society (2012). In the context of globalization, the Western world cannot isolate itself from the revitalizing influence of Christian movements from other parts of the world, claims Coffey (2013). Hamberg (2011) views the current attitude of youth towards religion and religiosity as an indicator of desecularization. Lambert (2003) signals a diminished pace of secularization and a re-intensification of Christianity in youth, along with the development of a believing without belonging. Dobbelaere (2011) believes that the revalorization of religion in Russia and in the other former Communist countries as part of their citizens' redefined identity indicates the reversibility of the secularization process.

Lee Ellis et al. (2017) also support the idea of the reversible character of secularization. They build their arguments on previous studies on the positive correlation between religiosity and fertility, and the negative connection of intelligence with each of the two. As a result of these correlations, the authors formulate three previsions that are neither quite politically correct nor too comforting: the religiosity level of the whole world will increase, the weight of presence of the Islam among the religions of the world will also expand, and the average level of intelligence worldwide will gradually decrease.

Other critical positions focus on characterizing the contemporary age as post-secular. The term "post-secular" was coined by Habermas and is used to indicate, on one hand, the retrieval of Christ's love through contemporary viable forms of love of the neighbor (democracy, charity, responsibility, community development, and cohesion), namely the retrieval of the sacred through the profane (Rorty şi Vattimo, 2008; Girard şi Vattimo, 2009), or, on the other hand, by transforming the border between the sacred and the profane into a flexible one: religious tourism as a form of entertainment, churches used as concert halls, religious relics gathered in private collections, but also consumption as a spiritual, psychotherapeutic experience (Nikiforova, 2017), religious attitudes expressed in secular spaces, but also profane attitudes that are present in sacred areas (Pfister, 2017).

4.2.5 Rational choice theory of religion as a theoretical alternative to secularization

Rational choice theory of religion (RCTR) is one of the most rigorous (by the criteria of logical empiricism) structured alternative theories to the theory of secularization. RCTR, elaborated by R. Stark and W.S. Bainbridge (1980), and developed by Stark, L.R. Iannaccone and R. Finke, operates with human interactions as exchange forms in which actors tend to maximize their profit. In the case of religion, many of the desired benefits (for which the actors are willing to pay the costs) cannot be obtained in this world. People are willing to accept explanations concerning what they have to do in this world in relation with God or with gods in order to obtain benefits. In the case of complex societies, dealing with gods becomes an attribute of specialists and is part of organizational structures. The trust in gods as partners increases if the number of the faithful grows, and therefore religion is a collective phenomenon. Religious organizations are in competition for followers. They offer their products (benefits that cannot be obtained elsewhere, answers to the important questions on human life) at different costs. These are related to the social capital (the network of relations among the members of religious communities) and the religious one (a set of acquired religious knowledge and competences) of their potential believers (Stark and Finke, 2000). A broad religious market and competition among religious products offered (which incur recruitment of parishioners, assuming a missionary role, conversions) ensure meeting different needs of the faithful and thus the population's active and wide participation in religious life.

At this point, the opposition between the theory of secularization and RCTR becomes obvious. Pluralism and competition are considered in the case of the former as factors favoring the secularization process, sabotaging the authority of religious institutions, and encouraging religious indifference (Hamilton, 2011). According to RCTR, religion flourishes in the context of a free market with pluralism and competition. Lack of competition, religious monopoly, and/or the state's regulating intervention on the religious market cannot satisfy all people's preferences and leads to the loss of religious vitality. The case of the USA, difficult to explain through the theory of secularization, supports RCTR: there are a lot of denominations and an active and wide participation in religious life against the background of high technological development. On the other hand, in Europe, the cradle and reference point for the theory of secularization, there is low religious vitality and the religious market is controlled to the benefit of the dominant religion (Hamilton, 2011).

4.2.6 Correlating the status of parenthood with religiosity

Against the background of these theoretical criticisms of secularization, there is an increasing number of empirical studies that also show the inadequacy of secular discourse to the reality in the field. Here are some of these, worth mentioning for the theme of this research: bearing children leads couples closer to religion (Lundquist Denton & Uecker, 2018) and determines godless or pagan parents to find peaceful means of coexistence with the Christian majority (McClure, 2017). The level of religiosity is positively correlated with the joy of parenthood (Cranney, 2017) and religious belonging still models human groups shaping the way teenagers' networks of friendship build: parents' religiosity influences the forging of relations, and teenagers' religiosity stabilizes them (Cook, Schwadel, Cheadle, 2017).

Children's drawings suggest a differentiated relation of their religiosity with the characteristics that are theoretically highlighted by Western religiosity.

4.2.7 The process of secularization, not very relevant

Romania is one of the European countries ruled by a secular and secularizing political regime in the second half of the last century. The drawings about God made by the children 15 and 27 years, respectively, after the change of the regime in 1989 contradict the references to secularization as a continuous and irreversible process. The drawings from 2004 are predominantly canonical after 50 years of socialist education of the drawers' grandparents and parents. The 2016 drawings are made outside the 20-year time period that Norris and Ingelhart (2012) predict for the former socialist countries to become atheist.

Children's drawings rather show that Peter Berger's opinion (2012) is right: secularization within society is not necessarily related to secularization at the level of individual consciousness and that, even though churches have lost their influence at state level, religious faiths and practices are still present. In this context, the Orthodox hierarchs who minimized the problem of secularization for the ROC might have been right. They hardly admitted that secularization is a challenge for Orthodoxy (Conovici, 2009). Daniel Ciobotea, the current ROC Patriarch, shows the positive potential of secularization, which resides in a paradoxically forced shift from Christianity, as inherited tradition, to the conscious and insightful acceptance of a lively faith (Ciobotea, 2001). D. Popescu (1996) believes that Romanians will resist secularization by merging the lucid rationality of the West with Eastern mystical love. Their position might reflect more than a stubborn reluctance towards a theme of Western origin, and it could be the expression of authentic knowledge of both the resources of Orthodoxy and Romanians' religiosity.

The fact that historically and politically Romania surpassed a programmatically atheist and secularizing regime does not automatically generate a post-secular relation of Romanians with religion. The retrieval of Christian love through charity mentioned by Rorty and Vattimo (2008) has (momentarily) no reference point for Romanians. As already shown above, children's drawings indicate their relation with a lively religion that fulfils its traditional functions. Retrieval is about losing something first (Sorea, 2009). Since the influence of Christianity is not lost, the Christian love message does not need retrieval. Children's references to a God who requires/teaches us to be good can be considered, at the very most, discrete signs of post-secular charity.

4.2.8 Delimitation from the atheist trend

As I have previously shown, the reference point for children's representations of God is a religion that seems to be fulfilling its traditional latent and manifest functions as described by Wilson (2000). The multitude of codes pertaining to the main themes (*The Church mediates the relation with God* and *God is from another world*) show the proper catechetic education of the drawers and a personal acknowledgment of their relation with God. Children performed the task of drawing God with ease because they were knowledgeable about the subject. Only three of them confessed that they did not know how to draw Him. All this information indicates that undoubtedly the drawers are not atheists. Rather the contrary, I would say. The contemporary trend of spreading atheism is not reflected by children's drawings.

Some of the graphical solutions chosen by children and some of their explanations are both spectacular (because of their theological intuition) and touching (as pre-logical efforts to operate with abstract concepts). God can have a triangular head (since He is part of the Trinity). He can be drawn as red little hearts since He is love. Sometimes His halo is drawn as an antenna above the head. He has a very big hand that He is extending from the sky to support people and bring a sack of bread ("Our daily bread..."). In one of the representations of the Crucifixion, Jesus is holding the Bible (since that is how it was written to happen), in another God is drawn next to the Cross (so that He would hear "Eli,

Eli…"). Mary is wearing heels and God, who is old, is wearing glasses. Sometimes there are rockets flying past Him (He lives after all in Heavens), and in another drawing He does not have any legs because He does not need any since He does not walk on Earth.

The children who drew and explained their work in this way are not atheists. Their representations show the acknowledgment of their relation with God in accordance with their power of understanding. Coles (1990) has highlighted the natural religiosity of children, their growth in the horizon of an expected encounter with divinity. The children's representations of God show that Colen was right and stand as arguments that consolidate the conclusion about drawers' demarcation from the atheist trend.

4.2.9 Rational choice theory of religion requires amendments

The multitude of the main themes in *The Church mediates the relation with God* and *God is from another world*, the theme of catechistically correct codes and the theme of a God who is personally acknowledged, sanction RCTR. The majority of Romanians are Orthodox and yet the monopoly of Orthodoxy does not inhibit religious experience. The relation between the state and Orthodoxy does not seem to fit the theory since there is neither a multitude of denominations, which should support the religious effervescence as in the USA, nor religious apathy like in Western European countries, which are characterized by religious monopolies. This non-conformance to the theory might be the result of the religious freedoms, which Orthodoxy, through its priests, tolerates; I referred to them above. A more detailed description of this situation has already been provided in the previous chapters. By tacitly allowing for these domestic and controlled freedoms, Orthodoxy ensures the fulfilment of its believers' different needs. By bringing a (relatively) diversified offer within it, Orthodoxy ensures the faithful adequate support for fairly diverse religious experiences. RCTR could be amended in such a context as follows: in the case of religious cults with high tolerance to believers' transgressions from canons, religious monopoly does not inhibit religious experiences. Tolerance to believers' transgressions from canons represents religious specialists' tacit acceptance of certain faiths and local practices that belong to other religious traditions than the official religion, that is of compensators that are different from those attached to obtaining rewards in the dominant religious explanation. The acceptance is not related to the main expressions of the explanation, but to the negotiation of additional compensators.

Orthodoxy and Catholicism are the oldest Christian denominations. They officially separated in 1054 during the Great Schism. Orthodoxy is the dominant religion in the former territories of the Byzantine Empire and the Russian Empire. Orthodox Christians are organized in autocephalous churches (Greek, Romanian, Russian, Serbian church, etc.), and these acknowledge the same tradition and share the same beliefs and principles of religious organization. Orthodoxy, whose priests are ordained in apostolic succession, is very keen on upholding Christian tradition. Theologically speaking, Orthodoxy considers itself as the keeper of the original Christian teachings (it is the "right belief"). However, most local traditions that are tolerated by the Romanian priests date from before Christianity. I believe that in this case the dogma prevails to the detriment of its letter, which means a (re)anchoring in an older form of religiosity in which Christianity is at least partially rooted. Whether legitimate or not, this anchoring seems to be the winning choice since it supports religious experiences and avoids apathy.

4.2.10 The tendency to enlarge the scope of spirituality

Related to the tacit tolerance of Orthodoxy, children's drawings really do show their open attitude towards an enlarged spirituality that goes beyond the Christian one. This openness is mentioned by Hamberg (2011) and Dobbelaere (2011), who consider it a feature of contemporary Europe. Some of God's traits in *God is from another world* and some associated with the theme *God, the protector* are very little related to canonical Christianity. I have already mentioned them: God lives in the space among stars, He has a school in the skies (from where angles bring homework to the saints on Earth), He levitates and flies, there are rockets flying high past Him, He is a giant and only angels know what He looks like, people cannot see Him well. He has solar attributes – He radiates, He is wearing a garment in the colours of the Sun (because there is no life without the Sun), and He has a shining face. Green butterflies are His messengers and He gives people ideas. The enlarged definition of religiosity with which children operate is also reflected in the themes that are less frequent but which are spectacularly anchored in the anthropology of religion: *God is of female gender* and *God is in everything*. These themes subsume references to experiences of the Self, which are not highly valued by Christianity.

The comparative approach to the drawings from 2004 and 2016 by longitudinal analysis reflected parents' increasing catechetic role in 2016. As compared to 2004, those who talk to children about God in 2016 are more often their parents and not their grandparents (*Fig. 14*). The 2004 drawings display a canonical, ecclesiastic dimension more frequently than those from 2016, whereas the latter include a multitude of codes related to the theme *God is from another world*. As *Figs. 15* and *16* show, parents, as a source of religious education for their children, are less tied to canonical Christianity (they take more liberties in this respect) compared to their parents (that is, the grandparents of drawing children). The studies on the relation between religiosity and parenthood (Cranney, 2017; Lundquist Denton & Uecker, 2018) give reason (encourage) to draw the conclusions on six- and seven-year-old children's representations of God in the case of their parents too. Thus, related to this finding, children's drawings reveal a tendency of contemporary Romanians to evolve towards an enlarged scope of their spirituality.

5 Conclusions: Results, limitations, and further themes

The children who drew God are not atheist and, since those who tell them about God are their parents, nor are these. Their represented God is friendly and cheerful, and their drawings consolidate the status of Orthodoxy as a "religion of joy" as a result of its soteriological orientation towards the Resurrection. Girls' drawings of a God of female gender suggest a differentiation of primary religious intuitions by gender. Drawers' representations of God justify the amending to RCTR in the sense of limiting the effects of religious monopoly in the case of the cults that are highly tolerant with their believers' transgressions from canons. The different approaches to the theme in 2004 and in 2016 show a widening of spirituality in children's communities of origin.

These are the main results of the interpretation of available data. This study's interpretative approach to the drawings is almost implicitly interdisciplinary, since it relies on interweaving anthropology, psychology, sociology of religion, phenomenology, and theology.

Using the drawing technique to study children's religiosity is adequate and fruitful. I believe it was difficult to use other means to generate childish representations of God like those picturing Him as a female and which are correlated with the drawers' gender (in this respect, I would like to thank Florentina Scârneci-Domnişoru for the suggestion). In addition, employing the drawing technique was very pleasant. The drawings and the children's explanations provided a lot of surprises. The appropriation of the way in which children represent God generated a lot of joy.

At the same time, in terms of this study's limitations, it turned out to be risky to extrapolate the results of children's religiosity to the religiosity of all Romanians. Such an approach is only selectively justified. For example, Romanian students are upset with the Romanian Orthodox Church, and especially with its representatives, the priests, whom they view as more focused on material benefits than on their status-related spiritual responsibilities (Sorea, 2015; 2018). Concerning the approach of the Romanian Orthodox Church to Christianity, which is pretty relaxed, friendly, and permissive to pre-Christian traditions (and which is also aligned to the trend of expanding the scope of spirituality, already shown by children's drawings), students have a high regard. Students' anger is not directed against entire Christianity, but against the businessmen in church. However, this study does not reflect any echo of the aforementioned anger, which indicates that there might be some other features of Romanians' religiosity that are not captured by its findings. Therefore, I believe that the limitation is one of the approach to extrapolate and not one of the technique employed to conduct the research.

On the other hand, maybe the example above only reflects the impact of acknowledging parenthood in relation with the church, an effect already discussed by Lundquist Denton and Uecker (2018). Maybe the impact is so powerful that former objecting students transform into the parents responsible for their children's religious education that the study unveils. In this respect, I believe that this possibility is a research direction worth investigating. Another research line that may prove just as generous in findings and is opened by this study is related to students' objections too. This is about the transformation of the 2004 drawers who were friends with God into today's students, who are angry with the Orthodox priests. In my opinion, outlining the context and details of this evolution is really necessary in order to clarify the representations on the religiosity of today's Romanians.

The results of the study suggest, as desirable research themes, the potential invulnerability of Orthodoxy to secularization and the limits of Freud's view on religion as a collective neurosis which results from projecting Oedipus complex onto the entire humankind (Freud, 1991). There are some more themes. All these inviting research themes opened by the current study consolidate the drawing technique as an adequate and fruitful technique for studying children's religiosity.

Bibliography

Bainbridge, W. S. (2011). Atheism. In P. B. Clarke (Ed.), *The Oxford Handbook of the Sociology of Religion* (pp. 319–335). Oxford: Oxford University Press.

Bauman, Z. (2000). *Liquid Modernity*. Cambridge: Polity Press.

Berger, P. L. (1967). *The Sacred Canopy; Elements of a Sociological Theory of Religion*. Garden City: Doubleday.

Berger, P. L. (1999). The Desecularization of the World. A Global Overview. In P.L. Berger (Ed.), *The Desecularization of the World. Resurgent Religion and World Politics* (pp. 1–18). Grand Rapids: Eerdmans.

Berger, P. L. (2005). Orthodoxy and Global Pluralism. *Demokratizatsiya: The Journal of Post-Soviet Democratization, 13*(3), 437–447.

Berger, P. L. (2012). Further Thoughts on Religion and Modernity. *Society, 49*(4), 313–316.

Blaga, L. (1994). *Orizont și stil*. București: Humanitas.

Braun, V. & Clarke, V. (2006). Using Thematic Analysis in Psychology. *Qualitative Research in Psychology, 3*(2), 77–101.

Casanova, J. (1994). *Public Religions in the Modern World*. Chicago: University of Chicago Press.

Ciobotea, D. (2001). *Confessing the Truth in Love: Orthodox Perception of Life. Mission and Unity*. Iași: Trinitas.

Codoban, A. (1996). *Sacru și ontofanie*. Iași: Polirom.

Coffey, J. (2013). *Secularizarea: Este ea inevitabilă?* Timișoara: Excelsior Art.

Coles, R. (1990). *The Spiritual Life of Children*. Boston: Houghton-Mifflin Company.

Conovici, I. (2009). *Ortodoxia în România postcomunistă. Reconstrucția unei identități publice, vol. I*. Cluj-Napoca: Eikon.

Cook, J. B., Schwadel, P. &Cheadle, J. E. (2017). The Origins of Religious Homophily in a Medium and Large School. *Review of Religious Research, 59*, 65–80.

Cranney, S. (2017). Is There a Stronger Association Between Children and Happiness Among the Religious? Religion as a Moderator in the Relationship Between Happiness and Child Number. *Journal of Happiness Studies, 18* (6), 1713–1727.

Culianu, I. P. (1994). *Eros și magie în Renaștere*. 1484. București: Nemira.

Dobbelaere, K. (2011) The Meaning and Scope of Secularization. In P. B. Clarke (Ed.), *The Oxford Handbook of the Sociology of Religion* (pp. 599–615). Oxford: Oxford University Press.

Dueck, A., Ansloos, J., Johnson, A., Fort, C. (2017). Western Cultural Psychology of Religion: Alternatives to Ideology. *Pastoral Psychology, 66*, 397–425.

Eliade, M. (1991). *Istoria credințelor și ideilor religioase, vol. I–III*. București: Editura Științifică.

Eliade, M. (1995). *De la Zalmoxis la Genghis-Han*. București: Humanitas.

Foucault, M. (1984). Des espaces autres. *Architecture, Mouvement, Continuité, 5*, 46–49.

Franz, M.-L. von. (2016). *Pisica. O poveste despre răscumărarea femininului.* Bucureşti: Nemira.

Freud, S. (1991). *Opere, vol. I.* Bucureşti: Editura Ştiinţifică.

Girard, R., & Vattimo, G. (2009). *Adevăr sau credinţă slabă? Convorbiri despre creştinism şi relativism.* Bucureşti: Curtea Veche.

Hamberg, E. M. (2011). Unchurched Spirituality. In P. B. Clarke (ed.), *The Oxford Handbook of the Sociology of Religion* (pp. 742–757). Oxford: Oxford University Press.

Hamilton, M. (2011). Rational Choise Theory: A Critique. In P. B. Clarke (Ed.), *The Oxford Handbook of the Sociology of Religion* (pp. 116–135). Oxford: Oxford University Press.

Heelas, P. (2011). Spiritualities of Life. In P. B. Clarke (Ed.), *The Oxford Handbook of the Sociology of Religion* (pp.752–782). Oxford: Oxford University Press.

Jung, C. G. (1997). *Imaginea omului şi imaginea lui Dumnezeu.* Bucureşti: Teora.

Jung, C. G. (2005a). *Opere complete, vol. 9.* Bucureşti: Trei.

Jung, C. G. (2005b). *Opere complete, vol. 14.* Bucureşti: Trei.

Lambert, Y. (2003). New Christianity, Indifference and Diffused Spirituality. In H. Mcleod and W. Ustorf (Eds.), *The Decline of Christendom in Western Europe 1750–2000* (pp. 63–78). Cambridge: Cambridge University Press.

Linquist, G. (1997). *Shamanic Performances on the Urban Scene: Neo-Shamanism in Contemporary Sweden.* Stockholm: Stockolm University Press.

Lossky, V. (2010). *Teologia mistică a Bisericii de Răsărit.* Bucureşti: Humanitas.

Lundquist Denton, M. & Uecker, J. E. (2018). What God Has Joined Together: Family Formation and Religion among Young Adults. *Review of Religious Research, 60*(1), 1–22.

Martin, D. (2005). *On Secularization: Towards a Revised General Theory.* Aldershot/Burlington: Ashgate.

McClure, A. I. (2017). Becoming a Parent Changes Everything: How Nonbeliever and Pagan Parents Manage Stigma in the U.S. Bible Belt. *Qualitative Sociology, 40,* 331–352.

Nikiforova, B. (2017). Cultural and Religious Dimensions of the Sacred and Profane Ambivalence: The Vilnius Case. *Studies in East European Thought,* 69 (2), 153–164.

Norris, P., Inglehart, R. (2012). *Sacred and Secular: Religion and Politics Worldwide.* Cambridge: Cambridge University Press.

Otto, R. (1992). *Sacrul.* Cluj-Napoca: Dacia.

Pfister, L. F. (2017). Ubication: A Phenomenological Study About Making Spaces Sacred. *International Communication of Chinese Culture*, 4(3), 393–411.

Piaget, J. (1965). *Psihologia inteligenţei*. Bucureşti: Editura Didactică şi Pedagogică.

Popescu, D. (1996). *Ortodoxie şi contemporaneitate*. Bucureşti: Diogene.

Rorty, R., & Vattimo, G. (2008). *Viitorul religiei. Solidaritate, caritate, ironie*. Piteşti: Paralela 45.

Rountree, K. (2014). Neo-Paganism, Native Faith and Indigenous Religion: A Case Study of Malta Within the European Context. *Social Anthropology, 22*(1), 81–100.

Scârneci-Domnişoru, F. (2016). *Datele vizuale în cercetarea socială*. Cluj-Napoca: Presa Universitară Clujeană.

Sorea, D. (2009). Observations with Respect to the Future of Religion Prefigured by R. Rorty and G. Vattimo. *Bulletin of the Transilvania University of Braşov, Series VII: Social Sciences and Law*, *2*(51), 237–242.

Sorea, D. (2013). Two Particular Expressions of Neo-Paganism. *Bulletin of the Transilvania University of Braşov, Series VII - Social Sciences and Law*, *6*(55), *no.*1, 29–40.

Sorea, D. (2015). Între revoltă şi înfiorare. Religiozitatea studenţilor sociologi. In A. Buzalic, I. Duşe (Eds.). *Biserică şi societate* (pp.193–212). Cluj-Napoca: Presa Universitară Clujeană.

Sorea, D. (2018). The Way Romanian Students Refer Themselves to Orthodox Christianity. *International Conference KNOWLEDGE-BASED ORGANIZATION, Vol. XXIV, no.*2. Retrieved from https://www.degruyter.com/downloadpdf/j/kbo.2018.24.issue-2/

Stark, R. & Bainbridge, W.S. (1980): Secularization, Revival and Cult Formation. *Annual Review of the Social Sciences of Religion*, *4*, 85–119.

Stark, R. & Finke, R. (2000). *Acts and Faith: Explaining the Human Side of Religion*. Berkeley: University of California Press.

Stăniloaie, D. (1991). De ce suntem ortodocşi. *Teologie şi viaţă*, *I*(LXVII), 4–8, 15–27.

Surdu, A. (2010). *Şcheii Braşovului*. Braşov: Kron-Art.

Turner, J. (1985). *Without God, Without Creed*. Baltimore: Johns Hopkins University Press.

Weber, M. (2007). *Etica protestantă şi spiritul capitalismului*. Bucureşti: Humanitas.

Williams, R.R., & Whitehouse, K. (2015). Photo Elicitation and the Visual Sociology of Religion. *Review of Religious Research*, *57*(2), 303–318.

Wilson, B. (2000). *Religia din perspectivă sociologică*. București: Trei.

Zuckerman, P. (2014). *Living the Secular Life: New Answers to Old Questions*. New York: Penguin Press.

Zuckerman, P. (2016). *10-Revealing-Maps-Religion-Europe*. Retrieved from http://www.ucatholic.com/blog/.

Mihaela Gotea

VII Exploring social workers' perceptions of their marital partners in different family life stages, using visual methodology

Abstract: Family life interferes with or supports the professional performance of individuals; this idea has been explored and underlined by a growing body of research. While this work is critical, little research attempts to incorporate the views and perspectives of social workers about their family lives using visual methodologies have been made. Specifically, in the present study I aimed to explore the role of the family environment in supporting the professional life of the social workers. I investigated marital partner's identity aspects perceived by the subjects at different stages of their family life. The sample of the present study numbered a total of 22 participants, aged between 25 and 65, who were working in NGOs (13) or public organizations (9). The data collecting method was respondent-generated image production. In the present study, the participants have chosen to photograph an image or a series of images for illustrating or symbolizing her/his life partner. The portrait of the Romanian social worker's intimate partner is composed of a wide range of qualities and roles, as the results demonstrated. The most important features of their marital partners are represented by their domestic roles, and their psycho-behavioral qualities. In addition, the results of this study support the idea that in each stage of family life, the perception on the partner focuses on certain identity features, and their hierarchy changes from one stage to another. In the current study, the findings are discussed in connection with the specific features of this profession, marital satisfaction, and job performance.

Keywords: family life, marital partner, respondent-generated image production, auto-photography

1 Introduction

The role played by social work in society is to protect large sections of the population from the negative impact of the growing social and economic inequalities, which Asquith, Clark, and Waterhouse (2005) consider that will continue to characterize life for many individuals, families, and communities in the 21st century. Working with vulnerable social categories involves vocation, professionalism, and certain personality traits.

Social workers are parts of a social environment; they do not operate in a vacuum. The mission, the aims, and the functions of social work, on one hand, and the roles played by the social workers in contemporary society, on the other hand, have been influenced by major social changes which have occurred over the last decades and years, such as: changing demographic structures, increased poverty, exclusion, disadvantage, and the internationalization of social problems (N.A.S.W., 2016). As Asquith, Clark, and Waterhouse (2005) highlight, there is no doubt that these social changes, which social work has had to accommodate, will continue to impact on social work in the future.

In Romania, social work is a relatively "young" profession (Lazăr, 2015b). In 1990 undergraduate study programs in Social Work were re-established at the Universities of Bucharest, Cluj-Napoca, and Iasi, and the first generation of social workers after communism graduated in 1994. At present, social workers in Romania are "a mature workforce with an articulated critical mind, aware of its own importance in the social ensemble, and who would often want to be more valorised and recognized" (Lazăr, Dégi and Iovu, 2016: 93). The above-mentioned authors conducted a national study on the profession of social work in Romania, and one of the dimensions analyzed was professional exhaustion. Among the most important predictors of burnout, highlighted by this research, are the following: the feeling that the work is emotionally exhausting, the low job satisfaction, the intention to reduce the number of working hours in social work during the next 2 years (as a coping strategy), the feeling of work-related frustration and insecurity at work, and the reduced availability of continuing vocational training programs. In other words, those who feel burnout (25.6 % of the respondents) they are less satisfied, are dissatisfied with the workplace where they do not feel safe, and want to work fewer hours, being overloaded with job tasks (Lazăr, Dégi and Iovu, 2016).

The professional identity of social work is based on its core values and principles, such as: respecting the right to self-determination of clients, promoting the right to participation, treating each person as a whole, and identifying and developing strength (Roth-Szamosközi, 2003).

Romanian social workers' perception of their professional community is complex and ambivalent. On the one hand, there are positive opinions such as: the confidence in the social workers' strength, the social importance of the work of the social workers, a high degree of trust in the unity of the professionals, optimism about the future of the profession, and the willingness to make the voice of the social workers heard. On the other hand, different aspects of the professional and social environment are criticized. Among the problems identified by the respondents the following are mentioned: dissatisfaction with the public image of their profession, with the status of social workers in society and with the fact that their work is poorly valued by others, low responsiveness of decision-makers to social worker problems, poor financing of the field, insufficient services compared with the complexity of social problems, low remuneration that makes them having incomes, sometimes close to those of the beneficiaries, employing people without specialized studies in social worker positions, the need for continuous training, case overload, burnout, poor availability of supervision for social workers, and the exodus from the professional field of the qualified ones (Lazăr, Dégi and Iovu, 2016).

2 Interferences between family and professional life

From the employee perspective (with whom I have discussed during time), social work is an area that implies a high involvement in professional life with a high consumption of time, emotional, social, and sometimes even financial personal resources. This involvement, inevitably, interferes with family life and affects it. Work and family are having a reciprocal influence on each other, so that work interferes with family and family interferes with work. Maintaining the balance between the two sides is one of the daily challenges for those working in social services, and sometimes they can be in a conflicting situation between family life and work. Romanian social workers who participated in the study coordinated by Lazăr, Dégi, and Iovu (2016) perceive that their work keeps them away from home too much, considering that they barely manage to maintain a balance and that work issues do not affect their life or family so much.

The attempts to explain the interface between individuals' professional and personal lives generate various theoretical approaches. One of them is work-family border theory (Clark, 2000) which states that individuals are 'border-crossers' who transit between the two spheres on a daily basis. Another approach, resource-drain theory, explains the relation between work and family by referring to the transfer of finite personal resources, such as time, attention, and energy, from one domain to the other; because resources (time, money, and attention) are limited, available resources in the original domain are reduced (Edwards and Rothbard, 1999).

As I mentioned above, the influences between work and family life are not unidirectional, they are bidirectional ones. Thus, I can underline that the specific features of family life can interfere with or support the professional performance of individuals. In this context, several questions about the role of the family environment in supporting the professional life of the social workers have occurred: How do social workers describe their marital partners? How does the profile of social workers' couple partners look like in functional families? Does this perception have any connection to the characteristics of the stages from family life cycle?

3 Family development theory and family life cycle

Family development theory is an important approach for studying and understanding families and how they change over time under normal circumstances, which stems from the conceptual work done by Evelyn Duvall and Reuben Hill in the late 1940s. From this perspective, the development of a group of interacting individuals is more important than the development of the individual. Falicov (1988) characterizes it as an eclectic framework that merged concepts from structural-functionalism and symbolic interactionism. It takes the family as the unit of analysis and begins with the formation of family through marriage. Developmental processes are inevitable parts of life and they are important in understanding families. The main idea of family development framework is that families change in form and function over life cycle, and they follow a succession of specific stages.

This theory operates with two basic concepts: the *life cycle* (emotional and intellectual stages from childhood to retirement as a member of a family) and the *developmental task* (the activities required by or characteristics of each stage, the growth responsibilities that arise at certain stages in the life of the family). Family life cycle can, also, be seen as a set of predictable steps or patterns and developmental tasks families experience over time. The family life cycle concept facilitates studying the family from beginning to end. Family stage is a time period in the life of a family that has a unique structure. And the shifts from one family stage to another are named transitions (Duvall and Miller, 1985). In this matter, age does not matter; people can enter the stages at different points, for example, one person can have a baby at 18, and another one at 23 or 42.

The criteria used for dividing the life cycle into stages are the following: (a) changes in family size (addition or subtraction of family members through birth, death, and leaving home); (b) changes in age composition (chronological age of the oldest child); and (c) changes in the family's connection with other social systems (change in work status) (in Falicov, 1988).

This approach underlines that members need to adapt to family changes to ensure family survival and be successful. In each stage, challenges in family life cause members to build or gain new skills. But not everyone passes through these stages smoothly. Framo (1994: 90) states, "Each developmental stage of the family life cycle is a shock to the system because roles have to be reassigned, values reoriented, status positions shifted, loss and mourning dealt with, and needs met through new channels" (p. 90). Becoming proficient in the proper skills allows members of a family to move from one stage of development to the next. If they do not master the skills, they are more likely to have difficulty with relationships and future transitions.

One of the well-known models of family life cycle is the 8-stage model outlined by Duvall (1957 cited in Duvall and Miller, 1985), which describes family development as a succession of eight developmental stages: 1) beginning family; 2) childbearing family; 3) family with preschool children; 4) family with school children; 5) family with teenagers; 6) launching centre; 7) empty nest; and 8) aging family.

The beginning family stage is represented by the married couple who establishes a home, but the marital partners do not have children. The specific developmental tasks are establishing a satisfying home and marriage relationship and preparing for childbirth. It is an important stage of more in-depth knowledge and mutual adaptation, as each partner comes with their own background regarding role expectations in family life. The childless couple has more free time, they go to public places and to parties more often, the connections to the members of the social network are more intense. Marital satisfaction is higher during this initial stage and then begins to decline, but rises again in the later years of marriage (in Strong, DeVault, and Sayad, 1998).

Childbearing family, from birth of first child until that child is thirty months, implies adjusting to the increased family size and to providing a positive developmental environment to the new member (as specific developmental tasks). Aldous (1978) has noticed that the arrival of the first child often marks "the end of the honeymoon" and has a significantly negative effect on the marital relationship. This family event produces changes in couple dynamics, in leisure patterns, in sexual frequency, and in the professional area (in Lamanna and Riedmann, 1991).

The third stage is named family with preschool children (the oldest child is between two and a half and six years old). It is characterized by coping with demands on energy and attention, and with less privacy at home.

The next stage, family with school children (when oldest child is between ages of 6 and 13), involves promoting educational achievement and fitting in with the community of families with school-aged children. Parents need to coordinate schedules with another institution. They have to deal with conflicting beliefs and values as the child hears new ideas from peers and teachers (Lamanna and Riedmann, 1991).

The fifth stage, family with teenagers (the oldest child is between ages of 13 and 20), focuses on allowing and helping children to become more independent. This period brings a variety of difficulties that affect not only parent-child relationships, but also husband-wife relationships, especially in terms of how tolerant or severe they must be to adolescent riots. Parents may be dealing with more complex problems involving adolescent sexual activities, drugs or alcohol, accidents, or law violations (Lamanna and Riedmann, 1991). Within families with adolescents, increased family conflict may occur as adolescents begin to assert their autonomy and independence. Gecas and Seff, (1990 cited in Strong, DeVault, and Sayad, 1998) have concluded that despite the growing pains accompanying adolescence, parental bonds generally remain strong.

Family as a launching center lasts from the time the oldest child leaves the family until the youngest leaves home. This stage involves releasing young adults, accepting new ways of relating to them, and maintaining a supportive home base. Young adults may leave and return home several times.

During the empty nest stage (from the time children are gone until the couple retires), the family is challenged to renew and redefine the marriage relationship; they are also preparing for retirement years. The spouses are challenged to rediscover themselves as man and woman. If the children were the only reason for remaining together, the couple may divorce at this point in life. But when partners have other meaningful roles in various contexts, such as work, school, or hobbies to turn to, the outcome is more positive, as Lamanna and Riedmann (1991) underline. Glenn (1990 cited in Strong, DeVault, and Sayad, 1998) discovered that marital satisfaction generally begins to rise for the first time since the first stage of marriage.

The eighth stage is represented by the aging family (from retirement till the death of the marriage partner). Its specific development tasks are adjusting to retirement, coping with death, and living alone. Retirement is an event which generates significant life change, and it has the potential for both satisfaction and problems. Various factors affect marital satisfaction during retirement such as: good health (the key determinant for relationship satisfaction), financial security, contact with others, a sense of purpose, and the ability to structure time meaningfully. Johnson, White, Edwards, and Booth (1986 cited in Strong, DeVault, and Sayad, 1998) have noticed that retired couples can experience the highest degree of marital satisfaction since the first family stage.

There are various versions of the stages of the family life cycle. Aldous (1978) presented a seven-stage model, very similar with the previous one, which contains the following stages: 1) newly established couples, 2) childbearing families (preschool children), 3) families with school children, 4) families with secondary-school children, 5) families with young adults, 6) families in the middle years (post-launching), and 7) aging families (post-retirement). Compared with Duvall's theory, this model does not divide the preschool stage into different periods of time: one period when child is exclusively a member of family, and another period of time when he goes to kindergarten.

Several specific life events or problems can disrupt the family life cycle. Some of these family crises can be generated by the financial problems, infertility, severe illness, intense and frequent conflicts, stress, or death. These issues can produce significant effects on members' wellbeing, as well as consequences on developing (or not) the newly required skills. But if they miss the development of skills during one particular stage, members of family can learn them during later stages, in order to increase the functionality of the familial group.

Duvall's theory implies a traditional nuclear family. In contemporary society, there is a need for alternative stage theories which describe greater variations in types of family structures (e.g., childless couples, single-parent families, stepfamilies). New models of the family life cycle and family development need to underline which dimensions are universal and which are culturally specific, as Falicov (1988) considers.

In addition, the family life cycle approach underlines:

- Stages of family life cycle are not absolutely segregated, they can overlap. Children do not leave all at once the family and many times they return home for some time.
- Our experiences during the family life cycle have a major impact on our development; they affect who we are and who we become.
- Successful transitioning to another family stage may help to prevent disease and emotional or stress-related disorders.

Mattessich and Hill (1987) point out that life cycle stages provide an index of development. An analyst who is using the family life stages can place in categories the families that are experiencing similar events, facing similar crises, and attempting to accomplish similar development tasks. These stages are useful for describing groups of families without the implication that all families within the same stage are absolutely identical.

4 Methodology

The present visual study on family was conducted as part of a larger project whose main objective was to familiarize team members with diverse visual techniques and use some of them in the expertise areas of the researchers involved. In this context, in the first phase, I have suggested investigating the identity aspects of the couple partner perceived by the subjects at different stages of their family life, using visual techniques. After studying the literature, I chose to focus my attention on a specific category of subjects – whose family life is less described and analyzed, both nationally and internationally – social workers. Another reason for selecting this category was the accessibility of contacting future respondents, because in my professional activity I have built and developed collaborative relationships with practitioners in this field.

4.1 Aims and objectives

The purpose of this study is to examine how social workers perceive their partners at different stages of the family life cycle.

The specific aims are:

- identifying the common elements of perceptions regarding marital partners of members within this professional category;
- identifying the specific elements of each stage of family life in shaping social worker's perception of his or her partner;
- describing the relationship between the perception regarding the life partner, from the perspective of the social workers, the marital quality, and the characteristics of this profession.

In Romania, research on the specific characteristics and risks of the social work profession has just begun (Lazăr, 2015a; Lazăr, Dégi and Iovu, 2016). And the family life of the social workers is still an under-explored thematic area. In addition, neither of these objectives has been addressed in Romania or abroad, as far as I know.

4.2 Population and sampling

In the present study, there was female (21 respondents) and male (1 individual) participation, living in urban (19 persons) or rural (3 individuals) areas, with master degree (13) or university degree (9), working in NGOs (13) or public organizations (9), with high levels of marital satisfaction (12 are very satisfied, and 9 are satisfied). Participants were aged between 25 and 65 years old; most of them were in the interval of 31–40 years old (11 participants) (see Tab. 1). In Romania, this profession is dominated by women (88 %), with the average age between 30 and 49 years (over 60 %), most of them active in the urban area (89 %), with a rich experience in the field, most of them (62 %) having at least 3 years of professional experience, as described by Lazăr, (2015a) and Lazăr, Dégi and Iovu (2016).

I had known the participants for a number of years before I conducted this study. Most of them were my students and some of them collaborators in my professional field. I share different levels of familiarity with the research participants, which means I am an "intimate insider"; Taylor (2011) proposed

Tab. 1: Socio-demographic characteristics of the sample

Code	Age range	Latest school they graduated from	Type of work organization	Resi-dence	No. of chil-dren	The duration of the marriage	Marital satisfaction	The stage of family life
S 01	41–50 years	University studies	NGO	rural	3	16–20 years	satisfied	family with teenagers
S 02	41–50 years	Master's degree	NGO	urban	1	over 21 years	satisfied	launching centre family
S 03	31–40 years	University studies	public institution	urban	1	6–10 years	very satisfied	family with preschool children
S 04	31–40 years	Master's degree	NGO	urban	2	11–15 years	very satisfied	family with school children
S 05	41–50 years	Master's degree	public institution	urban	2	6–10 years	very satisfied	launching centre family
S 08	31–40 years	Master's degree	NGO	urban	1	6–10 years	neither dissatisfied nor satisfied	family with preschool children
S 09	41–50 years	University studies	public institution	urban	1	16–20 years	satisfied	family with school children
S 10	21–30 years	University studies	NGO	urban	-	less than 5 years	very satisfied	beginning family
S 11	31–40 years	Master's degree	public institution	urban	1	less than 5 years	very satisfied	childbearing family
S 14	31–40 years	Master's degree	public institution	urban	1	less than 5 years	satisfied	childbearing family
S 15	31–40 years	University studies	NGO	urban	2	6–10 years	very satisfied	family with preschool children

(*continued on next page*)

Tab. 1: (continued)

Code	Age range	Latest school they graduated from	Type of work organization	Resi-dence	No. of chil-dren	The duration of the marriage	Marital satisfaction	The stage of family life
S 16	41–50 years	Master's degree	public institution	urban	2	16–20 years	satisfied	family with teenagers
S 17	21–30 years	University studies	NGO	urban	1	6–10 years	satisfied	family with preschool children
S 19	51–60 years	Master's degree	public institution	rural	-	6–10 years	satisfied	beginning family
S 21	31–40 years	University studies	NGO	urban	2	11–15 years	satisfied	family with school children
S 22	31–40 years	Master's degree	NGO	urban	1	6–10 years	very satisfied	childbearing family
S 23	21–30 years	Master's degree	public institution	urban	-	less than 5 years	very satisfied	beginning family
S 26	61+ years	University studies	NGO	urban	1	over 21 years	very satisfied	"empty nest" stage
S 28	21–30 years	Master's degree	NGO	rural	-	less than 5 years	very satisfied	beginning family
S 31	31–40 years	Master's degree	NGO	urban	1	less than 5 years	satisfied	family with preschool children
S 33	31–40 years	University studies	public institution	urban	1	6–10 years	very satisfied	family with school children
S 34	31–40 years	Master's degree	NGO	urban	-	less than 5 years	very satisfied	beginning family

this term for the researcher who has pre-existing relationships (close, distant, casual, or otherwise).

In the first phase, I contacted social workers with whom I have had professional relationships in recent years and former students about whom I knew they are practitioners in social work. I presented to them the study I intend to make and I invited them to take part of it. In the second phase, I asked some of them to recommend me other suitable respondents.

All participants are social media users. They were recruited through Facebook Messenger.

Taking into account the topic of the study, I focused my attention only to married or cohabiting people, making it a criterion of the theoretical sampling process.

The sampling method is a non-probabilistic, theoretical one; the selection criteria of the respondents were dynamic, in a continuous change, to achieve theoretical saturation. Among the criteria used in this research, the following could be mentioned: marital status, age, gender, residence, level of specialized studies, type of organization in which they work, current occupation, duration of marriage, number of children, children' gender, children' ages, and marital satisfaction.

Some of the contacted people were not included in the sample because of the following reasons: (1) they were no longer working in social work (they were no longer eligible) or they did not have an intimate partner; (2) although they had initially accepted to participate, some social workers did not submit the requested data for reasons such as lack of time or because they forgot; (3) the visual and textual materials they had sent me did not meet the requirements and they did not restore the document; and (4) some social workers did not respond to the invitation to participate in the study.

Participants were fully briefed with regards to the research theme, my position as researcher, and how their responses would be used. I asked for and obtained individual consent to research participation and made clear the right to withdraw at any point prior to, during, or post-research.

4.3 Data collection methods

The data collecting method that I have used in my present study was respondent-generated image production. Pauwels (2015:128) considers that "...the purpose of respondent-generated image production in a research project is primarily to acquire unique data about the respondents' world (their visualized experiences and environment as an entry point to their culture) and thus to generate scientific knowledge". My reason for selecting this method was to give the respondents the freedom to express their perception on their spouses' current identity features in a creative and innovative way. In my previous researches on family life, I collected and analyzed other types of qualitative data (gathered using semi-structured interviews) as well as quantitative ones (using the sociological survey based on the questionnaire). By using the visual methodology of data collection, I have aimed to find out if I have access to other dimensions of investigating family life.

In this project of visual sociology, the data were collected from August to October 2017. The first step was to send the invitation to the potential subjects to participate in this study, using social media. Thus, they were informed about the topic of research (social workers' perception of their couple partners) and the ethical principles that underpin my investigation. After expressing their intention and agreement to participate in this study, the subjects received the following request: *Draw (or photograph or film) an image or a series of images illustrating (symbolizing) how your partner is currently, which features characterize him or her now. Add a short, suggestive text to explain each image taken*. The request sent to the participants can be characterized by flexibility, because the participants had the opportunity to choose between photography, drawing, or film regarding the form in which their visual data would materialize.

After receiving the visual and textual data from the respondents, I requested the following information from them: the agreement to publish the submitted photos; the socio-demographic data about the respondent (age, latest school they graduated from, current occupation, current work place, residence area, the year when they met their couple's partner, the marriage year, the number, gender, and the age of the children); as well as a self-assessment of the level of marital satisfaction (Generally, how satisfied are you with your couple relationship? Choose one of the following variants: 1 = very dissatisfied, 2 = dissatisfied, 3 = neither dissatisfied nor satisfied, 4 = satisfied, 5 = very satisfied).

Although the respondents had the opportunity to select between three alternatives of constructing their visual representations regarding their partners' identities, they have surprisingly chosen to synthesize their perception only through photography.

Photography can be seen from two perspectives: as a method in a complex of sociological methodology and as a text to be variously evaluated, analyzed, and de-coded (Banks, 2007; Rose, 2007 cited in Spencer, 2010). Both views involve the assumption that photographs offer a representation of knowledge and a connection to an empirical truth.

Photographs have become the most common visual data in a variety of studies using visual methodology. This fact shows their great potential in describing and explaining different phenomena (Scârneci-Domnişoru, 2016).

As I mentioned above, in the present study the respondents have chosen only to photograph an image or a series of images for illustrating or symbolizing her/his life partner. Each participant sent a different number of images (between 1 and 19 units), collecting a total number of 85 visual materials. Therefore, this paper explores especially the use of auto-photography as a participatory visual technique in describing and understanding the visions that social workers are holding regarding their life partners. The cameras, lenses, lighting choices, and framing are the photographer's way of creating visual statements. Therefore, words and photographs have their own importance in research.

Auto-photography, also called self-directed photography or auto-driven photo-production, refers to photography carried out by the research participant rather than the researcher as part of a research process (Lombard, 2012). This is one of the participatory visual methods which hand the control of the camera to the research participants.

Important parts of daily life are often left unspoken, which is why we must turn our attention to the social life occurring outside a talk. Auto-photography allows participants to show their life worlds as well as to interpret them. It has the potential to promote engagement (Robinson, 2011). Engaging the individuals in the research, and allowing them to actually produce artifacts, have generated the communication of their feelings, meanings, and understandings. In a research context, auto-photography is also accompanied with verbal research methods in the present visual study, due to the necessity of clarification. Pauwels (2015: 127) underlines this methodological requirement: "most if not all respondent-generated image production projects necessitate the verbal input of respondent to help make sense of visual outcome".

Using a flexible research request and encouraging the participants to take the control on image production, I have actively involved them in the process of my research; I have invited them to create their images and to make their own interpretations. Photographs do speak for themselves, but they speak in several "languages" and we do not really know which one was "spoken" by the respondent. In this context, words give meanings to pre-existing or provoked images. Images produced by respondents need verbal clarification by their producers. Pauwels (2015: 217) states that "such verbal clarification may elucidate aspects that even the image makers were not aware of during the image capture".

Participants had used their own cameras to produce the photographs.

The main types of social documents gathered from the participants in this study are: *pre-existing visual documents* (photographs from the personal archive of the subjects, as well as images from the Internet) and *provoked visual materials*, generated by the topic of the present research (photographs, collages of images produced by respondents).

4.4 Data analysis methods

Data collected from social workers was analyzed using thematic coding (Flick, 2009). The underlying assumption is that in different social worlds or groups (social workers in various stages of family life), differing views can be found. During the process of coding and analyzing the collected data, I have focused both on the content of the photographs and the explanations their subjects gave to them. Photos and accompanying explanations were considered as separate data sets and coded separately. I analyzed the images globally, I selected fragments from the text that accompanied each photograph, I identified and named codes that expressed different ideas, and then grouped them into categories. These are emerging categories, resulting from coding. Then, I have established links between the categories previously discovered.

The photographs and the short explanatory texts accompanying them were gathered in a separate file for each respondent. All these image-text documents were uploaded to NVivo 11 software and then coded.

5 How social workers in Romania perceive their marital partners? Presentation and analysis of visual data

Social workers associated a wide variety of objects, animals, places, activities, and people with their partners' identities.

5.1 Classification of collected visual data

I divided the photographs taken by participants into the following categories: pictures with personal objects, artefacts, cartoon characters; symbols of moral or personality traits photographs with the partner alone in different roles and contexts; images of partner with family members; and pictures alongside his friends.

Selections of photographs from some categories are illustrated in Figs. 1–3, with descriptions of their content.

The first category of photos (see Fig. 1) includes partner's personal objects, objects which are the results of his work, and neutral objects/animals/cartoon characters. All these symbolize inner personality traits or features of relationship with others. It is the most common category of photos, being found in the description of 12 participants, with a total of 51 images.

The majority of visual data from this category capture positive dimensions of personality, such as: attention to detail, sense of humor, responsibility, romance, gentleness, offers protection, support, love to family members, is capable of repairing or preparing food, and so on. For example, a social worker makes a picture of a cardboard box (labelled as "the box of shame"), to symbolize that her husband is taking responsibility for his own actions, for the consequences they produce.

Other images in this category, accompanied by explanatory texts, illustrate undesirable characteristics of their own life partner, elements that generate the participant's dissatisfaction. For example, the image from Fig. 1 shows an old motorcycle. In the subject's view, this object reflects the tendency of her partner to gather old, obsolete, and ugly things, as well as the difficulty of detaching from things gathered over time.

I have also discovered ambivalent images, which refer both to the positive and negative aspects of the couple's partner. Another subject captured an image of the flowing water which on one hand symbolizes the smooth flow of a river associated with the gentleness and calm of her husband, and on the other hand the respondent considers the same river may sometimes be turbulent and muddy to refer to the partner's irascibility that occurs when he does not succeed or when someone treats him with an attitude of superiority.

Fig. 1: Personal objects describing partner's personality traits, 2017 (author's archive)

Fig. 2: Image of marital partner alone in a specific role or context (practical skills in home renovation), 2017 (author's archive)

The second category of images (see Fig. 2) includes a total of 27 photos taken from 10 participants. Following the global analysis of images and the open coding of the explanatory texts, I have departed a wide range of roles, abilities, physical traits, and personality ones. Among these, I can mention: a satisfied and high-standard professional, good chef, involved in performing domestic tasks, skilled in technical activities, having developed time management skills, and individualized relaxation strategies, handsome, strong, dynamic, focused on what he does, trustworthy, cheerful, optimistic, appreciated by those around him, with well-defined hobbies, and so on.

Some photographs from this category reflect the full images of their partners, viewed from the front, being visible both their postures and facial expressions. Other pictures exemplify another type of images in which the main character is positioned back to the camera (as shown in Fig. 2); in this case, the subjects seem to emphasize rather the physical context and the activity in which their husbands are involved. And another type of photos from this category includes partial images of life partner, in which the face does not appear; this kind of images can reflect either the desire to keep the anonymity of the social actor or the photographer's intention to direct our attention to the elements that symbolize the role played by her husband: the role of the gardener (outdoor space and harvest) or the love for animals (the delicacy with which dogs are treated and how they react in the presence of their master).

The third type of images (see Fig. 3) was found in the descriptions made by seven of the investigated subjects, including 19 photos. All images gathered in

Fig. 3: Image of the partner beside family members (the whole family), 2017 (with permission of Mihaela Dişor and Alexandru Dişor)

this category are spontaneous visual data, existing in the family archive before the start of the present study.

In this category, I have identified images that reflect either the whole family (as shown in Fig. 3) or just the couple or the parent relationship. The most widespread situation is illustrating the partner beside their children, and the least common is the one of the whole family. This may indicate the focus of subjects on the paternal role of the spouse (most of the participants have children of different ages) or may be related to the technical way of making family photos: it is more accessible and easier for a family member to take a photo with the other members, rather than ask an outside person (professional or not) to take a picture of them together.

Most of the contexts in which men appear alongside their children are outdoor spaces. Participants had caught on camera images of their partner and children hiking in the middle of nature, visiting the historic sites, on holidays, during gardening activities, participation in street civic actions, or playing in parks. This kind of photos builds the image of fathers who transmit to their children the love for nature and history, develop their civic spirit, give them opportunities to explore the environment, and protect them; fathers are mentors and, at the same time, playmates. Rarely encountered, photos where the parental relationship is placed indoors reflect the image of a father with a postmodern mentality, actively involved in the care and feeding of his little child, a man who manifests affection towards his child openly and transparently, and is willing to become a cheerful, nonconformist playmate.

The pictures which illustrate the couple's relationship reflect either important events in their lives (for example, their marriage ceremony) or moments of tenderness (the two are tightly embraced).

The least common category of images is represented by pictures with marital partner alongside his friends, being illustrated by a single photo. The present social actors in this image reflect a modern role of the man, the cook. They prepare the menu for a meeting of several families of friends. It seems that for the participants in this visual study, seldom the couple partner is seen and described as a friend, relative to people outside the family environment.

The preference of respondents in this study to use symbols to describe their partners may have different explanations. One of these would be that pictures containing symbols could give respondents greater freedom to capture and illustrate personality traits with a high degree of abstraction. Another explanation could reflect the respondents' desire to keep their partner's anonymity within the research, although some of them are active social media users and constantly display photos with their families, including their husbands. Rarely, some respondents underlined that their husbands' socio-professional status requires special conditions of confidentiality and protection of personal data.

Instead, respondents who offered pictures with their marital partners have easily agreed to have their photos published. They said they have no problem to public exposure.

5.2 Social workers' perceptions on life partners' identity characteristics

Following thematic coding, I discovered 7 categories (see Fig. 4) and 112 subcategories with component codes. Aggregating this data, a pretty rich set of perceptions regarding social workers' intimate partners has resulted, perceptions that reflect character qualities and physical features, what hobbies color their lives, how they behave in the professional and domestic space, and which roles characterize them.

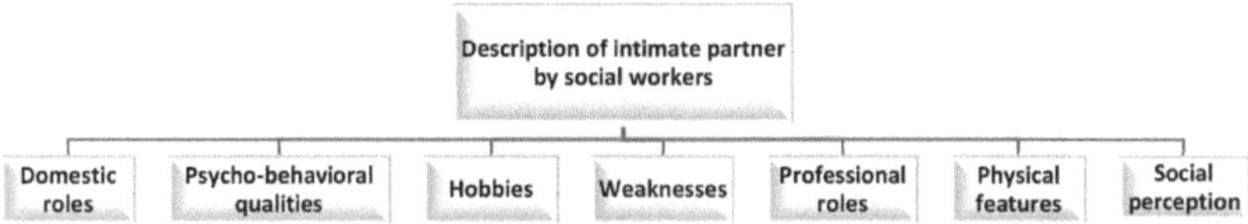

Fig. 4: Visual presentation of emerging categories resulting from coding

This section of paper will answer the question *how does the profile of social workers' couple partners is perceived in functional families?* and explore the main categories that were drawn from the project. The order of their presentation is given by their frequency.

5.2.1 Domestic roles

They represent the central element in the description of the life partner given by the social workers investigated. It is the category with the highest frequency, encountered in 21 sources (from the total number of 22 respondents), with 147 references present in the images and texts collected. In the case of this category, I encounter the role as couple partner (with an ensemble of qualities selected), of father, man cook (see Fig. 5), family man ("family above all"), skilled handyman, gardener, and the house accountant.

The role as couple partner was a focus for the majority of the respondents, 14 out of 22 subjects representing this role in their images and texts. Furthermore, its content is very rich, with various subcategories, such as: he provides security, is protective, loving, supportive, attentive, warm, conciliatory, adds dynamism to the relationship, empathetic, offers complementarity and independence in the relationship, respectful, romantic, with high personal goals, and unique.

The role of father is described by the majority of the respondents both in terms of responsible adult, a mentor to his child, as well as from a postmodern view, which entails attributes such as playful parent, close to his children, involved in caring for his children' education and leisure activities. This role is most commonly evoked by social workers who graduated from university with Bachelor's Degrees compared to those with a Masters' Degrees.

The domestic roles, presented by the respondents using images and accompanying texts, are a mix of traditional and modern elements. The photo from the Fig. 5 illustrates a modern role of the husband in some domestic contexts of nowadays. This result confirms the idea found in the literature, that the husbands of working women are less traditional than those whose wives do not work (Alwin, Scott, and Braun, 1992 cited in Alwin, 2004:145). Furstenberg

Fig. 5: Domestic roles (man cook), 2017 (author's archive)

(1992 cited in Alwin, 2004:145) called the neo-traditional family as "a renovated model of the gender-based division of labor when women share a greater measure of economic responsibility and men may assume a greater share of domestic chores than was deemed appropriate in previous times" (cited in Alwin, 2004:145).

It seems that, for the social workers who participated in the present study, the life partner is perceived as the one who assumes and accomplishes a wide range of domestic roles in an efficient manner, the one who offers security, protection, support in various domestic tasks, and is focused on the well-being of his own family group.

If in the professional space, the social worker is the one who offers support, protection, and encouragement for the beneficiaries of the social services, it

Fig. 6: Psycho-behavioral qualities (sense of humor), 2017 (author's archive)

appears that, in the private space, it is important for him to receive these elements from his own life partner to achieve inner peace and balance.

5.2.2 Psycho-behavioral qualities

These qualities cover a very wide range. After analyzing these types of data provided by 15 subjects out of 22, I discovered 47 subcategories.

Taking into account all the answers I received, it appears that some of the most important characteristics that social workers often identify are sense of humor (quality which is illustrated by Fig. 6), cheerfulness, and happiness. It is possible that these traits are so appreciated by the social worker because they help her/

him de-stress after working with beneficiaries which are dealing with problems of various degrees of gravity. These subcategories are equally encountered in subjects of ages between 31–40 years old and 41–40 years old, with postgraduate education or Bachelor's Degrees. In turn, I can also observe a difference in the frequency depending on the type of organization the social worker is part of. Therefore, it appears that it is mostly the respondents working in a public institution who evoke these characteristics, as opposed to those working in NGOs.

Furthermore, in the list of psycho-behavioral qualities I also encounter those that support interpersonal interaction (attentive to the needs of those around him, sociable, wise, kind, gentle, good listener, good storyteller, good friend, cute, interesting, offers support, affectionate, volunteer, attentive to his own personal image); those that reflect his views on life (he takes things as they come, loves live, nonconformist, optimistic, dynamic, full of energy); practical skills (good at technical activities, time-management skills, orderly, has good attention to details, focused on everything he does, good driver); athletic abilities (good swimmer); and attitude or character traits (calm, balanced, responsible, patient, cautious, capable, perfectionist, hardworking, charismatic, childish, animal lover, future planner, loves to be in the center of attention, selective of those around him, proud of his origins, with a civic responsibility, has his own relaxation strategies, is willing to do physical work, believer, foodie).

In the case of the subjects in the present study, it seems that patience is considered important predominantly by those in incipient relationships (less than 5 years) or with a still low level of experience (relationships of 6–10 years). In turn, the technical abilities are mostly mentioned by respondents with children.

5.2.3 Hobbies

In terms of activities performed with passion by life partners (9 subjects out of 22 transposed them in images), travels, nature outings, playing guitar, and fishing are evoked. Some of them are history, IT, aquariums, cars, or Elvis' music enthusiasts.

From the analysis of the images depicting the hobbies of life partners, I can identify two main categories of activity – those performed by themselves and those that entail the sharing of the moment or passion with other people (members of the family, friends, or even strangers). Fig. 7 presents the hobby of fishing. This hobby can be viewed as a relaxing activity that can be performed either in solitude or in the company of other people.

In terms of frequency of this category, I discovered that the perception of this identity dimension is predominantly evoked by social workers involved

Fig. 7: Hobbies (fishing), 2017 (author's archive)

in relationships lasting less than 5 years, compared to longer longevity marital relationships.

5.2.4 Weaknesses

Aside from the positive elements identified, some social workers (6 out of 22) also mention weaknesses of their life partners, trying to present an objective image of them.

In terms of weaknesses, the life partner is characterized using attributes such as: lack of self-confidence (he needs appreciation, has nervous ticks that express uncertainty); disorderly; vain; annoying; stubborn; isolated/withdrawn; lazy; too calculated (thrifty, frugal); forgetful; has cravings; lack of reaction; hardly finalizes projects (Fig. 8); likes old-fashioned things; keeps old things; takes over conversations; is late, etc.

The data obtained and analyzed show that also this category is mostly mentioned by social workers with a marital longevity that is lower than five years.

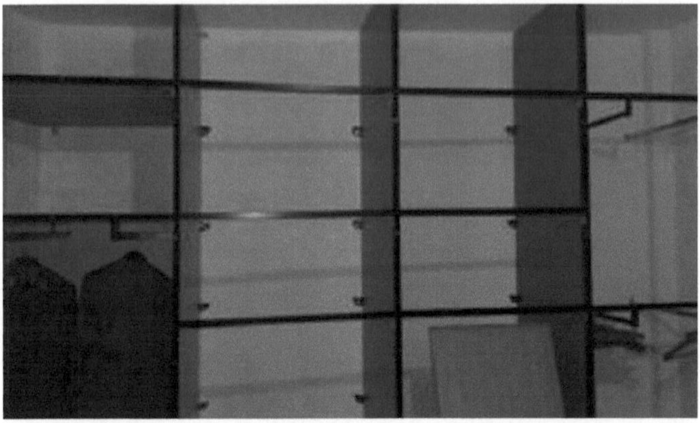

Fig. 8: Weaknesses (he hardly finalizes his started projects), 2017 (author's archive)

This tendencies in the descriptions of weaknesses seems to be the same as in the case of hobbies.

5.2.5 Professional roles

Out of a total of 22 respondents, 4 social workers refer to professional roles, mentioning that their partners are good professionals, who find joy and accomplishment in their careers.

The text accompaning the image from Fig. 9 clearly captures this role: "Professionally, he is an accomplished man because he does what he likes. He is an electrician and he doesn't see himself doing anything else. He is a good professional, meticulous, with high standards and big expectations from himself, first and foremost. He also has big expectations from other electricians, which is why he hardly finds collaborators".

This category is more frequent in the descriptions of life partners gathered from respondents with Bachelor's Degrees, as well as from those who work in public institutions.

Fig. 9: Professional roles, 2017 (author's archive)

5.2.6 Physical features

This category was found in the images and accompanying texts provided by three respondents. Strength or physical force (Fig. 10) of the partners is rather appreciated, but the general physical aspect is also evoked ("he is handsome"), although very rarely (only once).

It seems that the physical aspect of the male life partner does not matter very much to female social workers either. This conclusion matches the results obtained by other studies with a similar topic – the choice of a life partner (Iluţ, 2005).

Fig. 10: Physical features (physical power), 2017 (author's archive)

5.2.7 Social perception on him

This category is the least common; it is encountered in only one description out of a total of 22.

The social worker who brought this category to my attention believes that her life partner is appreciated by those around him (Fig. 11). At the same time, she mentions believing in her husband's potential by saying: "I know he can do more than he thinks he can".

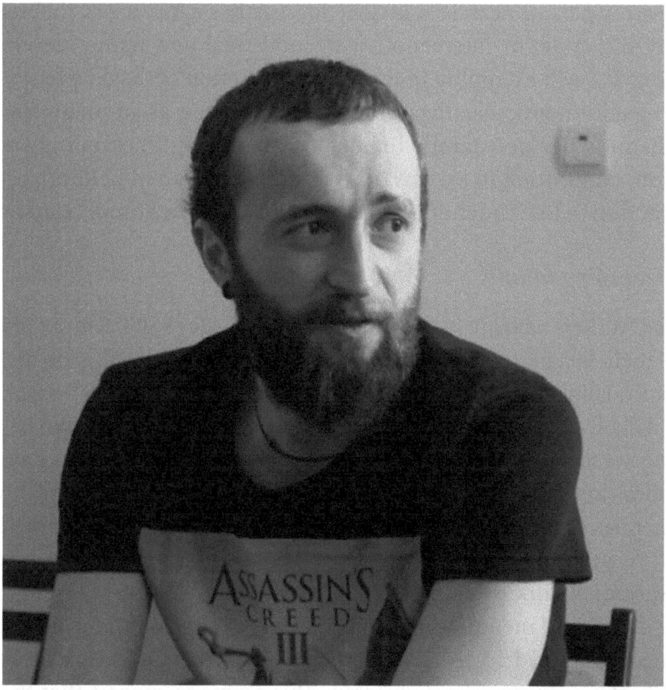

Fig. 11: Social perception on him (appreciation of those around him), 2017 (with permission of Mihaela Dişor and Alexandru Dişor)

5.3 Perceptions of marital partner through the family life cycle

After coding the images and texts, I have identified the list of categories and subcategories and analyzed them. Then I focused to find out if there are variations of these categories depending on the family life stages in which the subjects are. Thus, I have been pursuing the second research aim, which is identifying the specific elements of each stage of family life in shaping social worker's perception on his or her partner.

Using the same visual and textual database from NVivo, I have created sets of cases for each stage of family life. Then, using this software for processing qualitative data, I built a matrix that includes the variations of all categories and subcategories on the family life stages using the command "cross tabulate" from "query wizard". The data from the resulting matrix is detailed below.

The way a person perceives his/her life partner can vary at different stages of family life cycle, in interaction with individual and family developmental challenges, as I will exemplify in the following section of the chapter.

During adulthood, usually an individual starts up as an unattached young adult, then his/her new family life begins by moving to coupling and family formation, continuing to expansion (with the addition of children), and then to contraction (when the children prepare and leave the home) (Gerson, 1995).

5.3.1 Beginning family

The social workers who are in the childless family stage (5 subjects out of 22) characterize their life partners predominantly from the perspective of the psycho-behavioral qualities that they discovered, then by the domestic roles they accomplish in their daily lives. The appreciated and mentioned qualities are tidiness, sense of humor, social skills, responsibility, organizational and planning skills, faith, respect for tradition, and love of animals. In their households, the most frequently evoked domestic roles of the husband are those of cook, handyman, and gardener. In the romantic relationship, the social worker in the childless family receives protection, safety, warmth, kindness, and involvement from his life partner.

I also discovered mentions of the partner's weaknesses, though less frequently mentioned compared to the data gathered from the subjects who are in the stage of family with preschool children. This seems to suggest that the process of knowing each other is authentic and includes discovering both the qualities and the development areas in each other. In the description of the life partners, respondents also mention their hobbies. This stage of family life can be characterized by a larger freedom of action and a higher quantity of free time resources that can be invested in pursuing individual passions. The professional role of the husband is very rarely mentioned (only in one subject's description). A possible explanation is that this stage of family life generally overlaps with professional debut, meaning that the individual does not yet hold prestigious socio-professional positions. The marital satisfaction of the subjects in this stage is rather evaluated to a maximum level, compared to other stages of family life.

Coupling represents the process when two people come together and make a commitment to each other. But the individuals in the new couple bring behavioral and attitudinal patterns acquired from their families of origin into their new family system. That is why this stage is characterized by the joy of being together, getting to know the partner and yourself, and also the attempt to create a new system that will transcend generations. Gerson (1995) underlines that there is a big challenge in creating an identity as a couple while also continuing to hold ties to their families of origin. It is a struggle and a challenge at the same time, because it implies balancing their backgrounds, deepening their knowledge, and understanding each other.

5.3.2 Childbearing family

The addition of children to the marital couple is also named as the expansion stage in family life cycle (Gerson, 1995).

The social workers' perception of their own life partners in this stage of family life tends to contain predominantly psycho-behavioral qualities and domestic roles, as it was also encountered in the case of childless families. After the comparative data analysis, I discovered that there are similarities, as well as differences, compared to the previous family stage.

The similarity is represented by the appreciation of sense of humor, and the new qualities mentioned in this stage of family life are: patience, calm, kindness, attention to details, he is gentle but also selective with those around him, offers support, good storyteller, but also good listener, and attentive to the needs of those around him. The transition from dyad to triad generates changes in the social workers' perceptions regarding the domestic roles of their life partners. In this context, the marital role is evoked more often, probably due to the fact that, with the birth of the child, there were significant changes that affected the couple relationship as well. The marital role of the husband is rather presented in terms of protection, love, and romance. This is completed by the role of father, evaluated by respondents to a superlative level. Usually, in this stage, the social worker temporarily leaves the professional space and focuses on family life (she is in childcare leave). Therefore, only one source of personal satisfaction remains, which is the family one.

As reference points in partner descriptions, the social workers in this stage of family life also mention weaknesses and hobbies, but their frequency is lower compared to the beginning family stage. The responsibilities of the parental role diminish the previously available resources for doing activities that offer personal satisfaction.

Every parent discovers that children are wilful human beings who, from a very early age, play an active role in shaping their family environment. Presenting the characteristics of this stage, Framo (1994:99) states: "Since parenthood is romanticized in our culture, like marriage, the couple is often shocked by the reality of taking care of a baby, by the loss of freedom, and by the way their marriage is affected". This means that this stage brings both joy and stress. The adults' focus moves from a dyadic level to the baby or a child-centered perspective. New parents are challenged to balance these levels, to keep a sense of them as a couple, as well as to gain new skills in order to meet the demands of caring for children. Early in expansion, parents are setting the boundaries of the children's interactions with the outside world.

5.3.3 Family with preschool children

As children grow, they expand their social world to kindergarten, school, extracurricular activities, and friends. A tremendous challenge for parents is to gradually expand the boundaries to help children develop autonomy, but in a secure way.

The social workers in this stage of family life seem to give a greater importance to domestic roles in outlining the identity profile of their life partner. Therefore, the hierarchy of categories, depending on their frequency, is different compared to that outlined by analysis of previous stages, and it is built as follows: the highest frequency is that of domestic roles, followed by psycho-behavioral qualities and weaknesses.

The perception of respondents with preschool children seems to focus rather on the roles such as couple partner and father held by their husbands. Once the child goes to nursery school, the two parents seem to rediscover one another as romantic partners, bringing forward characteristics such as complementarity, love, and dynamism of the relationship. At the same time, during this time of their life, social workers tend to notice various behaviors and interpersonal qualities of their partners manifested in the parental relationship. Therefore, the characterization of the partner from the perspective of fatherhood is most notably found in this stage, compared to all of the other periods of family life. The combined experiences of greater participation in childrearing and living with a working wife may "affect the father's childrearing behavior and his assumptions of what the adult roles are for which he is socializing his children" (Hoffman, 1977: 655 cited in Alwin, 2004:145).

During this stage of family life, the psycho-behavioral qualities perceived in the partner and visually represented by the social workers occupy a second place, if I take frequency into account. Out of these, the most frequently mentioned quality is intelligence. It is found only in the descriptions of the respondents who are part of families with preschool children. References are also being made to sense of humor, kindness, attention to details, meticulousness, balance, or practical skills (good swimmer, driver, and handyman).

When analyzing perceptions of life partners in families with preschool children, I also find mentions of weaknesses. Surprisingly, this category contains the highest number of coding references, compared to all of the other stages. Once the process of knowing each other gets deeper, it seems that undesirable features of the intimate partner become more apparent. Also, in this stage, the woman has already returned to work, after childcare leave. In these conditions, she may experience high levels of professional stress or inter-role conflicts, factors that can also influence her perception of her life partner.

Changes in maternal work patterns and the changing work–family balance have had consequences for the culture of care, in which children are both recipients and providers. The new sociology of childhood rightly emphasizes that children are agents. Children are not passive victims of circumstance; they act and exert influence on the lives of others around them, particularly on their family members (Scott, 2004).

5.3.4 Family with school children

Social workers who are in the stage of family with school-age children characterize their life partners predominantly from the perspective of hobbies, then domestic and professional roles.

In this stage, hobbies have the highest frequency of references compared to the other stages of family life. It is possible that the higher level of independence that the child reached may also allow the adult to invest time in activities that offer him joy and relaxation once again.

At the same time, there are some changes of the content in the domestic roles category, compared to the previous stages. As such, in the characterization process of the intimate partner, there is a decrease in the frequency of the elements pertaining strictly to the couple relationship (there are only two references being made), as well as a decrease in the frequency of codes relating to the role of father. However, a new notion appears: the defining of the man as part of a larger unit, which is the family group. Therefore, the predominant perceived domestic role is that of family man, whose main priority is the common good of all the members of the family ("family above all").

The educational potential that families have, especially during the first part of their child's life, is decisive. Once the child enters the school community, parents have multiple goals, with well-defined outcomes: they are preoccupied with the future standard of living of their children, obtaining a higher income (instrumental goals), obtaining a superior social status that would offer them authority, income, access to resources, decisional capabilities (professional goals), teaching their children to live their school experience in a positive way (affective goals), finding ideals, cultural models, and personalities that can guide their journey in life (cultural goals).

In this context, social workers in the family with school-age children stage perceive and describe their life partners from the perspective of the professional roles they hold as well. In outlining the identity of marital partners, the category of professional roles has the biggest number of references in this stage. This can also have something to do with the fact that, as time passes, the moment of professional debut is surpassed and the process of career building has started to collect social, financial, and material benefits.

5.3.5 *Family with teenagers*

In this stage of family life, social workers tend to characterize their intimate partner predominantly by evoking psycho-behavioral qualities, then domestic roles and hobbies. A similarity can be observed in the ranking of the afore-mentioned categories in terms of frequency and the hierarchy observed in the childless family stage. Therefore, in the childbearing family stage as well, the most frequent codes evoked in the presentation of the partner were those from the first two categories mentioned earlier – the psycho-behavioral qualities and the domestic roles.

In the family with teenagers, social workers in the present study no longer characterize their partners in terms of weaknesses. Adults seem to have a higher degree of awareness of each other and probably along the years they have also developed coping strategies or solving-problems skills used for various issues occurring in their romantic relationship. The higher likelihood to practice hobbies in this stage of life could also be tied to the higher independence level of the children, which could lead to a higher degree of freedom for the parents.

During the adolescence of children, the family cycle begins to move toward and prepares for contraction. The relationship between the parents and the child needs to be continually renegotiated and transformed according to the specificity of each developmental stage (Gerson, 1995).

5.3.6 *Launching center*

Contraction begins as children prepare to leave the family. The main role of parents is to help their children to become confident in their newly expanded outside world while, at the same time, parents prepare themselves for their contracted new world. Couples move from the distractions of daily parenting to the stage when they have the time to focus on each other, to rediscover themselves as man and woman, as Gerson (1995) underlines. They may realize they have forgotten how to be a couple, or they may mourn the absence of their child, or they may find themselves in a honeymoon-like state.

Partners from families as launching centers seem to be characterized predominantly by domestic roles, psycho-behavioral features, and weaknesses. There are many similarities with the hierarchy of categories in families with preschool children.

In launching centre stage, the domestic roles characteristic of the intimate partner focus primarily on those related to couple relationship. Thus, social workers at this family life stage characterize their spouses as loving, protective, empathetic, supportive, attentive, sympathetic, and respectful partner. This set of features seems to suggest the installation of a companionate love, as it is defined by Kim and Hatfield (2004). Parental role is less frequently found in the descriptions of spouses at this stage, compared to those in the family with preschoolers or school children. In addition, in this category we can find other domestic roles such as the cooker, family man concerned with the good of the group, the accountant of the house.

The perception of social workers in this stage is focused on the psycho-behavioral qualities of the partner as well, the most frequently mentioned ones being: cheerful, funny, having personal strategies of relaxation, energetic, optimistic, and skilled at technical activities.

I have found references of partner weaknesses once again, of which there can be mentioned: uncertainty, taking over conversations, avarice, and lack of self-control in regards to eating. But there are also references to professional roles.

The reorganization and reinvention of the couple relationship, as a specific element of this stage in the family life cycle, were also outlined by Gerson (1995:94), who states "...parents must prepare for the contraction in their relational world and often must attend to both their individual needs and the needs as a couple for the first time in many years". In addition to this, parents who are willing to accept and promote autonomy in their children will be less likely to experience their own mid-life crisis (Gerson 1995:105).

5.3.7 Empty nest

In this stage of family life, the social worker's partner is perceived predominantly in terms of domestic roles played. He is described as a family man, a supportive and conciliating husband, and an extraordinary father.

When a child leaves, it is a significant event for both parents and child. And although many parents view it as a highly positive event, for others it is a conflicted time: a period of loving and letting go and a time when the day-to-day parental role is surrendered. For the child, it is a step toward independence; a symbolic marker of adulthood. However, we know very little about how fathers respond to and experience the transition to the empty nest (Mitchell and Lovegreen, 2009).

Although in Duvall's theoretical model the last stage in family life was the stage of aging family, in Romanian reality, I did not have access to subjects who had acted as social workers and, at present, to be retired. As I have already mentioned in introduction, social work is a relatively "young" profession in Romania (Lazăr, 2015b), and the number of retired social workers is very limited.

Using change in family size as a criterion for dividing the family life cycle into stages, another way to delimit family life cycle is mentioned by Falicov (1988), who identified five expanding, stable, and contracting stages: (1) stable stage – childless; (2) expanding stage – childbearing; (3) stable stage – childrearing; (4) contracting stage – launching; and (5) stable stage – empty nest.

6 Discussions and conclusions

This study had three research aims. First, I have focused on identifying the common elements of social workers' perceptions regarding their marital partners. The portrait of the Romanian social worker's intimate partner is composed of a wide range of qualities and roles. Besides the positively valued aspects, some of the social workers have also mentioned the weaknesses of their husbands, trying to provide an objective picture of their marital partners. For social workers from Romania, who participated in this study, the most important features of their marital partners are represented by their domestic roles, and their psycho-behavioral qualities. The findings demonstrate that each individual experiences and perceives the marital life differently, and that although respondents share some similarities in general perceptions on their marital partner, their personal experiences result in different rationales, associations, and memories about their spouses. Historically, men are responsible for the economic wellbeing of their families, but they also model morals, encourage persistence, perceptions of acceptance, contribute to gender schemata, and engage their children in rough and tumble activities. They also play and communicate actively with their children. In a recent qualitative analysis of interactions, Pinto, Cameron, Hancock, and Tapanya (2014) show that men can be an active partner in different activities at home. The same results were depicted from the present study. The movement of women into the workforce, longer working hours, and work intensification have resulted in less time for family, recreation, and community (Pocock, 2003, 2005), and this means she needs to share domestic responsibilities with a life partner she can constantly rely on, as some social workers from the present study seem to do with their husbands.

The second aim refers to identifying the specific elements of each stage of family life regarding the perceptions of social workers on their partners. According to the data gathered from the subjects, it seems that the dynamics of family life are also reflected in the variations recorded by the perception on the life partner. In addition, the results of this study support the idea that in each stage of family life the perception on the partner focuses on certain identity features, and their hierarchy changes from one stage to another. For example, in the beginning families, the most frequent elements detached from photos and texts refer to psycho-behavioral qualities of the intimate partner. Instead, in the family with preschool children, it seems that social workers are more focused on domestic roles in defining their life partner. And in families with school children, the most frequent coding references in photos and texts refer to partners' hobbies. These data can add new content to family development theory, offering examples for dynamics of perceptions regarding life partner in different stages of family life cycle.

During my study, I collected data which show that, in some cases, family life cycle approach is somehow a restricted perspective. It seems insufficient to capture and understand the diversity of family forms and the complexity of the family's life circumstances of contemporary times (e.g., childless couples which have a long marital experience, remarried couples).

The third objective focuses on describing the relationship between the perception of the couple partner, from the perspective of the social workers, the marital quality, and the characteristics of this profession. Social work is considered a vocational profession; the practioners from this area are motivated by the desire to do good, to help others, and to contribute to their well-being. It is a profession characterized by tact, empathy, and gentleness, which requires much dedication and openness, responsibility, and tolerance (Răşcanu, 2001). A large number of practitioners in the field of social work assimilate the values from the Code of Ethics and translate them into the interpersonal relationships in the professional area. These values are: affirmation of the beneficiaries' individuality, fighting against patterns and clichés in perceiving others, the right of individuals to have access to the necessary resources, respect for dignity and trust in the value of the human being, confidence in the self-determination capacity of assisted persons and in their ability to solve problems, and maintaining the confidentiality of information received from and in connection with clients (NASW, 2016). These values internalized by the social worker seem to shape also how they manifest in other contexts of life. In addition, the one who chooses social work as his/her profession has a vocation for diversity, tolerance, support, and a certain personality structure.

People tend to choose their life partners with a similar systems of values, attitude, and personality traits. Investigations on marital couples have shown that there is a high correlation between axiological and personality similarity and happiness in marriage. Also, there was a significant correlation between marriage satisfaction and the mutual perceived similarity between the two spouses. Moreover, in couples who evaluated themselves as happy, the perceived attitudinal similarity is greater than the real one (Iluţ, 2005). By comparing the predominant features, perceived by social workers at their life partners, with characteristic elements of the practitioners from this professional field, some elements of similarity can be detached: attention to the needs of others, gentleness, calmness, inner balance, responsibility, wisdom, optimism, patience, listening skills, and so on. The intimate partner is described by the social worker rather in positive, appreciative terms, with a series of personal and interpersonal skills and abilities. And such an appreciative perception of the partner strengthens marital satisfaction. In the case of the investigated subjects, the level of marital satisfaction is predominant at the maximum level, which may also indicate a high level of functionality in the marital couple. And a high level of marital satisfaction enhances job performance. Similar ideas are also found in spill-over theory, a particular theory regarding work–life balance. Spill-over is a process whereby experiences in one role affect experiences in the other, rendering the roles more alike; it refers to a direct relation between work and family. The experiences resulting from spill-over can manifest themselves as either positive or negative (Morris and Madsen, 2007).

This paper brings new directions in researching couple life of social workers, which consists both in the methodological approach (qualitative study of perceptions on marital partner, using visual methodology) and in its results (by the richness of details with which hetero-identification of partner is described).

During my first study of visual research, I have discovered that there are various advantages of using photographs in studying family life. First of all, participants assume themselves the roles of active actors and collaborators, rather than passive objects of study. And the degree of their involvement during the research process was higher compared with previous investigations that I conducted in the past. For example, time spent by respondents to produce visual and textual data was longer, some subjects noting that it took several days to create or search for relevant photos in order to characterize their husband. Also some of the subjects told me that the task they received was a constant element in their thoughts until they found the proper images.

Auto-photography has encouraged participants to take a leading role in directing the research focus and process. The production of visual material offered participants more freedom to select which data they transmit to researcher and encouraged them to become creatively involved in the research. I have noticed that photography combined the spirit of observation with the aesthetic sense of the participant.

The subjects' selection and interpretation of photographs allowed me as a researcher to access a deeper level of meaning. In addition to text, images can yield far richer data than word-only interviews. Photos combined with short explicative texts can aid participants in expressing their complex understandings, concerning their perspectives and experiences. For example, in my previous studies on family life (Gotea, 2014), using the semi-structured interview method, I have encountered the tendency of some subjects to give desirable answers or to change the theme of discussion when they were asked to talk about less pleasant topics such as marital conflict. Instead, through visual methodology, respondents provided information on their partners' qualities and weaknesses, from their own initiative.

Visual methods have also required very little intervention from me as a researcher. This means that I have spent fewer resources for the collecting data stage (less effort, less time, and fewer material and financial resources) compared with previous research studies. During my study, I have also noticed that images can aid researcher in recording, remembering, and rendering the research field visibly accessible to other specialists, albeit in a way that is always already partial, mediated, and constructed.

The present findings also suggested that using the photos opened up new ways of conceptualizing the hetero-identification of marital partner (as identified from the outside). All the categories and subcategories discovered in this visual study have enriched the content of this concept.

The findings suggest that auto-photography method is an effective technique for remotely eliciting individual's marital partner perceptions on a larger scale than would be possible using verbal methodologies. This makes it potentially very useful in a number of scenarios where participation rates are lowered by physical constraints.

Another advantage of using the visual methodology, which was recorded in the present research, was the positive feedback given by some subjects at the end of the data collection phase. Some people have described the experience of participating in this study as very interesting and provocative: "The received task is great". Others were interested in the results to be derived from the processing, analysis, and interpretation of the data: "I would like to know the outcome of the research project" or "I'm interested in seeing the results if possible". And sometimes participants were surprised and impressed because photo-production or photo-selection evoked particular feelings and memories about their couple life, that they had not anticipated "It was a great pleasure doing this collage of my husband… Even now I still have a smile on my face!" or " Thank you for this opportunity to express my feelings in all their purity… so I realize how rich I am having my family!"

The various advantages of collecting and analyzing visual data are also mentioned by other authors. For example, Scârneci-Domnişoru (2016) argues that visual data can reveal surprising details and things that are going too fast to be observed; they present reality in a holistic way; they are less selective than observations; they facilitate the elimination of cultural and linguistic barriers between the researcher and respondents; and facilitate empathic understanding; they are evocative; they are quite easy to gather; they offer the diversity of data gathered in research, providing an important type of triangulation; they represent a fascinating way for the researcher to collect data; and they are a welcome attempt to involve the respondents more easily in the research.

In different stages of the present investigation, I encountered some obstacles that required immediate solutions; they are illustrating possible disadvantages of working with photographs. For example, at the stage of presenting the task, some of the subjects showed insecurity, lack of confidence in them regarding their ability to cope with the novelty of the transmitted task. At the stage of visual data production, some of the participants were appealed to downloading images from the Internet, which may raise copyright issues for the researcher if he wants to use these visual data in his publications. And when I asked them for their socio-demographic data, some participants understood that they were asked to provide information about their husbands and they initially showed reluctance. Therefore, in visual studies, subjects can show extra caution in providing personal data compared to textual data-gathering studies (images may be more easily associated with participants, compared with texts resulting from transcripts of interviews).

New directions for continuing the current visual study would be to compare the perception of social workers on their couple partners with those of other professional categories (both professionals who offer help, but also professionals in technical or economic fields). Thus, several specific criteria for choosing a life partner could be captured, as well as elements that support longevity and quality of life for couple in the different socio-professional categories.

This chapter is meant to be an illustration of the potential for visual methods in family studies. Auto-driven photo-production combined with verbal explanations were useful for allowing social workers from this research project to select several aspects of their partners' identities that are meaningful to them. The photos taken or selected by participants reflect their "way of seeing" their marital partner at the present time or in a chronological manner. These artifacts symbolize feelings about their spouses and document important events, activities, or roles.

Bibliography

Aldous, J. (1978). *Family Careers: Developmental Change in Families.* New York: Wiley.

Alwin, D.F. (2004). Parenting Practices. In J. Scott, J. Treas and M. Richards (eds.) *The Blackwell Companion to the Sociology of Families* (pp. 142–157). Oxford: Blackwell Publishing Ltd.

Asquith, S., Clark, C. and Waterhouse, L. (2005). *The Role of the Social Worker in the 21st Century – A Literature Review*. Retrieved in January 15th 2018, from: http://www.gov.scot/resource/doc/47121/0020821.pdf

Clark, S.C. (2000). Work-family border theory: A new theory of work-family balance. *Human Relations*, 53 (6), 747–770.

Duvall, E.M. and Miller, B.C. (1985). Marriage and Family Development (6th edition). New York: Harper & Row.

Edwards, J.R. and Rothbard, N.P. (1999). Work and family stress and well-being: An examination of person-environment fit in the work and family domains. *Organizational Behavior and Human Decision Processes*, 77 (2), 85–129.

Falicov, C.J. (1988). Family Sociology and Family Therapy Contribution to the Family Development Framework: A Comparative Analysis and Thoughts on Future Trends. In C.J. Falicov (ed.) *Family Transitions: Continuity and Change over the Life Cycle* (pp. 3–51). New York: Guilford Press.

Flick, U. (2009). *An Introduction to Qualitative Research* (4th edition). London: SAGE Publications Ltd.

Framo, J. (1994). The family life cycle: Impressions. *Contemporary Family Therapy*, 162, 87–116.

Gerson, R. (1995). The Family Life Cycle: Phases, Stages, and Crisis. In R.H. Mikesell, D.D. Lusterman and S.H. McDaniel (eds.) *Integrating Family Therapy: Handbook of Family Psychology and Systems Theory* (pp. 91–111). Washington, DC: American Psychological Association.

Gotea, M. (2014). *Rețeaua socială și conflictul marital. Constrângeri și oportunități*. Cluj-Napoca: Presa Universitară Clujeană.

Iluț, P. (2005). *Sociopsihologia si antropologia familiei*. Iași: Polirom.

Kim, J. and Hatfield, E. (2004). Love types and subjective well-being: A cross-cultural study. *Social Behavior and Personality*, 32 (2), 173–182.

Lamanna, M.A. and Riedmann, A. (1991). *Marriages and Families: Making Choices and Facing Change*. Belmont: Wadsworth Publishing Company.

Lazăr, F. (2015a) *Profilul asistenților sociali din România*. Timișoara: CNASR, Editura de Vest.

Lazăr, F. (2015b). *Asistență socială fără asistenți sociali?* București: CNASR, Editura Tritonic.

Lazăr, F., Dégi, L.C. and Iovu, M.B. (2016). *Renașterea unei profesii. Sau despre cum este să fii asistent social în România?* Bucuresti: Tritonic.

Lombard, M. (2012). *Auto-Photography*. Manchester: University of Manchester.

Mattessich, P. and Hill, R. (1987). Life Cycle and Family Development. In M.B. Sussman and S.K. Steinmetz (eds.) *Handbook of Marriage and the Family (pp. 437-469)*. New York: Plenum Press.

Mitchell, B.A. and Lovegreen, L.D. (2009). The empty nest syndrome in midlife families: A multimethod exploration of parental gender differences and cultural dynamics. *Journal of Family Issues*, 30 (12), 1651–1670.

Morris, M.L. and Madsen, S.R. (2007). Issue Overview: Advancing work-life interaction in individuals, organizations and communities. *Advances in Developing Human Resources*, 9 (4), 439–454.

N.A.S.W. (2016). *Center for Workforce Studies*. Retrieved in 19 January 2018, from http://workforce.socialworkers.org/

Pauwels, L. (2015). *Reframing Visual Social Science: Towards a More Visual Sociology and Anthropology*. Cambridge: Cambridge University Press.

Pinto, G., Cameron, C.A., Hancock, R. and Tapanya, S. (2014). Thriving Toddlers and their Attentive Fathers and Grandfathers around the Globe during a Day in their Lives. Paper presented at 5th World Conference on Educational Sciences - WCES 2013, Roma. *Procedia - Social and Behavioral Sciences*, 116, 2039–2043.

Pocock, B. (2003). *The Work/Life Collision: What Work Is Doing to Australians and What to Do About It*. Sydney: Federation Press.

Pocock, B. (2005). Work-life 'balance' in Australia: Limited progress, dim prospects. *Asia Pacific Journal of Human Resources*, 43 (2), 198–209.

Răşcanu, R., (2001). *Metode si tehnici de asistenta sociala*. Bucureşti: Editura Fundatiei Humanitas.

Robinson, A. (2011). Giving voice and taking pictures: Participatory documentary and visual research. *People, Place and Policy Online*, 5 (3), 115–134.

Roth-Szamosközi, M. (2003) *Perspective teoretice si practice ale asistentei sociale*. Cluj-Napoca: Editura Presa Universitară Clujeană.

Scârneci-Domnişoru, F. (2016). *Datele vizuale în cercetarea socială*. Cluj-Napoca: Editura Presa Universitară Clujeană.

Scott, J. (2004). Children's Families. In J. Scott, J. Treas and M. Richards (eds.) *The Blackwell Companion to the Sociology of Families* (pp. 109–125). Oxford: Blackwell Publishing Ltd.

Spencer, S. (2010). *Visual Research Methods in the Social Sciences: Awakening Visions*. Abingdon: Routledge.

Strong, B., DeVault, C. and Sayad, B.W. (1998). *The Marriage and Family Experience: Intimate Relationships in a Changing Society* (7th edition). Belmont: Wadsworth Publishing Company.

Taylor, J. (2011). The Intimate Insider: Negotiating the Ethics of Friendship when Doing Insider Research. *Qualitative Research*, 11 (1), 3–22.

Ioana-Anisa Atudorei

VIII Studying students' moral emotions by visual techniques

Abstract: This chapter contains a study of moral emotions by visual techniques, and it demonstrates the importance of images in the field of social knowledge. Starting from drawings representing school context when students felt one of the following three moral emotions – embarrassment, shame and guilt – elements that can be associated with each of the three moral emotions are analysed. The chapter emphasises similar results obtained in this qualitative research where the drawings were used for studying emotions and a quantitative research that used a survey. It also focuses on new elements that can be drawn from visual data such as: lip expressions and the use of various colours to express the hierarchy of inner moral motions in social context. It could be said that the use of visual research and techniques or the combination of these two with research that collects statistical data by means of the questionnaire represent important ways of knowledge production in the field of sociology of emotions.

Keywords: moral emotions, drawings, visual data, visual techniques, social context, visual sociology

1 Introduction

In the last 40 years, the sociology of emotions found its definition and outlining due to the issuing of the papers *The Sociology of Feeling and Emotions*, published by Arlie Russel Hochschild (1975), *Conflict Sociology*, by Randal Collins (1975) and due to the conference on the topic of emotions organised at San Francisco, on the occasion of the reunion of the American Sociological Association. Numerous researchers have contributed to the support of the scientific research progress in the field of the sociology of emotions, among which are Izard (1971, 1977), Lewis (1971, 1992, 1995,1998) Ekman and Friesen (1971), Kemper (1978a, 1978, 1987, 1990, 2002, 2002), Scheff (1988, 2000), Frijda (1986), Ekman (1993, 1994, 2003), Lazarus (1991), Russell (1994, 1995), Frijda and Mesquita (1992, 1994), Barbalet (1998/2001), Fredrickson (1998), Fessler (1999), Haidt and Schweder (2000), Haidt (2003), Keltner and Haidt (1999, 2001), Fischer, Manstead, and Mosquera (1999), Parrott (2001), Turner and Stets (2005), Rimé, (2005/2007), Năstasă (2013) and Năstasă and Fărcaş (2015).

However, Emilé Durkheim [1912] (1995) is considered to be "the first great sociologist who has analysed the genesis, structure and functions of emotions"

(Chelcea, 2008, p. 68). He is followed by Charles Darwin [1872] (1967) with the basic paper for studying emotions *The Expression of the Emotions in Man and Animals*. I chose to research into moral emotions in social contexts due to the implications they have in creating the morals of humankind. Considered a multi-sensuous being, man can receive, according to a classification based on analysers, gustative, auditive, visual and tactile perceptions. We live in an era in which images, or better said communication via images, is in a continuous expansion, both in the offline medium and in the online one. But why is it that the image occupies such an important place?

Specialists in the field of philosophy – such as Nany (2015, 2013, 2011, 2010), Lopes (2005), Matthen (2005) and Hecht (2003) – have been preoccupied with the analysis of the visual particularities specific to image perception, and some other authors like Nany (2013), Abell and Bantilaki (2010) and Lopes (2005) have included the emotional component as well because the images transmit messages at an emotional level. In common language, we hear being used an expression which is representative in what the role of the image in concerned, i.e. "an image makes a thousand words". Why? Exactly due to the emotional load mentioned before, which makes it unforgettable.

The suggestion of my colleague, Florentina Scârneci-Domnişoru, to participate in the IVTSR project – the implementation of visual techniques in social research – has raised my interest to research moral emotions using visual techniques. I wanted to identify their pluses and minuses as compared to those of other methods because, ever since 1988, Douglas Harper has considered that "There have been, however, many sociologists who have used visual data, and their work has added unique knowledge to sociology" (Harper, 1988, p. 54). I chose to study moral emotions by means of visual techniques because, just like Edoardo Zamuner (2012), I consider that emotions can be best identified from images.

2 Defining emotions

In 1984, William James gave a simplistic definition to emotions, being of the opinion that these are behavioural answers. Afterwards, emotions were analysed in a much more complicated manner, notes bringing new information for defining them being issued. Thus, Peghy A. Thoits (1989) considers that emotions are spontaneous short-term reactions towards a person, an object, an event or a situation and comprise four strongly interconnected components: 1) situational signals (characteristics); 2) physiological changes (accelerated heart rate, etc.); 3) gesticulatory expressions (mimics) and 4) the definition of the emotion which refers to the integration of those certain components (Iluţ, 2008). Additional knowledge to the definition given by Peghy A. Thoits (1989) is brought by Gerrod W. Parrott who considers that "emotions are reactions to the events which are significant to people, including physiological, behavioural, cognitive and subjective experiences (feelings) of pleasure or annoyance" (Parrott, 1995/1996, p. 198). Interested in studying emotions, Nico H. Fridja (1988) thinks that these are not just the result of some situations analysed before, because they appear as tendencies which incite to a certain action and from behaviours which can be classified in a certain manner after the cognitive evaluation. Klaus R. Scherer (1984) considers that emotions are the stimuli which help us react in certain contexts, influence future behaviour and adjust social interactions.

But let us understand emotions as they are defined for the large audience by DEX (The Explanatory Dictionary of the Romanian Language). Why do I not rely on specialised dictionaries and books exclusively? DEX is the most widely checked dictionary and addresses all the persons who use the Romanian language frequently and need information regarding terms they cannot understand, offers the origin of a certain word and provides synonyms when necessary. According to it, "emotions are powerful emotional responses, sometimes unexpected, accompanied by alterations in the state and functioning of the body, which reflect someone's attitude towards the surrounding world" (Dex).

Now, after clarifying how emotions are defined, I would like to approach their nature to show where moral emotions come from.

3 The nature of moral emotions

The spectrum of emotions is wide, their classification deriving from diverse approaches and perspectives different authors interested in their analysis have had over them. Thus, Renė Descartes (1649/1999) divided emotions into two distinct categories: primitive and particular, conceiving an order of the appearance of feelings by saying: "there are only six such feelings, i.e.: surprise, love, hate, desire, happiness and sadness; all the others are composed of some of these feelings because these six feelings are species of them" (Descartes, 1649/1999, p. 53). But let us discover, in the following, from the papers researched into in the literature review, how emotions are classified and which of them enter the category of moral emotions and why.

Sociologist Theodor D. Kemper (1987) enlists fury, fear, pleasure and sadness as primary emotions. Paul Ekman (1992a, 1992b) takes into consideration the cultural factors and classifies them according to the facial expression. The moral emotions of shame and guilt were catalogued by Carroll Izard (1971) and

Robert N. Emde (1980) as primary emotions, while Silvian S. Tomkins (1984) included in this category only shame. Paul F. Griffith (1997) divides emotions into: emotions affectively programmed (primary emotions), cognitive emotions (social emotions) and socially built emotions. According to a tertiary division of emotions, Gerrod W. Parrott (2001) includes shame within both secondary and tertiary emotions, while embarrassment and guilt are included only in the category of tertiary emotions.

Completely dedicated to the study of emotions, Robert Plutchik (1962/1991, 1980, 2002) designs the classification of emotions as a scheme which ended up carrying his name, being known as "the Plutchik's circle" (1980). Here, shame is the result of the combination between disgust and fear, while guilt comes as a result between the combination of pleasure and fear.

Jonathan Haidt (2003) divides emotions into four categories: emotions concerning others (contempt, fury, annoyance); self-conscious emotions (shame, guilt, embarrassment); emotions linked to the sufferance of others (empathy) and emotions linked to the appreciation of others (gratitude, fear, veneration). The author states that embarrassment, shame and guilt differ from sadness, happiness, fury, fear, surprise and disgust because they are intrinsically linked to the well-being of the individual. Shame, embarrassment and guilt appear, according to Haidt (2003), against the background of a cognitive evaluation performed unconsciously. The basis of triggering moral emotion consists in the contextual factor or factors which determine the appearance of these emotions. They are named by Haidt (2003), "disinterested elicitors" or "event coding", and by Mesquita and Frijda (1992) "the tendencies which determine the actions", and are not favoured by the society.

As a result of the classification, it could be seen what the origins of the moral emotions are. It was identified the fact that embarrassment, shame and guilt presuppose a higher degree of evaluation because they interfere as a system which guides the decisions depending on anticipated emotions and establish the borders not allowed to be crossed in order to stay within socially accepted limits under certain circumstances. Hence, they are more complex, vary from individual to individual, are culturally influenced and occur in the situation where the norms favoured at a social level are disobeyed, meaning prejudices are brought to the concept of morality. Consequently, embarrassment, shame and guilt, being cognitive emotions, can be called moral emotions. In order for me to avoid for as much as possible the repetitive writing of the three emotions, I will gather them under the phrase "moral emotions", wherever necessary throughout the paper.

4 About shame, embarrassment and guilt

After defining emotions in general and establishing the origin of moral emotions, I will stop and focus on shame, embarrassment and guilt because they make the interest of the present paper. **Shame**, according to Lewis (1995, 1998); Tangney (1990, 1995); Tangney, Miller, Flicker, Barlow (1996) and Weiner (1993) is the emotion which precedes the situations in which the individuals feel responsible for their deeds, failings and failures, which tarnish their image as a result of analysing one's self. It can be said that "people lost face in the eyes of the others", reason for which they do not want to be seen anymore, they want to be alone (Joel R. Davitz, 1969, p. 83). Fessler (1999) is of the opinion that there are two major forms of shame: a lighter "proto-shame", determined by the simple presence of the dominating superiors, and a more complex shame which results from violating the norms, when the deed is exposed. A comparative analysis of the specialists' opinions regarding the study of moral emotions shows that, many times, shame is taken for embarrassment.

In the Chinese culture, shame is an extremely important emotion, reminding of the cultural heritage of Confucius. It is the result of the values inherited with the aim of self-improvement, of growth, of social development, based on harmony among individuals. For the Chinese people shame is self-conscious, presupposes focus on the self and is generated within contexts involving social relations which can lead to negative appreciations measured against one's own person. The negative appreciations linked to personal performances determine the emergence of shame (Fischer, Tangney, 1995).

Heidel's interest in researching shame (1991) emphasises the words used to render the emotion of shame in three cultures from Indonesia where the English language is not spoken. Thus, through this research, he observes that there are subtle differences between the words which signify shame among the populations of the three cultures, differences which cannot be accounted for among the speakers of the English language.

In Spain, more than in the Low Countries, shame is predominantly linked to family, to masculine honour and to feminine sexuality. The Spanish associate shame to a lower capacity of selection of the feminine persons to choose the partners whom they have sexual intercourse with (Fischer, Manstead, and Rodrigues Mosquera, 1999; Rodriguez Mosquera, Manstead, 2000).

Embarrassment is a variant of shame for Deborah F. Grenwald and David W. Harder (1998). The characteristics emphasised by Fessler (1999) for "proto-shame" are similar to the ones described by Keltner (1995), Keltner and Buswell, (1996) for embarrassment. In their research, Keltner and Harker (1998), Miller

(1996) and Frijda and Mesquita (1994) mention that the presence of embarrassment is dependent on the hierarchic position of the one the action is performed in front of and who participates in the creation of the embarrassing moment. When analysing the delineation between shame and embarrassment, it is estimated that if a deed is not perceived by the one who committed it as too tragical, the emotion felt will be embarrassment, while "if it was socialised in the spirit of honour and fairness, the perception of his/her deed being severely bad will lead to the emotion of shame", and the embarrassment will be "most likely associated to an accidental mistake, a temporary lack of attention, as different from shame which appears as the result of a constant characteristic of the person" (Chelcea, 2008, p. 216). Preoccupied by the distinction between shame and embarrassment, Miller (1996) noted down the conclusions of Eldman (1994), Leary and Meadows (1991), who emphasised that shame has private effects, while embarrassment appears when the one who did not observe the social norm considers that his/her deeds are exposed and connects them not to what he/she thinks about himself/herself, but to the opinions of the others (Chelcea, 2008, p. 217).

Goffman (1967), Jderu (2008, 2010) and Harré and Parrot (1996) consider that there are differences between embarrassment and shame, embarrassment being "a social control emotion", compared to shame perceived by Elspeth Probyn (2005) as an emotion reflecting who we think we are, considering self-esteem and a person's system of values. Haidt (2003) described embarrassment as a touch of the face, a nervous smile. Shame is more powerful, it creates pain (Lewis, 1971), touches the self, transmits that something is not all right and determines a state of abnormality.

Significant differences occur in the case of the Westerners who do not take embarrassment as shame, the explanation consisting in the importance these allocate to the virtues of truth. Turiel (1983) mentions that the Western societies separate moral order (problems caused by injustice, crime, evil determination) from social order (inadequate dress code due to the lack of being identified in a certain context). There can be distinguished two levels that emotions can affect. One of the social norms, when social norms are broken, and one of the moral norms (Keltner and Buswell, 1996; Tangney, Miller, Flicker and Barlow, 1996). Embarrassment is easier to handle, while the impact of shame should induce a higher degree of discomfort into the individual (Keltner and Buswell, 1997).

The last emotion, **guilt**, ends up many times being mistaken for shame. Under certain circumstances, it may happen for the ones who transgress the law to experience shame, guilt or both of them. I consider that guilt is related to both law and sanction, as well as morals and sanction. I will provide a relevant example. There are persons who broke the law (for example, they committed theft), are not caught and continue to steal. The explanation starts from who builds consciousness: morals or legislative coercion. I am of the opinion that guilt can be defined as a natural emotion, which should be felt when one's interior beliefs are broken and which should be in keeping with the moral and/or criminal code. There are persons who have been socialised in the spirit of morality and who, without having committed any wrong deeds, feel guilty, because they simply dared to think wrong. Consequently, I can say that guilt appears as a result of violating moral beliefs. Guilt is related to the one who broke the rules, meaning: broke an interdiction, accepted the legitimacy of the interdiction and admitted the authority of the court who placed the interdiction (Taylor, 1996, p. 57).

Personally, I consider that guilt is an emotion which registers different intensities depending on the person whom its effects are reflected on. When someone is late or misses the train and there is no other person affected by this he/she may feel guilty. But if his/her running late affects someone else, he/she will feel still guilty, but to a higher degree. Guilt is an emotion related to the trust the others have in you, to self-esteem, to image, to reputation, to stigmatisation in the case when the person is criminally sanctioned and he/she will have a criminal record for the rest of his/her life. Being difficult to render a definition, Septimiu Chelcea (2008, p. 219) mentions the conclusions of William Neblett, which make an analysis of the role of guilt starting from the following considerations: "1) Guilt can be experienced with intensity for a long period of time or, on the contrary, it can be on short-term and superficial; 2) Guilt sometimes constitutes a critical factor in motivating reasonable actions, but some other times a critical factor in motivating bad deeds; 3) Some persons experience this emotion very rarely, while other persons live the emotion of guilt excessively, a fact which prevents them from having a constructive life; 4) Guilt can be experienced towards a person, death, God or another authority (even impersonal); 5) We can feel guilty for both what we did not do, and for what we did; 6) We can feel guilty for both what we felt, and for what we missed to do; we can feel guilty for our feelings, as well as for the things we imagine we would have done if the opportunity had arisen" (Neblett, 1974, p. 652).

Charles Darwin [1872] (1967) opinionated, on the one hand, that shame and guilt appear when conventional rules or moral laws are not observed and are reflected in the behaviour of the guilty person who "avoids to look in the eyes of the accuser or just peeps an eye at him/her" while his/her eyes "become suspicious" or "run to and fro", while "the eyelids are partially closed" because "the guilty person cannot stand to meet the eyes of his/her accuser"; on the other hand, Darwin mentioned that he had observed a guilty look, without any trace of fear, in one of his children, at a very young age, due to an unnatural gleam of his eyes and a weird, affected attitude (Darwin, 1872/1967, pp. 150–151). Next, he was preoccupied with blushing, mentioning that this is not a biological natural reaction, as "it is not consciousness that generates blushing, because someone may sincerely regret, when alone, a minor mistake committed or can suffer the most profound remorse for an undiscovered murder, but he/she will not blush [...]. Not the feeling of guilt, but the thought that the others think we are or know we are guilty makes us blush" (Darwin, 1872/1967, pp. 191–192).

What I managed to trace was the fact there is a tendency to misinterpret moral emotions. The study of the relationship between emotion and culture were never short of theoretical and epistemological dissensions, which are prolific because they represent new challenges for researchers. It was in this way that different approaches took shape: universalist, positivist, relativist and interpretivist. The founders of the social and cultural establishment of emotion "rely on a series of different traditions, including ethnopsychology, on social and linguistic structures[...]", on the ethnographic description of emotions, being organised by means of a comparative frame which enables the approach of emotions form the perspective of the cultural expression necessary for overcoming the problems persistent in social relations (Lutz and White, 1986, p. 406).

Paul Ekman (1993) re-enforces the idea of the cultural architecture of emotions and mentions that he does not share the opinion according to which the emotional expression should be extended to other cultures, but considers that the future research done by specialists will not reach other conclusions. He thinks that the human effort to dissimulate facial expressiveness of emotions can be activated, but the success of these dissimulations is under a question mark (Ekman, 1993, p. 389).

Due to the differences discovered when defining emotions from one author to another, form one culture to another, I summarised the definitions which appear in The Explanatory Dictionary of the Romanian Language **for embarrassment, shame and guilt in order to be able to make a more detailed analysis**. The analysis of defining moral emotions, according to the terms and expressions used, prove that the Romanian vocabulary partially uses some similar descriptions for embarrassment and shame, which determines one to be taken for the other. Just as Taylor (1996) discovered, guilt is perceived as crime, as breaking the norm. For these reasons, guilt differentiates itself more clearly from embarrassment and shame (Taylor, 1996, p. 57) (Tab. 1).

Analysing the literature review, it can be observed that emotions are defined through the functions they have. Shame and guilt are negative emotions, "which pave the way to retreating from the public space (when the individual experiences the emotion of shame) or to performing some

Tab. 1: Defining embarrassment, shame and guilt according to The Explanatory Dictionary of the Romanian Language, Atudorei (2016)

Embarrassment	**Shame**	**Guilt**
– to be covered by embarrassment. – to shame, to blush, to be discomforted, to be disturbed, to be intimidated.	– uncomfortable feeling of shyness, of embarrassment, generated by a failure or mistake. – impertinence, senselessness, indecency; insult, scorn, offence, unfairness.	– the fact of being guilty, deed committed by the guilty one; the state of the guilty one. – guilt, culpability (the situation of a person who committed a crime);
– feeling of shyness someone may experience under an awkward situation; feeling of abashment. – difficult, unpleasant situation; entanglement, trouble. – to put someone in an awkward position.	– to be a scoundrel, whose deeds someone is ashamed of; to be the cause of someone's dishonour. – lacking common sense, nervy, insensitive, indecent. – to embarrass someone, to dishonour someone.	– crime (violating the law, punished by means of criminal fine or correctional facility; medium-gravity crime).

prosocial behaviours, to compensate for the pain or annoyance produced sometime" (Chelcea, 2008, p. 40). It can be seen that emotions are concurrent with reason and have the capacity to influence the behaviours of the individuals in social contexts.

5 Autochthon studies of moral emotions

Moral emotions have been analysed by Chelcea (2007, 2008) and Atudorei (2016) in different social contexts and were correlated to the importance the exposer of the one who committed a deed has, as a consequence of which he/she should have felt moral emotions.

The sociological survey conducted by Septimiu Chelcea (2008) represents the first research which dealt with the study of moral emotions in Romania. The research was done on a sample of 674 students in their 1st and 3rd year of study from seven academic establishments in Romania, from faculties with a humanities and technical-engineering profile. The instrument used for collecting the data was the structured questionnaire, and it aimed at registering data regarding behavioural assessment according to the TOSCA scales. Tangney, Wagner and

Gramzow (1989) were of the opinion that "the TOSCA scales is the most frequently used instrument for measuring the disposition of the subjects to experience shame or guilt on the basis of scenarios" (Chelcea, 2008, p. 274). The TOSCA scales comprise 15 scenarios which represent daily situations in which people should note down their predisposition to feel shame or guilt. The respondents were asked to imagine themselves in the situations described and to evaluate on a scale from 1 to 5 what they thought they would feel in the context mentioned. The subjects were included in the sample *ad libitum*, the data being generalised over the ones interviewed. The author thinks that "without being representative at a national level for the socio-occupational category of students, the sample that was used describes the state of affairs regarding the moral climate in the universities of Romania" and allows the testing of the research hypothesis "The less the disposition to experience the emotions of shame and guilt appears, the bigger the tendency to commit acts of intellectual fraud in universities becomes" (Chelcea, 2008, pp. 270–272). Septimiu Chelcea (2008) investigates what emotions are considered by the students to occur when copying in an exam, handing in a paper written by someone else, using information from the Internet without mentioning the source, taking over passages from printed papers without specifying where they appeared first and helping a colleague pass an exam by fraud. All these are analysed in three different contexts: when this fact is known by the colleagues, when he/she is sanctioned by the professor and brought to the attention of the colleagues and when this stays their secret. The results of the research show that there are significant differences in what experiencing emotions of shame and guilt are concerned, depending on the context. The students could note down whether they experienced feelings of shame or guilt or both of them. In the case when the intellectual fraud (copying, plagiarism, handing in papers from the Internet without mentioning the source) is exposed by the professor and sanctioned before the colleagues, there is registered the highest number of students mentioning that they would feel moral emotions. The number of the ones experiencing shame and/or guilt starts to decrease if the fact is known only by the colleagues and stays unpunished. The lowest number is registered when the deed remains secret. For all the contexts in which the facts listed before were committed, the answer "both" was registered, as well. It can be seen that the two emotions can be taken one for the other. It has been observed that exposing the acts of fraud in the presence of the others (of the colleagues) determines the emergence of shame, while disapproval in the private space, the emergence of guilt (Chelcea, 2008, p. 271). We can conclude that the public sanction of fraud is facile because the number of students in the universe of research "who state that they would feel neither shame nor guilt" is decreasing (Chelcea, 2008, p. 286).

In conclusion, it can be said, on the one hand, that in the context in which the acts are socially penalised the number of those who experience moral emotions increases, while, on the other hand, the greater the importance of the exposer is, the more the respondents state that they would feel shame or guilt. The exposer is named "the significant other" and his/her influence was tested in an autochthon context.

Being interested in the study of moral emotions, in 2014, I carried out quantitative research on a sample of 384 students from *Transilvania* University of Braşov, enrolled in the undergraduate programme. The sample was stratified by the 18 existing faculties. The number of the students selected was balanced according to the total number of students per each faculty. From all these, 51,6 % were female students and 48,4 % male students. What I also considered were the different aspects of the contexts in which the emotions would manifest themselves. Thus, I analysed the emergence of moral emotions in different contexts: when facts are exposed, when facts are not exposed, when they are exposed by the colleagues, when they are exposed by the professors, when others commit deeds which can be catalogued as intellectual fraud, when the doer is the only one who breaks the rule, when students work at the same time while attending faculty and when they do not work at all. Within my qualitative research, I analysed emotions considering previous intellectual fraud, i.e. the one from high school. For the students who declared that they had copied in high school too and that they continued to copy at faculty as well, I observed that: in the case of unexposed facts there is no difference between the moral emotions experienced in high school and the ones experienced at faculty; the degree of experiencing moral emotions is lower when the intellectual fraud is exposed by colleagues compared to when the students are identified by professors. Consequently, the hypothesis "The social context influences moral emotions" does not confirm in the case of unexposed moral emotions, but it is confirmed in the case of the emotions exposed by colleagues and by professors.

My quantitative research on moral emotions confirms Charles Darwin's [1872] (1967) conclusion which stated that shame appears when it is exposed. The values registered are higher when the acts of intellectual fraud are exposed. Moreover, for the moral emotion of shame differences appear depending on the significance of the other, reason for which it can be stated that shame is directly proportional to the importance of the exposer for the one who breaks the rules. Being alone when the acts of intellectual fraud are exposed or being one of the others represent two contexts which influence the type and the intensity of the emotion in a different manner.

The majority of the students stated that when the other colleagues did not copy, but they did and were not caught they felt guilty. Thus, I observed that they interiorised the most powerful moral emotion of the three, because the phenomenon was not generalised. In other words, they perceived themselves as being "the black sheep". In this situation, some students mentioned that they felt embarrassment, shame quantifying the lowest rate. It also happens for the respondents to mention that they felt embarrassment when the one who found out was not important to them and shame when the importance of the one who found out about their deed was higher.

In conclusion, the reference to the context in which the acts of intellectual fraud are reproduced by other colleagues of the students as well determines a decrease in the process of interiorising moral emotions (Atudorei, 2016), reason for which this was named "tolerant deviation" by Ştefan Boncu (2002). I can say that, the more sympathisers one has to repeat the act of intellectual fraud, the more this phenomenon becomes a practice due to the lack of sanctions. The respondents stated that the ones who commit acts of intellectual fraud and do not have a job should feel guiltier than the ones who already work. I discovered that the analysis is not objective. The same deed, in the same context, but influenced by the fact that some students have a workplace determines lower culpability from the part of the respondents for the ones who have a workplace in parallel to attending faculty. The decrease of blame can be explained through the fact that the respondents took into consideration the time resources available, which decrease for the ones who work.

6 Methodological aspects of the research

The aim of my research consisted of analysing, on the one hand, the contexts in which moral emotions occur with students as part of the school activities, and, on the other hand, the elements that can be associated to the emotion experienced under those circumstances. The visual data collected between the 20th of July 2017 and 30th of October 2017 consisted of drawings. In the universe of my research, there were included the students of *Transilvania* University of Braşov, from the undergraduate programme and from different profiles: social and humanities, technical and engineering and vocational.

The data are of a visual type and came as a result of collecting the generated social documents. On one side of the paper, I asked them to produce images (drawings) to emphasise the moral emotions which occurred in school contexts. On the other side of the paper, I asked them to describe in words what the image represented to reduce the subjectivity of the researcher when interpreting the significance of the drawings. For drawing, I presented them with coloured pencils, pencils and ball pens. They had total freedom in choosing both the way in which to draw and the colours to use when drawing. In order for me to avoid suggesting to them a certain hierarchy of the intensity of moral emotions: embarrassment, shame and guilt, I changed the order in which I asked them to draw. I required them to divide the paper into three parts and to draw, first of all, a situation when they felt shame, then embarrassment, the last part being dedicated to guilt.

With the social and humanities profile, predominant were the female students, with the technical and engineering one, the male students. The vocational profile was more equilibrated regarding gender distribution. For collecting the data, I relied on students from faculties with different profiles. My aim was to eliminate all possible similarities which could occur in the drawings due to possible similar characteristics of the students belonging to a certain profile.

The sample was based on availability, the respondents being chosen on the basis of volunteering. The database comprises 39 respondents: 13 from the technical-engineering profile (5 female students and 8 male students), 7 from the vocational profile (4 female students and 3 male students) and 19 from the social and humanities profile (19 female students and 3 male students). Gender balance is dependent on the profile each faculty is included in.

7 Data analysis and interpretation

For processing the visual data, I used the NVivo software. I classified moral emotions into shame, embarrassment and guilt, and within each of them I worked with emergent categories. In the first category, I included the drawings which represented shame, in the second one, the ones picturing embarrassment and in the third one, the ones portraying guilt. The emotions were correlated with the context in which they appeared.

8 The analysis of school contexts in which students experienced shame

The first moral emotion that I analysed was shame because it was the first one that I collected visual data about by means of drawing. I will start with the analysis of the contexts in which shame appeared, then I will stop at the characteristics that were associated to it. It is only by means of visual techniques that aspects related to mimics, gestures and colour accompanying the manifestation of emotions in a certain context can optimally be highlighted.

Tab. 2: Deeds committed in school contexts in which students portrayed the emergence of shame

Deeds committed in school contexts in which students portrayed the emergence of shame	Frequency
A minor mistake in the presence of another significant person – involuntary situations	1
Intellectual fraud exposed – moral norms	10
Not applying oneself to the tasks adapted to the role – moral norms	3
Confessing not passing an exam to significant persons/parents – moral norms	3
Handing in a bad project/material – moral norms	5
I didn't do my homework/I didn't learn/not assuming the role of the student – moral norms	11
I was late – conventional rules	4
Involuntary exposure of intimate body parts – involuntary situations	2

The school contexts sketched in the drawings in which shame occurred reflect **the presence of another person or of other persons**. Of the 39 situations in which shame is portrayed, in two of them there are colleagues present and in other two, parents. Professors are present in other 35 contexts where colleagues always appear, as well. The occurrence of other persons in the context of describing the emotion of shame coincides with what Septimiu Chelcea (2008) and Elspeth Probyn (2005) observed: they stated that shame appears in the presence of "the significant other" and is perceived in relation to who we consider we are, taking into consideration one's self-esteem and a person's system of values. Also, the presence of other persons in the drawings in which shame is pictured confirms "the theory of blushing" in which the author states that "someone can feel profoundly ashamed of having said a little untruth without blushing, but, if he merely suspects that he might be discovered, he will blush immediately, especially if he is discovered by a person that he respects" (Darwin, 1872/1967, pp. 191–192). The contexts analysed show that there appears a higher frequency of breaking moral norms (32 out of 39), in comparison with the situations in which it has been observed that conventional/social norms are broken (4 out of 39) or with the situations which do not depend on free will (3 out of 39), but place the individual in a position that they associated with shame. In Tab. 2 I will exemplify the facts that generated shame.

Fig. 1: Highlighting the covering of the face when shame appears (author's archive)

8.1 The characteristics of shame in school-related contexts

Shame is one of the most powerful human emotions which appears, as shown before, in the social space of communication and distinguishes itself through a series of distinctive reactions. In this research, I captured the desire of the persons to cover their face or their eyes in the situations in which they experience the emotion of shame.

With the exception of one single drawing, in which the persons are not represented facing the viewer and the eyes could not be captured, in all the others the eyes are present in the drawings. In six pictures the subjects cover their face or the eyes area (Fig. 1).

The action performed becomes shameful for the one who committed it when he/she acknowledges that someone watched him/her or saw him/her. Being looked at by another person is equivalent to unveiling the secret which triggers tension and the introversion of shame, observation which is in perfect agreement with the theories about shame. Subsequently, shame is linked to the visual and, as it can be derived from the six drawings, the subjects wish they were not watched. The covering of the face plays the role of expressing the avoidance of the visual contact, a gesture translated into the desire not to be seen because of the facts that place them in shameful positions, just as Charles Darwin observed, as well [1872] (1967).

8.2 The expressiveness of the lip contour

The expressiveness of the lip contour represents another characteristic identified at the facial level for expressing shame. In nine drawings the lip contour has a horizontal shape (Fig. 2).

In the case of the contexts in which shame appears as a result of breaking conventional rules (he/she was late for a class) or in involuntary situations (the wind lifted her skirt and intimate body parts were exposed), the corners of the mouth

Fig. 2: Highlighting lip contour in the case of shame (horizontal shape) (author's archive)

have a horizontal position. The horizontal position of the lips can be interpreted as determining a lower introversion of shame.

In 22 out of 39 cases, the corners of the mouth are pointed downwards, as it can be noticed in the selection of drawings in Fig. 3. In the majority of the contexts in which students broke moral norms, the corners of the mouths appear pointed downwards. This aspect can be related to the fact that the impact of the deed committed has a higher intensity, that shame registers a higher degree when they commit deeds which break moral norms, compared to the situations when conventional or social rules are broken, or when the situation was involuntary.

However, some atypical situations can be mentioned. In three contexts, the shape of the mouth appears with the corners drawn upwards, which is not normal for a situation in which a person experiences shame. When this expression can be read on someone's face, we instinctively associate it with the state of a good disposition, with content, with happiness. But these emotions were drawn for the situations in which the students believed that they had produced good papers and they handed them in being content. When receiving feedback from the professor, the good mood disappeared because they became aware that the material handed in was of poor quality, reason for which the situation generated shame. Hence, the expressiveness of the corners of the mouth pointed upwards will change. The smile, as an expression of joy, appeared in the absence of the acknowledgement of the situation.

Fig. 3: Highlighting the shape of the lips in the case of shame (the corners of the mouth pointed downwards) (author's archive)

In five drawings, the shape of the lips is not highlighted. In some cases, the lips were not drawn, and in others, the persons positioned themselves from behind, so nothing could be observed. In the context of experiencing shame, the tilted position of the head appears in two drawings and in some other two drawings falling tears are highlighted.

Another important characteristic which suggests the introversion of shame consists in its overt manifestation at face level which is coloured in **red**, indicating blushing. I am reminding of the fact that all students had the whole range of colours at hand to use for colouring their drawings. When they drew, the choice was deliberate when using the colours, and was not caused by the context of not being provided with a certain colour. In 22 of the 39 drawings, the reddening of the face does not appear. In some of the drawings, the person is captured from behind and in some others, the faces are completely covered so this characteristic could not be captured. In 16 cases, the red colour is used to picture the reddening of the face, as it can be seen in Fig. 4, and in one case, the pink colour.

Fig. 4: Highlighting blushing for drawing shame (author's archive)

I observed that the tendency to colour the cheeks appears in the contexts in which the norms broken were the conventional/social ones (I was late for the class, I did not prepare enough and I took a bad mark, I failed the exam); the moral ones (I copied and the professor caught me, I had to run a distance, but I cut the road short, the professor caught me and he/she failed me because I was not fair, I took a paper from a colleague, I handed it in as mine, the professors caught me and they gave me a 2) as well as in involuntary situations in which intimate body parts were exposed (the wind lifted my skirt and a colleague saw me). Moreover, in the contexts in which shame appears and both the colleagues and the professors are present and the moral norms (I copied) or a conventional rule (I did not pay attention to the professor's explanations and he/she asked me something about what he/she had said and I could not answer) were broken, both the covering of the face and blushing appear, as well as the pointing downwards of the corners of the mouth. These observations can be linked to the importance of the person present in the context. It is presupposed that the presence of the professor should be more significant for the one who commits the shameful deeds. The colleagues can find out, but their duty not being supervision (they are sympathetic and do not reveal the facts even if they see them) and evaluation, we can derive that the professor has a more important role. He/she can discover and sanction. Consequently, his/her importance increases. Hence, the colouring of the cheeks in the majority of the cases and the pointing downwards of the corners of the mouth. The conclusion coincides with Charles Darwin's notes (1872/1967) who mentions that shame is directly proportional to the significance of the other for the one who did something wrong. In other words, the higher the respect for that person, the greater the intensity of the shame for the

Fig. 5: Involuntary contexts in which shame appears (author's archive)

exposed person. It may happen that in some situations, the exposer can experience shame as well, hence the expression: "I'm ashamed of his/her shame".

In the case of shame, some situations, which are not influenced by free will, may appear. Here, the context that can be highlighted is the one in which a female medical student, during her internship, caught a glimpse of the intimate body parts of a patient who had suffered burnings and could not be dressed or covered, or of another student in whose case her intimate body parts were exposed involuntarily because the wind had blown and had lifted her skirt, a colleague seeing that, according to Fig. 5.

Although in these contexts there appears the involuntary exposure of the intimate body parts in public, we can interpret it starting from the symbolic interactionism, more precisely from "a distance from the role", according to the opinion of Jean-Manuel de Queiroz and Marek Ziolkowski (1994). In the case of the medical student, for whom the context should not have produced the emotion of shame because it was an absolutely normal situation, normality which can be extended to the gynaecologist's professional practising act, before who the intimate body parts of the female patients are exposed, the problem which appears is that of the dual identity of a person. The sensation of entering another self, completely new, resulted from the professional role, cannot happen without having effects over the emotional. Practically, the person in the situation cannot give up the initial identity, built on a system of values, of conventions. If we had to compare the context of the student to that of the gynaecologist's, we would possibly be able to formulate a new hypothesis: "If the distance from the role decreases, the moral emotions diminish, as well". Subsequently, practising the actions within social contexts determines the diminution of the emotions' intensity. An approach of the problematics of the role can prove the necessity to practice the role, a role which will transform the person at the level of identity. The analysis of the visual data reflects the socialising importance of the social contexts. It surprises you at the beginning, it enables you to practice your role and it modifies your emotions because the more an action or a fact repeats itself, the weaker the intensity of the emotions will be (Atudorei, 2016). The identity distance "increases the feeling of control which presses upon us", determining us to mould ourselves according to the new context (Mead, 1963, p. 233). Consequently, we can conclude that sanctioning the deeds amendable from a moral point of view, respectively according to the social norms, must determine the implementation of both sanctions for introverting the moral emotions and the situations which should generate the introversion of some powerful emotions.

9 The analysis of the school contexts in which students experienced embarrassment

The second emotion expressed by means of drawings was embarrassment. The context referring to the presence of the other is interesting, because in 38 cases embarrassment occurs when the others are present. There is only one case of intellectual fraud, in which the respondent mentions that "I didn't learn, I prepared ready-made cheating-sheets and I went to the exam like that" and the presence of another person does not appear. In 13 situations, only the colleagues are present, while in 23 both the colleagues and the professor appear. There are two situations in which unknown persons appear. Even if their hierarchic position is different, embarrassment was experienced anyway.

Frijda and Mesquita (1994), Miller (1996), Keltner and Harker (1998), Chelcea (2007, 2008) and Atudorei (2016) analyse the significance, respectively **the hierarchic position of the person/persons present in the context in which embarrassment occurs**. These all highlight, as a result of their research, the relationship between the person who experiences embarrassment and the person in whose presence the embarrassing moment occurs. The authors reach the conclusion that the intensity of embarrassment is lower when this one occurs in the presence of persons who have a lesser importance for the ones who committed an embarrassing deed, for example, in the presence of an unknown person or whose significance is of little importance to them. In conclusion, the greater the importance of the one in whose presence the embarrassing deed was committed is, the higher the intensity of embarrassment will be.

Consequently, the conclusions reached after analysing the visual data strengthen Rowland S. Miller's statement (1996) who was of the opinion that embarrassment is very unlikely linked to what we think about our own person. It is closely linked to what we consider that the others might think of us. This observation must be correlated to the statements of other researchers, such as Edelman (1994) and Leary and Meadows (1991), who mentioned that embarrassment appears then when, either in reality or imaginary, another person is present who might expose the deed. In the following, I will reveal what deeds were committed by students in school contexts in which they experienced embarrassment and who appears around them. In all the contexts in which embarrassment appears, their faculty colleagues were present and in 24 there were also the professors. The deeds which triggered the emergence of embarrassment are included in Tab. 3.

I analysed the deeds which occurred in the contexts which generated embarrassment, starting from the possibility to decide over the occurrence of the actions. In 30 situations, it was the case of a deliberate act, in 20 cases moral norms being broken and in 10, conventional rules. The other nine situations were involuntary.

If in the case of shame, the tilting of the head appeared in two situations, in the case of embarrassment this posture does not appear at all. The eyes are portrayed in 34 drawings. In four they are not highlighted, and in another case the person positioned himself/herself from behind. If in the case shame, the covering of the face is pictured, in the case of embarrassment this one does not appear. The reaction illustrated by means of crying appears in two drawings, just like in the case of shame. The expressiveness of the lip shape is highlighted in 32 drawings. In seven cases, the lip contour is not pictured. In 15 drawings, the lip contour has a horizontal shape, as it can be seen in Fig. 6, in 11 drawings, the corners of the mouth are pointed downwards, according to Fig. 7. There are six atypical cases for the shape of the lips concerning the emotion of embarrassment. In three cases, the corners are pointed upwards, in two, they zigzag and in one drawing, only one corner of the mouth is pointed upwards, according to Fig. 8.

Tab. 3: The deeds committed by students in school contexts in which they experienced embarrassment

The deeds committed by students in school contexts in which they experienced embarrassment	Frequency
Lack of concentration in class/I was late for class – conventional rules	9
Exposed intellectual fraud – moral norms	5
Not applying oneself to the tasks adapted to the role/Handing in a bad project/material/I didn't help my colleague in matters concerning school even though I had promised – moral norms	13
I spoke badly of someone – moral norm	2
I religiously discriminated someone – conventional rule	1
I stained myself/I spilled food on me/A car splashed me and I got dirty/They were talking about me that I am an orphan of both parents/Being a boy and having long hair I was told by the professor that I had long hair and that I was slow in the uptake/Glimpsing at a naked patient during internship at a hospital/My friends were laughing at me on a topic that I was embarrassed of/Not observing some manners/I kept forgetting my colleagues' names at the beginning of faculty years – involuntary situations	9

Fig. 6: Highlighting the lip contour (the horizontal position of the corners of the mouth) (author's archive)

After analysing the drawings, I observed that there is a higher frequency for the lips sketched in a horizontal position for the contexts in which conventional rules were broken or for the deeds which triggered embarrassment in an involuntary manner. Even if in the literature review embarrassment is catalogued as being a moral emotion which affects the self in a lesser degree than that of

Fig. 7: Highlighting the lip contour (the corners of the mouth pointing downwards) (author's archive)

Fig. 8: Highlighting the lip contour (the corners of the mouth pointing upwards, in zigzag or lateral) (author's archive)

shame, the pointing downwards of the corners of the mouth reflects the discomfort which appeared at a personal level.

When the students exemplified situations in which they broke moral norms, they drew the corners of the mouth pointing downwards in a higher degree.

As a result of these observations, I can say that the more the perception of the gravity of the deed which produced embarrassment increases, the more the introversion of the emotion and the degree of discomfort increases. Probably, self-esteem decreases.

The context described for the atypical drawings in Fig. 7 reflects the incapacity of the students to anticipate the fact that they can be placed under an embarrassing situation (I was confusing the names of my colleagues, a car splashed only me from head to toes and all my colleagues were laughing at me, I wore a more generous cleavage at an oral exam and I felt bad when my colleagues asked me if I wanted to impress the professor, I was talking about a certain professor

Fig. 9: Highlighting the colours used in drawings to picture embarrassment (author's archive)

and this one overheard me, I was defending a project trusting that it was good and after the explanations of the professor I realised it was not the case at all, so my smile disappeared, etc.).

Other aspects analysed refer to the presence or absence of **a colour associated to embarrassment**. In 30 drawings, no colour was used to portray embarrassment. **In the other nine drawings, red appears in one case, yellow in three, pink in two, blue in one and orange in other three**. The chromatic range enlarges in the case of **embarrassment, as it can be seen in Fig. 9**.

If until now research has mentioned red as the colour associated to shame, starting with blushing, now I could see that red also appears reddening the face when the emotion of **embarrassment manifests itself**.

It is interesting to note that, as different from shame, the colouring appears in a lower degree (for shame, out of 39 cases, 16 used red and 1 person, pink). For **embarrassment they used more light colours**. Due to this reason, I consider that **embarrassment would be a** "softer" **emotion compared to shame for which red is used, a colour with a higher intensity**. The preference for lighter colours, less striking, would reflect, in my opinion, a dilution of the emotions, translated through introversions which affect the self a little less. Analysing the

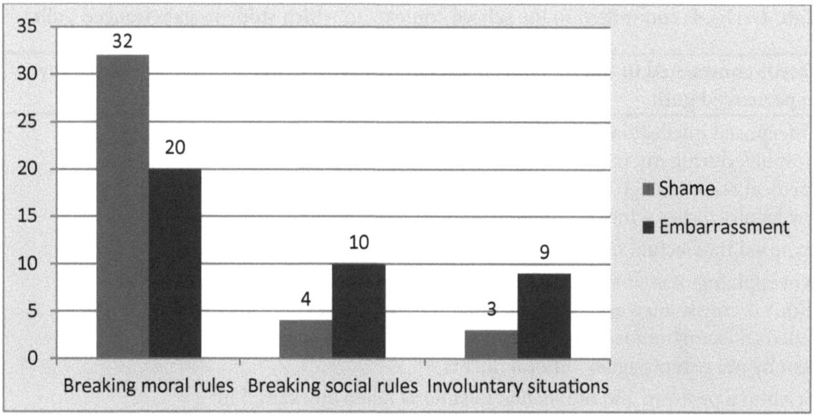

Fig. 10: The absolute frequency of cataloguing the deeds committed when exemplifying shame and embarrassment

choice for the colour which appears in a certain context, corroborated with the presence or absence of another person and its significance for the student, I could discover that it appears in involuntary situations, not being associated to the characteristic/trait of being moral, ethical. The deeds committed break, both in the case of shame and in the case of **embarrassment, moral norms and conventional rules**. In both cases, the moral norms and the conventional rules were broken deliberately. However, the visual data reflect a difference between shame and **embarrassment**. In the case of **embarrassment, more involuntary situations appear** (Fig. 10).

Moreover, the number of deeds which break moral norms decreases for embarrassment and increases for the cases reflecting shame. There are cases in which the same drawing was made to designate both the situation in which shame and embarrassment appeared, conclusions reached by Chelcea (2008) and Atudorei (2016) by means of sociological surveys implemented at an autochthon level, for which the data were collected using the structured questionnaire.

In contrast with the autochthon results, the research carried out at an occidental level by Turiel (1983) prove that the two emotions can be confounded. What I can see is that in Romania, the importance given to the virtues of truth registers lower quotas, considering that the emotions are confounded, justice being done proportionally by law and morals. But here, the ones which interfere are the values that the individuals adhere to and the way in which these have been assimilated.

Tab. 4: Deeds committed in the school contexts in which students experienced guilt

Deeds committed in the school contexts in which students experienced guilt	Frequency
Unexposed intellectual fraud/I received money from a patient in hospital, during my internship/I motivated my skipping an exam on medical reasons to go in the mountains/I lied to my parents regarding my faculty duties – moral norms	14
Exposed intellectual fraud and unpassed exam – conventional rules	3
Not applying oneself to the tasks adapted to the role of the student/I didn't do my homework/I didn't learn/I skipped classes and seminars/I failed an exam because I hadn't learned enough and I spent the money sent by my parents again – moral norms	12
I caused a problem and others had to suffer/I failed an exam, I hit a door in my hostel with my foot and I broke the door – conventional rules	2
I didn't help my colleague at an exam and she failed/I didn't help my colleague in an unpleasant situation/I embarrassed a colleague/I told a colleague that she didn't look good dyed blonde and she was sad – moral norms	4
I committed a minor mistake in the presence of the professors/ Inattentive in class – conventional rules	4

10 The analysis of school contexts in which students experienced guilt

The last emotion analysed is guilt. Out of 39 school contexts in which guilt is portrayed, in eight cases no other person is present. In the other 31 drawings, only the colleagues appear in 12 situations, the parents in 2 and both the professors and the colleagues appear in 17 situations. In Tab. 4, I will exemplify the deeds which occurred in the drawings to illustrate guilt. The contexts which reflected the manifestations of shame or embarrassment contained situations generated involuntarily. In the case of guilt, all the deeds drawn were committed voluntarily. In 30 cases, moral norms were broken, while in other 9 situations, conventional/social rules. The conventional rules are socially amendable and are lawfully regulated in order to be sanctioned according to the deed committed either through warning, fine or confinement.

If in the case of shame, there was a more accentuated tendency of the desire of the respondents to cover their face, in the case of guilt, in only 2 out of 39 drawings this similarity appears. Analysing the context in which the persons

Fig. 11: The tilted position of the head in the case of guilt (author's archive)

cover their face, I observed that the deeds are exposed by persons important to the students (parents, respectively the professor, in the second drawing).

The deeds which are associated to guilt are more linked to the idea that they are publicly disapproved of. Although in 10 cases of intellectual fraud the deed was not exposed by the persons present, the students drew a situation in which they felt guilty.

The tilted position of the head can be noticed in seven drawings which highlight guilt, as it can be seen in Fig. 11. In all the contexts in which the head appears tilted, the deeds were exposed in the presence of a significant person. In only one case, there is no person physically present, but the subject states that "I felt relieved I didn't fail, but guilty because I copied. It was cloudy in my soul, so to say. It's God, if not anyone else, and someone still sees you!" The presence of someone else in the person of God is interesting to note. The student mentions that he was seen and exposed, after all. I can say that someone knows and that this is significant considering that he feels that he was seen.

If the theory states in the case of guilt that the accused one avoids eye contact, we can see that in the drawings highlighting guilt there are several persons, 13 subjects, who look down or have their head tilted to avoid eye contact.

The expressiveness of the lip contour does not appear highlighted in 10 drawings.

In 17 cases, the lip contour is drawn pointing downwards, according to Fig. 12, while in 8, it has a horizontal shape, as it can be seen in Fig. 13.

Fig. 12: The expressiveness of the lip contour (the corners of the mouth pointing downwards) (author's archive)

Fig. 13: The expressiveness of the lip contour for guilt (the corners of the mouth have a horizontal position) (author's archive)

Fig. 14: The expressiveness of the lip contour for guilt (the corners of the mouth are pointed upwards or in zigzag) (author's archive)

Four situations in which the shape of the lips have an atypical shape can be distinguished. In two drawings, the corners of the mouth are pointed upwards, and in the other two are drawn in zigzag, according to Fig. 14.

The lip contour pointed upwards, as a sign of a good disposition, cheerfulness or happiness appears, in the first case, in a hilarious context. Finding themselves in the student hostel, two colleagues decide to steal the clothes of another colleague who was taking a shower, who could not go back to their room but naked (the showers were common). In the other context, the student

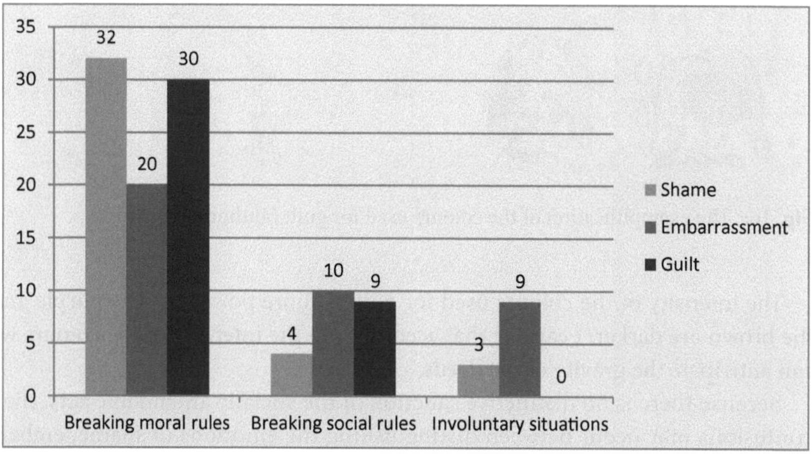

Fig. 15: The absolute frequency of cataloguing the deeds committed when exemplifying shame, embarrassment and guilt

mentions that he was happy at a party, and that, afterwards, he seated an exam which he did not pass because instead of learning he had fun at the party. There is the tendency to draw the situation as perceived positively at the beginning, but which, analysed afterwards, determines the experience of guilt. It can be observed that guilt appears reflected at facial level by means of the lip contour, both in the presence and in the absence of other persons. Here too, guilt ends up being presented in some cases under similar contexts as the ones of shame. In the case of guilt, crying is not associated to exteriorising this emotion, as it appears in only one case in which the respondent lied to her parents about an exam.

A possible explanation would rely on the fact that the mistake once assumed and interiorised is correlated to breaking a rule which presupposes social disapproval and, consequently, it is of no importance whom it was done wrong to because the deed remains. The drawings reflect a close frequency between shame and guilt, according to the type of norm broken, as it can be noticed in Fig. 15. Compared to the drawings which picture shame and embarrassment, with guilt no involuntarily triggered situations appear. In all contexts in which guilt is portrayed, I could see that the deeds committed were deliberate.

The colouring of the face for the emotion of guilt appears in five cases, as it can be seen in Fig. 16. Just like in the case of embarrassment, several colours were used: red twice, yellow once, purple once and brown still once.

Fig. 16: The exemplification of the colours used for guilt (author's archive)

The intensity of the colours used for guilt is more powerful. The purple and the brown are darker. I can say that according to the intensity of the colours we can anticipate the gravity of the deeds.

Because there is no distinctive sanction of the socially amendable acts, then confusions may occur between distinguishing the emotions of shame, embarrassment and guilt, a fact confirmed as a result of analysing the visual data. The similarity of the contexts for describing the introversion of different emotions reflects the impossibility to identify the nature of the order which should regulate the commitment of some deeds or, more correctly said, to stop certain facts. Moral order will be taken for social order. Hence, from here, that the capacity of the people to evaluate the gravity of the deeds will decrease. Turiel (1983) specified that, in Western societies, in which the virtues of truth are of utmost importance, different sanctions appear for the facts which do not observe the moral order, as compared to the ones which do not observe the social one. Moreover, there are described contexts in which similar facts were committed, but the emotions mentioned as having been introverted were different. Some experienced shame, others guilt. In order to eliminate the emotional differences interiorised in different contexts what is needed are clear-cut reference points and a so-called sovereign self, according to Abramovski's observation (1897).

11 Conclusions

As a result of the present research, I consider that I contributed to the addition of knowledge regarding the topic under analysis. The visual techniques used allowed me to associate moral emotions to new elements. The novelty was related to the lip contour and/or the range of colours associated to embarrassment or guilt. For embarrassment, pink, yellow and orange were used, and, in some drawings, red and blue. If we analyse the intensity of the colours used, we will see that they are lighter. This thing can highlight the perception of embarrassment as softer than shame and guilt, meaning the gravity of the deed committed is lower. For guilt, besides red and yellow, darker colours were sporadically used, such as purple and brown. Alongside the rules broken, the darker colours, associated to the tilted posture of the head and the expressiveness of the lips can render a more serious deed which triggers a more powerful emotion. The colours used, the shape of the lips, the tilted head and the presence of another/other person/persons situate guilt on the first position as intensity, shame on the second place and embarrassment on the last, as some other authors have concluded, as well: Lewis (1992), R. Miller (1985, 1994, 1995), Miyake & Yamazaki (1995), Chelcea (2008) and Atudorei (2016).

The analysis of the drawings supports the conclusions of the theory of blushing, according to which shame reddens one's face, because the students who used a colour chose red. The use, in some cases, of the same colour or the representation of the shape of the lips in a similar manner for different emotions reflects the fact that the emotion of embarrassment can be taken for shame or guilt or that there is a lack of perception in what the differences between shame and guilt are concerned. With the exception of the elements of novelty mentioned above, the rest of the aspects coincide with the conclusions reached by means of the sociological survey method used by Septimiu Chelcea (2008) and by me (Atudorei, 2016). I referred primarily to these pieces of research because they were carried out at an autochthonous level, still on students. I am of the opinion that the cultural identity of the respondents can influence the results.

Septimiu Chelcea did quantitative research on 674 students from the big university centres in Romania, and I carried out quantitative research on 384 students from *Transilvania* University of Braşov, just like for the present research. Both quantitative types of research used the method of sociological survey. The instrument used for collecting the data was the structured questionnaire. An advant`age of using visual techniques is rendered by the fact that a database of 39 drawings was able to confirm the results of the research done on much bigger samples, as exemplified above. Moreover, it brought elements of novelty, as well.

I consider that combining visual techniques with collecting statistical data by means of the questionnaire will contribute a great deal both in the field of sociological knowledge and in others. The selection of the subjects for collecting the data is done according to clear criteria. A questionnaire comprising open-ended questions, in which the subjects can also note what the drawings or the photos render, eliminates the possibility of an incorrect analysis or the subjectivity of the researcher when interpreting the image.

Bibliography

Abell, C., & Bantilaki, K. (eds.). (2010). *Philosophical Perspectives on Depiction*. Oxford: Oxford University Press.

Abramovski, E. (1897). Les bases psychologiques de la sociologie. *Revue internationale de sociologie*, 8-9-10. Paris: Giard et Brière.

Atudorei, I. A. (2016). *Emoţiile morale în contextul crizei din România*. Cluj-Napoca: Presa Universitară Clujeană.

Barbalet, J. M. [1998] (2001). *Emotion, Social Theory, and Social Structure: A Macrosociological Approach*. Cambridge: Cambridge University Press.

Boncu, Şt. (2000). *Devianţa tolerată*. Iaşi: Editura Universităţii "Al. I. Cuza".

Chelcea, S. (2007). Emoţiile în viaţa socială. Ruşinea şi vinovăţia în spaţiul public postcomunist din România. *Sociologie Românească*, 5(1), 24–43.

Chelcea, S. (coord.). (2008). *Ruşinea şi vinovţia în spaţiul public*. Bucureşti: Editura Humanitas.

Collins, R. (1975). *Conflict Sociology. Toward an Explanatory Science*. New York: Academic Press.

Darwin, C. [1872] (1967). *Expresia emoţiilor la om şi animale*. Bucureşti: Editura Academiei.

Davitz, J. R. (1969). *The Language of Emotion*. New York: Academic Press.

Descartes, R. [1649] (1999). *Tratat despre sentimente*. Bucureşti: Editura IRI.

Durkheim, É. [1912] (1995). *Formele elementare ale vieţii religioase*. Iaşi: Editura Polirom.

Edelman, J. R. (1994). Embarrassment and blushing: Factors influencing face-saving strategies. In S. Ting-Toomey (ed.). *The Challenge of Facework* (pp. 231–267). Albany: State University of New York Press.

Ekman, P. (1992a). An argument for basic emotion. In *Cognition and Emotion*. 6(3,4), pp. 69–200. San Francisco: University of California. [Online]: http://www.csun.edu/~gk45683/Ekman%20(1992).pdf

Ekman, P. (1992b). Facial expression and emotion. *American Psychologist*, 48, 384–392.

Ekman, P. (1994). Strong evidence for universals in facial expressions: A reply to Russell's mistaken critique. *Psychology Bulletin*, 115(2), 268–287.

Ekman, P. (2003). *Emotions Revealed: Recognizing Faces and Feelings to Improve Communication and Emotional Life*. New York: Times Books.

Ekman, P. & Friesen, W. V. (1971). Constants across cultures in the face and emotion. *Journal of Personality and Social Psychology*, 11, 342–353.

Emde, R. N. (1980). Toward a psychoanalytic theory of affect: vol. I. The organizational model and its propositions. In S. Greenspan & G. Pollock (Eds.), *The Course of Life: Psychoanalytic Contributions toward Understanding Personality Development*. Vol. I: Infancy and early childhood (pp. 63–83). Washington, D.C.: U.S. Government Printing Office.

Fessler, D. M. T. (1999). Towards an understanding of the universality of second order emotions. In A. Hinton (ed.), *Beyond Nature or Nurture: Biocultural Approaches to the Emotions* (pp. 75–116). Cambridge, UK: Cambridge University Press.

Fischer, A. H., & Manstead, A. S. R. (2000). The relation between gender and emotion in different cultures. In A. H. Fischer (ed.), *Gender and Emotion: Social Psycho-logical Perspectives* (pp. 71–96). Cambridge, UK: Cambridge University Press.

Fischer, H. A., Manstead, A. S. R. & Rodriguez Mosquera, P. M. (1999). The role of honor-related vs. individualist values in conceptualizing pride, shame, and anger: Spanish and Dutch cultural prototypes. *Cognition and Emotion*, 13(2), 149–179.

Fischer, K. W., & Tangney, J. P. (1995). Self-conscious emotions and the affect revolution: Framework and overview. In J. P. Tangney & K. W. Fischer (eds.), *Self-Conscious Emotions: The Psychology of Shame, Guilt, Embarrassment, and Pride* (pp. 3–22). New York: Guilford.

Fredrickson, L. B. (1998). What good are positive emotions? *Review of General Psychology*, 2(3), 300–319.

Frijda, N. H. (1986). *The Emotions*. Cambridge: Cambridge University Press.

Frijda, N. H. (1988). The laws of emotion. *American Psychologist*, 43, 349–358.

Frijda, N. H. & Mesquita, B. (1994). The social roles and functions of emotions. In S. Kitayama, S. & H. R. Markus (eds.), *Emotion and Culture: Empirical Studies of Mutual Influence* (pp. 51–87). Washington, D.C.: American Psychological Association.

Goffman, E. (1967). *Interaction Ritual. Essays on Face-to-Face Behavior*. New York: Anchor Books.

Griffith, P.E. (1997). *What Emotions Really Are*. Chicago: University of Chicago Press.

Haidt, J. & Shweder, R. A. (2000). The cultural psychology of the emotions: Ancient and new. In M. Lewis & J. Haviland (Ed.), *Handbook of emotions* (2nd edition, pp. 397–414). New York: Guilford.

Haidt, J. (2003). The moral emotions. In R. J. Davidson, K. R. Scherer & H. H. Goldsmith (eds.), *Handbook of Affective Sciences*. Series in affective science (pp. 852–870). New York, NY, US: Oxford University Press.

Harder, W. & Grenwald, D. (1998). Domains and shame: Evolutionary, cultural, and psychotherapeutic aspects. In P. Gilbert & B. Andrews (eds.), *Shame: Interpersonal Behavior, Psychology, and Culture* (pp. 225–245). New York: Oxford University Press.

Harper, D. (1988). Visual sociology: Expanding sociological vision. *The American Sociologist*, 19(1), 54–70.

Harré, R. & Parrott, G. W. (1996). *The Emotions. Social, Cultural and Biological Dimensions*. London: Sage Publications Ltd.

Hecht, H., Schwartz, R. & Atherton, M. (eds.). (2003). *Looking into Pictures: An Interdisciplinary Approach to Pictorial Space*. Cambridge: MIT Press.

Hochschild, A. R. (1975). The sociology of feeling and emotions: Selected possibilities. In M. Millman & R. M. Kanter (eds.), *Another Voice* (pp. 180–307). Garden City: Ancor Press.

Iluţ, P. (2008). Capital social, informaţie şi implicare emoţională. In Chelcea, S. (coord.). *Ruşinea şi vinovţia în spaţiul public* (pp. 113–137). Bucureşti: Editura Humanitas.

Izard, C. E. (1971). *The Face of Emotion*. New York: Appleton-Century-Crofts.

Izard, C. E. [1977] (1992). *Human Emotions*. New York: Plenum Press.

Jderu, G. (2008). Teoria dramaturgică a emoţiilor. În Septimiu Chelcea (coord.). *Ruşinea şi Vinovăţia în spaţiul public. Pentru o sociologice a emoţiilor* (pp. 69–76). Bucureşti: Editura Humanitas.

Jderu, G. (2010). Ordinea interacţională şi emoţiile. Homo sentiens în perspectiva sociologiei dramaturgice. *Sociologie Românească*, 8(2), 48–64.

Keltner, D. & Buswell, B. N. (1996). Evidence for the distinctness of embarrassment, shame, and guilt: A study of recalled antecedents and facial expressions of emotion. *Cognition & Emotion*, 10, 155–171.

Keltner, D. & Haidt, J. (1999). Social functions of emotions at four levels of analysis. *Cognition and Emotion*, 13, pp. 505–521. .

Keltner, D. & Haidt, J. (2001). Social functions of emotions. In T. Mayne & G. A. Bonanno (eds.), *Emotions: Current Issues and Future Directions* (pp. 192–213). New York: Guilford Press.

Keltner, D. & Harker, L. (1998). The forms and functions of the nonverbal signal of shame. In Gilbert, P. & Andrews, B. (eds.), *Shame: Interpersonal Behavior, Psychopathology, and Culture* (pp. 78–98). New York: Oxford University Press.

Kemper, Th. D. (1978). *A Social Interactional Theory of Emotions*. New York: Wiley & Sons.

Kemper, Th. D. (1987). How many emotions are there? Wedding the social and autonomic components. *American Journal of Sociology*, 93, 263–289.

Kemper, Th. D. (1990). Social relations and emotions: A structural approach. In T. D. Kemper (ed.), *Research Agendas in the Sociology* (pp. 207–237). Albany: State University of New York Press.

Kemper, Th. D. (2002). Predicting emotions in groups: Some lessons from September 11. In J. M. Barbalet (ed.), *Emotions and Sociology* (pp. 53–68). Oxford: Blackwell Publishing.

Lazarus, R. S. (1991). *Emotion and Adaptation*. London: Oxford University Press.

Leary, M. R. & Meadows, S. (1991). Predictors, elicitors, and concomitants of social blushing. *Journal of Personality and Social Psychology*, 60, 254–262.

Lewis, M. (1971). *Shame and Guilt in Neurosis*. New York: International Universities Press.

Lewis, M. (1992). *Shame: The Exposed Self*. New York: The Free Press.

Lewis, M. (1995). Embarrassment: The emotion of self exposure and embarrassment. In J. P. Tangney & K. W. Fischer (eds.), *Self-Conscious Emotions: The Psychology of Shame, Guilt, Embarrassment and Pride* (pp. 198–218). New York: Gulford Press.

Lewis, M. (1998). Shame and stigma. In P. Gilbert & B. Andrews (eds.). *Shame. Interpersonal Behavior, Psychopathology, and Culture* (pp. 126–140). New York: Oxford University Press.

Lopes, D. M. (2005). *Sight and Sensibility: Evaluating Pictures*. London: Oxford University Press.

Lutz, C. & White, G. M. (1986). *The anthropology of emotions. Annual Review of Anthropology*, 15, 405–436.

Matthen, M. (2005). *Seeing, Doing and Knowing: A Philosophical Theory of Sense Perception*. Oxford: Oxford University Press.

Mead, G. H. (1963). *L'Esprit, le soi et la société*. Paris: PUF.

Mesquita, B. & Frijda, N. (1992). Cultural variations in emotions: A review. *Psychological Bulletin*, 112, 179–204.

Miller, S. (1985). *The Shame Experience*. Hillsdale: Erlbaum.

Miller, R. (1995). Embarrassment and social behavior. In J. P. Tangney & K. W. Fischer (eds.), *Self-Conscious Emotions: The Psychology of Shame, Guilt, Embarrassment, and Pride* (pp. 322–339). New York: Guilford Press.

Miller, R. S. (1996). *Embarrassment. Poise and Peril in Everyday Life*. New York: The Guilford Press.

Miller, R. S. & Tangney, J. P. (1994). Differentiating embarrassment and shame. *Journal of Social and Clinical Psychology*, 13, 273–287.

Miyake, K. & Yamazaki, K. (1995). Self-conscious emotions, child rearing, and child psychopathology in Japanese culture. In J. P. Tangney & K. W. Fischer (eds.), *Self-Conscious Emotions: The Psychology of Shame, Guilt, Embarrassment, and Pride* (pp. 488–504). New York: Guilford.

Nanay, B. (2010). Inflected and uninflected experience of pictures. In C. Abell & K. Bantinaki (eds.), *Philosophical Perspectives on Depiction* (pp. 181–207). Oxford: Oxford University Press.

Nanay, B. (2011). Perceiving pictures. *Phenomenology and the Cognitive* Sciences, 10, 461–480.

Nanay, B. (2013). *Between Perception and Action*. Oxford: Oxford University Press.

Nanay, B. (2015). Trompe l'oeil and the dorsal/ventral account of picture perception. *Review of Philosophy and Psychology*, 6, 181–197. doi:10.1007/s13164-014-0219-y.

Năstasă, L. E. (2013). Personal and professional development of future melotherapists. *Journal of Experiential Psychotherapy*, 16, 2(62), 3–11.

Năstasă, L. E. & Fărcaş, A. D. (2015). The effect of emotional intelligence on burnout in healthcare professionals. *Procedia - Social and Behavioral Sciences Elservier*, 187, 78–82.

Neblett, W. (1974). The ethic of guilt. *The Journal of Philosophy*, 71(18), 652–663.

Parrott, G. W. [1995] (1996). Guilt and shame. In A. S. R. Manstead & M. Hewstone (eds.), *The Blackwell Encyclopedia of Social Psychology*. Oxford. Blackwell Publishers Ltd.

Parrott, G. W. (2001). *Emotions in Social Psychology*. New York: Psychology Press.

Probyn, E. (2005). *Blush: Faces of Shame*. Sydney: UNSW Press.

Queiroz J. M. de, & Ziolkovski, M. (1994). *L'Interactionnisme symbolique*. Rennes: Presses Universitaires de Rennes.

Rimé, B [2005] (2007). *Comunicarea socială a emoţiilor*. Bucureşti: Editura Trei.

Russell, J. A. (1994). Is there universal recognition of emotion form facial expression? A review of the cross-cultural studies. *Psychological Bulletin*, 115, 102–141.

Russell, J. A. (1995). Facial expressions of emotion: What lies beyond minimal universality? *Psychological Bulletin*, 118, pp. 379–391.

Scheff. T. J. (1988). Shame and conformity: The deference-emotion system. *American Sociology Review*, 53, 395–406.

Scheff. T. J. (2000). Shame and the social bond: A sociological theory. *Sociological Theory*, 18(1), 84–99.

Scherer, K. R. (1984). Les emotions: Functions and components. *Cahiers de Psychologie Cognitive*, 4, 9–39.

Tangney, J. P. (1990). Assessing individual differences in proneness to shame and guilt. *Journal of Personality and Social Psychology*, 59, 102–111.

Tangney, J. P. (1995). Shame and guilt in interpersonal relationships. In J. P. Tangney & K. W. Fischer (eds.), *Self-Conscious Emotions: Shame, Guilt, Embarrassment, and Pride* (pp. 114–139). New York: Guilford Press.

Tangney J. P., Wagner P. E. & Gramzow R. (1989). *The Test of Self-Conscious Affect (TOSCA)*. Fairfax: George Mason University.

Tangney, J. P., Miller, R. S., Flicker, L. & Barlow, D. H. (1996). Are shame, guilt, and embarrassment distinct emotions? *Journal of Personality and Social Psychology*, 70(6), 1256–1269.

Taylor, G. (1996). Guilt and remorse. In R. Harré & W. G. Parrott (eds.), *The Emotions. Social, Cultural and Biological Dimensions* (pp. 57–73). London: Sage Publications Ltd.

Thois, P. A. (1989). The sociology of emotions. *Annual Review of Sociology*, 15, 317–342.

Tomkins, S. S. (1984). Affect theory. In K. R. Scherer & P. Ekman (eds.), *Approaches to Emotion* (pp. 161–195). Hillsdale: Erlbaum.

Turiel, E. (1983). *The Development of Social Knowledge: Morality and Convention*. Cambridge: Cambridge University Press.

Turner, J. H. & Stets, J. E. (2005). *The Sociology of Emotions*. Cambridge: University Press.

Weinblatt, U. (2018). Shame regulation therapy for families. *Communicating with Shame: Monitoring the Presence of Shame in Conversations*. Retrieved from: https://link.springer.com/chapter/10.1007/978-3-319-77470-1_3

Weiner, B. (1993). On sin versus sickness: A theory of perceived responsibility and social motivation. *American Psychologist*, 48(9), 957–965.

William, J. (1884). What is an emotion? *Mind*, 9(34), 188–205.

Wilson, J. Q. (1993). *The Moral Sense*. New York: Free Press.

Zamuner, E. (2012). *The Role of the Visual System in Emotion Perception.* Retrieved from: https://link.springer.com/article/10.1007%2Fs12136-012-0151-7.

Giuseppina Cersosimo

IX Concluding notes: Applications and developments in visual techniques

> Visual representations have, as Michael Lynch and Steve Woolgar state, 'little determinate meaning or logical force aside from the complex activities in which they are situated (1990 [1988]: viii).
> The image is the sum total of one's attitudes, beliefs, values, memories, aspirations, motivations, presuppositions, predilections, perceptions, worldview, and thought processes--all filtered through the grid of the symbolic transformations of the mind to give meaning and interpretation to life. *(Darrell Wood,* June, 2017)

Abstract: The chapter analyzes previous chapters and adds other research situations where visual techniques could be applied; it tries also to introduce other visual techniques that were not used in this project and which were not presented in this book. The chapter also contains a look into the future of the visual research; it discusses some development directions in the use of the images in social research and mentions some new and creative visual research techniques that probably will be used more and more in research.

Keywords: photo-elicitation, photovoice, visual methods, further applications

1 Introduction

This volume, edited by Florentina Scârneci-Domnişoru in collaboration with the other researchers, is full of problematic ideas which lean toward a dual articulation of the visual medium in social research: photo, images and drawing give voice to the research subjects, while acquiring further interpretative data from the researcher. In particular, we highlight an interpersonal face-to-face working relationship in the research experience citing, the data contained in the introduction to Scârneci-Domnişoru's *The Relevance of Visual Data in Social Research*, which has been a central reflection.

The various contributions of *Studying social change through the re-photography technique in a rural romanian community* by Codrina Csesznek, *Are the volunteers different from non-volunteers? A comparative analysis based on visual data (drawings)* by Marinela-Cristina Şimon, *A visual perspective on adolescent identity* by Ada Dobrescu, *Using the drawing to identify post-retirement identity transformations* by Diana-Cristina Bódi, *God, as the children of Romania draw it* by Daniela Sorea, *Exploring social workers' perceptions of their marital partners in different family life stages, Using visual methodology* by Mihaela Gotea and finally *Studying students' moral emotions by visual techniques* by Ioana Anisa Atudorei highlight the relationship between various social actors from Romanian communities, based on the emerging themes analyzed such as voluntary expressions, emotions, adolescence and old age; which the researchers, through their cognitive process, sorted and returned to redefine the ultimate purpose of the text in relation to the *relevance of visual data in social research.*

In the volume considered, however, we could refer to even further applications of the visual method. Just think about the usefulness of these methods in urban studies, beginning with Jabos Riis (Riis, 1890) famous photographs, or how many laboratories of visual research have sprung up – also in Italy – by linking visual methods (Abbatecola, 2017); the study and documentation of migratory phenomena, and the essential use of images in studies on deviance and crime, to highlight and interpret the roles of offender and assassin (Gilardi, 2009). We may also bear in mind the countless fruitful developments in the application of this methodology to the sociology of health and illness. Several studies further represent this topic such as Brieber et. al. (2014), Yang and Yang (2013), Reilly and Duke (2005), Jordanova (1987), Pryce (1989) and Stoeckle and White (1985), and there is a long and profound history of relationships between 'art' and 'medicine'.

I refer to this object as an example through which I intend to synthetically reason with the reader, presenting part of a research study to illustrate an innovative adoption of the visual method, like others present in this volume, revealing the effectiveness of the visual method in the study of social phenomenon (see paragraph no. 2).

The main objective of our research and analysis is to precisely respond to the recent debate on developments in visual sociology, including the analytical deepening that occurs, inclusivity and enrichment in comparison to and combination with other classical methods (of the ethnographer and the sociologist); or whether it can and must be established with its own specificity and autonomy. Many have already attempted to answer this debate, including: Stasz (1982), Henny (1986) and Harper (2000). Rather than reconstructing the debate from a historical point of view, in this conclusion we will examine visual sociology in a qualitative methodology framework.

2 Further applications of the visual method in sociological research: Illness, disease and sickness

Sociologists of health and illness will have interests in a variety of these representations and discourses in both historical and contemporary contexts. This includes imagery produced or used for research and forms of 'visual culture' such as publicity related to health education, photographs, paintings, advertising and everyday images. There are correspondences and continuities in signs and symbols within great works of art and in everyday advertising, and in a way this dictates the effectiveness of advertising in a consumer society.

My research stems from an epistemological base in which knowledge (about health and illness) is not pre-existing or fixed, nor is it stable. Rather, I work from a theoretical position that knowledge is gained through practice, interaction and experience. From this perspective, I argue that methodologically, photographs are visual products that simultaneously produce meaning. My interest is in both the meaning captured in a photograph, and the photograph itself. The word *fotografia* – photography – is both a noun and a verb; it is both a product and a process.

The symbolic interactionist Dewey (*apud* Guillemin 2004, p. 51)) explained that: It is no "linguistic accident" that *building, construction, work* and *design* are words referring to a process and its finished product. Without the meaning of the verb, the noun remains meaningless (Art as Experience, p. 51). There is an opportunity inherent here to apply these ideas to the case study methods of healthcare patients. In considering photography as the medium to explore, I am equally interested in the process of production, and the final images. To further explain the potential I see here for the field of Healthcare and the Sociology of Health, I will refer to my forthcoming article (Cersosimo, 2019).

The themes observed in our research were dialysis patient's perceptions of health, disease and illness, their new lifestyles, the improvement of relationships between patients and physicians, as well as the relationships between patients and their own families.

We investigated:

a) Perceptions of well-being post dialysis and social implications
b) Changes in lifestyles
c) Educational models for people with or without illnesses

Our sampling was comprised of patients with kidney problems, physicians, other healthcare professionals and family members of dialysis patients. The research period was from 2015 to 2017.

Sampling is based on patients with kidney problems, physicians, sanitary professionals and the families of patients

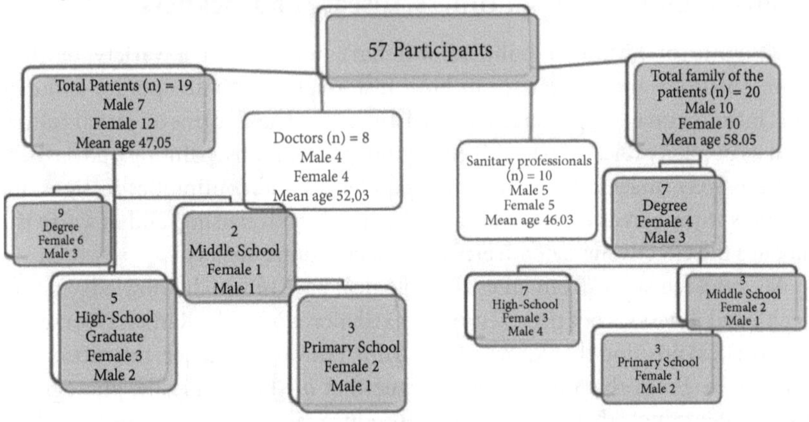

Fig. 1: Sampling

Total patients (n) = 19, Male 7, Female 12, Mean age 47.05
Total family of the patients (n) = 20, Male 10, Female 10, Mean age 58.05
Doctors (n) = 8, Male 4, Female 4, Mean age 52.03
Sanitary professionals (n) = 10, Male 5, Female 5, Mean age 46.03
See Fig. 1.

2.1 Visual research: Choosing a method

Visual Research has been used in the fields of Community Development, Education and Public Health among others. It is particularly useful in communities with marginalized or disadvantaged populations, for example, the Mexican and Latino migrant populations studied in *Sufferers of Illness* (Jurkowski and Paul-Ward, 2007; Levin et al., 2007).

2.1.1 Interpretations and meanings of health and illness

Methods such as using photographic images that the participants take themselves, and then discuss in an interview setting, sustain engagement between the researchers and the group being studied around a particular topic. Here, visual modalities and the resulting symbolism lie at the core of conduct and strategies for successful participation within different community contexts. In our particular study, photographs were taken by three different groups: researchers, ill patients and healthcare professionals.

In this work we use the terms *photovoice* and and *photo-elicitation* to refer to any method whereby participants are asked to take photographs that represent something about their community, daily life or point of view as the basis for an interview. In the process, photographs are selected for discussion by the interviewer and/or participant, and the participants then contextualize them by telling stories about what the photographs mean, or what emotions or memories they evoke. This is often in a group setting, but sometimes individually with a researcher. From this data collection, the researcher can codify the emerging themes.

2.2 The first question

The participants in our research study were asked to draw and write something at the side of the photo to explain the images. This method is a time effective way to begin the interview process while collecting qualitative and quantitative data.

Questions related to ethics and the forces of influence on researchers and participants are important to consider here, and the implications of this methodological distinction are very important, but unfortunately on this occasion, there is no time or space to elaborate.

2.3 Visual research like verbal data analysis

In some respects, the use of visual data is simply a technical means to an end, that is, the generation of verbal data for analysis. In other studies, however, it may become an integral part of the data and have a distinct relationship to verbal data and eventual text.

In the following images from our research study, the photo elicits different perceptions and meanings dependant on the bias of the viewer be it: the patient himself, their family, their doctors and/or healthcare professionals. As researchers we can investigate the meaning and implications of these varied perceptions of one photo.

In Fig. 2, it is evident that the perception of the elderly woman is very different than that of her healthcare providers. Her relationship to the photo of her is positive, because she feels blessed and happy to be alive and well cared for. The doctor and nurse have a different perspective that is that her quality of life is bad, and that she would not be alive at all without medical technology. As researchers, it begs the question, what is quality of life? This question placed within the realm of relative health or illness is defined by WHO – the subjective perception that an

Power or Afraid

This women has had Breast Cancer, and now she has kidney problems, but she is 90 years old today.
She said: I am power

When the Doctor saw this photo, they said: she is alive thanks to medical research

When the Nurse saw this photo, they said: she is alive but her quality of life is poor

Sick
Elderly women
Family

Fig. 2: Three Narratives: Patient, Doctor and Nurse (author's archive)

individual has of their own life position and relative quality, in the context of that culture and value system, in relation to other goals, expectations and concerns. So in discussing quality of life, we must recognize the plethora of interdependent variables that come to play. These can be traced back to four domains:

- physical state and functional abilities
- psychological state and well-being
- social interactions
- professional and economic status

In this context of a bio-psycho-social system, the quality of life question highlights the development of meaning from the first moment of detection, recognition of the subject of the image – a person who is ill, to the interpretation of that illness outside of subjective experience. This process goes beyond defining illness and actually contributes to the social construction of illness. In this way, the conscious perception of the illness by the patient is determined by the structuring and consolidation of awareness and meaning on the part of other research participants as well as the patients' own perceptions. That is to say, the way I feel about myself is influenced by others' perceptions of me.

In the words of one such male patient: *I'm a problem for my family and other people. I'm here, and I'm alive I'm lucky.*

In the words of one such female patient: *I'm lucky, because I am here despite my serious illness.*

Figure 3 highlights the importance of technological advances in the means and methods of practitioners and participants in everyday medical health practice,

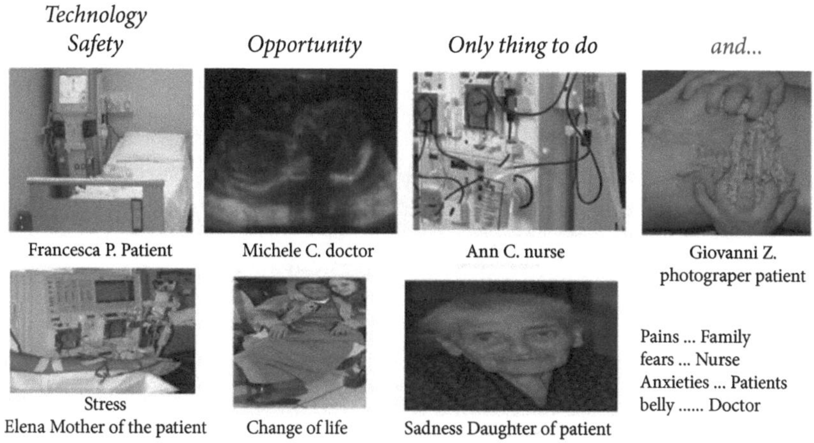

Fig. 3: Different Perceptions of the Illness (author's archive)

through a series of increasingly refined and widespread tools. Such varied data in relation to the theme of *disease* are noted and related to new and individual perceptions of other social actors such as the patient's family and their perception of how to survive disease.

Another interesting observation here is shown in our sampling of interlcutors subjected to the stimulus of photo-elicitation, be they young and old, male or female, medical or health professionals, their perception and language related to the sick person and or the healthcare situation is reflected in the words of the patients themselves (see Fig. 4). What changes is the attribution and importance of some words for the sick individual. The same words will carry different meaning and importance amongst family members and/or healthcare workers. For example, patients subjected to an image of an electro-medical device place significant value on the device in terms of their care and therapy, while this same equipment may be perceived as less valuable by doctors, nurses and relatives of the patient. The suffering and the sadness of patients can arouse an awareness and feeling related to a situation that does not translate to the experience of the other parties involved. This is rich datum which points to the ways that visual methodology can bridge the gaps for doctors and health professionals between the cultural and contextual understanding of patients with chronic pathologies and healthcare training processes, improving relationships between doctors, patients, nurses, healthcare professionals and the family members of patients.

The most common words during the patients interview	The most common words during the interview with health professionals and doctors	The most common words during the families interview
• Technologies 46%	• Technologies 21%	• Technologies 21%
• Opportunity dialysis 38%	• Opportunity dialysis 38%	• Opportunity dialysis 18%
• Malaise 17.5%	• Malaise 6.5%	• Malaise 30.8%
• Stress 13%	• Stress 11%	• Stress 26%
• Change of life 26%	• Change of life 1%	• Change of life 12%
• Illness 21%	• Illness 47%	• Illness 80%
• Sadness 9%	• Sadness 0.7%	• Sadness 3%
• Suffering 7%	• Suffering 2%	• Suffering 7%

Fig. 4: Same Words, Different Meanings

Asking respondents to interpret images of themselves and/or others elicits processes of 'making sense' of meanings assigned. It is not necessary for images to be self-generated so that those visual materials to be read as texts. Our interest in a painting, drawing or photography is not about the author's world of meaning, but rather about that of the audience. It is much more about 'ways of seeing' and creating meaning than simply the act of seeing a created work.

There are theoretical and empirical questions implicit here, about how these worlds of meaning and of the self are distinguishable from each other, yet interdependent in such interpretative work and, in my view, the idea of 'audience' remains the most underdeveloped and problematic area for the visual sociologist.

Mining data from a visual research process can also be keystone to studying personal orientations. The images produced can be analyzed in conjunction with in-depth interviews or ethnographic field research as eliciting techniques. It is in fact the reflexivity between image and verbalization which produces relevant data for the investigator, and in some respects, the use of the visual prompt is simply an efficient technical means to an end: that being, the generation of verbal data for analysis.

In other studies, parts of the relevant data may relate to both spoken and written text. An example of the former was provided in Gillian Bendelow's 1993 study of individual associations with pain. Pain is a difficult concept for participants to verbalize, and so they were asked to talk about pain in relation to a series of images, and only later to do so in relation to their own context. A complex array of ideas and associations was revealed by way of this method, as well as the finding that notions of pain vary by gender. It is perhaps not surprising to note that many artists have historically used their work to give voice to pain and suffering – suggesting that visual expression is a 'way of telling'. A world of drawing, painting and photographic projects have been created with the explicit aim to self-generate images that symbolize and make visible, hidden aspects of the self. Other examples include the work by Barbara Harrison (2002) and Deborah Lupton and Christine Heyes LaBond (2017), which discuss the use of video techniques for generating empathetic encounters. They focus on how these techniques might be rendered useful in research conducted through sites of action and experience that are explicitly constituted through forms of digital materiality. They argue for a processual view of digital materiality and of the research process. Empathetic imagining is itself understood as emergent from the research encounter, and they propagate ethnographic data from visual research through video recordings collected in collaboration with participants which document and decode their experiences of self-tracking and cycle commuting.

2.4 First conclusion on the use of this method in a healthcare context

The increasing popularity of qualitative methodologies in the study of health, illness and healthcare reflects the epistemological commitment to codify the ways in which participants themselves interpret, give meaning to and make sense of their experiences. These might be 'ordinary' everyday experiences and events, or those which disrupt and require new responses by the self and others; including the construction of new identities. Interest has focused mainly on the mutual relationships between self and society, which has been articulated within the developing field of auto/biographical studies in general.

Illness and other physical changes constitute one particular form of disruption well suited to these approaches. A number of studies have focused on the impact of chronic illness or death in relation to families. Personal narrative approaches have tended to dominate within this tradition, and it is here that the potential of visual methods has been clearly demonstrated, both alone and in conjunction with spoken and/or written responses.

For doctors, patients and family members, this type of study demonstrates the extent to which the interpretation of meanings inherent to interactions between the sick and doctors, nurses and families had important therapeutic implications for the patients' lifestyle. It also demonstrates that not all healthcare providers could be described as 'skilled' in interpersonal aspects of patient care.

Such research could educate nurses, doctors and family members as to what can and should be done in such brief encounters to improve their relationships with patients.

This line of research has its limits however, and although it is not possible to generalize the results, it is possible that these results could be a first step toward improving the relationships between patients and physicians on the topic of new treatments or technologies.

But since the images cannot speak for themselves and are subject to multiple interpretations, they can either shout their meaning or be totally silent. The caption restricts the range of possible content analyses, allowing the observer to also understand what goes beyond the denotatum.

This visual accountability recalls the concept of H. Garfinkel (1967), providing a framework for the adaptation of actions, and the production of activities and mediated events. It also contributes to understanding and empathy toward "the others'" perspective, with specific qualities and conformity to 'social pre-assumptions' (Goffman, 1981) within this health universe comprised of varied social actors, with diverse roles, from the doctor to the patient, from the nurse to the family, all with one single goal, to improve health.

3 Re-opening the old questions

The question of a central method for visual sociology has been reopened since there is not sufficient evidence to legitimize it cognitively. This is because, in order to translate the relevant concepts into visual indicators, the social scientist must constantly refer to epistemological premises. The theoretical framework directs the selection of the emerging themes to be considered, without constituting a rigid and predictive grid for understanding the phenomenon.

Visual research involves a constant dialogue between theory and research in all phases of the work, leaving open the possibility of redefining the analytical categories. The real responds only when 'questioned', and the theory is fundamental to the elaboration of research questions on which to define the empirical practice, in its non-predetermined sequencing.

The selected quantitative and visual tools must be constantly rethought according to the specific case study at hand, making correct methodological choices that are not based on positivistic rules. The centrality of the selective gaze, with respect to exact and quantifiable recording, is characteristic of all visual sociology: it relies on a researcher's own sensibility and personality as a means to penetrate and immerse oneself in the observed phenomena. It means constantly renewing, through empirical practice, the precious legacy of Georg Simmel, for whom vision is the main sense of modernity and "between the individual sense organs the eye is made to offer an absolutely unique sociological performance: the connection and reciprocation between individuals, which consists of looking at each other" (Simmel 1908 [1998]: 550). To gaze into another's eye is the most immediate and pure reciprocal relationship that exists, because it takes and gives at the same time. In the face of an individual, aside from his actions, one finds himself, and on a symbolic level, all that he has presupposed in his life. The face "offers to the eye the intuitively more complete symbolism of permanent interiority, and of all that our lived experiences have deposited in the foundation of our being" (Simmel, ivi: 552), even if it yields and moulds itself to changing situations. As in the face we can view the subject, "the precipitate of the past in the substantial form of his features, [...] the succession of his life in the moment" (ibidem), thus in the present sociological context, and in its potential in terms of documentation, the dynamics of past events are condensed into the present time. The sociologist who aims his gaze at the other and does not hide from the latter in the observable scene, and intends to reveal seemingly irrelevant aspects while appreciating the concreteness of individual clues, placing focus on interior and exterior worlds in order to highlight their mutual influences.

Opening your eyes to the world through authentic investigations means knowing how to grasp uniformity, but more importantly difference: a commitment which aids all forms of improvisation, and which implies a scrupulous dedication to understanding others, as small totalities, as well as objects through their complex layers of meaning. The strength of visual sociology therefore lies in its ability to investigate reality in a new way, with specific attention to the sphere of the sensible. It allows us to fill our eyes with specially selected images, which constitute a 'richly informative repository' of a historical epoch and its culture.

4 The empirical and the visual: A challenge for visual sociology

The first attempt to analyze relations in social research through the use of visual sociology consisted of creating a means for the production of data in the form of images, in particular in the form of photographs.

This is a classic path for the use of imaging techniques in field research, in particular as a complement to anthropological studies (Malinowski, 1985) or as a recognized method of collecting and returning data collected in the field (Bateson & Mead, 1942; Becker, 1981).

In the case of research like *In A Rural Romanian Community* by Codrina Csesznek, it is a matter of collecting a body of work that can be used later for a deferred observation of the sociological research study. The images produced, such as the notes collected in the field or the recordings of interviews will be resources for analysis. In this way images are used for empirical data collection purposes, and visual instrumentation imposes itself as a technical prosthesis for the researcher's eye. It becomes the lens and the vector of details invisible to the naked eye, in particular for the observation of sub-results and the interpretation of detailed interactions.

We talked about the impact of images realized by the researcher, but it should also be noted that the images may also have been produced by the subjects themselves, as in the work by Diana-Cristina Bódi: *Using the drawing to identify post-retirement identity transformations* as well as work by Marinela-Cristina Şimon: *Are the volunteers different from non-volunteers? A comparative analysis based on visual data (drawings).* The documentary collection of iconography produced by research participants can lead to reflections on its content; the composition and the intermediality of the images thus enter into the perspective of visual study (Rose, 2001). Whether these images are the product of the researcher or the research subject, this first level use of them in social research holds that photography is a trace of reality, with the potential to attract and channel our attention, which is prolonged in a potential provocation of the sense, observes John Grady (1996, 2001, p.86): "in a certain sense, the images scream at us to make them meaningful and it is this, above all, that gives them the unique ability to involve us". This ability to attract the attention of a person, the object of the scientific question, represents the first heuristic capacity of the image.

Another methodology to discuss in relation to images within social scientific research begins with what we call 'image-work', that is, the activities that lead a researcher to produce images during the research. Here the product of the work, the object-image, is of less interest than what is implied by it's production, including the "reactions" generated by way of comparisons between the visual fields from which it derives. In other words, the photographic act, which consecrates the production and consumption of an image, can be considered to be an indicator of the place and the actions/reactions it contains.

In some of the research presented in this volume, the possibility of taking photographs is an opportunity to reflect on the challenges of negotiations (Strauss, 1992) in the presence of the research photographer. More specifically, we need to consider ways of regulating the institutions of childhood and adolescence in the light of an external gaze, potentially controlled through daily practice. These forms of intervention (research and 'resumption'), specific to the work-image, are full of possibility in terms of relating research photography to the context of adolescence and childhood, as in *A visual perspective on adolescent identity* by Ada Dobrescu and *God, as the children of Romania draw It* by Daniela

Sorea, in which the control and production of a particular representation of adolescence and childhood are constant and repeated challenges. In these cases, a sociologist who is equipped with a photographic device must be able to reflect on the rules and modifications that this approach will determine.

The now indicated capacity of research-based images now goes beyond the more general attention of the researcher, to the work that surrounds the production of photographic clichés. The possible alteration of reality must be integrated into the scientific practice in a positive way through the photographic act, while providing elements for reflection related to the context of image creation in the research. Photography – in its practice and in its reading – must allow for reflection on the position of the researcher, as well as on his relation to the object of study, and the representation of the subject in the context of camera itself.

The use of images here should be seen as the primary source of information, which allows for direct observation derived from the re-union between the observer and the subject. The latter is, in a sense, the materialization of the close relationship that unites the observer and the observed through every attempt at ethnographic understanding. Photography in this case enables us to investigate the dynamics between the researcher and the subject, as well as the challenges between the gaze and the frame to be grasped. These considerations are of particular importance in the case of the qualitative study *Exploring social workers' perceptions of their marital partners in different family life stages, using visual methodology* by Mihaela Gotea, the image and its mediation remind the researcher of his role as an observer, that is a full participant within the institution; and the awareness of this status opens the way for epistemological reflection on his role in that context, a challenge that reveals again the capacity of an image to 'define' the work and the status of the researcher. In fact, through the image produced or the process that produces it, the technical work of the photographer is revealed – as a practical fulfillment – but also the research project and researcher. More precisely, the photographic work refers the scholar, in the course of the research, to a reflection on the scientific nature of the approach and the knowledge gained through observation. This reflexive activity, aimed at conceiving the work-image on this side of the object-image, questions the statute of the data derived from the researcher's gaze. Rather than displaying the relationship between protagonists in the study, the image makes visible and solidifies the shared nature of visual data production. It is not only what the researcher has seen that is recorded and becomes the subject of the work; it is the researcher, in his totality, who participates in the visibility of the situations studied.

Photography elicits the power of the gaze. Through it we discover the omnipresence of culturally significant images that bind observation, observer and observed in a social relationship based on visualization. The sociological gaze of the researcher as well as that of other social actors, and the requested gaze of the ultimate reader of a sociological analysis are all equally important and must be included if we are to comprehend a global economy and culture of visibility and exchange. This potential for condensation and shifting of the gaze in relation to epistemological challenges is made viable through the reciprocal relationship between visual research methodologies and the scholar himself through his search for reality in the field. It is his image, his presence and his turmoil at the heart of his understanding. Here we consider photography according to its definition by Maresca in 1996, as a 'device of thought' which could contribute, through analysis of the social sciences, to a better understanding of the world. In this relationship between science and reality, we are encouraged to "think even with our eyes" (Maresca, 1996, 29): "In this title, photography more than any other form of image, designates an intellectual challenge: that to understand without abstraction, that is to say, to elaborate a mode of analysis which is not closed ipso facto on itself, which does not necessarily separate itself from the world it claims to explain" (Maresca, quoted, 224).

Can visual sociology, as defined and practiced at present, claim to be an independent discipline? Or rather, does it limit itself to providing new tools to confirm previous knowledge gained through theoretical and disciplinary systems? The implications of the human gaze and visual culture as explored and presented in this volume can give us a first possible answer when considering the interactions of researchers, objects and subjects of social research. That is, they can be considered separately, in the service of specific fields where the use of image-based techniques can be aimed at the production of data, and then be re-contextualized in a pre-existing intellectual space. In our case, the images produced in the field constitute a reservoir of data for the field of sociology, but there is potential for reflection use of these images in qualitative research studies in various fields and contexts. We have first examined the image as an icon for data analysis, and then looked at the varied roles of researcher and research subject; finally we have reflected on images as the source of epistemological questions in relation to the visual learning of social phenomena.

5 In Conclusion

Undoubtedly, the contributions we have considered here deserve to be read carefully. The multiplicity of the perspectives analyzed reveals the ways in which visual sociology is not only a method, but a very good method for social analysis which in time could even transform our current power structures by way of a new public perspective based on the power of images. This perspective could expose the full dimension of social analysis in relation to its various actors with their respective roles and statuses. According to Burawoy (2007, pp. 24 et seq.) public sociology is primarily "a return translation, bringing knowledge back to those from whom it came, turning private problems into public issues". Public sociology therefore cannot be a neutral science, it is a partisan science (Gouldner, 1968, Niemonen, 2010), and an instrument to be wielded not only for the purposes of pure knowledge, but also as a device to strengthen civil society through autonomy in relation to global concerns politically and economically. In other words, visual sociology can address the needs of the most vulnerable members of society: adolescents, the aging, the poor, criminals, the sick, single mothers, volunteers and other victims of neo-liberalism, not by way of controlling them, but by empowering them to be self-determined (Padovan, 2007, pp. 3–5).

In this perspective the practice of visual sociology expresses multiple points of view rooted in the research practice and orientation of the authors. If we take up the Gramscian lesson on cultural hegemony (1975), we intend to intervene and transform symbolic relationships by affirming the public nature of knowledge and the cultural significance of the images we produce. One of the main objectives of this volume therefore, is to produce resistant cultural objects, carriers of autonomous knowledge on invisible themes and subjects and to guarantee the willful distribution of the understanding gained through encounters with them.

Bibliography

Bateson, G. & Mead, M. (1942). *Balinese Character: A Photographic Analysis*. New York: New York Academy of Sciences.

Becker, H. S. (dir.) (1981). *Exploring Society Photographically*. Evanston: Nothwestern University Press.

Becker, H. S. (1986). *Doing Things Together. Selected Papers*. Evanston: Northwestern University Press.

Brieber, D., Nadal, M., Leder, H. & Rosenberg, R. (2014). Art in Time and Space: Context Modulates the Relation between Art Experience and Viewing Time. *PLoS One*, 9(6), e99019. doi: 10.1371/journal.pone.0099019.

Burawoy, M. (2005). The Critical Turn to Public Sociology. *Critical Sociology*, 3, 313–326.

Burawoy, M. (2007). For Public Sociology. In Clawson D., Zussman R., Misra J., Gerstel N., Stokes R. & Anderton D.L. (eds.) *Public Sociology Fifteen Eminent*

Sociologist Debate Politics and the Profession in the Twenty-First Century (pp. 23–64). Berkeley: University of California Press.

Dewey, J. (1934). *Art as Experience*. Rahway: The Barnes Foundation Press.

Garfinkel, H. (1967). *Studies in Ethnomethodology*. New York: Englewood Cliffs.

Gilardi, A. (2010). *Wanted! Storia, tecnica ed estetica della fotografia criminale, segnaletica e giudiziaria*. Milano: Mondadori.

Goffman, E. (1981). *Forms of Talk*. Blackwell: Oxford.

Gouldner, A. (1968). The Sociologist as Partisan: Sociology and the Welfare State. *American Sociologist*, 3, 103–106.

Grady, J. (1996). The Scope of Visual Sociology. *Visual Sociology*, 11(2), 10–24.

Grady, J. (2001). Becoming a Visual Sociologist. *Sociological Imagination*, 38(1/2), 83–119.

Gramsci, A. (1975). *Quaderni del carcere*. Torino: Einaudi.

Harper, D. (2000). The Image in Sociology: Histories and Issues. *Journal des Anthropologues*, 80(81), 143–160.

Harrison, B. (2002). Seeing Health and Illness Worlds – Using Visual Methodologies in a Sociology of Health and Illness: A Methodological Review. *Sociology of Health & Illness*, 24(6), 856–872.

Jordanova, L. (1987). *Sexual Visions: Images of Gender in Science and Medicine between the Eighteenth and Nineteenth Centuries*. Brighton: Harvester-Wheatsheaf.

Jurkowski. J. M. & Paul-Ward A. (2007). Photovoice with Vulnerable Populations: Addressing Disparities in Health Promotion among People with Intellectual Disabilities. *Health Promotion Practice*, 8(4), 358–365. doi/10.1177/1524839906292181.

Lupton, D., LaBond C. H. & Sumartojo S. (2017). Empathetic Technologies: Digital Materiality and Video Ethnography. *Visual Studies*, 32(4), 371–381.

Lynch, M. & Woolgar, S. (1990). *Representation in Scientific Practice*. Cambridge, Mass.: MIT Press.

Maresca, S. (1996). *La photographie. Un miroir des sciences sociales*. Paris: L'Harmattan.

Niemonen, J. (2010). Public Sociology or Partisan Sociology? The Curious Case of Whiteness Studies. *The American Sociologist*, 41(1), 48–81.

Pryce, A. (1989). *An anxious hour': visual imagery, death, loss and domestic ideology in the nineteenth century*. Unpublished M.Sc. Dissertation, London: South Bank University.

Reilly, J. M., Ring, J. & Duke, L. (2005). Visual Thinking Strategies: A New Role for Art in Medical Education. *Family Medicine*, 37(4), 250–252.

Riis, J. (1890). *How the Other Half Lives. Studies Among the Tenements of New York*. New York: Charles Scribner's Sons.

Rose, G. (2001). *Visual Methodologies. An Introduction to the Interpretation of Visual Materials*. London: Sage Publications.

Simmel, G. (1981). *Sociologie et épistémologie*. Paris: Presses Universitaires de France.

Stasz, C. (1979). *The Early History of Visual Sociology*. In Wagner Jon (ed.) *Images of Information. Still Photography in the Social Sciences* (pp. 119–136). London: Sage Publications.

Stoeckle, J. D. & White, G. A. (1985). *Plain Pictures of Plain Doctoring: Vernacular Expression and New Deal Medicine*. Cambridge, Mass.: MIT Press.

Strauss, A. L. (1978). *Negotiations: Varieties, Contexts, Processes, and Social Order*. San Francisco: Jossey-Bass.

Wood, W. D. *The Image in Symbolic Interaction: A Systems Approach to Communication & Social Change*, https://www.linkedin.com/pulse/image-symbolic-interaction-darrell-w-wood, on 28th June 2017.

Yang, K.-T. &, Yang, J., H. (2013). A Study of the Effect of a Visual Arts-Based Program on the Scores of Jefferson Scale for Physician Empathy. *BMC Medical Education*, 13(142). doi: 10.1186/1472-6920-13-142.

List of Figures

Florentina Scârneci-Domnişoru
The relevance of visual data in social research
Fig. 1: 'Typical Romanians from the Upper and Lower Class in today's Romania', drawn by a 21-year-old woman, 2012 (author's archive) 25
Fig. 2: 'God', drawn by a 7-year-old girl, 2016 (with permission of Daniela Sorea) 26
Fig. 3: 'A life full of mistakes and garbage', photograph taken by a 1 6-year-old boy, 2012 (with permission of Noemi Bernad) 27
Fig. 4: 'I have a whole collection of watches, but now … they count my hours …', photograph taken by a 50-year-old man, 2013 (with the permission of Hospice Casa Speranţei Braşov) 28
Fig. 5: 'A volunteering/A non-volunteering person', drawn by a 24-year-old woman, 2017 (with the permission of Marinela Simon) 32
Fig. 6: 'Me before retirement/Me after retirement', drawn by a 81-year-old man, 2017 (with the permission of Diana Bódi) 36
Fig. 7: 'Me in adolescence', drawn by a 19-year-old girl, 2017 (with the permission of Ada Dobrescu) 36
Fig. 8: Drawing by a medical student, 2017 (with the permission of Ioana Atudorei) 39

Codrina Csesznek
Studying social change through the *re-photography technique* in a rural Romanian community
Fig. 1.1: Drăguş – view from the South, 2004 (author's archive) 71
Fig. 1.2: Pizza Drăguş – restaurant, 2017 (author's archive) 71
Fig. 2.1: Luţeanu family house, 2004 (author's archive) 72
Fig. 2.2: Luţeanu family house, 2017 (author's archive) 73
Fig. 3.1: Panoramic view towards the South, 2004 (author's archive) 74
Fig. 3.2: Panoramic view towards the South, 2017 (author's archive) 74
Fig. 4.1: Uliţa Mare, 2004 (author's archive) 75
Fig. 4.2: Uliţa Mare, 2017 (author's archive) 76
Fig. 5.1: Dineti family house, 2004 (author's archive) 77
Fig. 5.2: Dineti family house, 2017 (author's archive) 78
Fig. 6.1: Old house, 2004 (author's archive) 79
Fig. 6.2: Ethnographic museum, 2017 (author's archive) 80
Fig. 7.1: Ms. Sucaciu's courtyard, 2004 (author's archive) 81
Fig. 7.2: Ms. Sucaciu's courtyard, 2017 (author's archive) 81

Fig. 8.1: Jurcovan's family courtyard, 2004 (author's archive) 82
Fig. 8.2: Jurcovan's family courtyard, 2017 (author's archive) 82
Fig. 9.1: Racu's family courtyard, 2004 (author's archive) 83
Fig. 9.2: Racu's family courtyard, 2017 (author's archive) 84
Fig. 10.1: Poparad's family living room, 2004 (author's archive) 85
Fig. 10.2: Poparad's family living room, 2017 (author's archive) 85
Fig. 11.1: Bobeica's family living room, 2004 (author's archive) 86
Fig. 11.2: Bobeica's family living room, 2017 (author's archive) 86
Fig. 12.1: Jurcovan's family kitchen, 2004 (author's archive) 87
Fig. 12.2: Jurcovan's family kitchen, 2017 (author's archive) 88
Fig. 13.1: Potinteu's family summer kitchen, 2004 (author's archive) 88
Fig. 13.2: Potinteu's family summer kitchen, 2017 (author's archive) 89
Fig. 14.1: Drăguş Commune Town Hall, 2004 (author's archive) 89
Fig. 14.2: Drăguş Commune Town Hall, 2017 (author's archive) 90
Fig. 15.1: Secondary school, 2004 (author's archive) 91
Fig. 15.2: Secondary school, 2017 (author's archive) 91
Fig. 16.1: The nursery school, 2004 (author's archive) 92
Fig. 16.2: The nursery school, 2017 (author's archive) 93
Fig. 17.1: Community centre, 2004 (author's archive) 93
Fig. 17.2: Community centre, 2017 (author's archive) 94
Fig. 18.1: Clinic, 2004 (author's archive) 95
Fig. 18.2: Clinic, 2017 (author's archive) 95
Fig. 19.1: The Orthodox Church, 2004 (author's archive) 96
Fig. 19.2: The Orthodox Church, 2017 (author's archive) 97
Fig. 20.1: Greek Catholic church, 2004 (author's archive) 98
Fig. 20.2: Greek Catholic church, 2017 (author's archive) 99
Fig. 21.1: The pub, 2004 (author's archive) 100
Fig. 21.2: The bar "The Brothers", 2017(author's archive) 100
Fig. 22.1: Old women on the bench (lăicioară), 2004 (author's archive) 101
Fig. 22.2: Old women on the bench (lăicioară), 2017 (author's archive) 101
Fig. 23.1: Old couple on the street, 2004 (author's archive) 102
Fig. 23.2: Old man on the street, 2017 (author's archive) 103
Fig. 24.1: Cleaning in front of the houses, 2004 (author's archive) 104
Fig. 24.2: Cleaning in front of the houses, 2017 (author's archive) 104
Fig. 25.1: Children on Nicheşti street, 2004 (author's archive) 105
Fig. 25.2: Nicheşti street without children, 2017 (author's archive) 105
Fig. 26.1: Children in cart, 2004 (author's archive) 106
Fig. 26.2: Children on a tractor, 2017 (author's archive) 107
Fig. 27.1: The Trâmbiţaş family – the millers of the village, 2004 (author's archive) 107

Fig. 27.2: Viorica Trâmbițaș, 2017 (author's archive) 108
Fig. 28.1: Zorița Poparad, 2004 (with permission of Ovidiu Poparad) 109
Fig. 28.2: Zorița Poparad, 2017 (with permission of Ovidiu Poparad) 109
Fig. 29.1: Emigrants from Spain, visiting home, 2004 (author's archive) 110
Fig. 29.2: Emigrants from Spain, visiting home, 2017 (author's archive) 110
Fig. 30.1: Women in traditional costumes, 2004 (author's archive) 111
Fig. 30.2: Women in traditional costumes, 2017 (author's archive) 112
Fig. 31.1: Little girls' costumes, 2004 (author's archive) 113
Fig. 31.2: Little girls' costumes, 2017 (author's archive) 113
Fig. 32.1: Herods, 2004 (with permission of Ovidiu Poparad) 114
Fig. 32.2: Herods, 2017 (author's archive) 115
Fig. 33.1: Bride and groom exiting the church, 2004 (with permission of Ovidiu Poparad) 116
Fig. 33.2: Bride and groom exiting the church, 2017 (author's archive) 117
Fig. 34.1: Ritualistic wedding gate, 2004 (author's archive) 117
Fig. 34.2: Ritualistic wedding gate, 2017 (author's archive) 118
Fig. 35.1: Wake held in the house of the deceased, 2004 (author's archive) 119
Fig. 35.2: Wake held in the house of the deceased, 2017 (author's archive) 119
Fig. 36.1: In the cemetery, 2004 (author's archive) 120
Fig. 36.2: In the cemetery, 2017 (author's archive) 120
Fig. 37.1: Alms, 2004 (author's archive) 121
Fig. 37.2: Alms, 2017 (author's archive) 122

Marinela-Cristina Șimon
Are the volunteers different from non-volunteers? A comparative analysis based on visual data (drawings)
Fig. 1: The symbolic representation of the volunteer in the social field (drawing made by a person of feminine gender, aged 66) (author's archive) 136
Fig. 2: Clippings of drawings (symbolic representations of the volunteer in the social field) (author's archive) 138
Fig. 3: Representations of volunteers drawn by subjects under 30 years. Drawings sketched by a 21-year-old man, a 23-year-old man and 29-year-old woman *(from left to right)* (author's archive) 138
Fig. 4: Clippings of drawings – Portraits of volunteers/non-volunteers (author's archive) 140
Fig. 5: Clippings of drawings – The availability of volunteers to help (author's archive) 141
Fig. 6: Clippings of drawings – Representation of non-volunteers (author's archive) 142

Fig. 7: Educational differences between volunteers and non-volunteers. *Drawings made by a 22-year-old woman (to the left) and a 21-year-old woman (to the right)* (author's archive) 144
Fig. 8: Social interactions of the volunteers. Drawings made by a 23-year-old man, a 28-year-old woman and a 24-year-old woman (author's archive) 148
Fig. 9: Beneficiaries of volunteering in the social field. Drawings made by a 67-year-old woman, a 29-year-old woman and a 21-year-old man (author's archive) 149
Fig. 10: The visual representation of the data concerning the characteristics of the volunteer in the social field (author's archive) 152

Ada Ioana Dobrescu
A visual perspective on adolescent identity
Fig. 1: *The representation of the relation with friends, in photographs, featuring adolescents*: The trip with friends without parents (author's archive) 165
Fig. 2: The representation of the friendship relations with adolescents (author's archive) 166
Fig. 3: The representation of the relationship with the girlfriend by female adolescents (author's archive) 167
Fig. 4: The representation of the nuclear family, as envisioned by adolescents (author's archive) 167
Fig. 5: The representation of family and of home, as envisioned by adolescents (author's archive) 168
Fig. 6: The representation of pets as friends of adolescents (author's archive) 168
Fig. 7: The representation of the extended family of adolescents (author's archive) 169
Fig. 8: The representation of the high school where the adolescents studied (author's archive) 170
Fig. 9: *The representation of the relationship with the adolescents' colleagues, in photographs*: End of high school – Waiting for the final exam (author's archive) 170
Fig. 10: *The representation of the significant events in adolescence:* The sweet 18th party (author's archive) 171
Fig. 11: The representation of adolescents' discrimination by their colleagues (author's archive) 172
Fig. 12: Representation of adolescents' vices (author's archive) 173

Fig. 13: The representation of some role models such as teachers or form masters, as envisioned by adolescents (author's archive) 174
Fig. 14: The representation of the relationship with the partner, as envisioned by adolescents (author's archive) 175
Fig. 15: The representation of divinity, as envisioned by adolescents (author's archive) 176
Fig. 16: The representation of the adolescence period (author's archive) 177
Fig. 17: *The representation of the adolescence stage through photographs:* Freedom in adolescence – no worries or problems (author's archive) 178
Fig. 18: The representation of the symbols associated to the period of adolescence by girls (author's archive) 178
Fig. 19: The representation of some symbols associated to the period of adolescence by girls (author's archive) 179
Fig. 20: Taking the driving license as an accomplishment of the adolescents (author's archive) 180
Fig. 21: *The representation of accomplishments with female adolescents, in photos:* I was a model for a time (author's archive) 181
Fig. 22: The representation of hobbies with adolescents through drawings (author's archive) 181
Fig. 23: *The representation of hobbies with adolescents through photos:* Trip to Bran, Moeciu (author's archive) 182
Fig. 24: The representation of the artistic activities of adolescents as hobbies (author's archive) 183
Fig. 25: The representation of free time activities of adolescents as hobbies (author's archive) 183
Fig. 26: The representation of sports as hobbies with adolescents (author's archive) 184
Fig. 27: The representation of significant experiences in adolescence (author's archive) 185

Diana-Cristina Bódi
Using the drawing to identify post-retirement identity transformations
Fig. 1: Life before retirement. Symbols drawn by women (author's archive) ... 199
Fig. 2: Life after retirement. Symbols drawn by women (author's archive) .. 200
Fig. 3: Me, before and after retirement (up), drawings made by women (down) (author's archive) 200
Fig. 4: Life before retirement. Symbols drawn by men (author's archive) 201
Fig. 5: Life after retirement. Symbols drawn by men (author's archive) 201
Fig. 6: Drawing of subjects with medium education. (author's archive) 202
Fig. 7: Drawing of people with higher education (author's archive) 202

Fig. 8: Family role drawn by a woman (author's archive) ... 203
Fig. 9: Activities and roles before and after retirement (author's archive) .. 204
Fig. 10: The roles of the subjects before and after retirement (author's archive) ... 205
Fig. 11: Professional roles before retirement (author's archive) ... 206
Fig. 12: Responsibility as obligation- professional roles described by women (author's archive) ... 206
Fig. 13: Workplace usefulness (author's archive) ... 207
Fig. 14: Professional roles illustrated by men (author's archive) ... 207
Fig. 15: Withdrawal, drawn by men (author's archive) ... 208
Fig. 16: Family roles before retirement, drawn by women (author's archive) ... 210
Fig. 17: Family roles before retirement, drawn by one man (author's archive) ... 210
Fig. 18: Family roles after retirement, drawn by men and women (author's archive) ... 211
Fig. 19: Drawings presenting the continuity of family roles with women. On the left side, before retirement. On the right, after retirement (author's archive) ... 211
Fig. 20: Activities performed with grandchildren (author's archive) ... 213
Fig. 21: Household roles before and after retirement, drawn by women (author's archive) ... 213
Fig. 22: Household roles after retirement, drawn by women (author's archive) ... 214
Fig. 23: Household roles drawn by men, after retirement (author's archive) ... 214
Fig. 24: The decrease of the social network in the view of one of the subjects (author's archive) ... 215
Fig. 25: Social roles, before (left) and after retirement (right) (author's archive) ... 216
Fig. 26: Leisure activities before retirement (author's archive) ... 217
Fig. 27: Leisure activities after retirement (author's archive) ... 217
Fig. 28: Watching TV, as a leisure activity after retirement (author's archive) ... 218
Fig. 29: Reading as hobby, before retirement (author's archive) ... 219
Fig. 30: Reading as passion, after retirement (author's archive) ... 219
Fig. 31: Positive feelings before retirement (author's archive) ... 220
Fig. 32: Negative feelings after retirement (author's archive) ... 220

Fig. 33: Positive feelings after retirement (author's archive) ... 221
Fig. 34: Retirement period for women (author's archive) ... 221
Fig. 35: Third Age problems (author's archive) ... 222
Fig. 36: Ageism, drawn by a woman (author's archive) ... 222

Daniela Sorea
God, as the children of Romania draw It
Fig. 1: God's halo (author's archive) ... 236
Fig. 2: God's face representation and His garments (author's archive) ... 237
Fig. 3: The Crucifixion (author's archive) ... 237
Fig. 4: God's triangular face (author's archive) ... 238
Fig. 5: God's celestial nature (author's archive) ... 242
Fig. 6: God's prestige (author's archive) ... 243
Fig. 7: God and His angels (author's archive) ... 243
Fig. 8: God is cheerful (author's archive) ... 246
Fig. 9: God as love (author's archive) ... 248
Fig. 10: God hugging the world (author's archive) ... 249
Fig. 11: God as a father (author's archive) ... 250
Fig. 12: God is of female gender (author's archive) ... 251
Fig. 13: God in the things of the world (author's archive) ... 252
Fig. 14: Who tells children about God ... 257
Fig. 15: What children's grandparents told them about God in 2004 ... 257
Fig. 16: What children's parents told them about God in 2016 ... 258

Mihaela Gotea
Exploring social workers' perceptions of their marital partners in different family life stages, using visual methodology
Fig. 1: Personal objects describing partner's personality traits, 2017 (author's archive) ... 296
Fig. 2: Image of marital partner alone in a specific role or context (practical skills in home renovation), 2017 (author's archive) ... 296
Fig. 3: Image of the partner beside family members (the whole family), 2017 (with permission of Mihaela Dişor and Alexandru Dişor) ... 297
Fig. 4: Visual presentation of emerging categories resulting from coding ... 299
Fig. 5: Domestic roles (man cook), 2017 (author's archive) ... 300
Fig. 6: Psycho-behavioral qualities (sense of humor), 2017 (author's archive) ... 301
Fig. 7: Hobbies (fishing), 2017 (author's archive) ... 303

Fig. 8: Weaknesses (he hardly finalizes his started projects), 2017 (author's archive) 304
Fig. 9: Professional roles, 2017 (author's archive) 305
Fig. 10: Physical features (physical power), 2017 (author's archive) 306
Fig. 11: Social perception on him (appreciation of those around him), 2017 (with permission of Mihaela Dişor and Alexandru Dişor) 307

Ioana-Anisa Atudorei
Studying students' moral emotions by visual techniques
Fig. 1: Highlighting the covering of the face when shame appears (author's archive) 335
Fig. 2: Highlighting lip contour in the case of shame (horizontal shape) (author's archive) 336
Fig. 3: Highlighting the shape of the lips in the case of shame (the corners of the mouth pointed downwards) (author's archive) 337
Fig. 4: Highlighting blushing for drawing shame (author's archive) 338
Fig. 5: Involuntary contexts in which shame appears (author's archive) 339
Fig. 6: Highlighting the lip contour (the horizontal position of the corners of the mouth) (author's archive) 342
Fig. 7: Highlighting the lip contour (the corners of the mouth pointing downwards) (author's archive) 343
Fig. 8: Highlighting the lip contour (the corners of the mouth pointing upwards, in zigzag or lateral) (author's archive) 343
Fig. 9: Highlighting the colours used in drawings to picture embarrassment (author's archive) 344
Fig. 10: The absolute frequency of cataloguing the deeds committed when exemplifying shame and embarrassment 345
Fig. 11: The tilted position of the head in the case of guilt (author's archive) 347
Fig. 12: The expressiveness of the lip contour (the corners of the mouth pointing downwards) (author's archive) 348
Fig. 13: The expressiveness of the lip contour for guilt (the corners of the mouth have a horizontal position) (author's archive) 348
Fig. 14: The expressiveness of the lip contour for guilt (the corners of the mouth are pointed upwards or in zigzag) (author's archive) 348
Fig. 15: The absolute frequency of cataloguing the deeds committed when exemplifying shame, embarrassment and guilt 349
Fig. 16: The exemplification of the colours used for guilt (author's archive) 350

Giuseppina Cersosimo
Concluding notes: applications and developments in visual techniques
Fig. 1: Sampling 362
Fig. 2: Three Narratives: Patient, Doctor and Nurse (author's archive) 364
Fig. 3: Different Perceptions of the Illness (author's archive) 365
Fig. 4: Same Words, Different Meanings 366

List of Tables

Codrina Cseszneк
Studying social change through the *re-photography technique* in a rural Romanian community
Tab. 1: Visual dimensions and sub-dimensions of the research 67

Marinela-Cristina Şimon
Are the volunteers different from non-volunteers? A comparative analysis based on visual data (drawings)
Tab. 1: The matrix of the sample 137
Tab. 2: The empirical evaluation of the benefits of volunteering (Chinman and Wandersman, 1999, p.52) 145

Diana-Cristina Bódi
Using the drawing to identify post-retirement identity transformations
Tab. 1: Matrix of socio-demographic data 198
Tab. 2: Categories resulted after coding the drawings 204

Daniela Sorea
God, as the children of Romania draw It
Tab. 1: Main themes 233
Tab.2: Drawings. Structure of the theme "The Church mediates the relationship with God" 234
Tab. 3: Drawings. Structure of the theme: "God is from another world" 241
Tab. 4: Decreasing order of themes by children's residential environment and religion 254
Tab. 5: The Church, People find God in church, God requests faith 255
Tab. 6: God's Heaven 256

Mihaela Gotea
Exploring social workers' perceptions of their marital partners in different family life stages, using visual methodology
Tab. 1: Socio-demographic characteristics of the sample 291

Ioana-Anisa Atudorei
Studying students' moral emotions by visual techniques
Tab. 1: Defining embarrassment, shame and guilt according to The Explanatory Dictionary of the Romanian Language, Atudorei (2016) 329

Tab. 2: Deeds committed in school contexts in which students portrayed the emergence of shame 334
Tab. 3: The deeds committed by students in school contexts in which they experienced embarrassment 342
Tab. 4: Deeds committed in the school contexts in which students experienced guilt 346